TREATING
PROBLEM
BEHAVIORS

TREATING PROBLEM BEHAVIORS

A Trauma-Informed Approach

RICKY GREENWALD

Routledge
Taylor & Francis Group
New York   London

An earlier version of this book's treatment approach was presented in: Greenwald, R. (1999). *Eye Movement Desensitization and Reprocessing (EMDR) in Child & Adolescent Psychotherapy.* NY: Jason Aronson and is used by permission in modified/revised form. Portions of Chapters 1, 2, 3, 7, 11, and 12 have been modified from the following two books: Greenwald, R. (2005). *Child Trauma Handbook.* NY: Haworth, and Greenwald, R. (2007). *EMDR Within A Phase Model of Trauma-Informed Treatment.* NY: Haworth, and used by permission. Chapter 10 is based on Greenwald, R. (2008). *Progressive Counting: Treatment Manual.* Greenfield, MA: Trauma Institute/Child Trauma Institute, and used by permission. The scripts in Appendix C are reprinted, by permission, from: Greenwald, R. (2005). *MASTR manual, revised.* Greenfield, MA: Child Trauma Institute.

Routledge
Taylor & Francis Group
711 Third Avenue
New York, NY 10017

Routledge
Taylor & Francis Group
2 Park Square
Milton Park, Abingdon
Oxon OX14 4RN

© 2009 by Ricky Greenwald
Routledge is an imprint of Taylor & Francis Group, an Informa business

International Standard Book Number-13: 978-0-415-99801-7 (Softcover)

Library of Congress Cataloging-in-Publication Data

Greenwald, Ricky.
   Treating problem behaviors : a trauma-informed approach / by Ricky Greenwald.
      p. ; cm.
   Includes bibliographical references and index.
   ISBN 978-0-415-99801-7 (pbk. : alk. paper)
   1. Psychic trauma--Treatment. 2. Psychotherapy. I. Title.
   [DNLM: 1. Stress Disorders, Post-Traumatic--complications. 2. Stress Disorders, Post-Traumatic--therapy. 3. Psychotherapy--methods. WM 170 G816t 2009]
   RC552.T7G74 2009
   616.85'21--dc22   2008034969

Visit the Taylor & Francis Web site at
http://www.taylorandfrancis.com

and the Routledge Web site at
http://www.routledge.com

Contents

Acknowledgments

Thanks to the hundreds of clients who provided feedback on their treatment experiences. I told you it was so I could learn more and better help others. Here's one result.

Thanks also to the hundreds of workshop participants who took the trouble to provide detailed evaluations. I do pay attention, and your feedback makes the learning better for the next ones.

Thanks to Cynthia Cushman, who improved the Map Out a Problem format, and to Nancy Smyth, who improved the Case Formulation format.

Thanks to those I supervised on projects researching this treatment approach: Kris Bertelsen, Kimball Cutler, Shirleyan Ebert, Robert Godbout, Ellen Irving, Thomas Lebeau, Jacques Lemay, Thomas Owens, Glenn Soberman, and Nancy Van Cleave. You helped to improve the treatment approach and to improve how I teach it.

Thanks to the following individuals, who each reviewed a draft of the book and provided helpful feedback: Teresa Descilo, Galyn Forster, John Hamel, Thomas Lebeau, Annie Monaco, Mark Nickerson, and Nicole Rizzo.

Introduction

Why are you looking at this book? Perhaps because you work with people who are trying to control their anger and aggression, their temptations to abuse alcohol or drugs, their criminal or addictive or self-destructive behaviors—people who are trying to get or keep themselves on a positive, productive path. Perhaps because you know how hard it can be to really help your clients to improve their behaviors.

Clients with Problem Behaviors Are Often Unresponsive to Treatment

Sometimes the client has no active interest in changing. Often, even when someone does want to change, willpower, social support, and prayer are not enough. And even when your client is working hard with you, the standard treatment approaches (e.g., self-control skills training, problem solving, communication skills) may not really do the job.

Why not? One strong possibility is that the client's posttraumatic stress symptoms have not been taken into account. Exposure to trauma or loss is extremely common among those with problem behaviors and can lead to a range of treatment impediments. Trauma-exposed individuals may have impaired empathy and not care about the pain they cause others. Posttraumatic stress symptoms may cause your clients to feel reluctant to trust you, dubious about the value of treatment (nothing good's going to happen anyway, so why bother?), fearful of facing emotions, and highly reactive to apparently minor provocations or other stressors. In short, posttraumatic stress symptoms may not only contribute to the client's behavior problems but also prevent you from being able to help your client to resolve the problems.

Solving the Problems

The treatment approach presented here features a structured sequence of research-supported and field-tested interventions to systematically address these issues. A trauma-informed treatment style is used to help clients feel safe, secure, and in control within the treatment itself. A structured motivational interview is used to facilitate the client's identifying and committing to working toward positive goals. Problem solving and constructive avoidance are used to help clients reduce their exposure to temptations and stressors. Cognitive-behavioral training is used to help clients improve self-management skills and affect tolerance. Then clients are guided to face and resolve any disturbing trauma or loss memories that may be contributing to ongoing reactivity or stress. Once clients are doing well with daily functioning, the focus turns to anticipated future challenges, using relapse prevention and harm reduction methods.

Summary of the Book

The first chapter summarizes the evidence for the relationship of trauma and problem behavior and on that basis presents a trauma-informed treatment approach. This chapter also includes a review of research in support of the component interventions and of the approach as a whole.

The following chapters go through the treatment approach step by step, with scripts and practice exercises along the way. A case example, including the complete transcript of the entire course of treatment, further illustrates the interventions. Following each chapter you will see the case sessions in which that chapter's interventions were utilized. Each session transcript is followed by a copy of the official notes, a copy of the therapist's personal notes, and further commentary to highlight questions of clinical judgment in implementing the various interventions.

This treatment approach was initially designed for adolescents with acting-out behaviors, and the book primarily focuses on this population. However, with minor modifications, this approach can also be used with preadolescents and with adults as well as with clients with other types of self-management problems. Each chapter includes a final section providing any necessary age-appropriate modifications of that chapter's interventions.

The final chapter of the book teaches how to use this book's treatment approach with existing clients whose treatments were started before you read this book. It also teaches a system for using the trauma treatment framework to problem-solve challenging cases. This method can be used for your own cases or for providing supervision or consultation to others.

Appendix A provides a listing of Internet resources on trauma-informed treatment for problem behaviors. Appendix B provides a reprint of the article "The Role of Trauma in Conduct Disorder" (Greenwald, 2002b), which addresses the research base and theoretical issues in somewhat more detail than elsewhere in the text. Appendix C provides session forms for each intervention, including scripts and room for notes. These forms can be copied and used to guide treatment, whether to promote treatment adherence in a research protocol (as was done in Farkas et al., 2007) or simply to help you remember what to say in your own practice setting. The scripts are especially helpful while you're learning and getting used to the various interventions.

The book's treatment model is taught in part through a story, in which elements of the story correspond to treatment components. The story, alas, uses some gender-role stereotypes. Although I have been writing in a nonsexist style since long before it was considered acceptable, in this case I am sticking with the story as is. It is archetypal, it works, and every time I tried to make it more politically correct it worked less well. I hope you will be able to take the good from it, and if you want to tell it to your own clients in a different way, of course you are free to do so.

Trauma Resolution

Readers may use their preferred trauma resolution method when the time comes. For those readers using Eye Movement Densensitization and Reprocessing (EMDR), there are special instructions along the way about how to introduce eye movements and incorporate eye movements with some of the other interventions. Those not using EMDR can skip these sections and ignore the occasional "EM" notation, which is a signal for the EMDR therapists to elicit eye movements. Although EMDR was used in the case example, it is too complex to teach in this context. This book teaches Progressive Counting (in development, based on the research-supported Counting Method) which, like EMDR, appears to be well suited to the problem behavior client in that it is efficient, allows for privacy regarding details of the trauma memory, and is well tolerated by clients.

Limitations

This book does not teach every intervention that may be needed for every client problem such as dissociation, self-harm, or fear of attachment. You still need to attend to your clients and whatever special issues they may face. Sometimes the approach in this book will be sufficient, and sometimes it will have to be supplemented. For example, the book's self-management interventions may be more than adequate for an angry or aggressive client, but more extensive interventions may be needed for a client who self-harms. For another example, using the book's scripts may promote the development of a good therapy relationship, but with a client for whom a good relationship feels threatening, you'll have to address that.

Similarly, you'll also have to integrate the book's material with your clients' unique situations. For example, your client may be involved in the justice system or group treatment—perhaps for anger management, substance abuse, domestic violence, or a sexual offense—and may have unique inputs and requirements on that account. Also, this book's focus is primarily on teens, and although age-related modifications are provided at the end of each chapter, these suggestions may not take into account the full complexity of your clients and their situation. The purpose in this book is not to address every eventuality but to provide the core of the treatment approach.

In this book the focus is on the individual portion of treatment, even though the individual approach may not always be sufficient to achieve the treatment goals. This emphasis on the individual is not intended to be dismissive of the importance of working with the key people in the client's environment, including parents, teachers, corrections officers, social service providers, spouses, employers, and others. In the text, the reader is referred to other sources for guidance on this often essential aspect of treatment.

Doing What Works

Mental health professionals have been under a lot of pressure to use empirically supported interventions whenever possible, for both ethical and economic reasons. Although the current emphasis on empirically supported treatments has merit, unresolved issues remain. One problem with this trend is that many such methods may be perceived by clinicians as inapplicable to their practice settings. In the treatment of problem behaviors, another problem is that most such interventions have had only minimal success in practice settings.

The present treatment approach offers the prospect of improved outcomes by integrating motivational interviewing and trauma treatment with the more typical approach of cognitive-behavioral skills training. This treatment approach also offers direct application to clinical practice, because the interventions have already been adapted to practice settings. This treatment approach has been used with juvenile delinquents, teens and preteens with school-related problems, youth in foster care and residential treatment, and adults in a range of outpatient and court-mandated treatment settings.

The advantage of using field-tested interventions is that, more often than not, they work. Here's how you can make them work as well as possible for you. First of all, practice using the scripts, *word for word*. The scripts are like sales pitches that have been developed and refined for one purpose: to get the response you are hoping for. I encourage you to practice with the scripts verbatim several times, with colleagues and then with clients, until you have them more or less memorized (it doesn't take long). Over time, as you start changing the words to fit your situation and to suit your personal style, you will notice whether you are still getting the responses you want. If you are, carry on; if not, go back to the script and see if you can identify the difference that makes the difference.

This book teaches a highly structured treatment approach that guides the client step by step from beginning to end. This approach entails mastery of a number of complex clinical skills. Workshop participants who have repeated (e.g., as part of the process of becoming a supervisor) have consistently reported learning a lot more the second and even the third time around. If you are using the book without the benefit of the supervised practice that a training program affords, it is worthwhile to go back to the book repeatedly over time as you gain more practical experience. This will help you to better understand why you are doing what you are doing and to master the finer points. With practice, study, and experimentation, you should be able to integrate this book's approach with your existing skills for maximum effect.

Chapter 1

Trauma-Informed Treatment for Problem Behaviors

The purpose of this chapter is to tell you what you're getting into in this book, and why. It starts with a brief discussion of problem behaviors and the current standard of care for their treatment. Trauma (and posttraumatic stress) is proposed as a key to understanding the serious limitations of the current standard of care and to coming up with solutions. A comprehensive phase model of trauma-informed treatment is presented, incorporating a series of interventions designed to address the trauma-related obstacles to treatment success. Finally, the empirical support for each component of treatment is reviewed, as well as the research on the treatment as a package.

The Problem of Problem Behaviors

Problem behaviors are a big problem. As a society we are extremely concerned about youth and adult aggression and crime, domestic violence, child abuse, alcohol and drug abuse, and other addictions (e.g., gambling, pornography). We are also concerned about the angry acting out, sexual acting out, and poor self-discipline that can lead to distressed relationships, unwanted pregnancy, school or work failure, health problems, and impaired quality of life.

Because such problems are so serious and so common, we have tried long and hard to solve or at least mitigate them. The primary standard of care, across problem behavior types, is self-management skills training, most notably focusing on anger management or relapse prevention. The other most common ways we try to control or eliminate problem behaviors include the following:

- Parent training, especially for parents of children and preteens with problem behaviors.

- Success experiences such as trying to rehabilitate criminals by finding them a job.
- Education and peer support, often in groups such as Alcoholics Anonymous.
- Legal and social sanctions against the problem behaviors, sometimes leading to loss of privileges, financial penalties, incarceration, or social isolation.
- Telling the perpetrator of the problem behaviors to stop it.
- Prayer.
- Positive thinking.
- Willpower.

We try these because they work—at least a little, sometimes—and that's better than nothing. But it may not be much better than nothing! Individuals with problem behaviors are notoriously difficult to help, and (with the exception of discipline training for parents of younger children) the standard of care tends to entail many more misses than hits. Indeed, many individuals with problem behaviors have learned, from repeated experiences, to feel hopeless regarding the prospect of treatment leading to meaningful change. And many therapists have learned, from their own experiences, to share that hopelessness.

For example, in the well-known "Willie M" study, comprehensive assessment and intensive case management were employed to individualize treatment from a menu of options for aggressive/violent adolescents who had at least one additional disability such as emotional disturbance. In this model program, no expense was spared to provide each individual with the optimal interventions. Even so, compared with participants who were in the program so briefly (average 26 days) that virtually no treatment was provided, participants with at least 1 year in the program (average 896 days) showed no benefit in either number of posttreatment arrests or time until first arrest (Weisz, Walter, Weiss, Fernandez, & Mikow, 1990).

Although that study focused on juvenile delinquents, the reality of minimum-impact treatment is familiar across treatment of sex offenders (Brooks-Gordon, Bilby, & Wells, 2006; Seager, Jellicoe, & Dhaliwal, 2004), drug abusers (Shearer, 2007), spouse batterers (Babcock, Green, & Robie, 2004), and others with problem behaviors. The bottom line is that the treatment often fails to lead to client change. We typically encounter one or more of the following obstacles:

- Many clients are not motivated to change.
- Many clients do not engage in or commit to the treatment.
- Many clients stop attending or participating in the treatment.
- Many clients who make an effort in treatment fail anyway. The problem is just too hard to overcome.
- Many clients who appear to succeed in treatment then relapse, or they go back to their old problem behaviors.

Therapists often acknowledge a reluctance to work with problem behavior clients, because the obstacles to treatment are so difficult to overcome. This is understandable; therapists don't like feeling ineffective and helpless any more than anyone else does. However, recognizing the problem, and perhaps avoiding it, does not solve it. The key to solving a problem is understanding it. What is there about problem behavior clients—what do they have in common—that tends to lead to these treatment obstacles?

Trauma's Role in Problem Behaviors

Trauma exposure has been definitively implicated as leading to a higher risk of problem behaviors in comprehensive literature reviews of violence/aggression (Widom, 1989), substance abuse (Ouimette & Brown, 2003; Steward, 1996), sexual offending (Ward & Siegert, 2002), antisocial/criminal behavior (Greenwald, 2002b, which is reprinted in Appendix B in this volume), and even pathological gambling (Scherrer et al., 2007). The underlying process that leads from victimization to development of problem behaviors does not seem to require direct correspondence of victimization history and type of problem behavior. For example, a victim of sexual abuse is at higher risk of becoming a sexual abuser but is also at higher risk of becoming a substance abuser or developing some other problem.

Although we have long been aware of the prevalence of trauma exposure among problem behavior populations, we have until recently done nearly nothing to address trauma-related issues. An early example of an enlightened approach to this issue among juvenile delinquents was the Boys Town model: Take them out of their bad environments and they will do better (Girls and Boys Town, 2007). This is also the prevailing model for children removed from abusive situations: Put them in a safer environment and the problem is over. Although that strategy can work with a few people, it fails to take into account the long-term psychological processes that trauma exposure can engender and that interfere with improvement.

This book's treatment approach is based on the proposition that trauma is the key to understanding the treatment obstacles experienced by problem behavior clients. Therefore, it is essential to explain trauma and its role in the development and persistence of problem behaviors (including obstacles to treatment). On the basis of this understanding, solutions to the treatment obstacles are presented within the framework of a trauma-informed treatment approach.

Prevalence of Trauma

Not long ago, trauma was defined as a horrific event "beyond the scope of normal human experience" (APA, 1980). To qualify as traumatic, an event should be subjectively perceived as threatening to a person's life or physical integrity and should include a sense of helplessness along with fear, horror, or disgust. Such events might include being in a car accident, house fire, or natural disaster, being raped, or being assaulted. Through research we have learned to identify a wider range of events as being possibly traumatic—for example, witnessing a parent or sibling being beaten, or being diagnosed with a life-threatening illness.

The bad news is that traumatic events are not beyond the scope of normal human experience. By the time most individuals become adults, they will have been exposed to one or more traumatic events. This is not just true for those growing up in high-crime urban areas. Even our (presumably) best-protected children experience trauma. For example, a study of second-year college students (modal age of 19) found that 84% had already experienced at least one major (Criterion A) trauma (Vrana & Lauterbach, 1994). Among disadvantaged populations, very few escape exposure to major trauma events (see Greenwald, 2002b). Trauma during childhood and adolescence is so common as to be normative. And of course, the longer someone lives, the more opportunity there is for exposure to trauma. When we are working with a client, we should assume trauma exposure.

The *Diagnostic and Statistical Manual of Mental Disorders*, 3rd ed. (*DSM-III;* APA, 1980)'s definition of a traumatic event is overly restrictive from a clinical perspective, because other adverse life events can have a trauma-like impact. For example, a person's response to a significant loss can be virtually identical to a posttraumatic response, except that following loss, hyperarousal may not be present (Pynoos, 1990). The research on so-called adjustment disorder shows that many children and adolescents do not adjust to or recover from a range of adverse events (Newcorn & Strain, 1992) but maintain some symptoms indefinitely. Research with adults has shown that distressing life events such as divorce, chronic illness, or unemployment tend to lead to equal or greater posttraumatic stress disorder (PTSD) symptoms than do those events that are technically defined as traumatic (Mol et al., 2005).

When working with a distressed client, we do not ask if the adverse past event technically qualifies as a trauma. We offer essentially the same treatment regardless of whether the source of the distress is an earthquake, a sexual assault, or a death in the family. In this book, the term *trauma* is intended to apply to major trauma as well as loss and other adverse life events, as long as the event has had a trauma-like impact on the client.

The Trauma Wall

A popular saying is, "What doesn't kill you makes you stronger," or, less colloquially, that we grow from adversity. Although this certainly can be true, it is not always the case. Sometimes what doesn't kill you may still hurt you or cause damage. So how does this work—why does it go one way rather than the other?

Here a food analogy is helpful. Usually, we chew food, swallow it, and digest it. Ideally, we do something similar with an upsetting experience, such as what Kübler-Ross (1969) described in the stages of processing grief.

For example, let's say your dog dies. Maybe you don't think about it or process it every minute of the day, but now and then you do think about it, remembering different aspects: how frisky she was when you first got her, how she liked to have her belly scratched, how badly you feel about having let her out the day she got hit by a car. You remember, you talk to others, you take a walk, you write, you cry, you laugh. Little by little—or bite by bite—the hurt becomes smaller as more gets processed, integrated, "digested."

When an upsetting experience is digested, it becomes your nutrition, something you grow from. Then it becomes part of integrated long-term memory, part of the past. It is not as fresh or upsetting anymore. Along with the emotional processing, we have organized the elements of the experience into a coherent story, including a perspective that allows us to move on. For example, you might say to yourself, "Well, she loved to play outside. I guess there was always the risk of an accident, but she would have been miserable tied up," and "She was a great dog. I'll always love her."

However, sometimes upsetting experiences do not get processed in this ideal way. Sometimes it's just too much to face, to take bites out of. Maybe the event was too upsetting and overwhelming; maybe you try to talk about it and are punished for that (perhaps by parents getting upset or peers rejecting you); maybe just when you are ready to take a bite out of this upsetting memory, another challenge comes along. It can be so difficult to face this upsetting memory, to tolerate it, that many people try to push it aside, push it behind a wall (Greenwald, 2005a; see also Foa, Steketee, & Rothbaum, 1989; Lang, 1977). This brings quick relief, so the strategy is experienced as helpful. Unfortunately, it provides only a temporary solution.

Here the food analogy does not quite match what happens with trauma memories. If you eat food that is bad for you, you get rid of it. If you have an experience that's bad for you, you may try to get rid of it (by pushing it behind the wall), but it's not gone. The only way out is to go through—through the memory processing system into long-term memory. Until the memory is processed, or digested, it stays behind the wall.

Although the wall may provide temporary relief, this system has problems. First, the memory stays fresh and keeps its power indefinitely, until it is digested. I have worked with people months, years, and even decades after the trauma, and the quality of the unprocessed memory is the same. When asked to concentrate on the memory, they say things such as, "It's so vivid it's like it just happened yesterday," or, even more telling, "I'm there."

Also, although the memory retains its freshness and power, it is still behind the wall, so we can't get at it with the rest of our psychological resources the way we can with processed memories. This means that the memory, or parts of the memory, can negatively influence us and we may feel helpless to stop it. For example, many rape victims will say, "I know in my head that it wasn't my fault, that I didn't do anything wrong, that I didn't deserve that. But I can't help feeling ashamed, dirty, to blame." In other words, the healthy part that knows better can't manage to influence the powerful beliefs and feelings that are shielded behind the wall.

Furthermore, the memories stored behind the wall are always waiting for a chance to come out, go through the system to be digested, and become part of the past. Sometimes the memory-related thoughts and emotions burst out from behind the wall. When this happens, we say that the memory-related material was "triggered" or activated by a reminder, something thematically related. It is as if the memory is seeing its chance and saying, "Me too! Can I finally come in and get processed already?" Another way of explaining this is that the stuff piled up behind the wall is like a sore spot (Greenwald, 2005a), and when some kind of reminder hits that sore spot, the reaction is stronger than others might expect. This is because the person is not just reacting to what's happening right now; the old stuff is kicking in, too.

For example, consider a certain 12-year-old boy who has been routinely physically abused at home. Behind the wall is piled-up fear of being attacked, a sense of helplessness, and rage. When he is accidentally bumped in the hallway, he experiences the modest irritation that the situation might objectively elicit, plus the sore spot reaction from the stuff piled up behind the wall. Now he has such a strong reaction it is as if he is being traumatized on the spot; subjectively, he believes that he is being attacked. He experiences this as "too much" (as with the original trauma) and becomes desperate to get rid of the fear, anger, and helplessness. How to get rid of it as quickly as possible? Fortunately, he knows what to do: He punches the attacker.

This so-called "problem behavior" is actually a solution; it pushes the fear and helplessness away. For this boy, the real problem was the sore spot reaction's overwhelming affect. The technical term for that sore spot reaction is *affect dysregulation*. In a nutshell, this is a primary reason that problem behavior clients persist with their symptoms: because the symptoms provide quick relief or protection from the overwhelming affect of the sore spot reaction.

Trauma and Reinforcement for Coercive Behavior

Several reviews have outlined a range of theories about how trauma exposure and posttraumatic stress symptoms may lead to antisocial behavior (Ford, 2002; Garbarino, 1999; Greenwald, 2002b; Steiner, Garcia, & Matthews, 1997). Here, an existing model of antisocial behavior will provide a foundation from which to understand trauma's possible role.

Patterson and colleagues (Patterson, DeBaryshe, & Ramsey, 1989; Reid, Patterson, & Snyder, 2002) have developed a dynamic developmental model for antisocial behavior. Briefly, the *reinforcement for coercive behavior* model describes an at-risk child who is reinforced in the family environment for acting-out behavior and who learns to favor this behavior as a way of managing impulses and frustrations to the exclusion of prosocial alternatives. This leads to school problems, adult hostility, and peer rejection, as well as increased anger or depression. The child becomes progressively more oppositional and socially disenfranchised. Later affiliation with deviant peers provides a measure of social acceptance while the peer influence leads to progressive escalation and diversity of antisocial behaviors. A number of trauma-related processes, described next, may contribute to this reinforcement cycle.

Affect Dysregulation

Affect dysregulation (the sore spot reaction), which is characteristic of many traumatized individuals (Chemtob, Novaco, Hamada, & Gross, 1997; van der Kolk et al., 1996), may play a critical role in the early development of antisocial tendencies. In one set of studies, affect dysregulation was found to be as powerful a predictor of conduct problems as parental reinforcement for coercive behavior; furthermore, each exacerbated the other (Snyder, Schrepferman, & St. Peter, 1997). Unstructured, ambiguous, or chaotic situations can also engender a fear response that is enhanced by the sore spot reaction. Then "punishment" can actually be reinforcing when, by forcing an ostensibly aversive parental response, the youth has turned a chaotic environment into a predictable one (Wahler & Dumas, 1986). Such reinforcement would be particularly salient for a traumatized child with a strong need for predictability.

Hypersensitivity to Threat

Trauma may also play a central role in the persistence of antisocial behavior. A hypothesized core effect of traumatization is the activation of a "survival mode" orientation (Chemtob, Roitblat, Hamada, Carlson, & Twentyman, 1988) in which the trauma victim becomes hypersensitive to possible indicators of threat, leading to misinterpretation of social cues, heightened arousal and anger, and inappropriate aggression in the perceived cause of self-protection. This information processing style is consistent with the "hostile attribution bias" commonly noted among antisocial youth (e.g., Dodge & Frame, 1982), and its use increases as a result of increased feelings of vulnerability or threat (Dodge & Somberg, 1987). This information processing style is subject to a positive-feedback cycle because the perception of threat increases the likelihood of aggression, engendering hostility in others and thus confirming the perception of others as dangerous. Similarly, anger in traumatized individuals may serve the function of dampening fear and thus be self-reinforcing (Novaco & Chemtob, 1998).

Situational Reactivity Leading to a Cycle of Problem Behaviors

Furthermore, trauma-related affect dysregulation may trigger reactivity to a variety of situations and stimuli perceived as thematically related to the trauma. One study found that situations triggering trauma-related helplessness, and to a lesser extent fear or horror, accounted for initiating 81% of the "offense cycle" patterns of a sample of adolescent sex offenders, according to therapist ratings (McMackin, Leisen, Cusack, LaFratta, & Litwin, 2002). While the acting-out behavior may provide immediate relief from the trauma-related thoughts and feelings, the consequences of that behavior often serve to confirm the negative lessons initially learned from the trauma, thus reinforcing reactivity and continued susceptibility to reoffending (see Figure 1 in Greenwald, 2002b).

Pessimistic Future

Trauma exposure can diminish the expectation for a positive future (Fletcher, 1996; Terr, 1991), fostering an instant gratification orientation and precluding regard for delayed consequences or investment in the long-term—an attitude also characteristic of problem behavior clients. The effects of trauma exposure can have wide-ranging secondary effects on development, becoming a focus around which personality and behavior are organized (Terr, 1991; van der Kolk et al., 1996).

Trauma-Related Treatment Challenges

If trauma is one of the keys to the development and persistence of problem behaviors, then trauma treatment should be part of the solution. Unfortunately, adding a trauma treatment component would tend to make the treatment even more challenging to accomplish. Like treatment for problem behaviors, trauma treatment has also been plagued by high dropout rates (Solomon, Gerrity, & Muff, 1992) and in particular, both children and multiply traumatized individuals are considered especially challenging to treat (James, 1989). Antisocial adolescents are notoriously resistant to engaging in treatment in general (Kazdin, Mazurick, & Bass, 1993; Patterson & Forgatch, 1985; Santisteban, Suarez-Morales, Robbins, & Szapocznik, 2006; Sommers-Flanagan & Sommers-Flanagan, 1995) and may be particularly difficult to engage and maintain in conventional trauma treatments. Trauma-related obstacles to treatment of problem behavior clients include challenges related to treatment engagement and to treatment tolerance and persistence.

Treatment Engagement

Mistrust of, and anger toward, adults and authority figures, as well as a peer subculture hostile to authority, can make it difficult for the client to engage or form an alliance with the therapist. Also, the pessimistic future orientation creates a disregard for long-term consequences and a preference for immediate gratification. Someone with such an orientation may find it easy to deny that he or she even has a problem, since the problem behaviors bring immediate gratification and the long-term consequences may seem irrelevant. Furthermore, treatment seems unattractive, because it would involve boring or hard work with no anticipation of benefit.

Treatment Tolerance

Affect dysregulation and poor affect tolerance may increase the intensity of reactions to discussion of conflict, negative emotions, and trauma-related material and may enhance the usual avoidance associated with trauma memories. Problem behavior clients themselves routinely express concern that merely talking about upsetting things will lead to volatility and increased acting-out problems. Also, such affect dysregulation-related acting out makes the client destabilized and crisis prone, distracting from a focus on skill development or trauma-focused treatment.

In sum, problem behavior clients are characterized by trauma-related affect dysregulation (i.e., the sore spot reaction) and poor affect tolerance, leading to avoidance as well as impulsive acting out for quick relief. Neither the standard self-management training nor straightforward trauma treatment is likely to be effective with problem behavior clients, who are unlikely to engage or to tolerate the treatment. Thus, if treatment with this population is to succeed, it should include components specifically addressing the trauma-related engagement and tolerance issues.

Selecting a Trauma Treatment Structure

The mental health field has been strongly influenced by physicians and psychiatrists, who have advocated for the medical model of diagnosis and treatment. In the medical model, the doctor determines what's wrong and, based on the diagnosis, implements the designated treatment. The medical model is ideal for broken bones, diseases that respond to a particular medicine, and many other medical conditions. In many instances, the correct diagnosis does lead to the correct treatment, which leads in turn to cure.

However, when treating someone for posttraumatic-stress-related problems, the medical model is not appropriate. Traumatized people already feel damaged and helpless; that's part of the problem. What happens when a helping professional takes an authoritarian role with a traumatized "patient" and says, "I know your diagnosis and I can treat you"? The professional conveys the message that "I know what's wrong with you and I will fix you." This only confirms the traumatized person's perception—"I guess I really am damaged and helpless"—and reinforces the problem. Even the word *patient* implies that the person's role is to sit and wait, presumably until the doctor gets around to providing the treatment and effecting the cure.

Trauma-informed treatment requires a different attitude on the part of the helping professional. An empowerment model is needed that can allow and encourage the client to take initiative, to actively participate in each stage of the treatment, to recover from the trauma, and to grow from it.

Quite a bit of research has been conducted to determine which types of interventions help traumatized clients the most; these include psychoeducation, stabilization, development of coping skills, and trauma resolution. Such interventions are typically sequenced within a phase model of treatment (e.g., Bloom, 1997; Herman, 1992; Shapiro, 2001), which represents the current standard of care (Foa, Keene, & Friedman, 2000; International Society for the Study of Dissociation, 2005). I've organized these interventions, plus treatment components specific to problem behavior issues, into a systematic approach that I call the Fairy Tale model of trauma-informed treatment (Greenwald, 2005a, 2007). In this model, the fairy tale is used (loosely) as an analogy, with elements of the story corresponding to the various treatment components. The Fairy Tale model will guide this book's treatment approach. First, the story.

The Fairy Tale

Once upon a time ...

There was a small kingdom, about the size of a small town. Things were pretty regular there: People did their jobs, kids went to school, some people went to church or temple or mosque and some didn't. Sometimes people would get together to share food, play games, play music, talk. Most people got along, but not everyone. And that's the way things were.

Until one day ...

The dragon came. One day the dragon ate a cow right out of a farmer's pasture. Another day the dragon ate a dog right out of someone's front yard. The parents told their kids that they weren't allowed to go outside anymore. But they found out that kids aren't very good at not going outside. So the parents stayed home to guard their kids, to keep them safe from the dragon. And even people who didn't have kids were staying inside; they were nervous about the dragon, too.

Things really slowed down in this kingdom. When people did get together, here's what they talked about: "How come our kingdom has a dragon, anyway? The other kingdoms don't have one." They didn't know, and they wanted to know. So they started coming up with ideas. This group of people blamed that group of people; that group of people blamed some others. Pretty soon, everyone was blaming someone, and they were all mad at each other.

It didn't take long until this kingdom got a bad reputation. People from the other kingdoms, well, they didn't know about the dragon, but they sure knew what was going on. They would say, "The people in that kingdom don't go to work, the kids don't go to school, nobody gets along, they're all mad at each other. They're messed up."

And that's the way things were.

Until one day …

A knight in shining armor came along. Well, he wasn't really a knight, and he didn't have any armor. He was just some guy who happened to be passing through. But the people in the kingdom saw something in him. "You!" they said, "You can slay the dragon; you're just the one to do it!" The guy said, "No, sorry, I'm not a dragon-slayer; you have the wrong guy. I've been walking a long way, and I'm looking for this girl I'm in love with. But I don't know where she lives." He pulled a picture out and showed it around. "Have you seen her?" The people said "Yes, she's our princess; she lives here. And what a coincidence: She really wants to get married—to whoever slays the dragon!" When the guy heard this, he said, "Well, in that case, I'm your man. Take me to your dragon!"

So they took him to the dark place where the dragon was sleeping. The guy saw the dragon and said, "Whoa, this is a bad idea! I can't handle this dragon; no way! It's huge, looks really strong, it's covered with scales, it breathes fire. Let's just forget the whole thing!"

The people said "No, you can do it; we know you can! Look, you can work out, do exercises, build yourself up. We'll help—we'll get you a personal trainer. And remember the princess!" The guy said, "Oh yeah, the princess!" He was in love with this princess, and he really wanted to marry her. "Okay, I don't know about this personal trainer stuff, but I'll give it a try and see how it goes."

So they gave him a personal trainer and took him to the schoolyard to start on his exercises. But he couldn't stay focused! Every time he got started on some exercise, he would suddenly stop and look all around—he was afraid the dragon would get him while he was out there, exposed. So he wasn't making any progress. This was clearly not working.

So they took him to a clearing at the edge of the forest where there were high trees on one side. Then they worked to build a high fence around the rest of the clearing. Everybody pitched in, cutting lumber, putting it up, securing it, cooking for the workers. Even the little kids were helping: bringing water to people, carrying messages, doing whatever they could. And it wasn't long until they had a high fence around the rest of the clearing. Then the guy could concentrate on his exercises.

Then he really got to work. He did push-ups and sit-ups, lifted weights, ran laps, did all kinds of exercises. Every day the trainer added a pound or two to the various weights. Every day the guy became a little stronger, a little faster, a little more agile. After a while, he started looking pretty good. When they thought he was almost ready, they had a couple of athletic teenagers dress up like dragons to give him some practice. He didn't use the sword, just a stick, but he got to practice his dragon-fighting moves.

Finally, the day came: He was ready. He faced the dragon, fought it, and slew it.

He did marry the princess. But things didn't just go back to exactly the same way that the kingdom used to be.

For one thing, they now had a hero in their midst. People from the other kingdoms were saying, "That kingdom has a dragon-slayer; I wish we had one."

And everyone in the kingdom felt proud and walked a little taller; they knew they'd all helped out and been a part of it.

But they were still asking each other, "How come our kingdom had a dragon, anyway? I wonder if we'll get another one?" And they didn't know. And they wanted to know. So they hired a consultant.

The consultant looked everywhere and interviewed everyone, and she finally called a meeting to tell them her findings. "You have two problems here. First of all, you throw all your garbage in the dump; it's this huge pile of garbage that stinks for miles around. That smell attracts dragons." So they decided that everyone would put their garbage in a compost pile in their own yard. Then there'd be no big smell to attract dragons—and compost is good for the gardens anyway.

The consultant also told them, "Here's your other problem. On the edge of the kingdom where the farms are, there are all these low fields; it's flat, flat, flat for miles! Dragons are lazy, and this place is just too easy for a dragon to cruise right in." So they decided to plant clusters of apple trees here and there in the fields. It wouldn't be impossible for a dragon to come, but with all the barricades it wouldn't be as easy as before.

Then they had a lot of apples. So every year at harvest time, they had a big Apple Festival, and people would come from all the kingdoms for miles around. There were all kinds of contests for the tastiest apples, the biggest apples, the best apple pies, and plenty of food, games, music—everything a festival should have.

The highlight of the festival was on Saturday night, the event everyone would go to: the dragon-slaying contest. Of course, they didn't have a real dragon, so whoever had won the year before got to play the dragon. All year long, young people from all the kingdoms were practicing, training, hoping that they'd be the one to win the big contest at the next year's festival. Not only was this great fun, but also, if another dragon ever did show up, they would be ready!

Then, they did live happily ever after—more or less.

The end.

The Fairy Tale Model of Trauma-Informed Treatment

The fairy tale was presented as the metaphorical basis of a phase model for an effective, comprehensive approach to trauma-informed treatment. Each step in treatment is related to the corresponding portion of the fairy tale. The treatment steps follow.

Evaluation

This includes the history of trauma/loss, strengths/successes, and circumstances in which the problem symptoms/behaviors occur.

■ In the fairy tale, the kingdom just seemed "messed up" from the outside. If you knew about the dragon, what people were doing was still unfortunate, but at least it made sense.

■ It is also important to focus on the client's strengths and resources, which are the foundation for success in treatment. In the fairy tale, some guy came along who eventually became the dragon slayer. In real life, the client is his or her own knight in shining armor and becomes the dragon slayer himself or herself. We need hard facts so that when we say to the client, "You— you're the one who can do it," we have good reasons for believing this.

■ Remember that famous expression, "It takes a kingdom to slay a dragon"? The guy in the story didn't do it by himself. So part of the evaluation is to learn about the resources available in the kingdom, or in the family and community.

Motivational Interviewing/Goal Setting

It takes a great amount of work, persistence, and courage to overcome trauma-related problems. Clients are not likely to commit to this unless we can help them identify their own goals—what they want for themselves—and understand how doing these treatment activities can help them to achieve their goals. This is the motivational component; most people won't do all this work just because someone else says they should.

In the fairy tale, without the princess, nothing would happen. With the princess in the picture, it's still a daunting task, but the guy says, "I guess I'll give it a try and see how it goes."

Trauma-Informed Case Formulation and Psychoeducation

Based on the evaluation, we communicate our understanding to our clients, including the connection between the trauma/loss history and the presenting problem, as well as an emphasis on the client's strengths and resources that can be brought to bear on solving the problem. This shared understanding becomes the basis for the treatment plan, which includes trauma treatment.

Treatment Contracting

The treatment contracting involves coming to an agreement to pursue specific activities in service of the client's goals, in light of the strengths and challenges highlighted in the case formulation. The treatment plan typically includes doing activities to become more safe and stable, to gain better self-control skills and emotional strength, and to face and work through the trauma memories.

In other words, fence-around, personal training, and slay the dragon.

Case Management, Avoiding High Risk, and Parent Training for Safety and Other Needs

It is very difficult to focus on building up strength and skills when an ongoing threat exists. If we want to help clients to get over their trauma memories, we must first make sure that the trauma is not ongoing. We also must ensure, to the best of our ability, that their basic needs are being met. Otherwise, they will be too distracted by survival to focus on trauma recovery. We often work with parents and other caregivers to help them provide a more consistent and supportive environment, for example, by becoming more consistent in their discipline style. This helps children feel safer and more secure so they can relax and concentrate on their tasks. With teens and adults, we may still work with family members, but we also focus more on what clients can do for themselves to create a safer and more secure environment. In general this entails resolving problematic situations and avoiding high-risk situations.

In the fairy tale, the people had to find a safe place and build a fence around it so the guy could focus on his personal training tasks.

Self-Management Skills Training

This training contributes to physical and psychological safety as well as improved affect regulation. We often train clients in various self-management and self-control skills. This also enhances their sense of safety and security, because the more they are able to control themselves the better they are treated by others and the more supportive their environment becomes. At the same time, clients become more competent and confident, as well as emotionally stronger, and are able to handle progressively greater challenges.

Once the fence is up, the guy can work with the personal trainer to become stronger and faster, and (in role plays) practice fighting the dragon. It takes more than strength and skill to slay a dragon; it also takes affect tolerance, the ability to persist in the face of pain. If you're going to fight a dragon, you'd better be able to take a punch or two.

Trauma Resolution

Remember the digestion metaphor? Digestion cannot happen while we are in survival mode. We need to feel safe and relaxed first. That's partly what all that preparation was about: helping the client to become safe enough and strong enough that success is likely here. Then it's a matter of facing the memory, taking a bite at a time, chewing it up—even if it tastes bad!—and digesting it. In treatment, this typically involves thinking and talking about it over and over again in a structured, systematic way.

> The guy in the fairy tale faced the dragon, fought it, and slew it. Actually, in treatment we'll probably start with a snake or two, and then a baby dragon or two before we go for the big one. Remember, we're the personal trainers here! We want to build on successes, not overwhelm our clients.

Consolidation of Gains

Once the trauma is resolved, or digested, the other problems may melt away, but sometimes they don't. The client may have some bad habits or be missing some skills. Now that the trauma is no longer driving the problem, the client is in a position to respond more positively to other interventions, to solve remaining problems, and to get firmly on a better track toward his or her goals.

> Now that the dragon is out of the way, the guy can marry the princess.

Relapse Prevention and Harm Reduction

It's not enough just to recover from the trauma and get on a better track in life. It's better to also learn from this experience and to take measures to prevent a recurrence of trauma or problem behaviors. This is the time to work with the client and others in his or her life to identify potential risks and take specific actions to mitigate those risks. This makes other bad things less likely to happen in the future. And since you can't guarantee that trauma or problem behaviors will never happen again, this is also the time to anticipate a possible recurrence and to make specific plans to recognize that and to minimize the damage.

- Stop using that dump; compost instead so that dragons are not attracted by the stink.
- Plant clusters of apple trees to make it harder for dragons to just cruise in.
- If a dragon should ever come again, be ready with some dragon slayers.

Stage of Treatment	Corresponding Element of the Fairy Tale
Evaluation including: • Strengths/resources • Trauma/loss history.	You have what it takes to slay the dragon. We need to know about the dragon to make sense of the problems.
Motivational interviewing, goal setting.	Without the princess, nothing will happen.
Trauma-informed case formulation and psychoeducation.	Identify the strengths/resources as reason to hope for a chance of success. Take the dragon into account, then the problems make sense.
Trauma-relevant treatment contracting.	Recommend fence-around, personal training to get stronger, and slay the dragon.
Case management for safety and other needs. Avoid high risks (and parent training) for safety and security.	Build the fence around so you're not worried about being attacked at any moment. Then you can concentrate on your tasks.
Self-management skills training for physical and psychological safety as well as improved affect regulation.	The personal training approach to build skill and strength.
Trauma resolution.	Slay the dragon.
More stabilization and self-management, to go farther now that the sore spot is gone.	Marry the princess.
Relapse prevention and harm reduction.	Compost instead of using the dump, to stop attracting dragons; stands of apple trees so it's harder for dragons to get in. Teens training for the dragon-slaying contest, so if another one does come along, we'll be ready.

Figure 1.1   The Fairy Tale Model of Trauma-Informed Treatment

Figure 1.1 provides a summary of this treatment approach. The Fairy Tale model as applied to problem behavior populations does not strictly follow this order; for example, some strengths are identified in the first session, and further strengths are identified in the Goal-Setting session. Although there are a number of ways to implement the treatment approach, the chart outlines the basic structure and treatment components.

Principles of Trauma-Informed Treatment

Each of the steps in treatment is made up of a number of specific interventions. These are taught in detail in the coming chapters. For now, I wish to introduce a few key principles that pervade the trauma-informed treatment approach: safety, structure, sensitivity, and success.

Safety

The traumatized client's primary concern is safety. People feel safe when they know what to expect and what to do—when they feel that things are under control. Therapists can do many things to help clients to feel safe in therapy, such as the following:

- At the beginning of the first session, introduce rules and expectations including the schedule for meeting, the purpose/goals of meeting, conditions of confidentiality, and what the client is expected to do in sessions.
- Keep your promises. Be ready and start the session on time. (If you can't do this reliably, don't make the promise.)
- Start each session the same way. Routines are reassuring. The starting routine can be as simple as a check-in; for example, many therapists start by saying, "Tell me something good and something bad that happened since last time we met." In addition to the predictability value of the fact of the routine, this is also a good way to find out what's going on in the client's life. Often this material can be used in support of the treatment plan. For example, if the client reports having handled a confrontation poorly, this event can be used for practicing self-management skills.
- End each session the same way. Routines can be developed around putting toys or materials away, talking about what's next in the client's day, or asking the client to say something he or she liked and something he or she didn't like about the meeting. Again, part of the value is the fact of the predictability of the routine, and part of the value is helping the client to gain closure on the session, regain composure, and to be ready for what's next in his or her day.

Structure

When we are working our way through the treatment steps in the Fairy Tale model, we are asking our clients to face progressively greater emotional challenges. For example, as early as the second meeting, we are asking the client to tell us all the worst things that ever happened to him or her. Most people habitually avoid talking about this kind of thing because it makes them upset. So what happens when they answer our questions, get upset, and then the session is over—what then?

In many circles, therapists have a bad reputation because this issue is managed poorly. Many therapists are trained to believe that their job is to help the client to "open up"—to be expressive, get out feelings, work on issues. Then the difficult material is activated, the client is upset, and the client is sent on his or her way. How many school teachers have had to complain, "It's bad enough that she gets taken out of my class—my class is important, she comes to school to learn! But then when she comes back after a meeting with the counselor, she's all upset, she can't concentrate, she's a mess!" Similarly, many family members have complained that the client is "a mess" in one way or another for some period after therapy.

Although some therapists believe that this is just the inevitable fallout that comes from doing therapy, these therapists are wrong. They are not trained in trauma treatment. Remember, like the rest of us, clients learn from experience. What do clients learn from the experience of being "a mess" after their therapy session? They learn that bad things happen if they open up with you. One client said, "Last time, after I left here, I was still heated, and I ended up getting into a stupid argument. It wasn't good. I don't want to talk about that [upsetting personal] stuff anymore."

When clients and their families regularly experience bad outcomes from therapy sessions, it gives therapy (and the therapist—you) a bad reputation. Spouses, parents, teachers, and others feel that therapy is an imposition, a disruption to the day. They don't see it helping the client but instead actually doing harm. So these others are more likely to press for termination of the client's therapy, or at least not to support it as actively as you would prefer. Also, the clients in this situation are likely to become more resistant and more reserved. Why trust the therapist who keeps setting you up for problems? Why open up if it only gets you upset and gets you in trouble?

The wise trauma therapist minimizes the risk of bad outcomes to sessions by using the following strategies:

- Carefully control what is discussed in a session so that the challenge (level of distress) is consistent with what the client can be expected to tolerate or handle. Using the personal trainer metaphor, if your client lifted 15 pounds in the previous meeting, you don't give him or her 50 pounds this time—you give the client 15 again, or maybe 18 or 20 if you think the client is ready. With this approach, the client experiences repeated successes with progressively greater challenges and is unlikely to become overwhelmed.
- Use the cognitive-affective-cognitive sandwich. This jargony term (sorry about that!) means that you surround the emotional/expressive component of your session with more structured components grounded in rational thinking. For example, you might start out by reminding the client of the reason he or she is going to talk about the hard thing, how this relates to his or her goals. In the middle you do work with the emotion, at whatever

level the client is ready to handle. The emotional component is finished with calming activities so that the level of upset or arousal is diminished. Then you go back to the cognitive, perhaps by discussing what was learned or by reorienting to what's next in the client's day. This helps the client contain the emotion and regain composure. Although no strategy works 100% of the time, therapists who make a practice of using the sandwich tend to have far fewer problems with their clients being "a mess" later on.

Sensitivity

No matter how carefully we follow the Fairy Tale model, no matter how well we plan, surprises can always occur. We are working with humans! So it's important to continually monitor how your clients are doing and what is going on with them. Frequently, when things are not going according to plan, it's because the client does not feel safe anymore. If we are paying attention, we have a chance of catching this and addressing it.

- A 55-year-old woman has been doing well in treatment and is ready for trauma resolution. The therapist prepares her for this, and they plan to start on it at the next meeting. Then for the next two meetings, at the last minute something comes up and the woman cancels. The therapist calls her up and asks her to please show up for the next scheduled meeting and tells her that the plan to talk about the trauma is off for now. When the woman shows up at the next meeting, she eventually explains that she does not feel ready to talk about the trauma yet and was afraid to come to sessions for that reason.
- A 22-year-old man has been very cooperative in treatment for the first four sessions with his employee assistance program counselor. Today he seems angry, refuses to answer questions in any detail, and keeps looking at his watch. The counselor asks him if he is in a hurry today. The man says, "Yes, I'm under a deadline, and I really should be working right now!" The counselor thanks the man for saying that; after all, he is here to do better at his job, not to miss his deadlines. They agree to reschedule their meeting so the man can leave and fulfill his work obligation.
- A 10-year-old boy has been working well in treatment and has completed several sessions of trauma resolution work already. However, in this session he refuses to talk about the memory that is already partly resolved. The therapist is stumped and is unable to get a decent explanation from the boy. Later, the therapist mentions to the boy's mother that he seemed different today and did not accomplish as much as usual. The mother reports that she had blown up at her son a couple of days earlier and threatened to send him to live with his father if he didn't get a better attitude.

In each of these cases, some pressing concern prevented the client from moving forward according to the therapist's plan. If the therapist just barges ahead, the client's concern is not addressed. Then the client might feel disrespected or pressured and take protective action.

On the other hand, when the therapist notices when things are not going smoothly and shows respect and concern, the client learns that the therapist cares and wants what is good for the client. In general, the more the therapist can do to help the client to feel safe and supported, the more work the client will be able to accomplish in therapy. Our goal is to create a "fenced-in" safe area in the room, in the therapy relationship itself. This allows the rest of the work to proceed.

Success

Remember the princess? The entire therapy enterprise is in service of the client's goals. In the trauma treatment approach, we may be part of the kingdom (providing safety and support), and we are also the personal trainer (and later, the consultant). As the personal trainer, our job is to help the client to make progress toward winning the princess. Remember, nothing succeeds like success. So one of our primary strategies is to help the client to build a track record of success, achieving smaller goals one step at a time. This track record helps to build confidence that the next steps will also be worthwhile and successful and to build hope that the larger goals can be attained.

The Research

The following reviews the empirical support first for each of the primary components of this treatment approach—the Fairy Tale model, as adapted for problem behavior clients—and then for the treatment approach as a package, as presented in the remainder of this book. The primary treatment components are motivational interviewing, self-management training, trauma resolution, and relapse prevention/harm reduction. In addition, this treatment also supports many of the so-called nonspecific factors that have been shown to promote positive outcomes.

Nonspecific Factors

Among the "common factors" that predict positive outcome of treatment, across-treatment approaches are presenting a convincing rationale for treatment activities (Messer & Wampold, 2002) and agreement on treatment goals and tasks (Horvath & Greenberg, 1994). Although these are complex and difficult interventions to implement (Mallinckrodt & Nelson, 1991), the scripted interventions for case formulation and treatment contracting facilitate the process even for less experienced therapists. Empathy, warmth, and positive regard, also among the common factors leading to positive outcomes (see Norcross, 2002), are generally considered therapist characteristics rather than treatment characteristics. Even so, this treatment approach may be likely to guide the therapist toward conveying these qualities. For example, in the Goal-Setting session, one portion of the script focuses on identifying the client's strengths and resources as a basis for the therapist's stated belief that the client will probably succeed in achieving his or her goals. This intervention almost certainly supports and conveys positive regard.

Motivational Interviewing

Motivational interviewing (MI) is a directive counseling approach—involving both style and specific procedures—designed to elicit motivation and action for positive behavioral change (Miller & Rollnick, 2002). It explicitly avoids the authoritarian, confrontive approach which has been shown to increase client resistance (Patterson & Forgatch, 1985). Intervention components are the following (Miller & Sanchez, 1994):

1. Individual assessment and feedback focusing on the discrepancy between behaviors and goals.
2. Emphasizing the individual's free choice and responsibility for his or her own behavior.
3. Providing advice to make a positive change.
4. Offering a "menu" of ways to accomplish the change.
5. Attitude of empathy and acceptance of the client's perspective.
6. Interventions to enhance self-efficacy, reinforcing self-confidence and optimism regarding goal achievement.

MI has been applied successfully to engaging clients in treatment for a wide range of client issues including substance abuse, health-related behaviors, high-risk behaviors, and compliance with treatment for a wide range of problems (Hettema, Steele, & Miller, 2005). A number of MI studies with adolescents have also yielded consistently positive outcomes (Colby et al., 2005; Gowers & Smyth, 2004; Kelly & Lapworth, 2006; Stein et al., 2006; see also Suarez & Mullins, 2008). A similar approach, focusing on positive future goals (and not merely on self-restraint), is also catching on within sex offender treatment (Ward & Gannon, 2006). MI has contributed to positive outcomes even in lieu of subsequent treatment; however, the gains deteriorate over time (Miller, 2005). It is essential to capitalize on the client's motivation by offering further treatment activities likely to lead to more robust and lasting change.

In this treatment approach, MI contributes to engagement, goal identification, and commitment to treatment. Modifications to Miller and Rollnick's (2002) manual were made for developmental appropriateness, problem-specific content, and enhanced treatment acceptance. An additional modification is the visualization of behaviors leading to desired goals; this type of intervention has led to increased performance of target behaviors (Taylor, Pham, Rivkin, & Armor, 1998). Finally, in addition to adopting an MI style throughout treatment, the Goal-Setting session—

the primary MI intervention—is scripted to promote treatment adherence and consistent effectiveness.

Cognitive-Behavioral Therapy

Cognitive-behavioral therapy (CBT) refers to an array of structured intervention strategies designed to provide corrective experiences, to develop more constructive ways of thinking and behaving, and to enhance specific self-management skills (Kendall, 2000). A review of treatments for antisocial youth found CBT approaches—particularly those focused on interpersonal problem-solving skills, reappraising social cues, connecting behaviors to consequences, and punishing maladaptive choices while reinforcing prosocial choices—to be of modest but significant benefit in reducing problem behaviors (Kazdin, 1997). "Seeking Safety," a structured package of trauma-sensitive CBT interventions, has also been found effective in treatment of substance abusers with PTSD (Najavits, 2002).

In a controlled anger treatment study in an adult PTSD population, severely volatile veterans' participation in anger management therapy led to increased self-control as well as reduction of apparently unrelated trauma symptoms (intrusive thoughts and images), whereas standard trauma treatment did neither (Chemtob et al., 1997). Anger treatment completers maintained their posttreatment gains at 18-month follow-up. These findings were consistent with another study, in which a multicomponent treatment for combat-related PTSD found incremental effects for both the exposure and the anger management components (Frueh, Turner, Beidel, Mirabella, & Jones, 1996).

Why should self-management training lead to reduced posttraumatic symptoms? Perhaps because when problem behaviors are reduced, the environment responds by becoming less hostile and more supportive. When the environment is experienced as being safer, survival mode can be relaxed and the trauma is less pressing, more part of the past. In other words, a side effect of effective personal training may be that the fence becomes stronger.

In this treatment approach, CBT contributes to establishing and maintaining the sense of safety and self-efficacy. Modifications to the Chemtob et al. (1997) manual were made for developmental appropriateness and enhanced treatment acceptance, also adding the consequence-oriented component found effective in the Kazdin (1997) review.

Trauma Resolution

Reduction of problem behaviors has often been noted as one of the incidental outcomes of child/adolescent trauma-focused treatment (Cohen, Berliner, & March, 2000). Trauma treatment has also been successful with problem behavior populations, including cognitive processing therapy (CPT) for incarcerated juveniles (Ahrens & Rexford, 2002) and Eye Movement Desensitization and Reprocessing (EMDR) for high-risk acting-out adolescent girls and young women

(Scheck, Schaeffer, & Gillette, 1998). Although these studies focused only on posttraumatic stress symptoms and did not track behavioral outcomes, they at least established that problem behavior populations can successfully undergo trauma-focused treatment.

Few studies have tested trauma treatment with reduction of problem behaviors as the primary targeted outcome. Datta and Wallace (1996) provided three sessions of EMDR to 10 adolescent sex offenders, focused on their own memories of having been victimized. Following treatment, many of the participants spontaneously initiated attempts at victim restitution, and empathy may have also increased (measurement problems made this outcome difficult to interpret). Soberman and colleagues (Soberman, Greenwald, & Rule, 2002) compared standard care plus three sessions of EMDR with only standard care for 29 boys aged 10–16 with serious conduct problems who were either in residential or day treatment. In this randomized study, EMDR led to significant reductions in reactivity to the trauma memory as well as severity of the primary identified problem behaviors (29% mean problem behavior reduction for EMDR recipients vs. 9% for controls). These findings provide further support for the proposition that effective trauma treatment can lead to reduced problem behavior.

It is noteworthy that all of the aforementioned trauma treatment studies used either CPT or EMDR, which each have features likely to make the treatment more tolerable than exposure, particularly for problem behavior clients. CPT involves writing down the trauma story rather than speaking it aloud (Ahrens & Rexford, 2002), as would be required with standard exposure procedures. EMDR uses brief bursts of exposure to the trauma memory and may therefore be better tolerated in session than prolonged exposure. Furthermore, EMDR treatment does not require the client to describe the trauma memory orally or in writing, which allows the client to work through the memory without having to disclose specific details of abuse he or she may have experienced. EMDR may also be more efficient than other trauma resolution methods (Rogers & Silver, 2003), making the ordeal more rapid and thus more tolerable. Finally, EMDR does not require homework, which problem behavior clients are unlikely to follow through on.

In this treatment approach, trauma resolution contributes to reducing the full range of posttraumatic symptoms, including pessimistic future, affect dysregulation, maladaptive beliefs, avoidance, and intrusive memories. Those using this treatment approach have so far primarily used EMDR (Greenwald, 2007; Shapiro, 2001) with modifications for developmental appropriateness and to enhance treatment acceptance (Greenwald, 1999). However, any effective trauma resolution method can be used as long as it will be tolerated by the client. For example, the Counting Method, which was shown to be as efficient as EMDR in one controlled study (Johnson, Lubin, & Ochberg, 2007), has been modified for enhanced efficiency and acceptability. Progressive Counting (PC), the method taught in this book, may be particularly well suited to the problem behavior client, because it is efficient, disclosure of details is not required, and the dose of exposure can be controlled by the therapist to minimize the risk of overwhelming the client (Greenwald, 2008a, 2008b; Greenwald, Schmitt, & Borton, 2009). Further research will indicate which trauma resolution methods are most suitable for problem behavior clients.

This treatment approach also manages the challenge of trauma resolution work by first targeting recent, minor upsetting events, and then discrete relatively minor trauma memories, to establish a track record of competence prior to approaching more distressing trauma memories.

Relapse Prevention and Harm Reduction

Cognitive-behavioral relapse prevention and harm reduction interventions (Marlatt & Gordon, 1985) focus on strategies for avoiding anticipated problematic situations and stressors, coping with them, and coping with anticipated relapse to prevent further deterioration. This approach has been used with some success in treating a range of addictions (Marlatt & Donovan, 2005) as well as with sex offenders (Dowden, Antonowicz, & Andrews, 2003), although when used as a stand-alone intervention its limitations have also been noted (Polaschek, 2003). It has not yet been widely applied to other types of problem behavior treatment. In one study, this approach was used in combination with other skills training with adults arrested for driving while disqualified (often as a consequence of a drunk driving conviction). Compared with a matched control group, this treatment reduced incidence of driving while disqualified; other criminal offending was reduced as well (Bakker, Hudson, & Ward, 2000).

The CBT skills training component of this treatment approach includes a module on avoiding high-risk situations. Following the trauma resolution phase, the treatment returns to a skills focus using relapse prevention and harm reduction methods to anticipate and prepare for future challenges and support maintenance of gains.

Trauma-Informed Treatment Approaches for Problem Behaviors

With the growing recognition of trauma's contribution to a range of problem behaviors, trauma-informed comprehensive treatment approaches have been developed. For example, a similar phase model approach has been recommended for domestic violence offenders (Hamel, 2005). Recent research supports such approaches. Ten adult sex offenders were given treatment including a motivational component, a skills component, and a trauma resolution component (with EMDR) focused on their own trauma/victimization history. Along with reduced posttraumatic stress symptoms, their interest in so-called deviant sexual objects decreased; this was confirmed with physiological measures (Ricci, Clayton, & Shapiro, 2006). In another study, adult female substance abusers were provided a treatment including trauma-sensitive self-management skills training plus trauma resolution (also

EMDR). Although 34% refused the trauma resolution phase, treatment completers had an 83% rate of completing drug court graduation criteria compared with only 33% of noncompleters and 35% of those (screened out for "no trauma") in the no-treatment program-as-usual (Brown, Gilman, Fava, & Smyth, 2009).

The Trauma-Informed Treatment Protocol

The treatment package, previously called the Motivation–Adaptive Skills–Trauma Resolution (MASTR) protocol, consists of a multicomponent treatment approach in which these validated interventions are systematically sequenced to address the engagement/motivation-, skill deficit-, and trauma-related treatment needs of problem behavior clients.

Treatment Development

The protocol was initially developed while providing treatment to about 50 adjudicated youth in two residential facilities in 1995–1996. Early anecdotal reports of MASTR for adolescent girls in residential treatment (Stewart, 1998) and incarcerated adolescent boys (Greenwald, 1996, 2000) were encouraging. However, only vignettes were presented, and no objective psychological or behavioral outcome measures were used.

An open trial was conducted with six youth referred for school-related academic and disciplinary problems (Greenwald, 2002a). Treatment completion was a problem in this school-based outpatient setting, because symptom reduction following the adaptive skills phase frequently led to premature termination. Only treatment completers were included in the study. Participants completed a psychological evaluation and received a variety of diagnoses including PTSD, conduct disorder, oppositional/defiant disorder, attention deficit hyperactivity disorder (ADHD), and dysthymia; most participants carried multiple diagnoses. Other interventions were also utilized as needed, especially parent consultation and training; however, MASTR was the predominant treatment. Therapist-administered standardized self-report measures were used to assess posttraumatic stress, anxiety, depression, and anger. Additional outcome measures included parent ratings of the youths' posttraumatic stress symptoms and the severity of the primary presenting problems, as well as school grades and discipline reports. Following treatment, participants showed consistently reduced posttraumatic symptoms as well as some decreases in other psychological symptoms. Participants also demonstrated clinically significant reductions in discipline problems at school and at home as well as improved academic performance.

A pilot study was conducted on the Goal-Setting session with 15 youth who had been expelled from school for at least 2 weeks, which warranted placement in an alternative school (Johnson, Greenwald, & Cameron, 2002). Following this single-session intervention, several of the participants showed immediate (next-day) behavioral changes such as talking differently to their teachers or wearing different types of clothing. Unfortunately, longer-term follow-up data were not gathered, so this can only provide an impression of possible effectiveness.

The treatment was introduced in a residential facility for youth with a variety of severe problem behaviors including violence. Facility clinicians, who provided weekly individual therapy to each resident, were trained to use the protocol. Compared with a 6-month baseline pretreatment period, following 2 months of treatment the total critical incident (defined by the facility as, e.g., assault, property destruction, runaway) count was down by at least 50% on all units (male conduct disorder, female conduct disorder, female sex offender, male substance abuser), with the most serious class of incidents showing the largest decrease (Greenwald, 2003).

In that study, the training intervention was not limited to the therapists who were focused on individual treatment. At the same time, the entire facility was involved in a review process focused on implementing trauma-informed milieu treatment system-wide. Therefore, it was not possible to determine the individual treatment protocol's specific contribution to this outcome. Of interest is the fact that facility therapists were already trained in EMDR prior to the MASTR training. It is not clear to what extent they may have already been using EMDR or to what extent they may have been unable to elicit cooperation for EMDR prior to MASTR.

A randomized controlled study was conducted in three secure facilities in New York with youth incarcerated for at least 6 months (Greenwald, Satin, Azubuike, Borgen, & Rubin, 2004). A group of 9 therapists treated 140 participants, who were compared with the standard care group of 160. Unfortunately, the randomization was fatally flawed in that those in the treatment group were systematically worse on factors that predicted outcome. Therefore, the equivalent outcomes of the treatment and control groups could not be interpreted with confidence (indicating that the treatment either did or did not provide benefit).

Even so, this project did yield considerable knowledge useful for further treatment development. Exit interviews with the therapists found that every therapist strongly endorsed the treatment approach, many indicating that this was the first time they felt they had something to offer to this difficult population. Indeed, the large majority of participants did engage in the treatment, especially the goal-setting and coping skills portions. However, only 12% completed trauma resolution, with another 34% at least doing some. Some of this failure to complete the treatment could be explained by unfortunate timing, in that some participants had not been in treatment very long when the study ended. Even so, it was clear that the treatment was not sufficiently persuasive regarding the value of persevering through the trauma resolution phase. Following this project, a number of treatment components were added to support perseverance through the full course of the treatment. These additions were extensively tested in a clinical setting prior to the next study.

One study has been completed since the protocol's revision. A group of 65 youth in foster or residential placement in Quebec were randomized to routine care (n = 32) or the MASTR treatment (n = 33) including motivational inter-viewing, skills training, and EMDR (Farkas, Cyr, Lebeau, & Lemay, 2007). Both therapists were trained and supervised by the protocol's developer (Greenwald, 2005b). The protocol's scripts were translated to Canadian French and included in the session forms to support treatment adherence, which was later deter-mined to be adequate by independent raters. Blind independent assessments were conducted, using validated structured interviews and objective measures, at pretreatment, posttreatment, and follow-up. At 3 months posttreatment, MASTR participants showed significantly superior outcomes on posttraumatic stress and behavioral symptoms compared with the (loosely defined) standard care control. Although MASTR has not yet been compared with another structured treatment approach, this study does establish MASTR as effective in a real-world clinical setting.

Don't Forget the Kingdom

This book's focus on the individual component of treatment does not negate the importance of working with others in the client's life. Although sometimes the individual treatment alone may be sufficient, success will probably be achieved more consistently when the environmental influences can be mobilized in sup-port of the treatment. This was exemplified in Greenwald (2003), in which the individual treatment was combined with a trauma-informed milieu, leading to dramatically reduced frequency of serious problem behaviors. Remember that old saying, "It takes a kingdom to slay a dragon"?

A variety of approaches are available for effectively mobilizing the kingdom. For example, parent training has been shown to be quite effective in reducing the problem behaviors of children and (to some extent) adolescents (Kazdin, 2005) and should be included whenever feasible. The Restorative Justice approach has been successful in engaging the community in support of criminals offering victim compensation as well as achieving reduced rates of reoffending (Morrison & Ahmed, 2006). Olweus' (1993) approach to reducing bullying has been consis-tently effective in school settings internationally (Limber, 2006). Szapocznik and colleagues' (Santisteban et al., 2006) family therapy approach has been success-ful in both engaging antisocial youth in treatment and achieving good outcomes. Hengeller and colleagues' Multi-Systemic Therapy (MST; Swenson, Henggeler, Taylor, & Addison, 2005), which integrates interventions with the individual, parents/family, school, courts, and other service providers, has also led to posi-tive outcomes for antisocial youth, although the effect in community settings has been much smaller than in university studies (Curtis, Ronan, & Borduin, 2004).

Promising "kingdom" approaches that are explicitly trauma informed have also been developed. For example, Saxe and colleagues' variant of MST, Trauma Systems Therapy (Saxe, Kaplow, & Ellis, 2006), showed promising outcomes with traumatized youth in challenging environments (Saxe, Ellis, Fogler, Hansen,

& Sorkin, 2005). Bloom's (1997) trauma-informed milieu Sanctuary Model has shown promise with teens in a residential setting (Rivard, Bloom, McCorkle, & Abramovitz, 2005). Greenwald's (2005a) Fairy Tale model involving individual, family, and community interventions had high retention rate and positive outcomes with impoverished minority youth and their families (Becker & Greenwald, 2008).

Family members' relationships with clients can be used as a source of motivation as well as of support. Family members as well as others in positions of authority over the client can also control reinforcements and punishments and can bring considerable influence to bear on the client. Even spouses and friends, who may not have authority over the client, do have control over their own behavior and in that way may have influence. Regardless of which approach is used to mobilize the kingdom, it is helpful (and often essential) that those with influence on the client do the following.

Provide Safety and Security

For clients to be able to concentrate on their treatment and make progress, it is important that they are, and feel, as safe and secure as possible. The clients themselves, especially adults and to some extent teens, are responsible for stabilizing themselves. However, depending on the situation, others may be in a position to contribute. Social service providers may be able to assist clients in obtaining adequate food or medical care or housing or in some other way to ensure that basic needs are met. Spouses and other family members can work to improve communication and relationships so that the stress level in the home is reduced. Residential facilities, prisons, and schools can make efforts to reduce violence, bullying, and harassment. Parents of teens and preteens can intervene in school and elsewhere to ensure that the client is in an appropriate environment, with sufficient supports and accommodations that success is achievable. Parents can also more consistently and calmly enforce the rules; for preteens and some teens, this will generally be a key element of treatment.

Make Sure the Client Gets to Treatment

You can't help the client if he or she doesn't show up. Many (or most) problem behavior clients will not show up unless they are compelled to do so. Therefore it's important to arrange such compulsion. Judges, and programs connected with the court system, tend to be pretty comfortable with requiring those under their authority to participate in treatment. Spouses may say, "Get treatment or get out." Parents tend to be more confused and ambivalent regarding whether to use their authority in this way. They often say, "But he doesn't want to go," perhaps followed by, "so of course I won't force him."

This parental stance, if left unchallenged, will almost surely lead to treatment failure. Even the occasional treatment-motivated problem behavior child or adolescent will sooner or later feel like quitting. This must be addressed up front to ensure strong parental support for treatment. This can be done by explaining to parents that the prospective client's lack of motivation is not a factor that prohibits treatment and by helping parents to understand that their parental role obligates them to get the child into treatment.

Motivation Is Not Required

Some therapists actually tell parents, "If she's not motivated, treatment is probably not worthwhile. There's nothing I can do." This is an absurd statement and really only means that the therapist does not know what to do. They might as well say, "I can't help your depressed child because he or she is depressed." Lack of motivation is part of the problem; it's a symptom and is simply a target for treatment. The therapist should be saying, "Don't worry about the motivation. You get your kid into my office, and I'll take it from there. That's my job."

Parents Have Responsibility for Their Children

When parents speak of therapy as something that their child should have a choice about, this reflects a lack of understanding about the meaning of treatment in the child's life. That's fair enough; most parents are not mental health professionals, and if they don't understand the therapist can explain.

First of all, the therapist can explain the possible consequences of no treatment. For kids with problem behaviors, the therapist might describe the client's coming years on the basis of the client's current behaviors and anticipated trajectory. This honest appraisal can be rather grim. On the one hand, to overdo this would be to use a coercive scare tactic, which should be avoided. On the other hand, if we don't tell parents what is likely to happen without intervention, we are not giving them adequate information on which to base their decisions. Informed consent is a central tenet of ethical and professional provision of services, and clients (and parents) have a right to know the likely consequences of the various options before they make a choice.

Second, the therapist can equate mental health treatment to medical treatment to help parents understand that as the parent they are responsible for making this type of decision on the child's behalf.

Therapist: If your child fell off his bike and scraped his arm, would you take him to the hospital?
Parent: Oh, no, just wash it and maybe put on a bandage.
Therapist: And if he broke his arm, just put on a splint?
Parent: No, for that, we go to the emergency room!
Therapist: And if he says he doesn't want to go?
Parent: He goes.

Therapist: Supposing your brain isn't working that day, and you let him talk you into not going. What would happen?

Parent: I guess his arm might heal wrong; maybe it wouldn't work so well anymore.

Therapist: Kind of a serious consequence.

Parent: Yeah. You don't mess with that stuff.

Therapist: I guess that's why kids have parents. Because kids might just see what they want right now. Parents see the long-term and can make better decisions for that reason.

Parent: I think I see what you're getting at.

Therapist: Yes. This treatment is like that. Kids usually don't want to go, because it's more fun to do something else that day. But parents don't just think about today; they think about the years to come and what kind of a life the child will have. That's why it's the parent's job to make the decision.

Enforce Consequences

The client's problem should be a problem for the client, not just for others. Then there is more of a chance for motivation to change. This concept is well known in the treatment of alcohol and drug abuse; we encourage spouses and others not to "enable" the substance abuser's behavior by covering for him or her or by somehow cushioning the impact of the behavior. The same concept applies to other problem behaviors. If the client does not experience a negative consequence for a problem behavior, those responsible for withholding consequences are—whether they like it or not—encouraging the behavior.

I once worked in a school system in which the disciplinarians refused to punish students for fighting and other serious problem behavior if that student happened to have a diagnosis of oppositional/defiant disorder or conduct disorder. One assistant principal explained, "You can't punish a child for his disability. That would be like punishing a blind student for not being able to see what's on the blackboard." He wouldn't budge on this, because he knew the laws and did not want to expose the school to lawsuits. This was a problem, because I did not want to treat students who were not being disciplined. We resolved the problem by systematically writing "school rules and consequences" into every such student's educational plan. Consistent discipline and enforcement of consequences is indeed essential to treatment of problem behavior clients.

I have known many teens and preteens with serious problem behaviors who did not perceive that they had any problem. This was in large part because they were not being effectively disciplined. When I pointed out their problem behaviors, they often said, "Other people might have a problem with me [or with my behavior]. But I don't have any problem."

What finally changed their tune? When the consequences were enforced and their problem behavior became a problem for them and not just for others. This transformed attitude was most striking following the client's first incarceration (especially if it is for more than just a few days). Then he or she said, "What do I have to do so I never get locked up again?" The bottom line is that if the client does not perceive a cost for the problem behaviors, he or she does not perceive a need for change or for treatment.

Chapter 2

Initial Interview

How does a trauma therapist say hello?

Actually, much goes into how we introduce ourselves and kick off the treatment relationship. The first goal is to establish a sense of safety and predictability in the therapy. We can do this by telling our clients what's going on and what to expect. The trick here is to tell them the truth and to offer a truth that is reasonably enticing.

Psychotherapy was initially considered suitable only for intelligent, articulate, psychologically oriented clients, but now we try to treat a much wider range of people. This brings special challenges. The psychotherapy literature tells us that clients from minority groups are more likely than others to drop out of therapy so quickly that treatment never gets a chance to work (Wierzbicki & Pekarik, 1993). The same is true for individuals who are not so intelligent, psychologically minded (i.e., insight oriented), or verbal. This does not imply that minority clients are unintelligent, but both groups tend not to understand the appeal of the traditional unstructured talk-therapy approach.

Adolescents (and children) in treatment have many similarities to these groups, in that they may not understand the purpose of unstructured talk and they may not be particularly psychologically minded or verbal. So it's important to understand that, along with many types of adults, teens as a group may be difficult to engage. This is in addition to the other obstacles to engagement (see Chapter 1) for teens who have been exposed to trauma and for teens who are affiliated with an antisocial peer group.

The literature also tells us that certain therapist practices can mitigate this problem and help these people stay in treatment (Nader, Dubrow, Stamm, & Hudnall, 1999; Sue & Sue, 1999). The therapist can acculturate the client to treatment by explaining what therapy is, what the procedures are, how it works (and why these procedures might help), and what is expected of the client. It is also helpful when the therapist's style is directive, goal oriented, and activity focused rather than unstructured.

Acculturation

Clients who are not "therapy-wise" do not generally understand why an undirected "talking about whatever you want" is supposed to help them. Experienced clients may also not understand this. As one incarcerated client said, "They've been giving me counselors for years, but all that talking doesn't make a difference. I still do what I do." Clients want to know what to do to solve their problem, and they don't see how this kind of talk will get results. When the therapist explains the therapy procedures and why these procedures can be expected to help the client, clients are more likely to engage and to stick around. Therapists can also tell the clients what to do—how to behave to be successful in treatment. Then clients know and have a better chance of doing it.

Even for clients with prior therapy experience, the acculturation process is critical. Otherwise, the experienced clients might believe that they already know what the treatment is about and how they should be participating. But we may not want our clients to do, with us, what they did with someone else. As the personal trainer, the one with the plan, it's the therapist's job to orient the client to this particular treatment approach.

Therapist Style

The other issue here is what actually happens in therapy. Just "talking about your feelings" doesn't necessarily help (and might actually do harm if the feelings are overwhelming). As noted in Chapter 1, this is especially true for problem behavior clients. The trauma-informed treatment approach consists of a series of tasks and relies on a directive therapist to guide treatment accordingly while also being sensitive and responsive to the client. When the client is helped to recognize the impact of his or her trauma (the dragon), to identify his or her goals (the princess), and to understand how the treatment plan might help him or her to overcome his problems and achieve his goals (personal training to slay the dragon and marry the princess), then the client is more likely to engage and to stick around.

Introducing Treatment

The therapist can start, then, by explaining what treatment is for and what is expected to happen in treatment. Here's an example of what a therapist might say at the beginning of the first session.

Therapist: Did your parents tell you why you had to come here?
Client: Not really.
Therapist: Usually people come here because someone is worried about them, someone thinks that they could be feeling better, acting better, doing

better in some way. My job is to learn a lot about you: what you care about, what you want for yourself, and what might be getting in your way. So I'll be asking you a lot of questions. Then I'll tell you what I learned. Then I'll give you some suggestions for how to get what you want, what to do about the things that are in your way. Is this what you expected when you came?

Client: I don't know. Sort of.

Note that we are not focusing on the client's problems at this point. We are acknowledging that problems exist and suggesting the possibility of solutions. However, the first focus is on acculturation, on what we're doing here, why, and how we are going to do it. This continues with an explanation of the rules and expectations.

The Rules

Therapist: Before we get started with the questions, I want to tell you what the rules are for our meetings together. The first rule is that I don't tell other people what you say. What you say here is private. But there are exceptions. One exception is if you give me permission to tell someone about a certain thing. Also, if I'm afraid someone's in danger, the law says that I have to tell.

This is the place to go over all rules and expectations regarding confidentiality, payment, cancellation policy, and any other conditions that apply. Stating the rules makes them explicit. Therapy is a new setting for most people, and knowing the rules and expectations up front helps them to feel secure because then they know what to do and what will happen. Here is an important one:

Therapist: The next rule is about what you say. You're not allowed to say anything in here unless you decide you want to. So what if I ask you a question that you don't want to talk about right now, how do you follow this rule; what can you do?

Note that this rule is not phrased as, "You don't have to answer a question if you don't want to." That's not a bad rule, but it carries the implication that the client can choose to not participate by not answering a question. That sets up both the client and the therapist to feel as if they have failed. If the client feels like a failure, and if that hits a sore spot, the client might be tempted to try some quick-relief strategy to get rid of the bad feeling. When a teen says, "I don't know," to everything you ask, she may simply be trying to transfer her own sense of failure and helplessness to you. Similarly, if the therapist feels that she has failed, and if that hits her own sore spot, she may be tempted to try to transfer her own sense of failure and helplessness to the client. Therapists often do this by pathologizing their client with epithets like "resistant," "unmotivated," "antisocial," or "border-line." Although such strategies (by either party) can provide quick relief, they do not contribute to the client's progress in treatment.

The rule, "You're not allowed to say anything in here, unless you decide you want to," carries the implication that the client is participating fully regardless of the choice. Later, when the client refuses to answer a question, the therapist can say, "I'm glad you remembered my rule!" Then the client is able to say to herself, "I did what I was supposed to," and the therapist is able to say to herself, "My client is following my directions." Thus, both the client and the therapist remain successful.

Helping the client remain successful is a core element of trauma-informed treatment for a couple of reasons. First, in the Fairy Tale model, we are focused on personal training to help the client develop strength and skills. When failure becomes habitual, it's difficult to keep up the morale necessary to persevere. Also—and this is related—even a small failure may hit a sore spot and trigger a trauma-related overreaction. If clients are getting habitually triggered in therapy, they will learn that therapy is not a safe place and they need to protect themselves. Then they are more likely to be resistant and with-drawn and less likely to get the job done. The more we can do to help clients feel successful when they are with us, the better chance we have of being successful with them.

After the rules we will ask questions. Consistent with the Fairy Tale model, it's very important to get the "once upon a time" information before we start focusing on the dragon and the problems it created. When we meet a client and focus immediately on his or her problems, the client feels as if he or she is a problem and that is how we see him or her. On the other hand, if we focus on the positives—interests, talents, successful relationships, and achievements—the client feels as if we are getting to know him or her, not just what's wrong with him or her. Also, because the client is expected to be his or her own knight in shining armor, we need to be able to see this potential in the client and to know his or her strengths. We get this information by asking, by learning much about the client, not just the problems.

Individual Interview Strategies

People can feel pretty nervous when a stranger starts asking them personal questions. The more we can do to help clients feel safe and in control, the more comfortable and more likely to cooperate they will be. Also, the more we can help them to feel safe and in control, the more they will learn to trust us and to believe that we care for them and have their best interests as a priority. A number of specific things can be done to foster the development of this therapeutic relationship and to help clients to feel safe with us.

Allow Certain Choices

Some teens and many preteens may prefer to occupy themselves with drawing, doodling, eating a snack, or fiddling with some found object. Although it is very important to get through the evaluation, we can allow clients to keep their hands occupied as long as they are also able to fully participate in the evaluation. Upon seeing the client begin to do something other than merely sit, the therapist might say something such as, "I don't know you very well. Will you be able to [do that] and concentrate on our conversation at the same time?" This gives the client the option of continuing the other activity, while also making clear that the conversation is a priority. Actually it can be helpful to have the other activity available as an outlet for restlessness and perhaps for containing emotion at challenging moments.

Help the Client Prepare

Before diving into the questions, remind the client about taking care of himself or herself regarding questions he or she may not want to answer. Think about driving a car fast. This can be a little scary, but fun too. Now think about how fast you'd be willing to drive if you weren't sure if your brakes worked! Or if you weren't sure where your turn would be coming up. For clients to be willing to take risks and move forward, it's important that they feel that they have the brakes and the map. When we are about to ask clients to "drive fast" or to take a new risk, it can be very helpful to remind and re-orient them to their treatment plan and their ability to use the brakes (e.g., by deciding not to talk about something).

Start Small

After the big build-up of "here come the questions," clients are relieved to be asked a series of "small talk" questions about, for example, their favorite color, favorite food, school, interests, and favorite activities. The questions only gradually become more personal as clients become more comfortable. People find these innocuous questions relevant—it's what we often want to know about one another—and like to be seen as a whole person and not just as a problem. Most clients will answer most or all of the questions and will feel good at having expressed themselves— even if no apparent emotionally laden disclosure has occurred.

Warn Before Any Potentially Challenging Shift

The trauma therapist avoids surprising clients with sudden shifts or potentially objectionable (personal or upsetting) questions. For example, in the Initial Interview script, after asking about what the client is good at, the next question is, "If you could be any animal, what would you be?" That is quite a shift. So first we give a warning: "Here comes a different kind of question." The goal is not to surprise clients but to help them feel that we are looking out for them. In general, the more clients feel that they know what to expect and are in control, the more they are willing to go ahead.

Give a Menu

When the client has trouble answering an open-ended question or some other question, the therapist quickly (after a couple of seconds) intervenes with a menu of possible choices—types of appropriate answers. This helps the client be successful and can preclude the tendency for acting out (e.g., "Don't know, don't care") in the interview. The 2-second rule (2 seconds of silence before jumping in) is a good guide, but you can use your judgment or even ask about the silence. For example, "This seems to be a hard question to answer. Should I just give you more time, or ask it in a different way?"

What's the difference between giving a menu and asking a leading question? Giving a menu is a way of showing what a right answer might look like, orienting the client to the possibilities, but clearly asking for the client's own answer. A leading question, on the other hand, pushes the client to give the particular answer that the therapist seems to be demanding. Here is an example of a follow-up when a client did not adequately answer the question, "How do you know when you're angry—what are the signals?" A menu might be, "Well, some people say they get swear words in their head, or fighting words, or their mind goes blank. Some people say that their face gets hot, or their heart starts pounding, or they fidget, or their hands turn into fists. What happens with you? What are your signals?" A leading question might be, "Then you want to kill him, right?" A leading question can feel coercive to the client and yields limited information of dubious value. Use the menu.

Provide Frequent Feedback

Therapy can feel safer for clients when the therapist offers frequent feedback. Many clients grew up around adults who, due to mental illness, substance abuse, or trauma-related reactivity, have been volatile. Children in this type of environment learn to (try to) read minds and read signs, to figure out when the bad thing might happen, so that it can be avoided or at least prepared for. When a therapist plays the "blank slate" game, clients don't know what the therapist is thinking, and they are liable to fear the worst. Then they will feel unsafe, afraid to say certain things for fear that you'll get angry or not like them anymore. Sometimes they will even tell us about this, perhaps after having disclosed a trauma or misdeed, saying, "Now you're mad at me," or, "Now you probably don't like me anymore."

On the other hand, if you provide frequent feedback, clients will feel that they know what's going on with you, and they won't have to wonder or worry about it. This doesn't mean that you make a habit of self-disclosure. Rather, it means that you let them know, selectively, what you think you are learning. For example, you might say, "Oh, so you did pretty well before you changed schools; I guess that means you're smart enough to do well in school."

This gives you a chance to convey a positive impression, focusing on the client's strengths even while implicitly acknowledging the problems. Another advantage of providing frequent feedback is that you get a chance to field-test the building blocks of your case formulation, the explanation of what's going on with the client. By the time you formally offer your full explanation, the client has already become familiar with many of its elements.

Offer Information

The therapist can share a couple of specific kinds of information during the initial interview. This strategy can also effect an informal psychoeducation regarding the impact of trauma. The goal here is to help clients understand themselves and their symptoms as within the range of normal responses to stressful past events. This also helps to build the case for the case formulation:

- Why you are asking that question: The therapist can simply explain this to provide information. For example, "The reason I was asking is that some people, after they got a concussion like you did, they notice that some things are different, like they might get headaches, or have more trouble concentrating than they did before, or have a shorter temper. Did you notice anything like that for you, after the concussion?"
- What other people say: At various points (e.g., when offering a menu or framing a question with multiple options) the therapist refers to what "other people" say. Traumatized individuals often feel strange, alien, isolated, different. This type of questioning effects some of the universality normally available in group therapy: that the things that have made the client feel different are actually things shared in common with other people. Clients feel relieved to discover that they are "normal."

Honest Praise for Self-Advocacy

Clients may be hesitant to tell you that they have to go to the bathroom, that they don't want to talk about a certain thing that you've asked about, or that they are in a hurry to get out of the session because of some other high-priority commitment or activity. They may feel that advocating for their own needs would somehow be disrespectful to you or to the treatment. Although this consideration may be admirable in some way, the risk is that the client ends up taking care of the therapist instead of the other way around. If the client believes that his or her needs are not as important as yours, then in that way the therapy relationship may be replicating a prior victimization or exploitation and will not feel safe to the client.

This does not mean that we should have no rules in therapy; to the contrary, rules and structures exist in large part to help the therapist maintain the focus on the client's needs. Traumatized clients respond well to structure and predictability; this helps them feel safe. However, the therapist should be sensitive to the client's apparent discomfort and supportive of the client's needs, which hopefully the client will learn to assert with more comfort and confidence over time. For example, the therapist might say, "Of course you can go to the bathroom now. How could I expect you to sit there and concentrate when you have to go to the bathroom? I'm so glad you said something!"

Sometimes the therapist might have to creatively "shape" clients—by reinforcing progressively better approximations of the desired behavior—to train them to advocate for themselves. For example, if the client hems and haws and eventually, with the therapist's help, admits that he does not want to talk about something, the therapist might say, "I'm glad you were able to find a way to let me know that you didn't want to talk about that. When you take care of yourself that way, we have a better chance of doing good work together."

For example, here's how a therapist responded to a 17-year-old boy who checked his watch at least 10 times within the first couple of minutes of a session. In this treatment setting, the sessions were not at a set time; rather, clients had other activities at the setting and waited their turn for the therapist.

Therapist: I notice that you're looking at your watch a lot. Are you in a hurry today?

Client: Yeah, it's my girlfriend's birthday; I told her I would take her out to dinner. She's already waiting for me.

Therapist: Oh! That sounds important.

Client: Yeah.

Therapist: Well, sometimes when someone's been working hard with me, once in a while I give him a break and let him out early. You've been working hard with me for the last few meetings; I figure you've earned a break. Is this when you want your break to be?

Client: Yeah!

Therapist: We have a lot to do though. So next time I see you, I expect you to work hard, right?

Client: Right. No problem.

Therapist: Have a good time with your girlfriend.

Client: Thanks!

What do clients learn when the therapist supports their needs being met? They learn, "This therapist cares about me and wants to make sure that I'm okay. This is not someone I need to defend myself against; this is someone who looks out for me and is on my side."

How Much Should the Client Talk?

If you were trained in a humanistic or psychodynamic approach, you were probably trained to encourage clients to be talkative and emotionally expressive. The trauma-informed treatment approach is different. As the personal trainer, it is your responsibility to guide the client not to take on too much too soon. "But she wanted to talk" is no excuse. You're the professional; you're the one in charge of guiding the session.

Imagine that you are a personal trainer. Your client has been handling 25 pounds pretty well. Supposing she comes in one day and says, "I feel good today. I think I'll go for 100 pounds!" You're the personal trainer. What do you say?

You probably say, "I'm glad you're feeling good. Let's go for 30." Because you know what will happen if she tries for 100. She may feel success for a moment but then is likely to collapse under the weight. Even if she is not injured, she will likely become discouraged and perhaps will say, "I didn't think this personal training stuff was going to work anyway." The personal trainer's job is to keep clients safe and to build them up, one step at a time, so they will be progressively able to handle greater challenges as they work toward their goals.

So how does a personal trainer run an initial meeting with a new client? Carefully! The therapist should be ready to actively discourage the client from overdisclosing. This is particularly important in regards to more sensitive topics such as details of troubled relationships or trauma memories. However, with children, teens, emotionally fragile or nonexpressive individuals, and clients who are not internally motivated for treatment, even more caution is required.

The therapist should err on the side of caution when considering whether, and how much, to ask in the way of follow-up to client comments in the first session. It is better to leave many stones unturned than to push a client into an area of discomfort or overexposure to upsetting content. Not asking a follow-up question can be counterintuitive and requires special intention and effort. Many therapists find it uncomfortable to just accept some short answer and move on; they say it feels mechanistic and uncaring. However, many clients report that when they learned the therapist was not going to "pry" it became easier and more comfortable to answer later questions. It's worth making the effort to help clients to feel safe and comfortable enough that they are willing to come back and take the next steps.

On the other hand, more interactive, in-depth conversation can be pursued at certain moments, and this can contribute to the development of rapport. The therapist should carefully choose safe and constructive topics for such conversation. It is usually both safe and constructive to focus more extensively on the client's accomplishments, skills, talents, or special interests. The client is unlikely to feel emotionally overwhelmed by talking about such a topic, and this type of conversation helps to establish the client as someone the therapist has a reason to admire and respect. This is a good foundation for the case formulation, at which time the therapist must be able to say, in essence, "You're the knight who can slay the dragon," and to provide data in support of that assertion.

Exercise: Practice the Initial Interview

Using the following script, practice this portion of the initial interview with a colleague; then change roles and have the colleague practice with you. If you are on your own, just go ahead and try this with a new client, bearing in mind that, with a real client, the script should only be used in the context of the complete session form (see Appendix C)—that is, when you've done the acculturation, rules, and other activities previously described.

If You Are the Client

- Role play a teenager—perhaps yourself as a teenager or one of your clients. Tell the therapist your name and age.
- Do not look at the script; don't do the therapist's job. Just respond as you would in the role you are playing. However, please don't give the therapist too much trouble either! This is not the time to role play your hardest case; give this therapist a break while he or she is trying to learn something new.

If You Are the Therapist

- Use the script verbatim.
- If you don't get the answer you want or need, optional follow-up questions are provided in parentheses. For example, if you ask, "What's your favorite color?" and the client says "Blue," then you've got your answer and you can move on. If the client says, "I don't really have one favorite," then you can use the parenthesized question and say, "Okay, what are your two or three favorites?"
- If the client declines to answer a question, thank him or her for remembering your rule, and move on to the next question.
- Do not ask extra questions to learn more about the client's responses. This might feel counterintuitive, but trust me for now and later you'll decide for yourself. There are two exceptions:
  - It's okay to ask a clarifying question if you really don't know what the client means. For example, if she says she smokes cigarettes, but not very much, you might ask, "Like how many cigarettes in a day?" However, in general, avoid these questions if you can.
  - It's okay to ask brief follow-up questions on one or two selected positive things that come up. In this exercise, only do this following the questions about what the client does with his or her friends, likes to do, or is good at. For example, if the client says he or she likes to draw, you might ask, "What kind of stuff do you draw?" This contributes to the focus on strengths.

- Write down what the "client" says. You would do this in a real session; these are your assessment data. It also shows respect by conveying that "what you say is important."
- Avoid expressing either disapproval or approval regarding the content of your client's responses. Even a positive judgment makes you a judge. Then if you don't express the same approval for something else the client says, he or she might think, "Oh, this response wasn't good enough for the therapist? The therapist didn't like this thing I said?" Also, if you seem to endorse certain content, the client might later choose the opposite content in order to generate conflict. It's not helpful for the therapist to get sucked into taking positions on the client's content. Try to find a way of indicating acceptance of what the client says while avoiding the role of judge.
- Use the script *verbatim*—word for word. Do not wing it, and do not improvise. You will have the rest of your career to do it however you like, so please, right now, take this opportunity to learn as much as you can from this. This script is as carefully crafted as a sales pitch and pulls for the responses you want. Please give it a try.

Script for Initial Interview

Okay. You remember I said I was going to ask a lot of questions to try to learn a lot about you? You know what do you do if there's a question you don't want to answer? So here come the questions, ready?

What's your favorite color? (If "No favorite," then: Okay, what are your two or three favorites?) What's your favorite food? What's your favorite music? What's your favorite TV show? What do you like in school? (Nothing? Not even recess?) What don't you like in school? (What else?)

Some kids like to keep to themselves, some like to mostly be with one or two good friends, some like to hang with a crowd. Which way are you? (If "crowd" then: Would you say there are certain kids who are better friends to you? Or everyone the same?)

You remember what to do if I ask you something that you don't want to talk about, right?

I'm going to ask you some questions about your friends. Your friends, do they mostly smoke cigarettes or don't smoke?

Do your friends mostly get high or don't get high?

Your friends mostly drink or don't drink?

Other drugs?

Would you say that your friends do pretty well in school, just get by, or are having trouble?

Do your friends get in trouble with the law or not?

Now some of the same questions about you. You smoke cigarettes or you don't smoke?

You get high or don't get high?

You drink or don't drink?

Other drugs?

What about school: You do pretty well, just get by, or not even?

You get in trouble with the law or not?

What do you like to do with your friends? (Possible follow-up to "hang out": So if I was watching you guys hanging out and having a good time, what would I see you doing?)

What else do you do with your friends?

What else do you like to do? (What else?)

What have people told you that you're good at? (What else?)

Here comes a different kind of question. If you could be any animal, who would you be?

What would be good about being a [insert animal choice]?

If you could have three wishes, what would they be?

If you could wave a magic wand right now and all your problems would disappear, what would be different tomorrow? (Possible follow-ups: If I'm watching on TV, what would I notice was different? Okay, so _____ would be better. What would be different that would make it better? Would the change be something inside you or outside you?)

Exercise Follow-Up Questions

For the clients: What was that like? How did it go for you? Can you describe what worked with you and what didn't?

For the therapists: What was that like? How did it go for you? Can you describe what worked with you and what didn't?

Many therapists balk at using a script, or indeed at doing anything they're not already good at or comfortable with. It's important to recognize that when you are trying to do something a new way, you are likely to feel deskilled for an initial learning period. The phases of learning are observation, imitation, and then integration. If you skip the imitation stage, you will have less to integrate. If you are willing to go through the growing pains of really learning the new thing, you are likely to improve your skills more, as eventually you integrate the new skills with your current level of competence and comfort. It will happen!

For at least the first several clients, I encourage you to use the session forms that are included in Appendix C. If one of your clients asks what you're doing with that book or piece of paper, you can just say, "I'm just making sure I don't forget any of the questions." You are the professional here; clients don't know how you're supposed to do your job, and they'll accept this answer. Some therapists continue to use the script as a regular practice.

Many therapists find it uncomfortable to just accept some short answer and move on; they say it feels mechanistic and uncaring. But what did your clients say; what is their experience? Many clients say things like, "I felt comfortable answering the questions because I knew you weren't going to pry." This is an important precedent to set, because in the next session we will be asking about trauma/loss history and want the clients to feel safe to answer those much more difficult questions without fear of prying. We want to keep the treatment carefully contained so that clients feel safe and are not overwhelmed by being asked to handle more than they're ready for.

Many teens, even the ones who gave one-word answers down the line, also say, "I liked being able to express myself, to tell you how I feel about things." When we ask these kinds of questions, people feel that we want to know them. Even if they don't elaborate on their answers, they may feel that they are showing themselves and being seen.

Clearly this script is designed to start off slow, to build rapport, and to help clients feel comfortable. However, we are also learning important things. For example, it is critical to obtain as much information as possible about the client's strengths and achievements. Later, these will be used as a basis for hope and commitment.

The three wishes and especially the magic wand questions are good for identifying not only treatment goals but also obstacles. These questions are also a good way to learn how the client perceives the problem—as coming from inside or outside the self. For example, a boy who sees his tendency to fight as an internal problem might say, "I wouldn't get so mad anymore." A boy who sees the same problem as external might say, "People wouldn't act so stupid [make me so mad] anymore." When we know how a client sees his own situation, then we know how to talk about it in a way that is consistent with his viewpoint. Then our case formulation is more likely to be accepted.

Routine for Ending Sessions

One way to create structure and predictability in treatment is to start and end sessions the same way every time. My preferred end-of-session routine is to ask, "Tell me something you liked about this meeting and something you didn't like." This trains the client to give both positive and negative feedback to the therapist, which can facilitate treatment progress. It also provides useful information to the therapist.

The initial interview can generally be easily covered in the first hour. The entire intake process may take up to several sessions, depending on how long your sessions are.

Age Variations

With Preteens

You can use the exact same script. However, if the child's initial responses to the cigarettes, marijuana, and alcohol clearly indicate that substance abuse is beyond the child's world, you can get away with skipping the "other drugs" question. However, if you're not 100% sure, go ahead and ask. You never know who might be sniffing glue, using ecstasy, or whatever.

With Adults

The script requires considerable modification. For example, you might not tell an adult "the rules" but rather explain expectations. It would also be inappropriate to ask most adults their favorite color, food, or TV show. However, the order of types of questions, and the basic principles exemplified in the teen script, do apply to adults and should be followed, albeit with age-appropriate modifications.

Case Example

Here is an entire course of individual treatment, transcribed verbatim except for intentional alterations. Case management and group and family work were conducted by others and are not featured here. Identifying information has been substantially altered to protect confidentiality.

You will notice that the scripts are generally used word for word and in order, and you will also see how the individual client's situation and responses affect this. The reasons for the various elements of the script, and the individual modifications, are addressed elsewhere in the text of this book. The purpose here is to illustrate this approach with an actual client.

Following each session are the official notes for the file as well as the therapist's personal notes, some of which also serve as documents in support of the treatment process and are shared with the client. Following that is a commentary on the session, in question-and-answer format, based on the questions of a number of readers.

"Alex" was a physically fit 15-year-old boy of mixed racial origins, slight Spanish accent, who was referred for treatment in an "after-care" program in his home city. He had recently completed 8 months of incarceration and was still legally in the state's custody for another year (the duration of his sentence) although he was allowed to live with his grandparents. Alex was required to come to the program site 4 days per week immediately after school until early evening. He was required to do his homework on site as well as to participate in a variety of groups (e.g., anger management, narcotics anonymous, and life skills) as well as in this treatment. Repeated failure to show up would be grounds for reincarceration. As per my own preference, I knew virtually nothing about him prior to our first meeting.

Session 1: Initial Interview

Mr. G: Hi, I'm Mr. Greenwald. Did Ms. Burns [the client's case worker] tell you why she wants you to talk with me?

Alex: I guess she thinks I have some kind of problem or something.

Mr. G: Actually she makes everyone in this program talk with me; it's not just you. You know that she wants you to do well in school and stay out of trouble, and she's hoping this will help. But when you're in the room, I don't work for her; I work for you. So my job is to learn a lot about you: what *you* care about, what you want for yourself, and what might be getting in your way. So I'll be asking you a lot of questions. Then I'll tell you what I think I learned, and you'll tell me if I got it right, or maybe you'll set me straight in some way. Once we agree on what's going on with you, then I'll give you some suggestions, things you can do to get stronger, to have better odds of getting to your goals. Then you'll decide what to do about the suggestions. Okay?

Alex: I guess so.

Mr. G: Before we get started with the questions, I want to make sure you know the rules. The first rule is about your privacy. Do you know what that rule might be?

Alex: I know: What's said in the room stays in the room. It's the same with every counselor.

Mr. G: Right. I don't tell other kids what you say. And I don't tell other grownups, either. What you say here is private. But there are exceptions. Do you know what those might be?

Alex: Yeah, like if I tell you something really bad.

Mr. G: Something like that. If I'm afraid someone might get hurt, the law says I have to tell. So let's say that you told me that you were in a bad mood, and when you leave here you're going to go home and eat all the pills in the medicine cabinet and then drink beer until you pass out. You might get hurt, so I would have to call someone who could try to stop you. Or let's say you told me that your family picks up a little extra money on the weekend watching the neighbor's baby. Just lock him in the bathroom all day long, no matter if he cries. The baby's not safe, so I would have to tell. Or let's say that someone was bothering a friend of yours, and you tell me that you have a knife and when you leave here you're going to go after that guy and make him back off. Someone might get hurt, so the law says I would have to tell so someone can stop you. So what if you did have that knife, and you were going to go after that guy, and you didn't want me to tell. What could you do?

Alex: I could say please don't tell anyone?

Mr. G: Nope. I don't break the law for anyone.

Alex: Okay, I could just not tell you.

Mr. G: Right. There are some other exceptions, too. If you give me permission to tell someone about a certain thing, then I can talk to that person about that thing. I don't need permission to give my own opinion, like if Ms. Burns wants to know if you're working hard with me or not, I'll tell her the truth. But I can't give any personal details you tell me, unless you give me permission. Also, you know that big file they have on you, with all those papers in it?

Alex: Yeah.

Mr. G: Well every time we meet, I have to put something in that file, for the records. That file is supposed to be private, too, with only people like Ms. Burns reading it. But the thing is, I don't know who's going to have Ms. Burns' job someday if she leaves. And I don't trust people I don't know. So I write down something to say what we did, but I usually don't put in personal details. For example, let's say that one time you're telling me about a fight you got in at school. And maybe the other guy deserved what he got, but still you're saying that you don't want to get in fights because it'll get you locked up again. So maybe we practice some other ways you can handle it next time. In the record, I would put down something like, "Practiced self-control skills" but without mentioning what happened at school. Like today, I'll probably fill a page with notes, but that's just to help me remember what you say. All I'll put into the file is something like "Explained the rules, talked about current situation, likes and dislikes." There's another rule just because you're in OCFS [the state program that has legal custody of Alex]. If you tell me details about a crime you committed while you were in OCFS [custody] that they don't know about—or about a crime you're planning to commit—the law says

I have to tell. I'm not talking about some little thing like jumping the [subway] turnstile; I mean if it's serious. So let's say that you and your friends are planning on going to the liquor store after midnight [when it's closed] to clean the place out. If you don't want me to tell, what can you do?

Alex: I know: Just don't tell you.

Mr. G: Right. But now just imagine that this is a couple of months from now, and you've found out that I don't tell other people your business, and you'd like to run it by me and get my opinion. How could you talk with me about it in a way that wouldn't force me to turn you in?

Alex: I could talk about this friend of mine that was thinking about doing it?

Mr. G: Sure, that would work. Or you could tell me in a general way without giving details like time and place, so I don't have anything to report.

Alex: I'm not going to be doing that anyway; I'm not looking for more trouble.

Mr. G: Yeah, I'm just giving examples to make sure you know the rules. So that covers the rule about what I can say to other people. The next rule is about what you say. The rule is: You are not allowed to say anything in here unless you decide you want to. So I'm going to be asking you a lot of questions; what if I ask you something you don't feel like talking about right now? How do you follow this rule? What can you do?

Alex: Just not say anything.

Mr. G: I don't think that'll work so well. If I see you not saying anything, I'll probably think that I just didn't ask it the right way, and I'll try again.

Alex: Oh. Maybe I can say, "I don't really feel like talking about that right now?"

Mr. G: That would be good; can I count on you to do that?

Alex: Okay.

Mr. G: Let's try it out. What's 143 times 96?

Alex: I don't know. I mean I don't really feel like talking about that right now.

Mr. G: Good. I'm sorry to take so much time on the rules; I know this is a boring way to meet someone. But I just want to make sure you don't have any surprises.

Alex: It's okay. I know you have to do your job.

Mr. G: Now you know that big file they have on you, with all those papers in it?

Alex: Yeah. I guess you know all about me.

Mr. G: Actually I don't look at that file. I don't want to know what other people think; I want to make my own impression. But this means that I'll have to ask you some questions that I could have found out by reading the file.

Alex: Okay.

Mr. G: Okay. You remember I said I was going to ask a lot of questions to try to learn a lot about you? You remember what do you do if there's a question you don't want to answer?

Alex: I know.

Mr. G: So here come the questions, ready? How do you spell your name?

Alex: A-L-E-J-A-N-D-R-O _____

Mr. G: What's your birthday?

Alex: March ____, 19_____

Mr. G: Were you born here [in New York City] or somewhere else?

Alex: Right here. I was born at Mt. Sinai [Hospital].

Mr. G: Yeah? I used to work there.

Alex: It's a good hospital. My cousins were born there too.

Mr. G: How long have you been back in the community?

Alex: Three days.

Mr. G: Oh, you're just back. Are you in school yet?

Alex: Not yet; they have to tell me what school to go to.

Mr. G: What's your favorite color?

Alex: Red.

Mr. G: What's your favorite food?

Alex: Fried chicken and Spanish rice.

Mr. G: What's your favorite music?

Alex: Rap, R&B.

Mr. G: What's your favorite TV show?

Alex: I don't really have one.

Mr. G: Okay. What do you like in school?

Alex: You mean from before, or from upstate [the incarceration facility]?

Mr. G: Either—both.

Alex: Not much!

Mr. G: Not even recess?

Alex: I like seeing the girls. And English is okay.

Mr. G: What don't you like in school?

Alex: The teachers. They're always trying to tell you you're doing something wrong.

Mr. G: Some kids like to keep to themselves, some like to mostly be with one or two good friends, some like to hang with a crowd. Which way are you?

Alex: Before, I had a lot of friends, a big crowd. Now I'm trying to stay out of trouble; I just come here and go home.

Mr. G: Would you say there are certain kids who are better friends to you? Or everyone the same?

Alex: Certain kids, a couple of my cousins, we've been tight since we were little kids. They're like my brothers.

Mr. G: You remember what to do if I ask you something that you don't want to talk about, right?

Alex: I know; you don't have to keep telling me.

Mr. G: I'm going to ask you some questions about your friends. Your friends— they mostly smoke cigarettes or don't smoke?

Alex: Mostly everyone smokes.

Mr. G: Do your friends get high or don't get high?

Alex: You mean the crowd, or my two cousins?

Mr. G: Each, I guess.

Alex: The crowd, yeah, a lotta weed. My cousins—it's not really their thing.

Mr. G: Your friends mostly drink or don't drink?

Alex: Both.

Mr. G: You mean both the crowd and your cousins?

Alex: Right.

Mr. G: Other drugs?

Alex: No, no one I know really goes for that other stuff.

Mr. G: Would you say that your friends do pretty well in school, just get by, or are having trouble?

Alex: The crowd—a lot of them don't even go to school. My cousins—they're doing okay, passing their classes.

Mr. G: Do your friends get in trouble with the law or not?

Alex: The crowd does; that's why I don't go around with them no more. My cousins—well they're not perfect, but nothing serious.

Mr. G: Now some of the same questions about you. You smoke cigarettes or you don't smoke?

Alex: (Pats his pocket where a cigarette pack is showing.)

Mr. G: That answers that. You get high or don't get high?

Alex: Before, yeah. But they check my urine now.

Mr. G: You drink or don't drink?

Alex: I like to drink. But I can't do it that much while I'm in OCFS. They're always calling and coming by and checking with my grandparents.

Mr. G: Other drugs?

Alex: Nope. That other stuff, that's just for business. You're not going to tell them I said that, are you?

Mr. G: I don't have to, if you were doing that before you were in OCFS. Anyway, you didn't give me any detail so even if I was supposed to, I couldn't. Y'know, you don't really have to worry about what I'm going to tell someone. If I ever have to do something like that, I'll tell you to your face; I won't go behind your back. What about school: You do pretty well, just get by, or not even?

Alex: In lock-up I did good in school. Before, though, I wasn't really doing much school.

Mr. G: Okay, and I don't have to ask you about trouble with the law. What do you like to do with your friends?

Alex: Chill.

Mr. G: So if I was watching you chill, what would I see you do?

Alex: Listen to music, joke around, talk to girls, maybe watch a movie.

Mr. G: What else do you do with your friends?

Alex: Play hoop [basketball]. That's about it, now. Before, that's another story.

Mr. G: What else do you like to do?

Alex: I like to cook.

Mr. G: Yeah? What do you make?

Alex: I can make Spanish rice as good as my grandmother. I can make lots of things. I've been cooking since I was little.

Mr. G: What have people told you that you're good at?

Alex: Cooking.

Mr. G: What else?

Alex: Talking to people. Writing. My teacher this last year said I'm a good writer.

Mr. G: What do you write?

Alex: Just whatever, like for school or for the journal I had to do.

Mr. G: Here comes a different kind of question. If you could be any animal, who would you be?

Alex: A lion.

Mr. G: What would be good about being a lion?

Alex: King of the jungle.

Mr. G: If you could have three wishes, what would they be?

Alex: Big mansion, a million dollars, and three more wishes.

Mr. G: If you could wave a magic wand right now and all your problems would disappear, what would be different tomorrow?

Alex: I wouldn't have to come here no more.

Mr. G: What else would be different?

Alex: I'd be passing my classes.

Mr. G: What would be happening different that would help you pass your classes?

Alex: The teachers, they'd try to help you instead of all the time telling you what's wrong with you. If I raised my hand, they'd ask me what do I want and try to help me.

Mr. G: Where you live now, who else lives there?

Alex: Grandmother, grandfather, and me.

Mr. G: Your grandmother, what's her name?

Alex: Carla.

Mr. G: (while writing the info into a genagram) How old is she?

Alex: I don't know, maybe 55?

Mr. G: Does she work a job or stay home?

Alex: She has a job; she works for the city, in housing.

Mr. G: And what's she like?

Alex: She's nice. Cooks good. Kind of worries too much.

Mr. G: And your grandfather, what's his name?

Alex: Everyone calls him "Pops"; I don't even know his real name. He's a little older, maybe 60.

Mr. G: And does he work a job?

Alex: He works in a hardware store; he's the manager.

Mr. G: And what's he like?

Alex: He works hard. He's nice too, but he's pretty strict. And he has a temper.

Mr. G: Anyone else live there?

Alex: No. My mother comes and goes, but they said she can't stay there now.

Mr. G: And your father, where is he?

Alex: I don't know.

Mr. G: You really don't know, or you don't feel like talking about it right now?

Alex: I don't feel like talking about it right now.

Mr. G: Okay. I'm glad you remembered the rule. Do you have any brothers or sisters?

Alex: I have an older sister and two older brothers.

Mr. G: Where are they?

Alex: The oldest one, Tamra, she's living in the Bronx, too, with her boyfriend, and they have two little boys. My brother Frank is in college to be a mechanic; he has his own apartment with some friends. And my other brother Julio is doing time [incarcerated]; he's got another couple years to go.

Mr. G: And your two cousins who are like brothers to you, are they on your mother's side or your father's?

Alex: My mother's.

Mr. G: What about your other grandparents; are they alive?

Alex: I think so; I never met them. I got a lot of cousins and stuff I never met, too; they all still in DR [Dominican Republic]. My father came from there when he was little.

Mr. G: Okay, so there's a lot of your family you haven't met.

Alex: Yeah.

Mr. G: I've been making a map of your family while you've been telling me about them. See?

Alex: The circles are for girls, and the squares are for boys.

Mr. G. Right; you figured it out. So who on this map do you feel most close to?

Alex: My cousins and my brother Julio.

Mr. G: And who next?

Alex: My grandmother.

Mr. G: And who do you feel least close to?

Alex: My father.

Mr. G: And who next?

Alex: Nobody. I'm good with everyone else.

Mr. G: Those were the questions I wanted to ask you for today. Because I like to learn, though, I will ask you one more thing before we finish. Can you tell me the thing you liked the most about this meeting we just had and the thing that you didn't like the most?

Alex: I like that you got to know me.

Mr. G: And what didn't you like?

Alex: Nothing, really.

Mr. G. Well, there must have been 1 minute that wasn't as good as the rest of it.

Alex: When you asked about my father.

Mr. G: Okay, thanks for telling me. What do you do now?

Alex: I'm not sure; I think they're having group now.

Mr. G: Okay. See you next week.

Session 1 Initial Interview, Official Notes

First meeting. Explained the purpose of this treatment program, rules and exceptions re confidentiality, etc. Intake interview for background information, likes/dislikes, friends, family.

Session 1 Initial Interview, Therapist's Personal Notes

Alejandro "Alex" _____   DOB: 3/__/19____
Born/lives in Bronx   Back 3 days

Red   Fried chicken, Spanish rice   Rap, R & B   No fav TV

School - L girls DL teachers

Crowd and 2 best friends, cousins

	Crowd	Cousins	Self
Cigs	Y	Y	Y
Weed	Y	Not much	before
Drink	Y	Y	Y
Drug	N	N	N
School	Probs	OK	Probs (OK in lockup)
Legal	Probs	OK	

W/ friends: Music, girls, joke, hoop
L: cooking
Good at: talking to people, cooking, writing
An: Lion/King of the J
Wishes: 1) mansion   2) million $ 3) more wishes
Wand: Not come here, better in sch. Diff: Teachers be more helpful.

Figure 2.1A   Session 1 notes

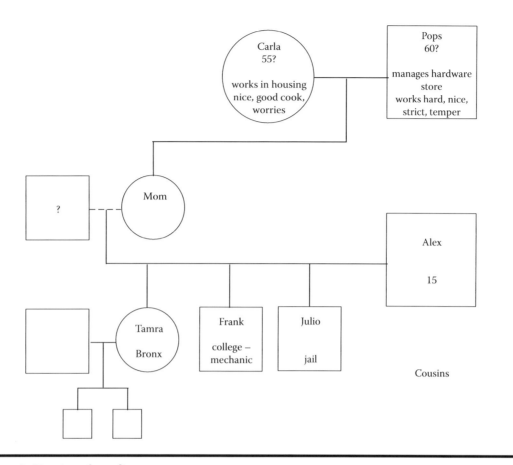

Figure 2.1B (continued)

Session 1: Questions and Answers

Q: Why did you go through that extra-long rap regarding the details of exceptions to confidentiality? That was much more than was in the script.

A: Part of what I added is what the script requires: that you state every exception to confidentiality that applies to your setting, even if the script doesn't mention it. So I was just making sure to include all the limits to confidentiality that pertained in the setting.

But I did go even further than that, as I routinely do with those clients who have been in a lot of trouble with the law. They have reason to be especially suspicious regarding authority figures, so I address this by providing plenty of specific examples. Also, I explicitly teach them ways to protect themselves, whether by not telling me something or by telling me in a careful way. In short, with clients who are likely to be extra cautious, I make a point to be extra careful in teaching them how to be safe with me.

Q: You really don't read the case files? And if not, why not?

A: I really didn't in that setting. For one thing, the files were too fat, and who has the time to sift through all that? Also, not reading the files gave me an excuse to ask all the questions I like to ask as part of building rapport. Also, when I tell the client that I want to make my own impression, I think that gives him the feeling that he's starting fresh with someone, which may create a sense of possibility. Finally, there wasn't much in those files that I really needed to know. My focus was on the client's own initiative and behaviors. If he doesn't want to tell me about some crime he committed, it doesn't really affect the treatment.

Q: Any reason why you ask for information about friends first instead of the client?

A: When it comes to the bad stuff, I think clients feel safer talking about other people, so I start with that. It also allows me to pass a test of being nonjudgmental regarding friends that may do drugs or crimes or whatever. This track record may make the client feel more comfortable in disclosing his or her personal badness.

Q: You really write just those skimpy little notes for the file?

A: Yes. I have it all on my computer, the standard notes for each session, and I just cut and paste for each client. Once in a while I'll add a little something extra about what's going on with the client. Many clients involved in "the system" have little privacy, and I don't want to make it worse by spreading their personal business around via their "confidential" file that so many people can access. The exception is if my notes would have legal implications, for example, if the client expressed suicidal intent. Then I include careful, thorough documentation.

Q: It is so tempting to ask additional questions about Alex's mother, cousins, his living environment. How do you stop yourself?

A: Good self-discipline. Also, I know from experience that such questions can bring trouble, in the way of too much heavy stuff too soon. Also I want to avoid dragging it out. This is the first session; just get the client through it intact, and that's good enough for today.

Q: How do you show acknowledgment of Alex's answer while staying neutral?

A: Nothing fancy here. I just pay attention, listen, write it down, and ask the next question. Clients seem to feel acknowledged and listened to.

Chapter 3

History

Routine for Starting Sessions

Starting every session the same way adds structure and predictability. To start every session (after the first one), I like to say, "Tell me something good and something bad that happened since last time we met," and also to ask, "Is there anything coming up that you're either worried about or looking forward to?"

These questions have several benefits in addition to the intrinsic value of ritual. It gives the therapist a fair idea of what might be on the client's mind at the moment. If the client is preoccupied with something, he or she may be distracted and unable to concentrate on the treatment activities. However, if these things can be identified and discussed immediately, if only for a few minutes, the client might then be able to focus on the rest of the session. Also, later on in the treatment, recent events may be used as examples for the various treatment activities (e.g., practicing self-management skills using the example of a recent confrontation). This helps the sessions to stay as relevant as possible to the client.

Also, in general, the clients who are in treatment for problem behaviors are not likely to maintain a journal, even though keeping a journal can be beneficial to therapy clients by helping them to become an observer of themselves and not merely being swept along by their experiences. Over time, the anticipation of being asked, "Tell me something good and something bad," can come to serve this function. Perhaps, in the moment a significant event is occurring, the client will say to himself or herself, "Oh, this is something my counselor will be asking about." When the client can be an observer of his or her experience, there is more opportunity for making choices about how to manage the experience.

Once the standard questions are asked, answered, and perhaps discussed, the next step is to reorient the client to the treatment by reminding of the prior work and transitioning to the present session. In the second session, the therapist might do this by saying, "Last time I asked you a lot of questions. Here come some more. Ready?"

Obtaining History While Focusing on Strengths

In the second interview, the therapist can ask about history and current status regarding the client's development including medical (including head injury), educational, work, legal, sex/relationship, and substance use. You'll need a sufficiently detailed history so you will later be able to tie together any trauma/loss history with possible onset or escalation of problems. It is also important to continue to learn about strengths, abilities, positive relationships, and successes, since these will be the foundation for the client's work in treatment.

With teens and preteens, it is ideal to get the history from a parent or guardian first before asking the client. Asking the adult first has several advantages. First of all, adults tend to know more than their children about some things, such as the child's early development. Second, adults will provide a different perspective, which is helpful to keep in mind as the child tells his or her own version. Finally, adults may provide information that the child does not. When it comes to the trauma history, it is especially nice, after the child has reported all the events he or she can think of, to be able to say, "Okay, and your Mom also told me you were in a car accident when you were 5." Then it can be added to the list, and the Trauma History session can be finished and left alone. If the information from the parent came afterward, the therapist would have to either reopen the trauma history to finish the job or leave the job unfinished. Better to get the information from the adult first if the adult is available.

Remember, this is the Fairy Tale model, not the medical model. This means that the interview style conveys a focus on strengths and resources, not on problems or deficits. For example, in asking about educational history using the medical model, the therapist might ask, "What problems do you have in school?" and perhaps "When did they start?" The trauma-informed therapist might ask about a client's educational history as follows:

- When you were in the first grade, did you feel like you were about as smart as other kids, a little smarter, or a little slower? How were your grades in first grade?
- Did you get in trouble in school more than other kids, less than other kids, or about average?
- Would you say you had more friends than other kids then, less friends, or about average?

Once the baseline of school-related functioning is established, the therapist can go forward from there and develop a time line of changes that may have occurred.

Therapist: So how long did things stay this way in school until something changed?
Client: Until about fourth grade.
Therapist: Oh. What happened in fourth grade? What was different?
Client: I started getting into fights more, and my grades weren't so good anymore.
Therapist: Like how much more? How many fights in a week?
Client: Not every day, but at least once or twice a week.
Therapist: How come you were fighting so much more than before? What was different?
Client: I just was more mad.
Therapist: And were you still passing your classes? What were your grades like then?
Client: I was still passing, but it was mostly Cs and Ds, and I failed one or two classes.
Therapist: And how long did things stay this way in school until they changed again?

The same type of interviewing can be practiced for the other topics. This results in a good timeline of the client's history of functioning in multiple areas. Not only have we learned about problem development; we also know how well he or she was doing before the problems started. Later, we can point to those times as proof that he or she has the capacity to do well if it were not for the impact of the trauma/loss history.

Incidentally, by the time you finish this part of the interview, you have learned quite a bit about the presenting problems, but you haven't done it by asking, "What's your problem?" or making the client feel as if he or she is a problem. Rather, you got to know the client, and in the course of telling his or her story, information about the client's problems were revealed. This client is likely to feel that you see the good in him or her, that you see him or her as a normal person—if with some problems—and that you care about him or her. That's a good start.

Trauma History

By partway through the second individual session, it's time to ask the big question: "What are the worst things that ever happened to you?" If we are going to conduct trauma-informed treatment, we need to get the trauma on the table so we can incorporate it into the case formulation and treatment plan. The problems, and the solutions, don't make sense unless you know about the dragons. Therefore, the trauma history must be taken during the evaluation. Fortunately, it can be done in a careful, intentional way that helps the client to feel safe and able to make progress in treatment.

Even the order of the different topics in the intake interview supports the Fairy Tale model. First we ask about the good things, the strengths, the track record of achievements and positive relationships—the "Once upon a time" stuff from when circumstances were better. (Hopefully such a time existed; if not, we still do the best we can in terms of identifying strengths and resources.) Then we ask about history up to the present, in various areas of life, and start to learn about the impact that the dragon might have made in terms of problem development. Only then do we ask about the dragon.

When we do ask about the dragon, we do it in a specific, limited way. Remember, the personal trainer does not ask the knight to go from 5 pounds to 100 all at once. The strategy is to provide progressively greater challenges, one step at a time, each one manageable with the therapist's help. You may have already taken the client through several challenges up to this point, such as the following:

- Trusting a stranger enough to cooperate and answer personal questions.
- Talking about family, relationships, and current life situation (some problems may be found here).
- Talking about the problem history (as part of education, legal, and other history).

That's a good start, but the client has a long way to go before he or she can be expected to slay the dragon. To invite this too soon is to risk failure. If the client is not ready to slay the dragon, then to allow him or her to talk about the trauma and face the emotions is only torture without benefit. So when we get the trauma history, we are careful to ask for and to allow disclosure of only the most basic facts—the bare minimum that will allow us to proceed with the case formulation.

Even though we are not asking for the whole story for each trauma event, the disclosure can be difficult for the client. It is probably the most challenging thing we have asked the client to do so far in treatment. So we continue to use the principles and practices of trauma treatment, to help the client to manage this experience, to feel successful, and to come out in reasonably good shape. Here are the steps we take.

Warn

"Here comes a hill. Why don't you check your brakes again, just to make sure they work?" In other words, we remind the client again about the rule: "Do you remember what to do if there's something you don't want to answer?"

Make a "List"

We say, "I need to make a list of the worst things that ever happened to you." What does the word *list* imply? Brevity. This is going to be quick and easy, perhaps even impersonal. We're not going to get into details. This establishes a limit and defines what will be happening. The client knows that he or she will not be expected or allowed to provide a lot of detail.

What Other People Say

This is a crucial opportunity for psychoeducation. When it comes to the trauma history, which is often a secret, people feel the strangest, most damaged, and most vulnerable. Here, the therapist offers the menu of possible trauma/loss events without even waiting for the client to be silent for 2 seconds first. This accomplishes several purposes:

- If you just ask the client to list the worst things that ever happened to him or her, you will get some answers. If you first give many examples of items that might be on the list, you will get more answers. This is the difference between multiple choice and fill in the blanks: Recognition is easier than recall.
- When you give these examples by saying, "Let me tell you the kind of things that other people say," you are normalizing the part of the client's experience that may feel most abnormal. You have transformed this question from, "How are you damaged and different?" to, "In what ways are you like other people?" This takes some of the pressure and stigma away.
- People often keep these experiences private and may be worried—for good reason—about how others might respond to a disclosure. When you describe what other people have said and you are calm and businesslike, you give the message that you can handle whatever this client will tell you. You've heard it before. You can talk about it; you will not freak out. This provides permission and safety.

Get the List

Once you have prepared the client, ask for the list of worst things. It is up to the client to determine what might belong on the list. The client may include items that surprise you yet fail to include items that you are sure should be included. It's okay to suggest additional events that you may be aware of from the earlier interviewing (including information from family members and others involved).

Age for Each Item

You also want to know at what age (or what grade) each event occurred. This can usually be done as the client is reporting each event, or it can be done just afterward. You need to know when events occurred to determine if the trauma/loss history can help account for problem onset or escalation.

Subjective Units of Distress Scale (SUDS) for Each Item

The Subjective Units of Distress Scale is the 0 to 10 scale for how bad it feels when you concentrate on it right now. Some tricks are involved in getting the SUDS scores:

■ Some clients will claim, "It doesn't bother me anymore." Although they are not exactly lying, what they often really mean is something such as, "I don't let it bother me anymore. I try not to think about it." You don't need to argue about this. Just ask your question in a way that will get you the answer you want (e.g., "When you make yourself concentrate on it now, just for a second, how bad is it from 0 to 10?").

■ Don't ask, "How do you feel?" That's not exactly the question. We are trying to help the client to keep some distance, keep it a little less personal. So the question is, "How bad is the feeling?" which is more objective, less intrusive. Or better yet, once they get used to the routine, "What's the number on this one?"

Asking for the SUDS is, in a way, doing exactly what we have been trying to avoid: having the client get into the feelings associated with the trauma memory. When therapists ask for the SUDS as they are asking about each event, they risk getting the client mired in the memory and unable to shake it. We do need to ask for the SUDS, so the best we can do is get it over with as quickly as possible. This is why we save it for last and do all of the events at once—well, one after another.

What If the Client Refuses?

Sometimes the client will refuse to disclose one or more of his or her trauma memories. This is good. It means that he or she is following your rules. So what can you do about that? How can you get the information you want and need while still respecting the client's decision (and keeping your own promise about the rules)?

Here's an interesting point: When you are talking about not talking about the trauma, you are in fact talking about the trauma. So when the client says he or she doesn't want to talk about it, you have already accomplished one of your goals, which is to have the client talk about it, at least a little, but not more than he or she can handle just now.

Another of your goals, though, is to get a timeline of when the bad things happened so that you can develop a case formulation. You can't just ask the client, "How old were you?" because that would be talking about it, and the client just told you that he or she doesn't want to talk about it. But you can ask her, "Is it okay to ask you how old you were?" Most people will readily disclose the age of the event they don't want to talk about. Later you can ask for the SUDS for that memory the same way you ask for the SUDS on the other memories on the list.

If the client will not even allow you to ask about the age of the event, don't worry; you can still do your job. Just write a question mark down on your list for the trauma and again for the age and SUDS. The fact that the client is not telling you more is itself important information. He or she is letting you know that it would be too much to handle that today. Does this mean that you have not established the trusting relationship that you were hoping for? Does it mean the client's testing you? Does it mean that the client's having a bad day but will have an easier time talking about the hard stuff next time? Does it mean that the client is more fragile than other people and will need that much more preparation before he or she is ready to slay the dragon? These are questions you will want to keep in mind.

What If There's Nothing on the List?

Sometimes a client who believes he or she is cooperating just doesn't have anything to put on the list. This can happen for several reasons. Sometimes even though you have provided the menu of common trauma/loss events, for some reason this doesn't jog the client's mind regarding his or her own similar experiences, and he or she can't think of any. Some people have a personal style that does not allow or acknowledge extremes, so they are unable to respond to your question about "worst things" or things that "really hit you hard." Some people do not consider the upsetting events in their own history to be severe or bad enough to merit being put on this list. Occasionally you will find someone who literally does not remember his or her past at all; this may be an indicator of major dissociative disorder, which is beyond the scope of this book. Perhaps most often, when the client says, "Nothing that bad ever happened to me," he or she is really saying something like, "So many bad things have happened that it is too much for me. So my strategy is to minimize. If none of it counts as really bad, none of it has to hurt me too much."

Just because there might be some good reasons why your list is empty (or nearly empty), don't stop there. In general, for reasons that will become clear later, it's good to have at least two or three items on a preteen's list and at least four or five items on a teenager's list. Adults should have at least a few items from childhood as well as whatever is on the list from postchildhood. More is fine too; less will often be a problem.

So what to do? We definitely don't want to tell the client, "No, I know you have more stuff to put on the list. Come on, give it up!" Fortunately, your clients don't know what your next question will be. So when you have a client who doesn't give enough events for the list, here are your next questions:

- How old were you for the worst thing that ever happened at school?
- How old were you for the worst thing that ever happened with other kids?
- How old were you for the worst time you ever lost someone you cared about?
- How old were you for the worst time you ever got disciplined or punished?
- How old were you for the worst time you ever saw parents or other grown-ups arguing or fighting?

These are the "greatest hits," but if you know about something else that happened to your client, just add it to the list—for example, "How old were you for the worst time you saw someone get hurt?" or whatever it might be. These questions seem to help complete the list. Occasionally the client will still say,

"Nothing like that ever happened," and we can accept that, as long as it's not the consistent answer for each question. Usually he or she will give the age that the event happened and explain a bit about it.

Notice that we do not ask, "Did this ever happen to you?" We already asked that and came up empty. This time we ask, "How old were you when this happened?" Now we get an answer we can use.

Finish the Sandwich

Whenever we expose a client to challenging emotional content, we follow it up with some calming activity and then with something more thought oriented to help with recomposure. Following the trauma history we have the client do a deep breathing exercise. This helps the client relax. However, it is rarely acceptable to tell a problem behavior client (especially an angry one) that he or she needs to relax. Thus, in the script you will introduce deep breathing without suggesting that the client needs it. Rather, the implication is that you have a lot of good tricks, but they're not all good for every client, so you'll be going through the bag of tricks and trying them out. If they work for this client, you'll do it again; if not, you'll try something else next time.

Then we ask about the best things that ever happened. This helps the client refocus on something more positive rather than staying stuck in the trauma. Once there's a good list of best things, choose one item on the list and ask about it in more detail. Although we avoid asking probing details about the trauma, it is okay to ask more about the good events; this helps to accomplish its purpose. The therapist should choose an event that is likely to engage the client without inviting access to one of the "worst things" events. For example, if the death of the grandmother is on the client's trauma list, do not ask for more detail about an event involving that grandmother—too much risk.

Finally, we end the session with the closing ritual questions as well as conversation about more casual topics, such as what the client will be doing later in the day or the week.

It is important to write down the details of the client's trauma history; you will need to refer to it on several occasions later in the treatment. Your notes on the trauma history might look like the "Worst Things" form in the case example (see the session at the end of this chapter) in the Therapist's Personal Notes. Please review those notes now. Perhaps you noticed the comment in parentheses after the "Breathing" notation. As a therapist, you may have a repertoire of interventions that can help clients calm down. Not every intervention works for every client. This is not the client's fault, and it's not a problem. We just want to keep track of what works and what doesn't with a given client so that we can proceed accordingly.

Exercise: Take a Trauma/Loss History

Work with a colleague. Use the script and form provided in the following section. When you have finished, change roles and do it again. If you're on your own, it is worthwhile to complete the form for yourself, but you'll be missing much of the learning experience.

If You Are the Client

- This is not a role play; be yourself. It is up to you to decide which events you wish to disclose. Remember the rule: You're not allowed to say anything here, unless you decide you want to. Disclose only to the extent that it feels comfortable and appropriate to do so.
- Do not use or look at the script; that's the therapist's job. Just be yourself.

If You Are the Therapist

- Use the Worst Things form provided, or duplicate the form on another piece of paper that you can write on. As you receive answers, write them into the form.
- In the script, the words in brackets are instructions for you. The rest is to be spoken aloud. Use the trauma history script verbatim. Say it word for word. Do not wing it or improvise.
- Remember to go in order. First, do the preparation, followed by the trauma/ loss events and ages. When you have all of those, get the SUDS for each event. Then practice the deep breathing. Next, proceed to the best things. The script will guide you.
- After you have completed the list, do the following, which is a nonscripted task: Ask a little more about one of the items on the Best Things list. Try to choose an item that will not bring up loss memories, and that will engage your client. This will help your client get more involved in the positive feelings that you are hoping will characterize the end of your session.
- Just because you will not be asking probing questions about the bad things that happened, this does not mean that you must shut off your humanity or your caring. You still can—and should—use your clinical skills to convey your compassion, your concern, and your comfort and ability to tolerate hearing what you are being told. How do you accomplish this? Different people have different styles, but the basic requirement is empathy, that combination of being both emotionally present and objective/composed.

Good luck.

Trauma History Script and Form

Now I'm going to ask you about something that some people don't like to talk about. You remember what to do if you don't want to say something? Good. I want to make a **list** of the worst things that ever happened to you. Maybe you already have something in mind, but let me tell you the kinds of **things that other people say** so you know what I'm asking about.

Some people, it would be maybe a car accident, or another kind of accident, or seeing someone else get hurt really bad. Some people, it's that someone in their family or someone else they care about got really sick or died. Or being taken away from their family or if someone hurt you, made you do sex things, threatened you, told you they would do something bad. Or seeing parents have really bad arguments or fights—you know, the kind of thing that could really hit you hard.

So what would be on your list? Okay, how old were you then? What else would be on your list?

(Keep going until the list is complete, including the event and the age for each.)

Now I'm going to ask you how bad the feeling is for these, on 0 to 10, where 10 is the worst feeling in the world and 0 is no bad feeling at all. I'm not asking about how bad it was at the time but, when you make yourself think about it right now, how bad the feeling is right now. So for [that car accident], how bad is that feeling right now on 0 to 10? (Ask about each memory on the list.)

Did anyone ever show you how to do deep breathing, like to relax? I'm going to ask you to try my way of doing it for a couple of minutes, then you'll tell me whether we should ever do it again or not. You will be taking a very deep, slow breath in, to my count of 3, then hold for 3, then breathe out slowly to a count of 3. Ready?

Breathe in 1, 2, 3; hold 1, 2, 3; out slow 1, 2, 3. Again, breathe in 1, 2, 3; hold 1, 2, 3; out slow 1, 2, 3.

This time, when you breathe out, look for any bad stuff: tension in your body, upsetting thoughts or pictures … and when you breathe out, imagine the air coming from that place, and the bad stuff going out with the exhale. Ready?

Breathe in 1, 2, 3; hold 1, 2, 3; breathe out the bad stuff, 1, 2, 3. Once more, breathe in 1, 2, 3; hold 1, 2, 3; breathe out the bad, 1, 2, 3.

How did that go? Would you say you feel better than before, worse, about the same?

Now I want to know about the best things that ever happened to you, or times that you felt really good. For some people it would be a really good birthday, or they did something they're proud of, or they went someplace special, or were having a really good time doing something. What are the best times you can remember? What else would be on your list?

(Then choose one thing on the list to ask more about.)

Worst Things

Age   Event   SUDS (0-10)

(Breathe)

Best Things:

Age   Event

Exercise Follow-Up Questions

If You Were the Client

How did this go for you? Please describe your experience if you are willing. Since people have a range of experiences, we can begin to learn from one another about the variety of possible responses. What did your therapist do that made you feel more or less comfortable than you might have expected? Did talking about the bad memories upset you? Did the breathing or talking about the good memories have any effect?

If You Were the Therapist

How did this go for you? Please describe your experience if you are willing. Were you tempted to encourage your client to talk more? How did you handle that?

For the Group

As a therapist in that exercise, please raise your hand if you found something your client said personally challenging to listen to or upsetting or hard to tolerate in some way. What did you tell yourself about that while it was happening? How did you handle it? Do you feel any remaining distress? How do you want to handle this distress now?

Many therapists find it uncomfortable to just accept some short answer and move on; they say it feels mechanistic and uncaring. But what did your clients say? What is their experience? Many clients report, "I felt comfortable answering the questions because I knew you weren't going to pry." This is good. We want to keep the treatment carefully contained so that clients feel safe and are not overwhelmed by being asked to handle more than they're ready for.

Many therapists who are new to trauma treatment struggle with the constraint of the list. When you ask clients about their trauma/loss history, some of them will try to tell you the whole story on the spot. It can be tempting to permit this. Many of us were trained to believe that when a client "opens up," that's a good session. He or she is choosing to open up; he or she obviously wants to talk about it, right? Wouldn't it be disrespectful to shut the client up once he or she has started? What kind of message would the client get from that?

Despite this temptation and these arguments, it is usually a bad idea to allow the client to disclose too much so early in treatment. The following reasons suggest that the therapist should exercise restraint on the clients' behalf:

■ People tend to be ambivalent about disclosing their trauma/loss history. They want to express it, yet they don't want to face it or expose themselves in that way. Just because the client is showing you one side or the other does not mean that he or she is not ambivalent. You must always take both sides into account. If you tell the client, "This is important. We don't have time now, but I hope we can talk about it in more detail when it's the right time," you have addressed both sides of the ambivalence. If you just allow the client to spill his or her guts, you have addressed only one side. The other side is likely to come out later. The client might feel overexposed and even tricked by the therapist into overdisclosure. Then the client is likely to feel unsafe and withdraw.

■ If you allow the client to discuss the trauma in too much detail too soon, you are inviting fallout after the therapy session is over. You haven't yet had a chance to do the self-management training to help the client learn to cope better with upsetting feelings. So allowing overdisclosure increases the risk that the client may become upset later on and perhaps act out or underfunction. This is bad for the client and gives you, and treatment, a bad reputation.

■ If you allow the client to talk too much about the trauma, you are less likely to have time to complete the follow-up activities in the session. The follow-up activities are critical to help the client manage and contain the emotion that may have been activated by recalling the trauma memories. Failure to complete the recomposure activities further increases the risk of after-session problems.

■ If you allow the client to talk too much about the trauma, you are less likely to have time to complete the trauma/loss history in this session, and you'll have to open it up again next time to get it done. The history is essential to making a case formulation. Once you have a case formulation and a treatment contract, things go much better, so you want to get to that point as soon as you can.

You are the mental health professional with the specialized knowledge of how to conduct a trauma-informed treatment. You are the one who is supposed to be providing a secure, supportive, and predictable environment, so the client can learn to feel safe. Chances are, the client is coming to you at least in part for problems related to judgment and impulse control.

So whose judgment do you want to trust—yours or the client's? If you allow the client's overdisclosure impulse to spoil your session and your treatment program, you have failed the client, and you have not kept your own implied promise.

Speaking of whose judgment to trust, some therapists make the mistake of asking the client which best thing he or she would like to talk about in more detail. Don't do that. Your client does not know your criteria for selecting just the right best thing. This is your job.

If this session has gone well, the client may have had a rather profound experience. He or she may have told you about something that he or she has never talked about before. Sometimes clients are afraid of how someone would react; sometimes they are afraid that they couldn't handle it. Hopefully you reacted in a calm and supportive manner, and hopefully the client was able to handle it well enough too, with your guidance. This is a great step! The client has learned some important facts about himself or herself, about you, and about what he or she might be capable of in treatment. He or she is stronger now than before and has more reason to hope.

It doesn't really take very long to ask the client about the trauma/loss history, but clearly much is involved. The follow-up activities—deep breathing, list of good things, and the less intense final conversation—are all very important to help the client regain composure and come away with a good experience. These take time. So here's some advice: Don't start on the trauma history with only 10 or 15 minutes left in your session. You might not make it through all the follow-up activities; it's too risky. If you have long sessions (close to an hour), then you can start partway through the session. If you have shorter sessions (closer to half an hour) it is best to start on the trauma history near the beginning of the session.

Age Variations

With Preteens

You can use the exact script as provided in the session forms (see Appendix C).

With Adults

Also use the script, with one slight modification. Where the script says "kids" you should substitute "people" as was done in the exercise (which you presumably did with another adult).

Session 2: History

Mr. G: Hi. Because last time was our first meeting, I just want to make sure that you remember the rules, about your privacy and the exceptions, and about what to do if there's something you don't want to say.

Alex: I remember: I just say I don't feel like talking about it.

Mr. G: Good. I like to start with a kind of a check-in. If you could tell me something good that happened since the last time we met and something bad that happened?

Alex: I got my school.

Mr. G: Is that the something good or the something bad?

Alex: It's good; I have a couple of friends there, and they didn't put me in the other school where there would be trouble.

Mr. G: Do you have your classes yet?

Alex: Yeah, I just got them this morning—look (pulls paper out of his pocket, with a computer printout of his schedule).

Mr. G: Did you get what you wanted?

Alex: I guess so; school is school. I don't know how my teachers are, though; that's the big question. I go tomorrow, I guess I'll find out.

Mr. G: And something bad?

Alex: Something bad? Had to come here today.

Mr. G: And is there anything coming up in the next week or two that you're either worried about or looking forward to?

Alex: Nothing really. Just to see how it goes at school.

Mr. G: I asked you a bunch of questions last time; now I have more. I'll start with something you might not even know the answer to. When your mother was pregnant with you, do you know if she might have been smoking cigarettes, drinking, or using any drugs?

Alex: I don't know, but I don't think she was drinking so much back then. Maybe once in a while. And she don't smoke.

Mr. G: Were you born early, or late, or on time?

Alex: On time.

Mr. G: Were you born big, or small, or average size? Sick or healthy?

Alex: I think I was normal, healthy, I don't know; I never heard nothing about being sick.

Mr. G: Did they tell you what you were like when you were a baby?

Alex: They say I was a happy baby. They say I didn't cry much. A little hyper though! I was always getting into everything.

Mr. G: When you were maybe a year old, were you the kind of kid who liked to explore and meet people? Or more shy, stay close to Mom?

Alex: I would just go, explore, play, whatever.

Mr. G: When you were maybe 2 or 3, old enough to play with other kids, were you like a bully, taking kids' toys? Or did that happen to you? Or was it more like playing fair?

Alex: No, nothing like that. Just play fair.

Mr. G: This question is about from being a baby all the way till today. Did you ever get sick or injured to the point that you had to go to the hospital?

Alex: Yeah, one time I fell out the window, and another time I broke my arm.

Mr. G: How old were you for those?

Alex: I don't know; when I fell out the window I was little—maybe 3 or 4. The broken arm—that was just a couple of years ago.

Mr. G: Did you ever have to take medicine for more than just a little while?

Alex: No. Just if I was sick or something.

Mr. G: Did you ever get hit on the head to the point that you were knocked out or got dizzy or headaches? Like when you fell out the window, or some other time?

Alex: I was knocked out for a little while when I fell out the window. I think I had a concussion.

Mr. G: Do you remember having headaches after that or being more tired?

Alex: No, I don't really remember much about it.

Mr. G: Do you remember any other changes? Maybe more trouble concentrating or shorter temper?

Alex, No, I don't remember anything like that. It was no big deal.

Mr. G: When you were in the first grade, do you remember feeling like you were about as smart as other kids, or a little faster, or slower?

Alex: About as smart—maybe smarter. I would always be waiting for the teacher to explain to everyone else.

Mr. G: What kind of grades were you getting?

Alex: Good—I passed everything.

Mr. G: Like just barely passing, or higher grades?

Alex: I think I mostly got Bs and As.

Mr. G: Were you getting in more trouble than other kids, less trouble, or about average?

Alex: About average, I guess. I wasn't no angel, but no big problems.

Mr. G: Did you have more friends than other kids, less friends, or about average?

Alex: I had a lot of friends; I always got along with everyone.

Mr. G: So that's how it was in first grade. How long did things stay that way for you in school, until something was different?

Alex: In third grade I started getting in more fights.

Mr. G: And were your grades still good?

Alex: Yeah, pretty good.

Mr. G: And you still had friends?

Alex: Always had friends.

Mr. G: How long did things stay that way for you in school, until something was different?

Alex: I was doing pretty good until I went to middle school [sixth grade, about age 12].

Mr. G: What was different then?

Alex: I got with a different group of friends, started cutting classes, getting high.

Mr. G: And how were your grades then?

Alex: In sixth grade I passed almost all my classes. By seventh grade I wasn't really doing much school anymore.

Mr. G: How old were you for the first time you ever did something that, if you were caught, would have gotten you in trouble with the law?

Alex: The first time? Getting high, I guess, in sixth grade.

Mr. G: Then how old were you for the next thing?

Alex: Later in the sixth grade, started doing some other stuff too.

Mr. G: Like what?

Alex: I don't really feel like talking about that right now.

Mr. G: Okay.

Alex: Okay, we were doing some robberies.

Mr. G: Like of houses or stores or of people?

Alex: People. We'd get a few of us together and look for the right spot. Then we'd tell someone to give us his money. If he didn't, we'd beat him up.

Mr. G: You also said something before about selling drugs?

Alex: Yeah, but I never got busted for that.

Mr. G: And what was it you finally got caught for, that got you locked up?

Alex: A&B [assault and battery]. I was on probation already for boosting a car, and then I was in a fight and got arrested. The other kid went to the hospital, and I went upstate [to the long-term incarceration facility].

Mr. G: Now I'm going to ask you about something that some kids don't like to talk about. You remember what to do if you don't want to say something?

Alex: I remember already! You don't have to keep telling me.

Mr. G: Good. I won't be asking for the stories today, but I need to make a *list* of the worst things that ever happened to you. Maybe you already have something in mind, but let me tell you the kinds of things that other kids say, so you know what I'm asking about.

    Some kids, it would be maybe a car accident, or another kind of accident, or seeing someone else get hurt really bad. Some kids, it's that someone in their family or someone else they care about got really sick or died. Or being taken away from their family or if someone hurt you, made you do sex things, or threatened you, told you they would do something bad. Or seeing parents having really bad arguments or fights. You get the idea—not just a bad day but the kind of thing that could really hit you hard.

Alex: I get the idea.

Mr. G: So what would be on your list?

Alex: I saw some pretty bad stuff between my parents.

Mr. G: How old were you for that?

Alex: It wasn't just one time; it was a few times.

Mr. G: How old were you the first time?

Alex: It started when my father came home; I was maybe 9 or 10.

Mr. G: And how old were you when it ended?

Alex: When my father left; I was maybe 11.

Mr. G: What else would be on your list?

Alex: Uncle died.

Mr. G: How old were you for that?

Alex: I was maybe 9; I was in the third grade.

Mr. G: What else would be on your list?

Alex: Being taken away from my mother.

Mr. G: How old were you for that?

Alex: 12.

Mr. G: What else would be on your list?

Alex: One time I got jumped [attacked]; I was 13. That's when my arm got broken.

Mr. G: What else would be on your list?

Alex: The first time I got high. That's what led into all my problems.

Mr. G: How old were you for that? Oh, you told me, sixth grade, right?

Alex: Yeah.

Mr. G: What else would be on your list?

Alex: Getting locked up, last year; I was 14.

Mr. G: What else would be on your list?

Alex: Nothing; that's it.

Mr. G: Oh, there was also the time you fell out of the window.

Alex: But that was no big deal.

Mr. G: Well, I put it on the list because it happened; but if it's no big deal, it's no big deal. Anything else?

Alex: Nah, that's it.

Mr. G: Now I'm going to ask you how bad the feeling is for these, on 0 to 10, where 10 is the worst feeling in the world and 0 is no bad feeling at all. I'm not asking about how bad it was at the time but, when you make yourself think about it right now, how bad the feeling is right now. So for the stuff between your parents, how bad is that feeling right now on 0 to 10?

Alex: 10.

Mr. G: Uncle died?

Alex: 10, no, maybe 8.

Mr. G: Father left, 0–10?

Alex: Zero; he should 'a left sooner. He was never really like a father anyway.

Mr. G: Being taken away from your mother, 0 to 10?

Alex: 10.

Mr. G: Getting jumped?

Alex: 5.

Mr. G: First time getting high?

Alex: 6.

Mr. G: Getting locked up?

Alex: 8.

Mr. G: Falling out the window?

Alex: 0.

Mr. G: Did anyone ever show you how to do deep breathing, like to relax?

Alex: They taught me that in anger management, but it doesn't work for me.

Mr. G: I'm going to ask you to try my way of doing it for a couple of minutes, then you'll tell me whether we should ever do it again or not. You will be taking a very deep, slow breath in, to my count of 3, then hold for 3, then breathe out slowly to a count of 3. Ready? Breathe in 1, 2, 3; hold 1, 2, 3; out slow 1, 2, 3. Again, breathe in 1, 2, 3; hold 1, 2, 3; out slow 1, 2, 3.

This time, when you breathe out, look for any bad stuff: tension in your body, upsetting thoughts or pictures—and when you breathe out, imagine the air coming from that place and the bad stuff going out with the exhale. Ready? Breathe in 1, 2, 3; hold 1, 2, 3; breathe out the bad stuff, 1, 2, 3. Once more, breathe in 1, 2, 3; hold 1, 2, 3; breathe out the bad, 1, 2, 3.

How did that go? Would you say you feel better than before, worse, about the same?

Alex: About the same. Maybe a little better.

Mr. G: Okay. Now I need to make a list about the best things that ever happened to you, or times that you felt really good. For some kids it would be a really good birthday or they did something they're proud of, or they went someplace special, or were having a really good time doing something. What are the best times you can remember?

Alex: When I was little and my Pops took me to a Yankees game.

Mr. G: How old were you then?

Alex: About 6.

Mr. G: What else?

Alex: First time getting high.

Mr. G: What else?

Alex: First time having sex.

Mr. G: How old were you?

Alex: 13.

Mr. G: What else?

Alex: I got an award for writing.

Mr. G: How old were you then?

Alex: It was in the lockup, just this last year.

Mr. G: What was that award about?

Alex: We had a rap contest, and I wrote the best rhyme; I won the prize.

Mr. G: Cool! What else?

Alex: When I was on the basketball team in school, before, one time in the playoffs I hit the winning basket.

Mr. G: I didn't know you were on a team. What position did you play?

Alex: I was playing forward; because I grew early, I was bigger than a lot of guys then.

Mr. G: So your team was in the playoffs?

Alex: We were good! We made it all the way to the semifinals.

Mr. G: So what happened in this game you got the big basket?

Alex: Okay, we're behind by 1, with 7 seconds left. I throw the ball in bounds, jump in, and I'm wide open so this kid Mike throws it right back to me. I just pop it up, and it goes in! Long shot, too, right on the 3-point line.

Mr. G: That must've felt good. So you're a pretty good shot?

Alex: I'm good at the whole game. I can rebound, block, steal, pass, everything.

Mr. G: Sounds like you can handle the pressure, too.

Alex: Sometimes, yeah.

Mr. G: Okay, that's it for today. Tell me something you liked about this meeting and something you didn't like.

Alex: It was good to get that stuff off my chest.

Mr. G: And what you didn't like?

Alex: Talking about all that personal stuff.

Mr. G: And where do you go from here?

Session 2 History, Official Notes

Further background info including developmental, medical, school, legal, trauma/loss, and best things.

Session 2 History, Therapist's Personal Notes

Pre-natal - cig? No drug?
Born normal, healthy, happy, active
Not shy/explore, play fair

Med: Fall age 3 or 4
Broken arm age 13
No meds
Head injury? With fall age 3/4 but no symptoms

School:
1st grade avg/high IQ, Bs & As, friends, not much trouble
3rd grade more fights
6th grade new school, new friends, cut classes, get high, pass most classes
7th grade more, fail classes

Legal: 6th grade get high, 7th grade robberies, boosting cars. Sell drugs. Charge: fighting/assault

Worst Things

Age	Event	SUDS (0-10)
9/10-11	parents (argue/fight?)	10
9	uncle died	8
11	father left	0
12	taken away from mother	10
13	got jumped (broken arm)	5
12	first time high	6
14	locked up	8
3/4	fell out window	0

(Breathe)   felt a little better

Best things:

Age	Event
6	Yankees game w/ Pops
12	first time high
13	first time sex
14	writing award
12	big shot in basketball game

Figure 3.1   History session notes

Alex: I have to leave early today because my grandmother asked if I would cook dinner today; she's watching my sister's kids.

Mr. G: And they're letting you go early?

Alex: Yeah, she called and checked it out with them.

Mr. G: What are you making?

Alex: Chicken.

Mr. G: Hope it's good! See you next week.

Session 2: Question and Answer

Q: There was no follow-up on how long the client was in the hospital at age 3 or 4. I would want to know if it was more than a very short stay since it could have a significant impact on attachment. A relatively short stay on a nonresilient child can have a big impact.

A: I'm not sure he even went to the hospital. But I did follow up by putting the fall on the list and later by asking his SUDS for it. This isn't perfect, but it does provide at least a rough indication of how distressful the memory is now.

Chapter 4

Motivation

The ultimate goal of the evaluation phase of treatment is for the client to agree to a treatment plan—preferably with at least a little enthusiasm. Before attempting to "close the deal" on the treatment contract, we must ensure that the client's motivation has been effectively developed and tapped.

Helping the client to "get the princess"—that is, to identify what he or she cares about and to commit to working toward that—is tricky, especially for problem behavior clients. Based on the comments and questions I have received over some years as a trainer, I have come to believe that in our field this is the component of treatment we are worst at. It doesn't help that this is also what we are worst at as a community. Parents and other authority figures are good at telling our clients what they should want but tend to be not so good at finding out what our clients really care about. So it's no wonder that problem behavior clients are notoriously hard to treat: because without the princess, nothing happens.

Motivational Interviewing

Motivational interviewing (MI) is the leading approach for helping clients to identify and commit to their goals and to make positive behavioral changes. MI is a well-established counseling style or approach primarily focused on conducting an evaluation and providing feedback, but the approach can be carried through the entire course of treatment as well. Although MI has been used primarily with adults with substance abuse problems, in recent years it's been applied more widely, including use with people with posttraumatic stress disorder (PTSD) and with teens.

The MI approach recognizes that people with problematic behaviors are generally ambivalent about these behaviors. On one hand, the problem behaviors solve some other problem for them (e.g., help to get rid of a bad feeling); that's why they persist. On the other hand, these behaviors cause other problems.

When others complain about why these behaviors are a problem, it's natural for an ambivalent client to respond by resisting, perhaps by saying, "I like it. I'll do it if I want to. It's none of your business." On the other hand, when the therapist supports the client's right to keep his or her behavior and acknowledges that some value must be found in persisting with that behavior, it's natural for the ambivalent client to respond by filling in the other side of the ambivalence, perhaps by saying, "Yeah, but I'm sick of getting in trouble because of what I do. It's getting old."

When we tell clients what they should do, then even if they accept this, they are accepting what we said. When we can guide clients to tell us what they should do, then they feel more ownership; it's what they chose—it's theirs. In this empowerment model of treatment, we want clients to take the initiative as much as possible. We want them to feel that they are participating in treatment activities because of their own determination to achieve their own goals. We may be the guide, coach, or personal trainer, but we can't do the client's work; the client does it. So the treatment has to be about the client's princess.

The following are the essential principles and procedures in the MI approach (Miller & Rollnick, 2002).

Free Will

What you do is up to you. The therapist is explicit about the fact that the client is making his or her own choices. The therapist might say, "It's your life; what you choose to do is up to you." This respects the client's autonomy while stating the truth—the client does make choices, not only of behaviors but also of his or her consequences. It's important for the therapist to be supportive of the client while also keeping some distance or neutrality, to avoid being sucked into a conflict about what the client should choose. For example, the therapist might say (or at least say internally), "I hope you make the choice that will help you get to your goal. But whatever choice you make, you know what happens at 6:30 tonight? I have dinner." In other words, root for your team, but don't bet your savings on what the team does. Another way of thinking about this is that we are supportive of the client but we are not invested in the behavioral choices he or she makes at any given time. When clients can't use their choices as weapons in a fight with the therapist, they are left fighting with themselves, and sometimes this leads to good things.

Empathy

Embrace the client's worldview. Empathy has been identified as one of the key components of effective psychotherapy, and it's central to this approach, too. When we embrace the client's worldview, he or she feels supported and respected; the client feels that we are with him or her. This doesn't mean that we necessarily believe everything the client says or that we only see it the way he or she does. But we do convey understanding and acceptance. This is often accomplished with an active–reflective listening approach. For example, the therapist might respond to a client's explanation of what happened by saying, "So you were just kidding around, but then he started really attacking you?" The alternative, to say, "It sounds like you started it," is nothing new; this is what others have probably been telling this client already. It hasn't helped; that's why they sent him to you. When you show empathy and acceptance for your client's worldview, then at least you are in the same conversation and the client feels that someone cares and understands.

Be Nonconfrontational

Getting in the client's face and telling the client what's wrong with him or her might work in the movies, but nowhere else. All you really get with the confrontational style is another free hour in your week. The research indicates that the in-your-face approach leads only to worse treatment compliance and increased dropout (e.g., Sommers-Flanagan & Sommers-Flanagan, 1995). Clients don't like to be "yelled at," so they block you out and write you off. The motivational interviewing style is nonconfrontational. We leave it up to the client to confront himself or herself.

Identify Goals and Enhance Investment in Goals

The therapist guides the client toward identifying goals, things that he or she cares about, wants for himself or herself. Even this can be challenging for a client with trauma-related avoidance of hope; the client may habitually deny having goals to preclude disappointment. The therapist also guides the client to increasing his or her investment and commitment to these goals. This is done by helping the client get in touch with how much he or she wants these goals and also by helping the client to believe that it's not just some fantasy; we can figure out practical steps that can make the goals seem more realistic and attainable.

Highlight Conflict Between Goals and Behaviors

The climax, or punchline, of the motivational interviewing approach is to highlight the conflict between the client's goals and his or her current behaviors. This is done, of course, in an empathetic and nonconfrontational manner. The therapist might say, "I'm confused. You told me that you want those good things to happen for you, and I believe you. I think you really do want that. But you also keep doing this stuff that you told me can get in your way and keep you from getting what you really want. So it's hard to tell what you care about the most."

When this dilemma is highlighted and given back to the client, it can have a strong impact.

Offer Specific Advice (for Concrete Actions)

Once the client has endorsed the positive goals and claimed them for his or her own, the therapist can offer advice and specific actions the client can take to help the client to achieve his or her goals. Even now, it's important to maintain the stance of supportive neutrality so that the client can retain ownership of his or her goals and initiative. The therapist might say, "Well, if that's really what you want, let me tell you what other people have done in your situation to get to the kinds of goals that you're talking about…." Then the treatment plan is offered in service of the client's goals.

Arrange for Some Quick Successes

It is important that the treatment plan include some early treatment activities that will lead to quick, if small, successes. What happens when the client quickly sees that he or she is actually accomplishing the first things on the list? The client believes, more than before, that this can really happen and that he or she is already on the road to success. The client becomes more confident, more hopeful, and more committed to treatment.

Future Movies

Future movies is a structured, scripted MI intervention designed to help clients to identify their goals and to elicit increased investment as well as commitment to working toward these goals. In essence, the client is told about a movie of his or her own life story and is asked to fill in the details from today until a good ending 10 years from today. It might be helpful to take a look at the Session Form for Future Movies in Appendix C to see how it goes before continuing here. The following features contribute to its effectiveness.

Uses MI Structure and Principles

The Future Movies intervention follows MI principles, both in language and in structure. For example, the client is never told what to do but is just guided in a way that the client makes his or her own positive choices. Also, the client visualizes both the good ending of the movie that would follow constructive behaviors and the bad ending that would follow continuation of the problem behaviors; then the client is asked to choose a preferred ending. The client's own preference for the positive outcome tends to push him or her to also choose the positive behaviors that lead to the outcome.

Provides Trauma-Based Case Formulation

The intervention provides a trauma-based case formulation—that is, an explanation of the client's situation (including presenting problem) from a trauma perspective. Such a case formulation is a necessary precondition to a treatment contract that addresses trauma, because if the client does not see trauma as part of the problem, why should addressing it be part of the solution? This is accomplished by telling the client's story according to the structure of the fairy tale starting with once upon a time, then the dragon/trauma leading to the symptoms, and then the client doing a series of constructive activities leading to achievement of his or her goal represented by the movie's good ending.

Counters Pessimistic Future

Many trauma-exposed individuals have developed a pessimistic attitude toward their own future as an avoidance strategy, in essence saying, "I don't want to get my hopes up; then I don't have to be disappointed again." When the client is busy avoiding becoming hopeful, it is difficult to get him or her to set goals or be willing to work toward them. The framework of a movie provides the psychological distance that allows the client to engage in imagining his or her own future. Many clients would be unwilling to talk directly about their own future, but most are willing to talk about what would be in the movie.

Fosters Investment in Positive Goals

Future Movies fosters investment in positive goals in two ways. First, the client is asked to identify, and then visualize, not only the good ending but also the series of small practical steps that could take the client from today to that positive outcome. Recognizing that achieving the goal is not merely a fantasy but is the plausible outcome of a series of small, achievable steps helps clients believe that they can actually do it. Incidentally, imaginal rehearsal of behavioral steps toward a goal also improves the odds of doing those behaviors (see Chapter 1). Later in the intervention, the client is guided to identify the strengths and resources (i.e., the knight and the kingdom) that can help to achieve the goals. This further increases the confidence and hope that make commitment possible.

Working the Movie Metaphor

This intervention, as well as many to follow, relies on the movie metaphor. To make this work, the therapist must be able to guide the client to identify images, actions, or situations that have such specificity that they can be as clearly visualized by the client as if watching it in a movie. Many therapists are not accustomed to extracting such specificity from their clients, but in this treatment approach it is an essential therapist skill and practice. The following guidelines will help you to become effective at working the movie metaphor.

Talk First, Picture Second

The purpose of an image is to symbolize something for the client. So it's important to develop the something first before asking the client to represent it or symbolize it. For example, when you are focusing on the good ending in the Future Movie, you will first ask your client to describe general details about his or her life (10 years from now). Only after the client has told you how he or she will be making a living, where he or she will be living (and with whom), what kind of car and other specific details, do you ask for the last picture of the movie, which represents how good the client's life has become. In other words, don't get the symbol until you have established what the symbol will be representing.

The Customer Is Always Right

This principle applies throughout the course of treatment, and it is central to the MI approach. We don't want to get into the position of arguing with our clients; rather, we artfully guide them to make their own choices. It can be challenging to accept the client's choice when it is not what we would choose for the client. In this instance, remember that you are the consultant, but it's the client's life. Whatever choice the client makes, you have still done your job.

It can also be tempting to "correct" the client when the client's answer is not in the format you need it to be. This often occurs when you are working the movie metaphor, because clients may not be used to giving the kind of answers that work in a movie. In this instance, try to avoid correcting the client or saying that the client is wrong. Rather, just ask your next question to build on what the client already said and to guide the client closer to an answer that fits what you are trying to get.

Client's Choice

The good ending picture that the client chooses is intended to represent, or symbolize, something meaningful and powerful for the client. When a client does not readily produce a suitable picture, it can be tempting for the therapist to jump in and suggest a picture. Don't do it! Remember, this good ending picture is supposed to be the client's princess, not the therapist's. If someone shows you a picture of a movie star, you will probably agree that the movie star is good-looking, but you will probably not suddenly be in love with that movie star. Similarly, it is essential to allow the client to choose his or her own symbol and princess. Therapists should avoid saying, "This is who I think you should be in love with."

Time, Place, and Action

A love story does not end with an abstract "happy together"—it ends with the couple walking into the sunset, hand in hand. A sports story does not end with an abstract "successful"—it ends with the ceremony where the hero is being given the championship ring. The picture is not specific enough until it has a time, a place, and an action—until you can see it as if you're watching it in a movie. If your client gives you an answer that is too general or that covers too many moments, you can ask, "So what's that last picture at the end of the movie that shows me how well you're doing?" If you still don't get a time–place–action picture, keep asking in different ways and hanging in there until you do get it.

Behaviors and Outcomes

When you're asking the client for the steps along the way, leading from today to the good end, sometimes clients will tell you only the outcome steps, for example, "I get good grades, then I graduate high school, then I get a scholarship …" It is important to have positive outcomes along the way, because who can wait 10 years for success and reinforcement? However, for this intervention to be most effective, the client must also be able to specify (and later visualize) the actual behaviors that lead to the positive outcomes. For example, if the client says, "I get good grades," the therapist might ask, "So if I'm watching this movie, what do I see the kid doing that leads to those good grades?" Then the client is more likely to provide behaviors such as, "Go to class, pay attention, do my homework."

Now we're back to time, place, and action. Can you see all that as if you're watching it in a movie? I can see some of it, but not everything. So I might ask, "In this movie, when would I see the kid doing her homework, and where?" Now the client might say, "After dinner, in the kitchen." This I can watch in a movie.

Can't Watch Someone Not Doing

When you are getting the steps along the way, sometimes a client will answer with a negative, for example, "I wouldn't be cutting classes." Although that may be an appropriate answer, you can't watch someone not cutting classes; what would you see in the movie? In this instance, you have to find out when the client would be doing the problem behavior, so you can find out what he or she would be doing instead that can be watched in the movie. For example:

Therapist: If you were going to be cutting classes, when would that be?
Client: At lunch, maybe some friend will say, "Hey, let's get out of here."
Therapist: So in this movie, when someone at lunch says, "Hey, let's get out of here," what would we see the kid in the movie doing to go toward the good end?
Client: Just say, "No, I gotta go to class today."

In this example, it was easy enough to identify the moment that the client will either engage in the problem behavior or resist. But sometimes it's trickier to identify the positive behavior, because it would involve a totally different situation than the one in which the problem behavior might occur. For example:

Client: I wouldn't be getting high anymore.
Therapist: If you were going to be getting high, when would that be?
Client: Mainly after school, with the crowd that hangs out in the park.
Therapist: So in this movie, if the kid was not going to be in the park getting high after school, what would we see her doing after school?
Client: Maybe get a job?

Now all we have to do is pursue this until it has a time, place, and action (this example is continued in the section below called "Keep the Movie Metaphor").

Don't Try to Solve the Problem

This session is not the time to help the client develop coping skills. That's personal training, and we wait for that work until we have an agreement with the client to do it—a treatment plan. If we go out of order and attempt personal training before the client has committed to a treatment contract, we increase the risk of treatment failure.

The sole focus for today's session is to guide the client to identify goals and enhance determination and hope in achieving the goals. One of the ways we do this is by having clients identify (and later visualize) the behaviors that lead to the desired outcome; this makes it seem more realistic and achievable. The following example shows how to identify a concrete time–place–action behavior without getting bogged down in trying to help the client develop the coping skill.

Therapist: What else would we see the kid in the movie doing to get toward that good end?
Client: I wouldn't be getting into fights.
Therapist: So in this movie, if I see someone trying to pick a fight with this kid, what would I see him doing to go toward his goals?
Client: Just ignore, walk away. But I can't do that; I get too mad!
Therapist: I'm not saying you will do it; no one knows what you'll really do. I'm just trying to figure out what we'd see in the movie if he was going to go toward the good end.

Keep the Movie Metaphor

Okay, it's no secret: You know that the movie is all about your client's future, and your client knows it too. Even so, there's considerable value in continuing to talk about "the one in the movie" rather than "you." Working the movie metaphor was helpful in the previous example in that it helped the client to get around the obstacle of not currently possessing the coping skills. Since it's just a movie, the client can simply see what happens without having to have the self-management skills already in hand.

The movie metaphor can be particularly helpful when a client appears hesitant to engage and may even be refusing to give an answer. The movie metaphor can be used to lower the stakes of the conversation so that it is safer for the client to continue. Then the therapist's message is, in essence, "I'm not going to back down; I'm going to hang in there until you give me an answer. But your answer doesn't have to 'count'; it doesn't have to mean too much, so it's okay, go ahead." This is illustrated in the following continuation of the example of the teen who proposed getting a job instead of hanging out in the park and getting high.

Therapist: What job?

Client: I don't know—anything to make money.

Therapist: Well, in this movie, what job would it be?

Client: How do I know? Could be anything.

Therapist: You're right, could be anything. Nobody knows what's really going to happen. Next week, another movie, it could be something different. For today's movie, what job would it be?

Client: In a store.

Therapist: What store?

Client: I don't know.

Therapist: In this movie, what store would it be?

Client: My aunt works in this clothing store downtown; she told me I could work there if I want to.

Therapist: What kind of work would you do there?

Client: Take the clothes from the dressing room, fold them, put them back on the racks. Maybe cash register if they let me, after a while.

In general, it's a good habit to stick with "the one in the movie" rather than sliding into talking about "you." Otherwise, the therapist might fall into the trap of appearing to be telling the client what to do. It is all too easy to start saying, "And then you'll do this, and then you'll do that," which violates the MI/empowerment stance you've been developing. Even though you are not intending to start bossing the client around, if you say "and then you'll do this," many clients will hear it the wrong way. If you stick with "the one in the movie," and "we don't know what you'll really do, we're just trying to figure out what would be in the movie if it was going to go to the good end," you'll be on safe ground. Then the client is more likely to get the message you are trying to convey: "My job is to help you see your choices. Your job is to make your own choices. It's your life." Then the client is less likely to feel pushed and more likely to cooperate.

Of course, you are carefully guiding the client along an intricate path designed to lead him or her to make good choices. Still, it's best to leave the sense of initiative to the client. If your client says, "You helped me so much," you only get one point. If your client says, "Look what I did," you get two points. And your client feels more empowered and more able to do whatever it takes to get to his or her goals.

Exercise: Try the Future Movies

If you are in a group, do this with a partner. If you are on your own and don't have a colleague to practice on, do it with a teenage client, and make sure that you get all the way through the whole session. This can be a long session (an hour or more) until you get practice and can keep it tighter, so try to allow enough time.

If You Are the Therapist

■ Stick to the script as much as possible, except that assuming your practice client is an adult, you will ask him or her first how many years ahead the movie should end, and you will use *people* instead of *kids*.
■ If something is in parentheses, that's for a follow-up or clarification; only use that if you need it. If you've already got your answer, accept it and move on.
■ If something is in bold, be extra sure to use those words verbatim.
■ If you are tight for time in this exercise, stop after the bad end with, "It's not worth it." Then you'll have time to switch roles. In real life, you would complete the session with the Strengths, Obstacles, and Today's Odds.
■ If you are trained in Eye Movement Desensitization and Reprocessing (EMDR), use the script with eye movements (EM), and do the eye movements where it says (EM).
■ If you are not trained in EMDR, use the regular script (No EM), and ignore the spots where it says (EM).

If You Are the Client

■ Be yourself. This is not a role play. (Alternately, role play a reasonably cooperative teenager.)
■ Do not look at the script during the practice. Just play your part, and let the therapist do his or her job.
■ Don't do your therapist's job, but be reasonably cooperative. She or he is just learning, so don't make it too hard.

Future Movies Script

I've asked about your past and about how things are now. Now I want to know about your future. Since you haven't been there yet, I can't ask it the same way, so I'm going to tell a little story, and you'll fill it in for me. Let's say that 10 years from now—how old will you be?—I stop at the video store on my way home from work and pick up a movie called *The (Client's Name) Story*. It's about this kid grows up in a city, starts out okay. Seems like a good kid but then some things go wrong for him, and he gets more angry, more stressed, the bad feelings piling up inside. He gets so stressed he ends up doing some things he doesn't really feel good about he gets himself into some trouble, and I'm getting sad, thinking of turning it off. But then things start to change. First one good thing, then another, then another, till finally, by the end of the movie—you know that last picture, when the music's playing and the credits are rolling?—I'm smiling and saying, "Way to go; you made it!" So tell me, if this was your story and things go the way you hope they do, what would your life be like? (Get details about, e.g., home, work, family, car.)

Okay, so if this is your life, what would be in that last picture to let me know how good you're doing? When you have this picture, what kind of feeling goes with it? Where do you feel that in your body? And what could you say along the way to encourage yourself toward this goal?

No EM: Okay, now I'm going to ask you to do a concentration exercise. I'll be asking you to concentrate on the picture, the feeling, where you feel it, and what you're saying to yourself. So concentrate on the picture, the feelings, the words. Take a deep breath. How did that go?

EM: Okay, now I'm going to ask you to do a concentration exercise. I'll be asking you to concentrate on the picture, the feeling, where you feel it, and what you're saying to yourself. At the same time, I'll be moving my hand back and forth, and you will be following with your eyes. A lot to focus on all at once. Ready? (EM) Were you able to concentrate on everything? Okay, let's try it again. Ready? (EM) How did it go that time?

The thing is, the movie didn't just jump from the middle to the end; there were all these things that happened along the way to get there step by step. So, tell me, if this is you, what happens in this movie? What would we see you doing tomorrow, next week, next month, next year?

So now I want you to imagine watching the whole movie in your mind, all the way to that good end you were telling me about—all the things you were saying would happen to get there step by step. So start from today, tell me when you're done. Ready? (EM if you're using them.)

How did it go? What happened in the movie?

I hope it goes the way you want it to, but what if it doesn't go the good way we've been talking about? What if you kept on doing the same old stuff, things got worse and worse; what would that last picture be? And what kind of feeling goes with this picture? Where do you feel that? With this picture, **would it feel true to say to yourself, "It's not worth it" to go that way?**

Okay, so just for a few seconds, I want you to concentrate on this bad ending, the bad feeling, where you feel it, the words, "It's not worth it." Got it? (EM) Okay. Did that "It's not worth it" feel more true, less true, or about the same? Okay, let's do this one more time; concentrate on this bad ending, the bad feeling, where you feel it, "It's not worth it." Got it? (EM) Okay. Is it more true, less true, about the same?

(Stop here if you're doing the shorter exercise.)

Commitment to Goals

So on 0 to 10, 0 is nothing 10 is all the way, deep inside, how much of you really wants to go for that good ending you were telling me about, or something like that?

Okay, now I know you don't want the bad end, but how much of you, on 0 to 10, still feels like doing the same old thing?

So most of you really wants to go the good way?

But sometimes that smaller part tries to take over and mess it up for all of you?

Strengths

I'm a gambling (man/woman). Let's say I'm going to put $100 down on you making it to the good end, or something like that. What would make me think this was a smart bet?

Well, I have some ideas about why this might be a smart bet. See if you think these ideas are right or wrong.

Motivation

Most people I know, if they really care a lot about something, they try harder than for something that doesn't really matter to them. You told me that on 0 to

10 you're a _____, you really want this. So would you say that you're determined, motivated—what's the best word?

Talent

To do what you said, you'd have to pass your classes. Now I know from some
other years that you're smart enough to do well in school if you decide to. You
think that's true?

Also, you're pretty good at _____, right? (Or whatever the skill is that's related
to the job goal.) So I might bet on you because you have talent.

Support

Would you say that people have a better chance of making it if they're all alone
in the world? Or if they have people in their corner that try to help them out
sometimes? You have people in your corner, yes?

Persistence

So are you the kind of person who, if something goes wrong, will just give up
and throw it all away? Or will you pick yourself up and keep trying? Because
something always goes wrong, right?

Track Record

Now it's one thing for someone to just tell me, "Yes, I want to make it." But
you've actually already been doing some of the things we've been talking about
that get you toward your goals (give examples). So this makes me think you're
serious about it, because you're not just saying it; you're doing it.

Obstacles

Now, you know what's gonna happen as soon as I put that money down.
Someone's gonna walk up and say, "Sucker! I'll bet you he goes the bad way."
What makes that guy think he's got some easy money coming?

(What could stop you from getting to your goals? What could get in your way?)

(If necessary, the therapist can generate a list, including typical things like wanting quick money, temptation [specify, e.g., smoke, drink, drug, unprotected sex],
stress, anger/temper, the don't-care feeling)

So I want to know what my biggest worry is—which of these is the biggest challenge? And which one is next?

So it sounds like there are some good reasons to believe that you really could make it on the good track and also some real challenges, some things that could get in your way.

Today's Odds

So I think I'm going to make my money, but nothing's a sure thing. Now I'm going to ask you to give me the odds, the way you see things right now. On a scale of 0 to 10, 10 is a sure thing 0 is no chance at all, so 0 and 10 are impossible because nothing's ever sure. What do you think my chances are of winning this bet?

And what would it take for you to tell me that it's not a (client's stated number) anymore, it's a (one higher) now? What would have to happen? (Follow-up questions/reflections as needed.)

Postexercise Discussion

What was that like for you as a client? What was it like as a therapist?

Telling the Story with Real Clients

The Future Movies intervention is one way to tell the fairy tale, not with knights and dragons but using the client's content. However, the opening part of the story is intentionally vague. This is not the place to name details of your client's trauma/loss history; we don't want to activate the trauma memories until it is time to slay the dragon, which is way down the road. Do make the story fit your client, in terms of general facts such as gender, place where he or she grew up (e.g., city, small town), what type of emotion gets piled up along with the stress (e.g., anger), and the general nature of the current problems at the halfway point, when the person in the movie is up to your client's current age (e.g., getting into trouble). The goal is to have a rather vague story that your client identifies with and that conveys the fairy tale structure.

Bad Ending Issues

If you did the short version of the exercise, some people comment that it feels wrong to end the exercise right after focusing on the bad ending. This is a good point. This was the end point in the exercise only to save time and focus on the trickiest part of the session. However, in a real session, you would never end there. Ideally, you get all the way to the end of this session's script. The intervention is most powerful when done all at once, as a single package, but it can take over an hour, even when you're good at it. If you have shorter sessions and can't get the whole thing in, end after the client has visualized the steps along the way to the good end. That's a feel-good stopping point, and in the next session, after your check-in, you can repeat that visualization and then move forward from there.

Some therapists express reservations about having the client visualize the bad end, even when integrated into the complete session. They may say, "Why do you do that? Doesn't that just make the client feel bad? Reinforce going the bad way? Focus on the negative?" In fact, you will also encounter clients who protest being asked to think about the bad end, even if only for a few seconds. This is not a surprise—people with poor affect tolerance don't like to feel bad. But it's an essential component of the intervention, so it's important that you understand its role.

First of all, the key to the MI approach is to challenge the client with a contrast between his or her goals and current behaviors. Having the client visualize the bad ending right after focusing on the good ending (and steps to get there) provides a stark contrast and inspires the client to choose to move toward the positive outcome.

This conflict is further developed by focusing on strengths and obstacles. At each step, while the conflict is being highlighted, the client is guided to identify with the positive goals while seeing the problem behaviors as a problem for himself or herself (and not just for others). And at each step, the client is gaining a better understanding of what to do to get to his or her goals and why he or she might really be able to be successful. By the end of this session, many kids will feel so capable and confident that they don't notice that they have shifted from talking about a movie to talking about their own plans.

If you skip the negative aspects (e.g., bad ending, obstacles), it would be easier for the client to convince himself or herself that he or she could continue with current problem behaviors, with no problem. If obstacles are not part of the conversation, some clients will not perceive them. If your clients don't perceive any obstacles to their goals, then they don't need your help. They're fine on their own—thanks anyway. When you can agree on significant obstacles or challenges, then you have something to offer, a strategy to help them to get stronger and to master the challenges. Don't think you can skip this part and get away with it; you'll pay later!

Finally, pairing the words, "It's not worth it," with the bad ending proves to be very useful to clients, both in making their choice in this session and subsequently. Many individuals, in the moment before a behavioral choice is made, actually flash on the bad ending, tell themselves, "It's not worth it," and make the positive behavioral choice. Having the client visualize the bad ending with, "It's not worth it," prepares the client with a useful tool.

Stacking the Deck the Good Way

Did you notice that the client gives a higher number (on the 0 to 10 scale) for wanting to go the good way than for wanting to do the same old things? That's intentional. Most clients will choose 8 or higher for wanting the good way and 5 or lower for doing the same old things. By the way, if you have followed the script and have less of a discrepancy, that's a bad sign, and you have a very challenging client on your hands. Fortunately, this is rare, except when the client is still actively being shielded from the consequences of the problem behaviors.

We follow this up by building on the momentum of the client expressing a stronger desire for the good way. We suggest that we will personally bet on the client making it, and then we establish the justification for our good judgment. The list of strengths should be approximately twice as long as the list of obstacles. Although it is important to identify and acknowledge the obstacles, we want to make sure that the client can feel that he or she has adequate strengths and resources to overcome them. In short, we make sure that the numbers add up the right way so that the client is more likely to feel confident and willing to commit.

Princess Rules

Future Movies is all about identifying, investing in, and committing to the princess (i.e., the client's personal goals). Many therapists new to Future Movies ask, "What about if the client chooses an unrealistic good ending?" This is an excellent question. The answer is that it depends. Following are the guidelines for when to accept the client's princess and when to ask the client to come up with another one.

Fantasy Good Ending: Okay

Yes, if your client wants to be president, a music star, or a sports star for his or her favorite team, that's fine—*as long as the client can identify constructive behaviors to go toward the goal.*

In informal surveys I have taken among mental health professionals, about two thirds of us had such fantasy goals at some point during our own childhood or adolescence. Having dreams probably didn't do us much damage; maybe it's okay for our clients, too. However, we would not want our clients to merely have the fantasy, which could even be counterproductive if the fantasy was so satisfying that it replaced a sense of need for action. Rather, we harness the fantasy to help our clients identify constructive behaviors that they can do to move toward their goal. For example, with a client whose good ending involved being a star basketball player, the therapist might guide the client to identify constructive behaviors as follows:

Therapist: So where do the pro teams find their players?

Client: In the draft. They draft them from the college players.

Therapist: How would someone get to be a college player?

Client: You have to play on your high school team, be really good, get a scholarship.

Therapist: How do you get to play on your high school team?

Client: Listen to the coach, practice, play hard, be good.

Therapist: So what if your coach is kind of hard on you, and you talk back?

Client: Can't do that; he'll kick you off the team. Just say, "Okay," and do what he says.

Therapist: What if you're starting and someone else wants your spot and he's jealous—he tries to pick a fight?

Client: Can't do that; can't fight, they kick you off the team for that, too.

Therapist: So in this movie, someone tries to pick a fight; what does the kid in the movie do if he wants to stay on the team and go for his goals?

Client: He just ignores the other kid and keeps playing hard. He keeps his starting spot, he has the last laugh.

Therapist: And what about grades? Don't you have to have passing grades to stay on the team?

Client: Yeah, you gotta get C or better in every class.

Therapist: So if I'm watching this kid in the movie and he's going for his goals, what do I see him do to keep his grades up?

Although much of the Future Movies intervention is scripted, it can take quite a bit of ingenuity to fill in the blanks and guide the client to come up with good endings and behaviors. Getting the steps along the way can be the trickiest part, especially when the princess is nowhere in sight. Not all fantasy endings are glamorous; some of the more mundane good endings may seem to be just as far out of reach for a given client.

The following conversation was with a 16-year-old girl who was spending a lot of her time on the street with various older men and under the influence of whatever substance she could find. She identified her good ending as being with a nice husband who has been to college and has a good job, and they live in a nice little house in the suburbs with their two children. She was able to visualize a good ending picture, and now it was time for the steps along the way. The therapist's task here was to transform this from an unrealistic fantasy ending to an ending that was attainable through a series of small, plausible steps.

Therapist: So what would we see this girl do tomorrow, next week, next month, next year if she was going to be going toward her goals?

Client: I don't really know. I guess one day she just meets this guy and, boom, they fall in love.

Therapist: Tell me more about this guy again?

Client: He went to college, he has a good job, and when he's mad he doesn't put his hands on me—he just takes a walk and comes back later.

Therapist: Is he kind of a party guy, always going out drinking and doing drugs and stuff? Or more kind of responsible and mellow?

Client: Oh, no, he's responsible. He comes home right after work; he wants to see me and the kids.

Therapist: Sounds like a pretty good guy. So what kind of girl would a guy like that want to marry? A street girl full of drugs? Or someone more responsible that he could count on?

Client: No, he'd want someone he could count on.

Therapist: Like what kind of a person might she be?

Client: She would probably have her own job and not be partying all the time.

Therapist: Where would he meet her?

Client: Maybe at work or at the library or something.

Therapist: So this girl in the movie, what would we see her doing tomorrow, next week, next month, next year to become that person and go toward her good ending?

Client: Maybe go to beauty school. I'm good at giving people haircuts. And it's good money.

Winning the Lottery: Not Okay

The key difference between the long-shot fantasy ending and the winning-the-lottery fantasy ending is that, with the latter, there are no constructive behaviors the client can do to achieve the goal. It's a passively attained outcome and of no use to the treatment process. Other examples of a winning-the-lottery type of ending include the following:

- My brother will be alive again.
- My parents will get back together.
- I'll live with my parents (when this is unlikely because the client has been removed from the parents' home and the parents have not taken steps to improve their situation).
- I'll be a rap star (if this is to be attained by lying around and then being "discovered" someday. If this is to be attained through practical steps, it's no longer a winning-the-lottery ending. The therapist can certainly give this a try and see if it can become a usable goal).

If you get a good ending that seems to be of the winning-the-lottery type, you will have to make a judgment. Are there a series of constructive actions that can conceivably get my client from here to there? Can this be converted to a long-shot but usable good ending? If not, then say to the client, "This is a more realistic movie; that kind of ending won't work. What else can you think of—something that you could actually have a chance of making happen?"

Being the Best Criminal: Not Okay

Once in a while, when asked for the good ending to the movie, a client will say, "I want to be the biggest dealer on the block, have all the people on the street out there working for me." When you use the script, you will be surprised at how rare this response is; even most young criminals, deep down inside, seem to want the conventional good life. However, once in a while you will get this type of answer.

I don't know about you, but my purpose in life is not to help my clients become better criminals. Also, clients with this type of goal are likely to (correctly) perceive that therapy has little to offer them. So the preferred strategy here is to try to negotiate the goal and see if the client will come up with a more prosocial good ending to work toward.

Therapist: You want to have your own family?
Client: Oh yeah, I want a wife, lots of little kids.
Therapist: Is your idea of a good family life to have your wife and kids always wonder, "Is he going to come home in a box today?" Or would you rather have more peace of mind?

Sometimes this works, and sometimes it doesn't. For the client who does not come up with a more prosocial goal, I have not found a way to help. Sometimes I have hung in there for another month or two, but it hasn't gone anywhere. Fortunately, such clients are much rarer than you might expect.

No Princess: Negotiable

On rare occasions, even with the movie metaphor the client will simply refuse to play along and state goals. The client may say, "This is stupid. How do I know what's going to happen?" or perhaps, "I don't talk about what might happen." Usually the therapist can cajole the client into cooperating by lowering the stakes while not backing down, for example, by saying, "Of course we don't know what's really going to happen. We're just talking about a movie. Even next week, the movie could be different. For today's movie, what would be happening 10 years from now?"

If even this doesn't work, the client is telling you how important it is to maintain the pessimistic future as an avoidance strategy. Then the best you can do is negotiate a shorter-term good ending that the client is willing to contemplate. This might go as follows.

Client: I don't like this movie thing: I don't talk about what might happen in the future.
Therapist: Are you trying to say that you don't like to get your hopes up?
Client: Exactly.

Therapist: Well, I understand that and I respect it. But if we're going to be working together, I have to have some way of knowing what you care about, what you want for yourself. Otherwise, how do we know what to work on?

Client: That makes sense.

Therapist: And this movie is the way I ask. Would it be okay to ask—but maybe not 10 years ahead but some shorter time ahead that it's easier to see your way to? (or alternately, "Would you rather tell me about your goals, what you want for yourself, in some other way?")

Once the client has agreed to talk about some shorter-term goal, the therapist tries to do the rest of the session the same way as far as is possible within what the client is willing to tolerate. For example, even if the client is not willing to visualize a movie of the steps along the way to the goal, the steps should still be identified.

People often comment that they feel hopeful after participating in this exercise. Many teens, at the end of the entire course of treatment, will say that this was the best session, the best thing about the treatment. We are helping clients to identify their goals and to recognize their own strengths and resources. This feels good, and it often inspires clients and mobilizes them. This is the session they thank you for.

This is perhaps the trickiest session to do well. When I have supervised therapists who frequently reported difficulty in getting the princess, it has always turned out that the therapist did not understand some critical component of the intervention or gave up too easily. With practice and with repeated attention to the many bits of advice provided here, you will get it. When you get it, your clients will engage in the treatment.

Clearly, the motivational interviewing approach supports the Fairy Tale model. It focuses on empowering the client and helping the client to identify the princess and then encourages the client to become more confident and to do what it takes to get ready to slay the dragon. Once the case formulation has been provided and the motivation has been identified and developed and enhanced as much as possible, it's time to offer the specific advice, which comes in the next session.

Age Variations

With Preteens

With preteens, do not use Future Movies. They do not have a 10-year plan; that timeline is developmentally tailored for teenagers. Preteens want to have a good day but also are able to look forward to the near future. Kids this age want to have more friends, get picked on less, get in less trouble. They want to stop wetting their bed so they can sleep over at a friend's house; they want to get a better report card so their parents will take them to the video arcade; they want to earn money to buy a special toy; they want to get better at a sport so they can get picked earlier for a team and so they can help their team win. This does not mean that they would choose to be in treatment, even if the treatment can help them to get what they want. We must still count on the adults to make sure that the child shows up.

Even so, it's the client who either will work with us or will throw obstacles in the way. So for preteens, it's still important first to identify what the client cares about and what he or she wants for himself or herself and then to make those goals the explicit focus of the treatment. Note that one goal clients may have is to not come to treatment anymore. This is a legitimate goal to work toward, and, of course, working hard on the other treatment goals will get the whole thing over with more quickly. It's also important to help children believe that their parents really want them to work toward their goals. In case clients believe that their symptoms help their parents in some way, this intervention helps them to believe that their parents will be okay and that they have their permission to get better. Also, when children and parents work together, this supports and enhances the relationship that may have been disrupted. Here are the steps in a relatively straightforward intervention (Greenwald, 2005) to accomplish this motivational piece with preteens.

1. Acknowledge that it may not be the client's choice to come to treatment: "Your parents told me that you're going to have to come here every week for a while. Does that sound good to you, or would you rather be doing other stuff?"
2. Identify goals by using a "greatest hits" menu of other kids' goals: Make sure to include the goals you suspect this client might have. "Here are some things that other kids have told me they wished for. You tell me if you wish for any of these things, too."
   • Some kids wish they didn't have bad dreams anymore.
   • Some kids wish they got better grades in school.
   • Some kids wish they had more friends.
   • Some kids wish they didn't get picked on so much.
   • Some kids wish their parents didn't yell at them so much.
   • Some kids wish they didn't wet their bed anymore.
   • Some kids wish they didn't get in so much trouble.
3. Align the child's goals with the parents' goals for the child: "So you wish that you had better grades and that your mom didn't yell at you so much? You know, when I was talking with your mom before, that's what she said she wanted for you, too. Did you know that?"
4. Mutually commit to these goals: "So while you are stuck coming here, is it okay if that's what we work on? Doing things to help you get better grades and to get your mom to yell at you less?
5. Get the picture: Regardless of the client's age, it is very important to get the client to generate a picture or image that represents the goal. So if the client says, "I'll be happier," the therapist should ask something such as, "What

picture could represent that?" If the client does not know how to respond, the therapist can carefully guide—without suggesting content—until the client is able to give a representative image. This should be specific—having a time, place, and action. This image becomes a symbol that helps the client to stay focused on the goal.

For example, an 11-year-old girl first said, "I wish my mom would stop yelling at me all the time!" The therapist said, "Okay, suppose 3 months from now you are telling me that your mother doesn't yell at you so much anymore. If I'm watching your life on TV that day, what would I see that would show me that?" With some guidance, the girl finally said, "Okay, I come home from school and I throw my stuff down on the floor like I always do, and my mom just asks what kind of cookie I want for my snack."

The time–place–action picture makes an emotional connection. It is more inspiring than the abstract idea of the goal and, thus, is a more powerful motivator. One way to understand the role of this symbol is this: If you're in love with a princess, you probably have her picture on the wall.

The aforementioned intervention will get the princess, but it does not provide a case formulation the way Future Movies does. It's okay; case formulation will be addressed again in the next session. Since the previous intervention for preteens only takes a few minutes, it does not require a dedicated session. Rather, it should be combined with the next session and should be done after the case formulation (with the circles and arrows; you'll see it) but before the treatment plan.

With Adults

When you do Future Movies with adults, don't use the 10-year plan. That's developmentally appropriate for teens but arbitrary for adults. Rather, first ask the client. You might say, "If we were watching a movie about what you're here to work on, how far into the future is the ending of the movie?" If the client says, "Three years," then when you tell your Future Movies story, say, "Three years from now …." The rest is the same.

Session 3: Motivation

Alex: (holding a bag of chips) It is okay if I bring these in?

Mr. G: Yeah, it's okay. Just throw the bag away afterward, okay?

Alex: Yeah, no problem.

Mr. G: So tell me something good that happened since the last time we met and something bad that happened.

Alex: Good, I got this girl's phone number. Bad, my urine came up dirty [in the weekly drug test].

Mr. G: Okay, one thing at a time; who's the girl?

Alex: She's in some of my classes at school.

Mr. G: What's she like?

Alex: She looks good! And she's nice, too. She doesn't try to play you, like some girls do.

Mr. G: So did you call her?

Alex: Not yet. I will though.

Mr. G: And the dirty urine. What's going to happen to you?

Alex: I have to go to Bridges [the local short-term secure facility] for the next two weekends. That sucks.

Mr. G: Yeah. Could be a lot worse, though. I guess they decided to give you a break. Have you been going to school every day?

Alex: Every day. And here every day, too. I been doing good other than that one mistake.

Mr. G: Maybe that's why they weren't harder on you. Is there anything coming up in the next week or two that you're either worried about or looking forward to?

Alex: Just those weekends in Bridges. Sucks.

Mr. G: In the last couple of meetings, I've asked about your past and about how things are now. Now I want to know about your future. Since you haven't been there yet, I can't ask it the same way, so I'm going to tell a little story, and you'll fill it in for me. Let's say that 10 years from now—how old will you be?

Alex: 25.

Mr. G: And I'll be having gray hair by then. So 10 years from now, I stop at the video store on my way home from work and pick up a movie called *The Alex [Last Name] Story*. It's about this kid grows up in a city, starts out pretty good. He has friends, does good in school, his family cares about him. They have their troubles, too, but it's a good family. But then something bad happens. The kind of thing you wish didn't happen to a kid, but it's a realistic movie. So the stress and anger starts piling up inside. Then more bad things happen, and he gets more angry, more stressed, the bad feelings piling up even more. He gets so stressed he ends up doing some things he doesn't really feel good about; he gets himself into some trouble, it doesn't look too good. By halfway through the movie, he's a teenager, he's locked up, and I'm saying to myself, "I don't even want to watch this movie. I used to work with kids like this. Looks like another good one going down the drain." But I just sit there, and then something good happens. A little thing—nothing stupid like him winning the lottery, it's a realistic movie. Just something he does to make his day go a little better instead of a little worse. And then something else good happens. And then something else. And I don't want to get my hopes up, but little by little, things are starting to go his way. Till finally, by the end of the movie—you know that last picture, when the music's playing and the credits are rolling?—I'm smiling and saying, "Way to go—you made it!" So tell me, if this was your story and things go the way you wish they would, what would your life be like?

Alex: I'd be doing good, have plenty of money.

Mr. G: What would you be doing for money?

Alex: Have my own business.

Mr. G: What kind of business?

Alex: I don't know; could be anything.

Mr. G: For this movie, what would it be?

Alex: A restaurant.

Mr. G: What kind of restaurant?

Alex: Spanish food, a little corner restaurant where people can get the food they like. But big enough that people can have parties there, like for graduation or Quinceanos [a girl's 15th birthday party] or whatever. You know what's Quinceanos?

Mr. G: Yeah, I know what it is. And where would you be living?

Alex: Where I am now. Well, not with my grandparents. In my own apartment.

Mr. G: By yourself? With friends? A girlfriend? Your own family?

Alex: Own family. Live with my girlfriend and two kids.

Mr. G: Boys or girls?

Alex: One of each: the boy first and then the girl.

Mr. G: And when you're 25 at the end of this movie, how old are the kids?

Alex: Like 2 or 3 years old. 3 and 2.

Mr. G: And what's your girlfriend like?

Alex: Pretty. Nice.

Mr. G: She kind of a party girl, or more mellow, responsible?

Alex: Well, she knows how to have a good time, but she's more mellow, doesn't drink or do drugs. She has her own job, too.

Mr. G: What kind of job?

Alex: Um … she's a nurse.

Mr. G: And are you taking the subway and taxis everywhere, or do you have your own wheels?

Alex: My own wheels.

Mr. G: What are you driving?

Alex: A Ferrari.

Mr. G: What color?

Alex: Red.

Mr. G: So if this is how things are for you when you're 25, what do I see in that last picture to let me know how good you're doing?

Alex: We're having the grand opening of my second restaurant.

Mr. G: So what's happening in the picture; what do I see?

Alex: I'm cutting the ribbon. Big crowd of people there—my girlfriend and my kids are next to me. And my Moms and grandparents. Lots of food in big dishes.

Mr. G: When you have this picture, what kind of feeling goes with it?

Alex: Good, happy.

Mr. G: Where do you feel that? Where in your body?

Alex: All over.

Mr. G: And what could you say along the way to encourage yourself toward this goal? Something like, "I can do it," or "I'm gonna make it"?

Alex: "Go for it."

Mr. G: Okay, now I'm going to ask you to do a concentration exercise. I'll be asking you to concentrate on the picture, the feeling, where you feel it, and what you're saying to yourself. At the same time, I'll be moving my hand back and forth, and you will be following with your eyes. Some people tell me this is weird, and I guess they're right, but I think you can handle it. It is a lot to focus on all at once. Ready? (EM)

Were you able to concentrate on everything?

Alex: Not really. As soon as I started watching your fingers go back and forth, I lost the picture.

Mr. G: Yeah, it can be hard to hold it all at once. So let's try it again. Ready? (EM) How did it go that time?

Alex: A little better.

Mr. G: Good. Try it again. Get the picture, ready? (EM) How did it go this time?

Alex: Good.

Mr. G: The thing is, the movie didn't just jump from the middle, where the kid's a teenager, to the end; there were all these things that happened along the way, to get there. So tell me, if this was your story, what happens in this movie? What would we see you doing tomorrow, next week, next month, next year?

Alex: Well, I wouldn't get locked up anymore.

Mr. G: If you were going to get locked up, what would it be for? Fighting? Getting high? What?

Alex: Yeah, those would be the main things.

Mr. G: So in this movie, if someone is trying to pick a fight, what would we see the guy in the movie doing to go toward his goals?

Alex: Just ignore, walk away. But I can't do that; I get too mad.

Mr. G: We don't know what you'll actually do. I'm just trying to find out what the guy in the movie would be doing to get toward his goals. So if you were going to be getting high, when would that be?

Alex: At a party or if I be with certain friends.

Mr. G: And in this movie, what would we see the guy do when someone passes him a joint at a party?

Alex: Just pass it to the next person. Don't take a puff.

Mr. G: And if you were going to be with those certain friends, when would that be?

Alex: My only chance now is on the weekends.

Mr. G: And if this guy in the movie wasn't going to be hanging with those friends so much, what would we see him do on the weekends?

Alex: I don't know, probably playing hoop or maybe get a little job.

Mr. G: Like what kind of job?

Alex: Anything. Keep me busy, make some money.

Mr. G: In this movie, what would the job be?

Alex: My grandfather said I could help him in the store if I want. Unload boxes, put things on the shelf, sweep the floor, stuff like that.

Mr. G: What else would we see the guy in the movie doing?

Alex: Graduate high school, get trained in how to run a restaurant.

Mr. G: What do we see the guy in the movie doing that leads to him graduating from high school?

Alex: Pay attention, do the work, don't cut classes.

Mr. G: And who's at his graduation?

Alex: My grandparents, my cousins, my brothers and sister, my Moms.

Mr. G: And how would he get trained to run a restaurant?

Alex: My school has this Culinary Arts program I was thinking of doing next year. You do regular school in the morning, and you do the cooking and stuff in the afternoon. Sometimes they get you a job, too.

Mr. G: So you'd start out getting jobs in other restaurants until you were ready to start your own?

Alex: Yeah.

Mr. G: And this girlfriend, where do you meet her?

Alex: At a party.

Mr. G: You mean one of those parties where everyone's getting high?

Alex: No, nothing like that. Like a family party for my cousin's graduation or something.

Mr. G: So now I want you to imagine watching the whole movie in your mind, not from the beginning but from today, all the way to that good end you were telling me about. All the things you were saying would happen to get there, step by step. Ready? (EM)

Alex: Done.

Mr. G: How did it go? What happened in the movie?

Alex: Just what we said.

Mr. G: Okay, we're going to do it again, same thing, step by step. Ready? (EM). How did it go this time?

Alex: Good. Same thing. I'm gonna do it.

Mr. G: I hope it goes the way you want it to, but just for a minute I want to talk about something else. What if it doesn't go the good way we've been talking about? What if the kid in the movie goes back to doing the same old stuff, things got worse and worse, until I'm looking at that last picture 10 years from now, I'm sad, I say, "What a waste of a good kid!" What would that picture be?

Alex: Locked up again, for longer this time, [a sentence of] 10 [years] to life.

Mr. G: So what's the picture that we see that shows us how bad things are for you?

Alex: I'm behind bars in an orange jumpsuit.

Mr. G: And what kind of feeling goes with this picture?

Alex: Bad. Sad.

Mr. G: Where do you feel that?

Alex: Right here (taps chest).

Mr. G: With this picture, would it feel true to say to yourself, "It's not worth it" to go that way?

Alex: It's not worth it. That's for sure.

Mr. G: Okay, so just for a few seconds, I want you to concentrate on this bad ending, the bad feeling, where you feel it, the words, "It's not worth it." Got it? (EM) Okay. Did that "It's not worth it" feel more true, less true, about the same?

Alex: More true. It's not worth it.

Mr. G: Okay, let's do this one more time; concentrate on this bad ending, the bad feeling, where you feel it, "It's not worth it." Got it? (EM) Okay. Is it more true, less true, about the same?

Alex: About the same.

Mr. G: So on 0 to 10, 0 is nothing, 10 is all the way, deep inside, how much of you really wants to go for that good ending you were telling me about, or something like that?

Alex: 10.

Mr. G: Okay, now I know you don't want the bad end, but how much of you, on 0 to 10, still feels like doing the same old thing?

Alex: 0. I'm not going to do that stuff anymore.

Mr. G: There's no such thing as a 0. We're not talking about what you will do— just how much urge there is. Like for me, when I was a kid I used to steal from stores.

Alex: For real?

Mr. G: Yeah. And now, sometimes when I'm in a store, even though I have enough money, I see something and I feel like just grabbing it. I don't do it, because if I got caught they'd probably put my picture in the paper, I'd lose my job, it's not worth it. But I'd say on 0 to 10 that I'm about a 2 or 3; still feel like doing that sometimes. So how much of you might still feel like doing that stuff?

Alex: Maybe half. About 5.

Mr. G: So most of you really wants to go the good way?

Alex: Yeah.

Mr. G: But sometimes that smaller part tries to take over and mess it up for all of you?

Alex: You could say that; I guess so.

Mr. G: I'm a gambling man. Let's say I put $100 down on the table says that you're going to make it the good way. What makes me think this is a smart bet?

Alex: I don't know. Cause you think I'm gonna do it?

Mr. G: Well, I have some ideas about why this might be a smart bet. See if you think these ideas are right or wrong. Most people I know, if they really care a lot about something, they try harder than for something that doesn't really matter to them. You told me that on 0 to 10 you're a 10—you really want this. So would you say that you're determined, motivated? What's the best word?

Alex: Determined.

Mr. G: Also, to do what you said and get that training, you'd have to pass your classes. Now I know from how you did before you went to middle school that you're smart enough to do well in school if you decide to. You think that's true?

Alex: Yeah. I did good in the school upstate, too. I got my credits all the way through ninth grade.

Mr. G: Also, you're a good cook, right?

Alex: Right.

Mr. G: So I might bet on you because you have the talent you need to run a restaurant.

Alex: That makes sense.

Mr. G: Would you say that people have a better chance of making it if they're all alone in the world? Or if they have people in their corner that try to help them out sometimes?

Alex: People in their corner.

Mr. G: Who are the people in your corner?

Alex: My grandparents, my cousins, my family.

Mr. G: So what should I say: People in your corner? People who care? People who help?

Alex: People who care.

Mr. G: Here's a question for you. Say you go up for an easy layup but you get jammed [the shot is blocked]. Are you the kind of guy who will mope around for the next 5 minutes while the play is going on down the court somewhere?

Alex: No way. I just hustle even harder, try to get the ball back.

Mr. G: Good. Because I don't want to bet on a guy who lies down and dies every time something goes wrong. Because things do go wrong.

Alex: That's for sure.

Mr. G: So should we say "persistence," "won't quit," "doesn't give up," "bounces back"?

Alex: Doesn't give up.

Mr. G: Now it's one thing for someone to just tell me, "Yes, I want to make it." But you've actually already been doing some of the things we've been talking about that get you toward your goals. Okay, you're not perfect, but you got your credits through ninth grade; you've been going to school, coming here, getting yourself on track. So this makes me think you're serious about it, because you're not just saying it—you're doing it.

Alex: I guess so.

Mr. G: So I'm going to write down, "track record." See, here's the list I made while we were talking. You think these are pretty good reasons to bet on you or not so good?

Alex: Pretty good reasons.

Mr. G: Now, you know what's gonna happen as soon as I put that money down. Someone's gonna walk up and say, "Sucker! I'll bet you he goes the bad way." What makes that guy think he's got some easy money coming?

Alex: Well, look where I been, what I was doing before.

Mr. G: Okay. What else would he say?

Alex: I don't know.

Mr. G: Maybe he'd say, "Sure, he's doing fine now, but pass him a joint and see what he does."

Alex: Oh yeah.

Mr. G: So I'll write down, "drug temptation." Or the guy might say, "Sure, he's doing fine now, but get him mad and he'll do anything; just forget about his goals."

Alex: I do get pretty mad.

Mr. G: So should I write down "temper" or "anger" or what?

Alex: Anger.

Mr. G: And the guy might say, "Sure, he's doing fine, but if his pockets are empty and some friend comes to him with a scheme, he'll just go do it."

Alex: Maybe. I don't think that's the big thing.

Mr. G: Okay. Or he might say, "Sure, he's doing fine, but some peer says, 'Hey let's get out of school and do something more fun,' and then he'll just go along."

Alex: Could be.

Mr. G: So I want to know what my biggest worry is about losing my bet. Drug temptation, anger, empty pockets, peers?

Alex: Anger.

Mr. G: And what's my next biggest worry?

Alex: Wanting to get high.

Mr. G: And next?

Alex: Peers.

Mr. G: So it sounds like there are some good reasons to believe that you really could make it on the good track. And also some real challenges, some things that could get in your way. So I think I'm going to make my money, but it's not a sure thing. Now I'm going to ask you to give me the odds, the way you see things right now. On a scale of 0 to 10, 10 is a sure thing and 0 is no chance at all, so 0 and 10 are impossible because nothing's ever sure. What do you think my chances are of winning this bet?

Alex: 6 or 7. 6 1/2.

Mr. G: And what would it take for you to tell me that it's not a 6 1/2 anymore, that it's a 7 now? What would have to happen?

Alex: If I keep going to school and no more dirty urine.

Mr. G: Okay, that's it for today. Tell me something you liked about this meeting and something you didn't like about it.

Alex: I liked talking about my plans and that you would bet on me. I didn't like that it took so long.

Mr. G: Yeah, this was a long meeting, wasn't it?

Alex: Was it more than an hour?

Mr. G: Yes, a little more. Where do you go now?

Alex: Group.

Mr. G: Okay, see you next week.

Session 3 - Motivation, Official Notes

Focused today on future goals, steps to achieve those goals, strengths and resources that can help him to achieve his goals, and possible obstacles.

Session 3 - Motivation, Therapist's Personal Notes

School ok so far
Dirty urine - next 2 wkends in Bridges

FM good end: own restaurant, gf nurse, boy 3 girl 2, live same area own apt, red ferrari
FM good end pic: cutting ribbon on 2nd restaurant

EM went okay

Steps:
anger: ignore, walk away
drug: pass it on; weekends: play hoop, get job at store w/ grandfather
school: pay attention, do work, don't cut classes
go to culinary arts program next year at school
grad: grandp's, cousins, mother, brothers, sister
jobs in restaurants
meets gf at party

Strengths:
determined
smart enough for school
talent - good cook
people who care
doesn't give up
track record

Obstacles:
drug temptation – 2
anger -1
money temptation
peers – 3

Today's odds: 6.5
To get to 7: keep going to school, no more dirty urine

Figure 4.1   Motivation session notes

Session 3: Questions and Answers

Q: How many moms does this kid have anyway?

A: Just one. Some kids say "my mom" and some say "my moms." He's only talking about the one.

Q: Why use eye movements to visualize the good end, bad end, and steps along the way? Aren't eye movements mainly for trauma processing (in EMDR)?

A: For those trained in EMDR, we start eye movements in this session for several reasons, such as to prepare clients for the mechanics of EMDR before we get into working on trauma memories and to avoid creating an association between eye movements and negative affect, as might occur if we wait to use EM until it was time to work on the trauma memories.

Eye movements are used in EMDR not only for trauma processing but also for development of positive/adaptive reappraisals of the situation and the self (e.g., in the Installation phase). Although the question of whether EM actually contribute to treatment effect is still controversial, the available evidence indicates a role for EM (Lee & Drummond, 2008). On the chance that EM also enhance the development of positives, why not add EM to other visualization activities? They might help and probably do no harm.

Q: Did you really steal from stores when you were a kid? And whether you did or not, why say so? Isn't that a rather personal disclosure?

A: We are trained to avoid personal disclosure because it can shift the focus from the client to the therapist. This is a real risk, and I avoid personal disclosures even when many therapists would make them, for example, to establish credibility with the "I've been there too" message. I don't tell my clients where I've been, because we're there to talk about the client, not about me. And I don't think I need to claim experience as, for example, a drug addict, combat veteran, or rape victim to be of service to clients. Being respectful, empathic, and offering practical skills and strategies seems to do the job.

I use personal disclosures for two main purposes. One is to build rapport with casual disclosures—for example, when talking about sports, music, or other possibly shared interests. The other is to use myself as an example or role model, when I believe my client might need help to make a stretch to a difficult but important position. For example, many clients resist acknowledging personal weakness, but it's essential to recognize one's weaknesses to address them. So I will illustrate the point with my own story of personal weakness (in this case, urge or temptation) to show that one can harbor such weakness without being a weak person. Similarly, later in the treatment I will offer another personal disclosure (of weakness in the face of temptation) to explain why I avoid certain high risks.

I know I still didn't answer the first question. Since neither of these purposes applies at the moment, I see no reason for personal disclosure now. Knowing won't help you to be a better therapist, will it? I will say that in general, I prefer telling the truth, and also I rarely tell anything to a client that I am not willing for others to hear.

Chapter 5

Treatment Contract

From the Future Movies session you have the princess (i.e., the client's goal), which provides an answer to the question, "Why should I care/bother?" You also have a good start on the case formulation, which provides a detailed understanding of the client's problem (i.e., the dragon and related symptoms) as well as the client's strengths and resources (i.e., the knight and the kingdom), which may contribute to achieving the goals. In the Treatment Contracting session the therapist further develops the problem side of the case formulation, which leads directly to, "What to do about it?" The therapist then offers the suggestions, which constitute the treatment plan: (1) build a fence around the client for stabilization; (2) engage in personal training to help the client to become stronger, and then (3) slay the dragon.

Both the treatment plan and the therapist's personal trainer strategy are shared with the client, in keeping with the therapist's stance as expert collaborator. In the medical model, treatment may be done by the doctor to the patient. In the Fairy Tale model, the therapist serves as consultant and coach but leaves the initiative and power in the client's hands.

Case Formulation

The case formulation is the explanation the therapist gives to the client about what is going on with the client. This is an opportunity to teach the client about the problem, how the client's trauma/loss history contributes to the problem, and what strengths and resources the client may have available to address this. The case formulation accomplishes several purposes.

It Transforms the Client From "Bad" to Hurt

It's tempting for a family member to be angry with a bad child or spouse, to reject him or her, or to give up on him or her. But what if the client isn't really bad but just sad, mad, or scared? How do you react to a wounded person? You want to help. Helping the family—as well as the client himself or herself—to see the client as wounded rather than as bad opens the door for a more empathic and constructive attitude toward the client.

It Externalizes the Client's Problem

As their family members may do, many clients also believe that they have become bad, damaged, or tainted in some way. The case formulation helps them to see themselves as basically good, with some problems that have intruded but that do not represent their core being. In other words, the dragon (and related symptoms) is the problem, not the once upon a time or the kingdom—not the client himself or herself.

It Normalizes

People suffering from posttraumatic symptoms and labeled as *problems* tend to feel that they are not normal, that they are bad, stigmatized, broken, sick. The case formulation helps them to see themselves as having normal and reasonable reactions to unfortunate events. The case formulation also calls for simple and normative actions (e.g., avoiding problem situations, becoming stronger, and then talking through the bad memory) to effect a cure.

It Emphasizes Strengths and Resources

The case formulation does not start with the dragon or the problems/symptoms. It starts with "Once upon a time," with the kingdom's predragon level of functioning, and with the knight in shining armor. It is the kingdom and the knight (i.e., the family/community and the client) who will work together to slay the dragon—thus, the list of strengths and resources made in the previous session, the reason the therapist will bet on the client making it the good way. These strengths and resources will be the foundation of the client's success in treatment.

It Mobilizes People to Productive Treatment-Related Activities

When the client and others can understand where the problem comes from, when they can feel empathy, connection, and protectiveness toward the client (instead of anger and rejection), when they can feel capable and empowered to solve the problem, and when they have reason to hope for improvement, watch out!

It Gives the Therapist Credibility

The therapist may have been the first one to ever really explain the problem. This enhances the therapist's credibility and improves the chances of acceptance of the proposed solution.

Treatment Contract

In the Future Movies session, the trauma-informed case formulation (and treatment plan) followed the structure of the fairy tale, filled in with the client's own details. The Treatment Contracting session builds on that groundwork with a more detailed analysis of the client's problems and a carefully presented set of suggestions for the treatment plan. It would be helpful to take a look at the Treatment Planning Session Form (Appendix C) before continuing here.

The treatment planning script leads the client to see the whole package as a rather obvious, commonsense proposition. This is good; people are more likely to accept something that, even if they couldn't articulate it themselves, they recognize as true. Clients may be unsure about the trauma resolution part, but that's also okay for now. The therapist just says that this part of the plan will be discussed further when the time comes, and the client can make his or her decision then. When the time does come, the client will be much further along and will have built up confidence not only in himself or herself but also in the therapist's advice.

Many therapists were trained to regard the treatment plan as something to keep in the therapist's mind or perhaps to put in the paperwork to make the insurance company happy. In the Fairy Tale model, the treatment plan is an explicit discussion about a recommended sequence of treatment activities, leading to an agreement or treatment contract. In this approach, the treatment plan and contract is an essential intervention.

One client, upon being presented with the treatment plan, said, "Oh, this is different from other times I've been to counseling." The therapist asked, "What do you mean?" The client said, "With other counselors, we talked about my feelings or we tried to solve problems. This is more like taking a class; you have to get through each step, and then you get your certificate." This is exactly the impression we are hoping to foster. This treatment contracting intervention offers the following benefits.

It Gives the Client a Sense of Initiative

This is a plan of action on which the client has decided. From here on, the therapist can refer to the treatment plan as a way of reminding the client that any given treatment activity was agreed on by the client in the service of achieving his or her goals. This maintains the client's position as the one driving the treatment and keeps the therapist from sliding into the trap of appearing to be bossing the client around.

It Gives the Client a Sense of Direction and Progress

Can good therapy be done even if the client does not know the treatment plan? Of course. But without a treatment contract, clients may feel that they are just mucking around and hoping that something good will come out of it. It is easy for a client to feel helpless and discouraged under such circumstances, especially when results are not quickly forthcoming. With a treatment contract specifying a sequence of tasks that make sense to the client, he or she knows what is going on in treatment and why. The client has more of a sense that he or she is doing each activity for a clear purpose and getting ever closer to the goal. Having a plan encourages the client to remain engaged and committed.

It Gives the Therapist a Mandate to Stay Focused

Once the client and therapist have agreed on a course of action to help the client to get to his or her goals, the therapist has an obligation to the client to follow this course. Imagine that, in the next session after you have done this treatment contract, your client comes in and tells you, "My uncle died yesterday." You will probably spend the session focused on that rather than on the next treatment task that had been on your agenda. Okay, this happens; if something is absolutely preoccupying the client, we have little choice but to talk about it. But then suppose that in the next meeting, the client has another crisis and then another crisis the next time.

Is the treatment derailed? Have you changed from directive therapy to supportive therapy? Not if you have a treatment contract. Now you can say, "I want to check in with you about something. A few weeks ago, we made a deal to do certain things together to help you get stronger toward your goals. Then the next week, instead of starting on that, well, your uncle died so of course that's what we talked about. Then ever since then there has been one big thing after another. So on one hand, I don't feel bad that we talked about that stuff, because it was important. On the other hand, I'm wondering if I might be letting you down, because we're not doing what we said we were going to do—to help you get to your goals. What do you think?"

Many clients were previously in supportive or nondirective therapy and have developed a habit of using their sessions for venting. When the therapist reorients the client to the case formulation, the princess, and the treatment plan, the client is offered an opportunity for real change.

Some clients might respond by saying, "Well, this is a hard time in my life. Can we meet twice a week for a while, so one time we can talk about whatever's going on and the other time we can do the stuff we were going to do?" More often, a client will say, "Well, if I'm really upset about something, I probably do have to talk about it. But can you, like, interrupt me after a few minutes and see if we can change the subject?"

If the therapist only has a secret treatment plan, he or she is left holding the tiger by the tail. If the therapist and client have a shared treatment contract, the therapist has a mandate from the client to make repeated efforts to try to get the client back on track—not because the therapist is trying to boss the client around but because the therapist is trying to keep his or her obligations in the service of the client's initiative and goals. This is a good position for the therapist to be in, and it really can help the treatment stay on track.

Practice Exercise

There is no official practice exercise in this chapter. The only tricky part of this session is filling in the circles properly, and you will get the skills you need for this by doing the practice exercise in Chapter 8 (Self-Control Skills). Otherwise, the script is fairly straightforward, and it takes care of itself. However, practice never hurts, so if you want to try this with a colleague by just going through the script, go for it. The "client" in the practice exercise should first identify and share with the therapist a problem behavior that he or she would like to improve. In the practice, just focus on that single behavior; do not look for other problems.

Obstacles to Following Through

It is worthwhile to anticipate treatment obstacles and to prepare coping methods in collaboration with the client and others who may be involved. The primary obstacles are lack of system support for treatment and the client's (and others') temptation to terminate treatment prematurely. These obstacles are addressed in the following text.

System Support

As mentioned earlier, it is absolutely essential that those with responsibility for the client's welfare and conduct (e.g., parent, guardian, school, court, treatment/ incarceration facility, employer, service provider) actively support the treatment, particularly in the following ways:

- Provide as safe, consistent, and supportive an environment as possible.
- Make sure the client comes to treatment and keeps coming until the therapist says treatment is over.
- Make sure the client is not being "enabled" in the problem behaviors but is facing real consequences for the behaviors. If the client is not experiencing

any problems related to the problem behavior, it will be difficult for the client to perceive obstacles. No obstacles, no need to change, and no need for treatment.

■ Make sure the client is being reinforced (rewarded) for good behaviors. It is important that the client can learn from repeated experience that the good behavior is worthwhile and contributes to progress toward his or her goals. Otherwise, the risk of discouragement is too high.

We're Done Now, Right?

The biggest crack in this treatment approach, paradoxically, is caused by its own effectiveness. The success of the fence-around and personal training phases of treatment may tempt the client (and others involved) to end treatment prematurely. Suppose the client has made good progress with symptom management, the crisis has passed, and the client's behavior has considerably improved. At this point clients often claim to be "better," and it can be difficult for others involved to know how to disagree with this claim.

Avoidance may also be an issue; not only do clients often prefer to avoid talking about the bad thing that happened, but others also often wish to spare them that experience. Therapists may collude (and yes, even good therapists can be reluctant to face trauma). Clients often say, "I'm doing fine now, so I don't need to talk about that [trauma memory]." Since many people do not appreciate the extent to which healing from trauma is possible, they may not really understand the purpose of the trauma resolution phase of treatment anyway, so it can be easy for them to let it go.

In this treatment approach, this obstacle is addressed in three ways: (1) by putting the trauma on the map; (2) by predicting the temptation to quit prematurely and preparing for it; and (3) by artfully persuading the client to go ahead with the trauma resolution work when the time comes.

Put the Trauma on the Map

In the Treatment Contract session, we create a graphic representation of the case formulation that illustrates how past trauma memories create the sore spot that make certain situations "high risk" for the client. In every subsequent session, we work from this piece of paper. Even when the work is focused on fence-around or personal training activities, the trauma is always on the map and in the client's face. This can help to convey that the unresolved trauma really is part of the underlying problem and must be dealt with sooner or later. Of course, the fact that this proposition is explicit in the treatment plan itself—on the same piece of paper—provides further reinforcement for the message.

Predict the Temptation to Quit

This intervention is particularly important to do with the parent or whoever is responsible for compelling the client to show up for treatment (including the client himself or herself, in the case of a self-referring adult). Remember that most people are not psychologically minded, and if they see the client behaving better they are likely to conclude that the client is better and that treatment is done. However, if you predict this and say, "That's like the third day of antibiotics," you can help them to understand that, although the client may appear to be better, the root of the problem has not yet been addressed. You can reiterate the case formulation and treatment plan and can suggest, "If the time comes that [the client] seems better and you are tempted to quit, I'd like to make an agreement. Will you agree to come and talk to me about it before you go ahead and make a decision to stop? Then we can talk about whether the client is really done or if it's just the third day of antibiotics."

Most people will agree to this, and many will even keep their agreement. Then when the time comes to talk about it, you will have a chance to reiterate the case formulation and treatment plan, to confirm how well the client is doing, and to explain the importance of persevering to treatment completion. Then you explain that otherwise there is a high risk that the client will relapse because the underlying vulnerability has not been addressed.

If you fail to predict the premature temptation to quit and then it arises, one of two outcomes is likely. Most often, the client simply stops showing up and no one in a position of authority bothers to do anything about it. Alternately, you have a chance to try to talk the responsible adults into getting the client to keep coming, but because they already believe the client is doing fine now, you look like a therapist who inappropriately wants to keep clients after they are better. On the other hand, if you predicted the premature temptation to quit and then it arises, you will have good credibility and a much better chance of prevailing.

Artfully Persuading the Client

In the Treatment Contract session, we only identify trauma resolution as a recommendation that will be discussed in more detail when the time comes. The time comes at the end of the Reduce Stress session, as the transition to beginning trauma resolution work. At that time, the script includes a sales pitch that has worked rather well, at least with the urban teenaged boys with whom it's been tried.

Age Variations

With Preteens

With preteens, the case formulation (circles and arrows) can be done about the same way as with teens. However, the treatment plan is quite different, in large part because the parents of preteens play a greater role in fence-around activities and in treatment as a whole. Here's how to put it together.

1. First complete the case formulation portion of the session as with teens, with the circles and arrows, through the part about the sore spot from the old memories.
2. Next, get the princess, as described in the preteen section at the end of the previous chapter.
3. Then, with the client's permission (which is normally forthcoming), bring in the parents and together with the client show and explain the case formulation (e.g., circles and arrows) to the parents.
4. Finally, offer the treatment plan with the client and parents together as follows (Greenwald, 2005a).

Fence-Around

Therapist (to parent): You know that course you took in high school on special parenting strategies for trauma-exposed kids? How did you do in that course?

Parent: Um, they didn't have that course in my high school.

Therapist: Yeah, I guess they don't have that course in most high schools. Too bad. Anyway, now you need the course, so you can get it from me. There are special things you can do to help your child feel extra safe and extra secure. This will help him or her to calm down and relax and be able to concentrate on the rest of the work so [he or she] can get better. I'm just giving you the overview now, but we can take some time to figure out which things you're already doing to help [him or her] feel safe and secure, and maybe I can help you to find even more things to do.

Personal Training

Therapist (to client): When you're older and bigger and stronger, do you think [these trigger situations] will still mess you up the same way? Or do you think you'll be able to handle them better?

Client: No; my cousin used to get mad all the time, but he calmed down. When I'm older like my cousin, I won't get so mad anymore either.

Therapist: There are special things we can do together to help you get bigger and stronger, so you can handle it better. I can show you things to practice, kind of like a coach.

Slay the Dragon

Therapist (to client): You know how we were talking about how those old memories make a sore spot inside? Down the road, when I think you're strong enough, and if you decide you want to, there are special ways of talking about those memories that can make the bad feelings get smaller. Then the sore spot is smaller and it's easier to handle the [trigger situations] that come along.

This treatment plan gives everyone a role. This is especially important for parents, who may feel guilty, inadequate, and disempowered. Parents can build the fence around the child by maintaining household routines, implementing a consistent discipline approach, implementing an incentive system, and taking other measures to help the child be, and feel, more safe and secure (see Greenwald, 2005a). Teachers or others can do their part in some situations. The child can work on becoming stronger, in anticipation of facing and working through the trauma memories.

With Adults

This session is the same with adults as with teens.

Session 4: Treatment Contract

Mr. G: Hi, tell me something good and something bad since last time we met.

Alex: Bad, spent the weekend in Bridges. It's not like it's so bad there, but I like my freedom.

Mr. G: And something good?

Alex: Nothing really good happened this week.

Mr. G: There must be 1 minute that was better then another. Doesn't have to be anything big.

Alex: I passed my first test at school.

Mr. G: What was the test?

Alex: English. You had to answer questions about a story. I got a 90 [out of a possible 100].

Mr. G: A 90—that's more than just passing.

Alex: It wasn't that hard.

Mr. G: Anything coming up that you're either worried about or looking forward to?

Alex: Just one more weekend at Bridges; that's all.

Mr. G: Last time we met, we talked about your goals, the kind of life you want for yourself. We talked about your strengths, things that will help you get what you want (the reasons I'm betting on you) and also about some things that could get in your way if you're not careful (the reasons that other guy was betting against me). Have you driven a car before?

Alex: A few times.

Mr. G: Here's a driving question: What do you do if you're driving along, and you see a patch of ice on the road ahead?

Alex: Better slow down, drive around it.

Mr. G: That's right. Do you know what drivers mean when they talk about "black ice"?

Alex: Not exactly.

Mr. G: It's from water that melts and then freezes a certain way so you can't see it; you think it's just the road, but there's ice on it. What happens if you're driving along and you can't see the ice ahead?

Alex: What happens, you slip and maybe have an accident.

Mr. G: That's right—anything could happen; you could be in big trouble. So I want to talk a little more today about the things that could be getting in your way. The goal is that you can see it clearly and make your own choices; I don't want you to have any black ice. Okay?

Alex: Okay.

Mr. G: You said that the main thing that could get in your way is your anger. So are you losing your temper every minute of every day or just at certain times?

Alex: Just once in a while; only if someone makes me mad.

Mr. G: Like what would someone have to do to make you mad?

Alex: Like if someone grills [stares at] me, bumps into me, or says something about my family.

Mr. G: Oh, so there are only certain situations that could lead to you losing your temper. I'm going to write these down as your "high-risk situations." So when's the last time that one of these things happened?

Alex: Just this morning.

Mr. G: What happened?

Alex: Today on the way into school, a guy stepped on my sneaker.

Mr. G: So when that happens, what are your thoughts and feelings?

Alex: I'm mad.

Mr. G: What are you saying to yourself; what are the words in your head?

Alex: I want to hurt him.

Mr. G: And what's happening in your body; what are the signals that you're mad?

Alex: My heart is beating, and my hands are fists.

Mr. G: So this is a pretty strong reaction. When you're like this, what do you feel like doing?

Alex: Feel like hitting the guy.

Mr. G: Okay. But you told me that this kind of thing would get you bad consequences. Like what kind of bad thing might happen to you if you hit the guy?

Alex: Suspended from school, maybe get locked up again, the guy might try for revenge.

Mr. G: Another reason that other guy would bet against me was drug temptation. Like when would you be most tempted to smoke? You said before, at parties or with certain friends?

Alex: Yeah, not every party, not the family parties, just certain ones.

Mr. G: And at that kind of party, what's the moment you might be most tempted?

Alex: When someone passes me a blunt. Especially if it's a girl.

Mr. G: At that moment, what are the words in your head, your emotions, the signals in your body?

Alex: Excitement; I want some.

Mr. G: And if you let that take you over, what do you do next?

Alex: Take a puff, inhale.

Mr. G: And you told me that leads to bad consequences?

Alex: Next time I don't think they put me in Bridges. Probably get locked up for longer.

Mr. G: Another reason the guy would bet against me is because of peers. Like what would a peer say that could take you away from your goals?

Alex: Well, like, on the way to school someone could say, "This girl has the keys to her apartment; let's go have a party." Or maybe at lunch [at school] someone could say, "Let's get out of here."

Mr. G: And in that moment, let's say at lunch when someone says, "Let's get out of here," what are the words in your head, your emotions, the signals in your body?

Alex: Excitement; I want to do it. Also, part of me knows I shouldn't go, and part of me I don't want to say no, these are my friends.

Mr. G: And if you let that take you over, what happens next?

Alex: I go.

Mr. G: And what consequences does that lead to?

Alex: Failing my classes, Ms. Burns [the case worker] on my case, my grandparents on my case.

Mr. G: So let me ask you another question. These high-risk situations you were telling me about, would you say that you mess up every time someone does one of those things?

Alex: Not every time. I didn't do anything bad this morning when that guy stepped on my sneaker. I'm trying to stay out of trouble.

Mr. G: Would you say that you have a better chance of controlling yourself when you are feeling good, relaxed? Or when you're already stressed?

Alex: If I'm relaxed. If I'm already stressed, don't mess with me.

Mr. G: So when you get these bad consequences, like failing your classes, or having dirty urine, or being suspended from school, or wondering if someone will try for revenge, does that make you more relaxed or more stressed?

Alex: Definitely more stressed.

Mr. G: See, I've made a chart of the things you were telling me [shows it]. So the more you handle these high-risk situations by doing the quick-relief behavior, the more you end up getting stressed from the consequences?

Alex: Yeah, I guess so. Oh, this is like a cycle!

Mr. G: Right, it can be. Then the more you're stressed, the harder it is to handle the high-risk situations. Does this cycle seem familiar from before?

Alex: Yeah. I kind of knew all this already, but it's good to have it laid out like that.

Mr. G: Now here's an interesting thing: You know how you told me the things that were your high-risk situations? Not everyone has the same ones. Some other kid might say, "I don't care if someone stares at me. What bothers me is when I can't figure out the problem in math class." And another kid might say, "Someone says Let's cut school, I just say forget it, no big deal. What gets to me is when someone in my family puts me down." Everyone has their own. I have an idea why these are the high-risk situations for you. Can I tell you?

Alex: Sure, go ahead.

Mr. G: Okay. To explain this, can I touch your shoulder lightly with this pen?

Alex: Okay.

Mr. G: Okay, pay attention, and tell me how much this hurts, on 0 to 10. (Taps client's shoulder lightly.) How much?

Alex: Nothing. 0.

Mr. G: Now I'm going to ask you to imagine something that I would never do and you would never let me do. Imagine that I have a baseball bat and that I swing this bat as hard as I can right to that spot on your shoulder—not just once but over and over again for 10 minutes. And then tomorrow, the same thing over and over again. Every day like that for 2 weeks. And then, you're walking down the hall, and someone bumps you in the shoulder—can I touch you there again?

Alex: Okay.

Mr. G: Okay, now tell me how much this would hurt if someone bumped you like this after that 2 weeks with the baseball bat [taps lightly as before].

Alex: A 10!

Mr. G: How come? I barely touched you.

Alex: Cause it's already all banged up and sore.

Mr. G: Okay, that makes sense. The thing is, not all of our sore spots are on the outside. Remember when we made that list of the worst things that ever happened to you, and I asked you on 0 to 10 how much the things still hurt inside? Some of the things on your list had pretty high numbers. For most people, those old memories make a sore spot on the inside, so when something else comes along that maybe feels like that in some way, like if someone does something to get you mad, it hits the sore spot and you react extra strong.

Alex: Maybe, yeah.

Mr. G: So this thing makes sense to you?

Alex: Yeah.

Mr. G: Okay, then we have a pretty good idea of what could get in your way keep you from getting to your goals. Remember when we first met, I told you I'd ask you a lot of questions, then tell you what I learned, then give you some suggestions?

Alex: Yeah.

Mr. G: Well, here come the suggestions. This is my best advice for what you can do to get stronger toward your goals, give yourself better odds. You might be doing some of these things already, and there might be some things you could be doing even better.

Alex: Okay.

Mr. G: First of all, let's say you have a friend, he's 21, he's an alcoholic but he's trying to stay sober. He's doing good so far; it's been 2 months without a drop, but every day's a struggle. He needs a job, and he says to you, "That bar down the street needs a bartender; think I should try for that?" What will you tell him?

Alex: No, don't do it.

Mr. G: Why?

Alex: Because there's gonna be beer all around, sooner or later he's gonna drink some.

Mr. G: Good answer. So you already understand the first thing I'm going to suggest for you: Avoid high risk. If you know where the trouble is, sometimes you can just decide to stay away from it. Then it doesn't even have a chance. So you see your friend a couple of weeks later. He tells you, "Thanks for the advice. I got a job at a clothing store; nobody drinks there, I'm doing great. But last Saturday I went to my friend's house for his birthday, I thought it was just going to be a few guys. There was a hundred people there! And kegs, bottles, everywhere." This is a good friend of yours. What do you hope he did?

Alex: I hope he left.

Mr. G: Good idea. Because even when you do everything right, try to stay away from trouble, sometimes trouble finds you.

Alex: That's for sure.

Mr. G: So you already understand my next suggestion: self-control skills. It's something you're already doing; my suggestion is to get even better at it.

Alex: Yup.

Mr. G: Now you told me that if you're stressed, it's harder to use your self-control skills. So my next suggestion won't be a surprise: Reduce stress. Now this one has different parts. One part is to get better at doing things every day to keep yourself feeling good so the stress doesn't happen. But no matter how hard you try, sometimes the stress comes, and then the question is, do you want to walk around all stressed out? Or catch it and bring it back down?

Alex: Bring it back down, calm down.

Mr. G: So there are also things you can do, get better at, to bring your stress down. The other part is to bring stress down from the old stuff, those old memories that make that sore spot inside. Down the road, when I think you're ready, and if you decide you want to, there's a special way of talking about those old memories; it can help to make the sore spot smaller. So something that's a 10 now could end up being a 5 or even a 3. Most kids tell me they don't like that meeting, because they don't like talking about the old memory. But afterward they say things don't make them so mad anymore. How does that sound to you?

Alex: I don't know; maybe it's good, but I don't think it'll work for me.

Mr. G: Well, it works for most people, but I can't promise if it'll work for you or not. Anyway, when the time comes, I'll tell you more about it, and you can make your decision.

Alex: Okay.

Mr. G: And here's my final suggestion: track record of small successes. Let me explain what I mean. Let's say you have someone just like you are today. He has his goals, but there are things in his way, too. So he's trying, and he's not perfect, but he's doing pretty good. Two or three steps forward, one step back. Two or three steps forward, one step back. A month from now, someone steps on his sneaker, and he has to decide what to do. And let's say there's another guy, also starts out like you are today. But every time he makes a step forward, he slides a step back. One step forward, one step back. He's not really getting anywhere. And a month from now, someone steps on his sneaker. Which one of these guys has a better chance of handling this in a way that will help him go toward his goals?

Alex: The first one.

Mr. G: Why?

Alex: He knows he can do it. Also he's doing good, don't do something stupid and mess it up.

Mr. G: And what's the other guy saying to himself?

Alex: Doesn't matter what I do—I got nothing to lose.

Mr. G: So when I suggest building this track record of small successes, I'm not just talking about the big things like graduating high school. I'm talking about things like what you did this morning when the guy stepped on your sneaker. The more you succeed at doing the things you said you cared about, the more strong you'll feel, the more confident you'll feel, and the harder you'll be willing to work on it. So what do you think of these suggestions; do they make sense to you?

Alex: Yeah, they make sense; some of it I've been trying to do already.

Mr. G: So is this something you think you might want to work on together when we meet?

Alex: Yeah, I want to do it. I think it's good.

Mr. G: Okay. So my suggestion is that when we meet next time, we start at the top. We figure out what you're already doing, and what else you could do if you want to, to get even stronger toward your goals. And in different meetings we kind of work our way down step by step. And if something comes up that you don't feel like talking about, what happens?

Alex: I just say I don't feel like talking about it.

Mr. G: Right. So tell me something you liked about this meeting and something you didn't like.

Alex: I like having the plan, things I can do to get to my goals. And I didn't like, um, just all the talking, but it wasn't so bad as last time.

Mr. G: And what's next for you now?

Alex: Homework.

Mr. G: And one more weekend at Bridges?

Alex: Yup. One more.

Mr. G: Okay, see you next week.

Alex: See you.

Session 4: Treatment Plan, Official Notes

Further focus on possible obstacles to achieving goals. Then presented suggestions/treatment plan, including avoiding high risk situations, improving self-control skills, reducing stress (via daily practices as well as resolving old trauma/loss memories) and building on small successes.

Session 4: Questions and Answers

Q: I have been waiting for you to tell your client the fairy tale. Wouldn't this session have been the perfect moment? When do you do it?

A: Actually I haven't told the fairy tale to clients! But many therapists I've trained have told the story to their clients with good results. They have told me that their clients gain a better understanding of the treatment process and seem to become more engaged and committed. So I finally got the message that if the story is worthwhile for therapists, it's good enough for clients, too. I will start giving my clients copies of my comic book, *A Fairy Tale* (Greenwald & Baden, 2007), and see how it goes. I don't know yet where it might be most beneficial for the client to get the fairy tale story: at the beginning of treatment or at the Treatment Contracting session.

If you are going to tell the actual fairy tale to your clients, I have several suggestions on how to pull this off.

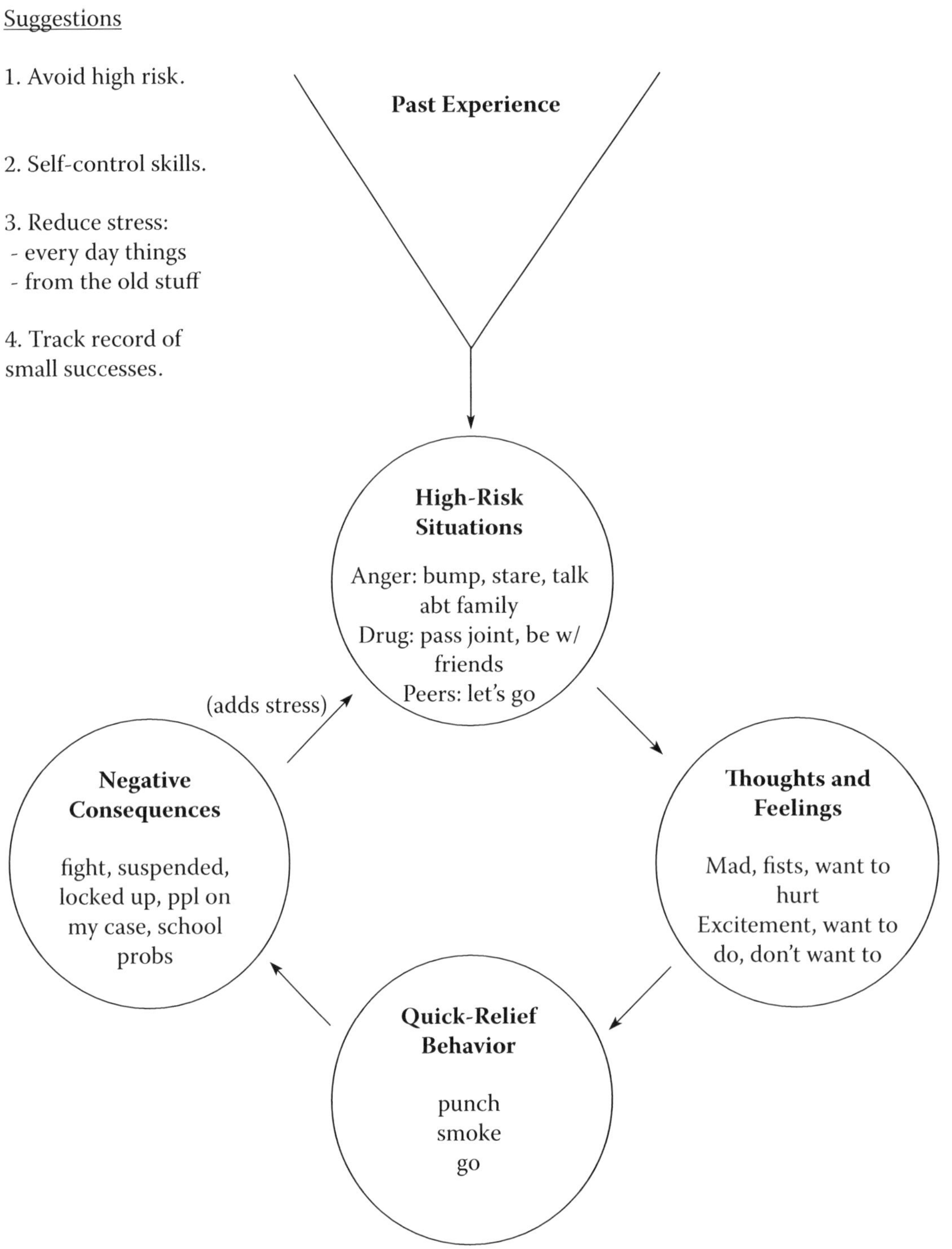

Suggestions

1. Avoid high risk.

2. Self-control skills.

3. Reduce stress:
 - every day things
 - from the old stuff

4. Track record of small successes.

Past Experience

High-Risk Situations

Anger: bump, stare, talk
abt family
Drug: pass joint, be w/
friends
Peers: let's go

Thoughts and Feelings

Mad, fists, want to
hurt
Excitement, want to
do, don't want to

(adds stress)

Negative Consequences

fight, suspended,
locked up, ppl on
my case, school
probs

Quick-Relief Behavior

punch
smoke
go

Figure 5.1   Session 4—Treatment Plan, Therapist's Personal Notes

■ Give them a copy of the comic book or, alternately, read the story verbatim from the book for your first few tries. Like any other script, you internalize it with practice.

■ Depending on your personality, you may not feel comfortable with the fairy tale as I tell it, for any number of reasons. So you might revise it a bit to suit your style and values. If you do this, I encourage you to still make sure to include all the elements. For example, if you want the guy to tame the dragon instead of killing it, the fence-around and personal training are still important, as is the experience of facing the feared thing.

■ You may also have clients for whom the story should be modified; for example, some girls or women may more easily identify with a female protagonist. Personally I haven't found that girls or women had trouble with the story, but you might find some clients to differ from this. So again, if you do modify it, make sure that you still find some way of including all the elements.

Q: Where do others in the system fit in? Isn't the treatment plan a good time to bring others on board?

A: Yes. In this particular case, the others were being taken care of in another way. In many cases, following this session I might bring in parents or significant others, guide the client to present his or her goals and strategies, and discuss what others can do to help the client achieve the goals. This is a great way to frame those behaviors that the client may not like, such as adults enforcing strict consequences, because now it is defined as being in the service of the client's goals.

Chapter 6

Avoid High Risk

Start With Fence-Around

Following the Treatment Contracting session, we start immediately with fence-around, for two reasons. First of all, the client should be, and feel, as safe, secure, and stable as possible to have the best chance of being able to concentrate on what's coming next: the personal training work. Second, the motivational interviewing (MI) and personal trainer approach requires us to facilitate some small, quick successes. It is important for the client to experience quick success so that the perhaps still tentative commitment to working toward his or her goals is reinforced and strengthened.

If you want some quick, easy success, fence-around is the way to go. Let's say that your client is trying to stop getting into fights. If you were to start by working on self-control skills, the focus might be on having the client ignore or walk away when provoked. Although this may be possible, it is quite difficult because it involves having the client overcome the strong anger reaction to behave according to plan.

On the other hand, if you can help the client to figure out where the fight is most likely to happen (e.g., at a certain street corner or lunch table where the antagonists hang out) and if you can get the client to avoid being in that place, voila! The client has managed to get through the day without fighting, without having had to deal with the strong reaction, and without having to try to control his or her anger. Instead, the client didn't even have to face the challenge in the first place.

This is why we start out by guiding the client to avoid high-risk situations. It's the easiest way to start doing better because it does not require mastering the strong emotional reactions. After the client has experienced some quick success with this, the momentum and determination is likely to grow. Later, building on the success, we can work on self-control skills, which are more challenging.

In addition to guiding the client to avoid high-risk situations, it is also important to implement, or at least facilitate, other fence-around interventions as needed. The goal is to help the client to be, and feel, as safe and secure as possible. Certain practical issues can and should be addressed early on, as soon as possible after the treatment contract has been made. Potential fence-around interventions may include, as needed, case management, parent training, problem solving, and lifestyle changes, in addition to the behavior changes to avoid high-risk situations. These may be done directly by the client, by the therapist, or by anyone in the client's system who can get the job done. These interventions can often have a significant impact on the client's ability to progress in treatment and should be effected as soon as possible.

What kinds of issues need addressing in the fence-around phase of treatment?

- Continued exposure to an abuser.
- Acute/pressing needs (e.g., medical, housing, financial).
- Client or family member at risk of being hurt (e.g., involvement with an abusive partner; suicide threats, medical fragility).
- Inappropriate educational or work placement, in which success is impossible.
- Disability without the needed accommodations.
- Bullying or harassment.
- Inadequate supervision or discipline.
- Any ongoing repeated and preventable exposure to an unwarranted trigger.

This does not mean that we should put a bubble around the client to protect him or her from every possible stressor. However, if we might be able to right a wrong, this is a good time to try. The purpose of the fence-around interventions is to actually solve problems that are currently forcing the client to remain focused on survival and other pressing concerns instead of being able to focus on activities that will progressively lead toward healing. Case management and parent training interventions for child/adolescent treatment are described in detail in Greenwald (2005a).

Many therapists eschew case management and problem-solving interventions as being beneath them—as being more suitable for case managers than for therapists. Don't be that way! Case management is good therapy. First, it establishes the therapist as someone who cares about the client and can help the client to achieve his or her goals. This provides an excellent track record for the therapist and for treatment. Second, if you don't do the case management, the client may not be in a position to benefit from the other treatment activities that you are hoping to get through. In the Fairy Tale model, fence-around is an essential phase of treatment and is quite as important as the rest of the phases.

The bottom line is that if we can't help the clients with their most pressing concerns, we are not useful to them. This does not mean that we must personally do all case management (although some therapists do), but we certainly better make sure that the important things get done.

The remaining focus here will be on helping clients to "manage their own cases" by avoiding high-risk situations.

Avoiding High Risk

There are two types of high-risk situations. One type is a safety high risk in that clients are in some kind of danger. When clients avoid this type of high-risk situation, they can feel safer because they actually are safer. The other type is when clients are at high risk of (being triggered or tempted to) acting-out behavior or some other symptom. In each case, helping clients to get better at avoiding high risk is an excellent step. And in each case, this is done by specifically identifying the high-risk situations, and then figuring out how these situations can be anticipated and avoided. Sometimes this can involve family members or others, and it may involve making practical changes in lifestyle, such as in the following examples:

- The client's ex-boyfriend, who assaulted her, has not been found and arrested. The client gets the lock on her door changed and asks several neighbors to be on the lookout for the man and to call the police if they see him.
- The client's high-risk time for getting into trouble or danger is during school, when he cuts classes and goes off with his friends. The client, parents, and teachers set up a system in which the teacher signs a card every time the client goes to class, and the client shows the signed card to the parent every day after school. This monitoring helps to keep the client in class.
- The client's high-risk time for problems is after work, particularly if he stops at the bar for "just one" drink. He arranges his schedule so that his friends expect to meet him at the gym right after work.
- One of the client's high-risk situations for becoming violent is when his wife brings up his low pay, which is a real issue in the family. However, to avoid high risk the couple agrees not to discuss this for consecutive periods of a month at a time (until the client gains better self-control).
- The client's sore spot is hit when a certain family member calls and harangues her. She starts to use her answering machine to screen calls so that she will not be surprised by this family member.

Some people object to the idea of encouraging clients to avoid normal stressors that they should be able to handle. Shouldn't we be helping them to face and cope with the stressors rather than trying to overprotect them? Parents of preteens and younger children often ask a similar question after their child has been exposed to a major traumatic event and then wants to sleep in the parents' bedroom. "Should we let him sleep in our room? We don't want to kick him out, because he's scared. But we don't want to baby him; maybe he'll want to sleep in our room for the next 10 years. What should we do?" I tell the parents, "If I only told you, 'Yes, let him sleep there,' and that was it, then maybe he would sleep in your room for the next 10 years. But there's more to it. Let him sleep there for now, because he's been scared and you can do this to help him to feel extra safe, for a little while. If he feels safe enough, he'll be able to do good work with me and get stronger. Then he'll go back to his room on his own; you won't have to push him."

This is the purpose of "overprotecting" clients by encouraging them to avoid high-risk situations that ultimately they should be able to handle. Often it is just one step, a short-term strategy to help clients to feel sufficiently safe, secure, and successful that they are ready to take the next step. For example, we might first encourage the client to avoid certain people who make provocative comments, and in subsequent sessions, we will coach the client to cope effectively with those. On the other hand, some of the client's high-risk situations may be worthy of long-term avoidance as well. For example, it is hard to live a productive life while spending all your time with a peer group that is focused on crime or substance abuse, so the client might permanently avoid this peer group and find new friends.

A high-risk situation is defined as any situation in which the symptom or problem behavior is significantly more likely to occur than usual. Typically this involves either a temptation or a trigger situation (in which something occurs that hits the client's sore spot, such as being insulted). Sometimes both elements are combined in a single situation, such as when a client is being pressured by peers to do something that is also tempting. Furthermore, some temptations (e.g., to partake of a mind-altering substance) might be particularly appealing because of the relief it may provide from trauma-related dysphoria. For present purposes, the relative contribution of temptation and trigger is unimportant. In treatment, the focus is simply on the situation and the associated behavioral choices.

Conducting the Session

The client's high-risk situations were already identified, at least in a preliminary way, in the Treatment Contracting session. Now, in the Avoid High Risk session, the high-risk situations will be more comprehensively identified and elaborated so that the client can develop strategies for avoidance.

Opening Routine

As always, the session begins with the standard check-in questions (and perhaps related conversation), including, "Tell me something good and something bad," "Is there anything coming up that you're worried about or looking forward to?" and some kind of recap or follow-up from the previous session and transition to the current session's activity. Now that the treatment contract has been made, that transitional piece is done in a new way. From here on, the therapist presents the piece of paper that includes the client's treatment plan (as well as the case formulation circles and arrows) and says, "We've been talking about the things you decided to do to get stronger toward your goals. Last week, [we talked about the steps you could take to give you a better chance of getting to your goals]. Is it okay if we start at the top, today, with 'Avoid High Risk'?"

Starting each new session with this invocation of the case formulation and treatment plan accomplishes several important things. First of all, it implicitly reminds the client, "I'm not here to boss you around. We're doing this because you said you cared about your goals." This reminder seems to help clients to stay motivated rather than trying to fight the therapist. Also, repeatedly referring to this page provides a silent but graphic reminder that the trauma and loss memories continue to lurk and to create sore spot reactions. Such awareness may help the client to accept the necessity, later in treatment, of working through the trauma memories. Finally, it clearly connects past work in treatment with present and future work in a way that repeatedly conveys to the client a sense of direction and progress.

Common Challenges

The Avoid High Risk session's procedure is straightforward. The therapist orients the client to the purpose of the session and reminds the client that the therapist's job is not to tell the client what to do but only to help the client to see what his or her choices are. Then the therapist and client work together to make a list of each significant high-risk situation and, for each situation, to identify a realistic avoidance strategy that the client can implement if he or she chooses to. It would be helpful to review the Avoid High Risk Session Form (Appendix C) before continuing here. It seems simple, but a number of challenges may arise; these are addressed in the following text.

Can't Find a High-Risk Situation

Most clients are not trained to identify the exact moment just before their problem behavior is most likely to occur. It's the therapist's job to help the client find these moments. For example, the client might say, "I'm most likely to get into a fight if someone bumps into me or pushes me." The therapist can follow up by saying, "Who would be most likely to do that? And when and where would it be most likely to happen?" until together they can identify the most common times, places, and actions that constitute this particular high-risk situation. Hang in there until the client finally says something such as, "In the hallway when I'm going from science [class] to English, there's these two guys there, they're always looking for trouble." Only when the high-risk situation is clearly defined as to time, place, and action does the client have a real choice about whether, and how, to avoid the situation.

Just Not Be There

Once the high-risk situation is identified, the next question is, "If you wanted to avoid this situation, what could you do?" Sometimes a client will propose the fact of avoidance without proposing a method of accomplishing this. For example, the aforementioned client (with the antagonists in the hallway between classes) might say, "Just not be in that hallway when they are." That doesn't work, because the client has not yet figured out how to avoid the situation and still get to the next class. If we want our clients to practice new behaviors, part of our job is to help them figure out exactly what those behaviors are. In this example, the therapist can follow up by saying, "What could you do? How could you get to your class and avoid those guys in the hall?" Now maybe the client will suggest, "I can hang back until the first bell. Then they'll be gone, and I can still make it to my class." Then the therapist pushes it even further so that nothing is left to the imagination. "If I'm watching this on TV and I see you hanging back, what do I see? Where are you, who are you with?"

The principle here is that, as with future movies, it is not sufficient to know what the client will not do. That can't be seen on TV. We have to know what the client will be doing instead, with time, place, and action. This specificity gives the client the best chance of really doing it.

How About This Coping Skill?

Sometimes the client may propose a coping skill instead of an avoidance strategy. For example, with a high-risk situation of being handed a bottle while with a certain group of friends after school, when the therapist asks, "If you wanted to avoid this situation, what could you do?" the client may answer, "Just say no thanks, pass the bottle to the next person." Although that may be a good coping skill in the situation, today we are trying to figure out how to avoid the situation. This is a whole different concept, which the therapist has to fully grasp to guide the client effectively.

We don't want to chastise or suggest that the client is flat-out wrong, or the client might feel unfairly criticized and thus unsafe with the therapist. Remember, the customer is always right. In this situation, the therapist might first praise the client's thinking and then guide the client to come up with an avoidance strategy, which is the right answer in this session: "You're ahead of me. In a week or two, I will be asking you what you could do in that situation. But today we're trying to figure out what you could do if you didn't even want to be in that situation in the first place."

But These Are My Friends!

Sometimes a client will come up with an avoidance strategy that he or she finds objectionable. Continuing the previous example of avoiding the situation of the bottle being passed, the client might say, "I could just go home after school instead of going with my friends." And then after considering this for a moment, the client might say, "But these are my friends! I'm not gonna just walk out on them!" In other words, the client has identified a perfectly good strategy but doesn't like it.

One good therapist option here is to try to help the client to find a way to make the avoidance strategy more acceptable. For example, the therapist might say, "Is there a time you could still be with your friends that doesn't have such a high risk? Like when they're doing something other than drinking?" This approach may offer the client a way to keep from completely abandoning the friends. Another way to make the avoidance strategy more acceptable is to help the client find an attractive alternative activity: "Going home doesn't sound like much fun anyway. Is there anything else you could do after school that you'd feel good about?"

The other good therapist option, whenever a client expresses objection or doubt regarding whether he or she will actually use the avoidance strategy, is to acknowledge the client's power to choose: "I'm not saying you should do this. I don't know what you will do. We're just figuring out what your choices are." This takes the therapist out of the fight and leaves the client to fight himself or herself.

I Don't Know What to Do

Sometimes a client may be unable to come up with a good avoidance strategy. When there is no alternative but to give clients suggestions, there are still better and worse ways of doing it. The worse way is to make the suggestion directly, as in, "Why don't you just ...." Then it is the therapist's advice, which is inherently tainted because the therapist is both an authority figure and someone who couldn't possibly understand this client's world (even if you actually do). The other problem with giving direct advice is that the client may perceive pressure (again, whether actual or not) to accept and embrace the advice. Then the client may respond not to the content of the advice but to the perceived pressure. Whether the client gives in to the pressure or resists it, neither leads to the desired outcomes. We want to take ourselves out of the equation so the client is more likely to feel his or her own power and autonomy and to do the effective behavior.

The better way is to offer a menu and invoke peer authority, for example, "Let me tell you the kinds of things that have worked for other people in this situation, and you see if you think that any of these might work for you." Clients are more likely to identify with peers and to seriously consider the suggestions that come from peer successes. Also, when the therapist offers a menu of peer examples, there is no one right answer and no obvious therapist preference, so the client is less likely to perceive pressure from the therapist to make a particular choice. The menu comes in pretty handy, and clients tend to respond well.

Can't Avoid This One

Sometimes the client can't think of a way to avoid a certain high-risk situation, and the therapist can't either. When you think you've found one of these, keep trying for a little while; sometimes creativity and effort pays off. For example, clients can avoid certain high-risk situations even with their own parents by staying in their rooms, getting involved with some activity that keeps them away from home, or completing the chore (that the parent would be yelling at them about) before the parent gets home.

Still, sometimes you will encounter high-risk situations that are, at least to some extent, unavoidable. In this case, you agree with your client and admit it. "I think you're right. It seems like this one can't be avoided. So I guess you're stuck with facing it and trying to deal with it." However, avoid getting involved with trying to come up with the coping skills; that's for future sessions.

Timing and Pacing in the Fairy Tale Model

This session is rather straightforward and tends to be over in a matter of perhaps 20 minutes. You may choose to let your client out early or to talk about something else to keep your sessions close to the same duration from one time to the next. It is okay to talk about something else, as long as you avoid moving forward in the treatment. You have just given the client something to practice. Now let him or her try it out before you pile on the next challenge.

This is a good moment to comment on pacing issues over the course of treatment. I'm a believer in getting as much done as fast as possible, within certain limits. The longer treatment drags on, the more chance there is for something to happen that disrupts the treatment. Friends and family members get hurt or die; someone gets pregnant; clients get betrayed, expelled, hospitalized, arrested, incarcerated, or run off to Florida. Get through treatment faster, and there are fewer days in which disruptive events have a chance to occur. Once through treatment, clients with improved mental health status and behavior are less prone to experiencing such events and are better able to cope with those that are unavoidable.

On the other hand, there are times when hurrying through treatment can backfire. For example, it is rarely productive to rush or skip a given step in treatment. If you skimp on the foundation, then your work on subsequent treatment tasks will have less chance of success. The following discussion outlines some considerations for pacing over the course of treatment.

The first sessions could, in theory, all be done at once, and in fact I do prefer to get them done as quickly as possible. People often show up for treatment in times of crisis and may be uniquely open to engaging in treatment at that time. Therefore, it is good clinical practice to get through the evaluation portion as quickly as possible—to get people hooked on the treatment plan while they are still in that open moment.

Once you start giving tasks involving actual behaviors, though, it's important to give the client a chance to practice in the world and then to follow up on that in the next session. So the fence-around and personal training portions of the treatment should be paced accordingly, one session and intervention at a time. Then the client is not overwhelmed and has the best chance of success with the task of the moment.

Once you are into slaying the dragon, the pacing depends on your trauma resolution method and on what your client can tolerate. There is no theoretical reason why you could not work more intensively during this phase, if your method allows it and if your client can tolerate it. In fact, the sooner the sore spot is gone, the better off the client will be.

Pacing after trauma resolution will depend on the client, the treatment issue, and the situation. The same general principle holds: if there is something for the client to do out in the world, stop and give him or her a chance to do it. If it's only a matter of getting some in-session work done, then you can go for it as long as you have the time and the client has the tolerance.

Age Variations

With Preteens

With older preteens, this session is done as per the script. With younger preteens, the session is skipped. Which way to go depends on the therapist's judgment as to how much control the client has over his or her own life situations and therefore how productive the session is likely to be.

Regardless of whether you do this session, fence-around interventions are crucial for preteens. In particular, parent training for consistent discipline is likely to be a core component of your overall treatment approach.

With Adults

With adults there is no variation; do the session as per the script. You should also explore other fence-around strategies in whatever ways make sense for your client.

Session 5: Avoid High Risk

Mr. G: Hi, tell me something good and something bad.

Alex: Something good, I tested clean and I don't have to go back to Bridges; something bad, I had to be there last weekend again.

Mr. G: And how's school going now that you've been there a couple of weeks?

Alex: It's good. Kind of boring, but I'm going every day, doing my homework; I'm doing okay.

Mr. G: Anyone giving you trouble there?

Alex: There's always people looking for trouble. But no one I have a real beef with, it's okay so far.

Mr. G: And how are the teachers?

Alex: Most of them are good. My math teacher, though, he picks on me; it's like he's already decided I'm no good and he's just looking for his chance to prove it.

Mr. G: So how do you handle it?

Alex: I just try to let it roll off me—just don't say nothing, do the work.

Mr. G: Is anything coming up that you're either worried about or looking forward to?

Alex: Not really. Well, I start working for my Pops this weekend, can make a little money.

Mr. G: That's good. Will you have some free time, too?

Alex: Yeah, well, I work all day Saturday, but Sunday they go to church and then I only work for a couple of hours after that. Then I'm free all afternoon.

Mr. G: Do you go to church too?

Alex: I do; they like me to go with them.

Mr. G: We were talking about the things you wanted to do with your life, the things that could help you get there—the reasons I bet on you—and the things that could get in your way if you're not careful. Last time we met, we talked about a strategy, things you could do to get stronger, give yourself better odds [pulls out the treatment plan page with circles/arrows]. The first thing on the list is "Avoid High Risk"; is it okay if we talk about that today?

Alex: Yeah, I guess so.

Mr. G: Remember, I'm not going to be telling you what to do. My job is to help you see what your choices are so there's no black ice. It will be up to you to decide what to do about it. Okay, one of the high-risk situations you told me about was if someone makes you mad. When is that most likely to happen?

Alex: I don't know; could happen any time.

Mr. G: But are there certain people who you know are more likely to give you trouble? Or certain times or places that it's more likely?

Alex: If I cut through the park after school on my way to the train, there are some guys who hang out there who I knew from before; some of them have a beef with me.

Mr. G: So if you wanted to avoid that high risk, what could you do?

Alex: Just walk around, I guess; don't cut through.

Mr. G: Are there other people or times or places that you're more likely to have someone getting you mad?

Alex: Not really, no.

Mr. G: What about that math teacher?

Alex: Oh yeah. But I can't not go to math class; I have to go.

Mr. G: Is there a certain thing that makes him worse or that sets him off?

Alex: He just goes off for any little thing. All you have to do is whisper something to the person next to you and he's on your case.

Mr. G: And if you wanted to avoid that high risk, what could you do?

Alex: Not talk to people in the class, I guess. But sometimes I have to, like if I don't understand what I'm supposed to do.

Mr. G: So what could you do about that, to keep him from going off on you?

Alex: I don't know.

Mr. G: Does he go off on people if they ask him a question?

Alex: No, he likes that. I think it makes him feel important. I guess I could just ask him.

Mr. G: Okay. And for the drug temptation, you said certain parties?

Alex: Yeah. Not the family parties, but parties just with kids.

Mr. G: Do you know ahead of time which kind of party it's going to be?

Alex: Definitely.

Mr. G: And if you wanted to avoid that high risk, what could you do?

Alex: I could just say no thanks and pass the blunt on when they pass it to me.

Mr. G: That would be a good self-control skill once you're in the situation. But we're trying to do like what you told that friend: Don't get the job in the bar in the first place, so the problem doesn't even have a chance to happen. So if you wanted to avoid the high risk, what could you do?

Alex: Oh. Just not go, I guess. But I like to go. I can't just be perfect all the time—gotta have some fun too.

Mr. G: You'll make your own decisions. Today we're just figuring out what your choices are. So when do these parties happen?

Alex: Could be any night, but mainly Friday or Saturday nights.

Mr. G: And if you didn't go to a party on one of those nights, what would you be doing instead?

Alex: I guess I could still do something fun, maybe catch a movie with friends or take a girl out or something.

Mr. G: You also said that one high risk for drug temptation was being with certain friends?

Alex: Yeah, my friends from before.

Mr. G: If you were going to be with them, when would that be?

Alex: Anytime—during school, after school, nights, weekends, whenever.

Mr. G: And if you wanted to avoid that high risk, what could you do?

Alex: Just be where I'm supposed to be, like I've been doing. Go to school, come here, go home. I'm trying to stay away from them, trying to stay out of trouble.

Mr. G: You also said that one high risk was peers telling you, "Hey, let's go and cut school," or whatever. You said that might happen mainly before school or at lunchtime?

Alex: Yeah.

Mr. G: If you wanted to avoid that high risk, what could you do?

Alex: I can't avoid that one. If I go to school, there's going to be kids there saying let's do this and let's do that. That's just how it is.

Mr. G: Okay, some high risks you can't avoid. Are there any other high-risk situations you can think of?

Alex: No, I can't think of any more.

Mr. G: Then that's it for today; this was a shorter meeting than usual. Tell me something you liked about the meeting and something you didn't like.

Alex: I kind of liked making that list of the situations; it helped me to see what I have to do. Didn't like … I didn't like thinking about maybe not going to parties anymore. I don't know about that.

Mr. G: And what's next for you today?

Alex: I don't know, I guess I'll just hang around until they tell me I can go home.

Session 5 - Avoid High Risk, Official Notes

Focused today on identifying high-risk situations, in which it might be particularly difficult to avoid problem behaviors. Discussed strategies for avoiding some of these situations; others seem to be unavoidable.

Session 5 - Avoid High Risk, Therapist's Personal Notes

High Risk Situation	Avoid High Risk Strategy
Guys in the park after school.	Walk around; don't cut through
Math teacher goes off.	Don't whisper; ask teacher the question
Someone passing a joint at a party.	Don't go to the party; catch a movie w/ friends; take a girl out.
Being with friends from before.	Go to school, to OCFS, go home.

Next time: ask how weekend was w/ new job.

Figure 6.1 Avoid High Risk session notes

Mr. G: Okay, see you next week.
Alex: See you.

Session 5: Questions and Answers

Q: That seemed like a really short session. How do you just let him go without finishing the 45 minutes or 50 minutes?

A: In this particular setting, I had the flexibility to make sessions be as long or short as I chose. The Future Movies session was well over an hour; this session was 20 minutes. Most sessions were closer to about 45. It was nice to be able to do what I needed to do, within reason, and not worry about the clock. However, I have also been in settings in which the clock ruled. In such settings, we just find something else to do for the rest of the short sessions and find a way to shorten or break up the longer ones.

Q: When do you do fence-around? What part of treatment? Do you stop the individual sessions and have parent or family sessions? Or do you add on sessions? Do it at the same time? Should the fence-around be simultaneously?

A: First of all, the Avoid High Risk session is fence-around; it's the fence that the client can build for himself or herself. But you're asking about how to work with the rest of the kingdom on this. There's no single right time or way to do this; rather, you do it whenever it's called for and however it's likely to work. For example:

■ Certain types of limits should be (and often are) set even prior to treatment or soon after treatment starts. For example, the court may require a substance abuser to undergo regular drug testing or a sexual offender to stay away from areas frequented by children. A spouse may state that one more act of violence will end the marriage. An employer may state that one more no-show will end the job. A school system may state and enforce its rules. Such limits help problem behavior clients to face the consequences of their problems, which is essential for motivation for positive change.

■ Pressing safety issues should be resolved as soon as possible, even before the treatment plan is completed. If the client is being abused or threatened or lacks adequate food, housing, or medical care, this should be corrected as soon as possible.

■ Pressing emotional safety issues should be resolved as soon as possible following the treatment contracting session. This may involve negotiating certain relationships, modifying a school situation to facilitate success, or some other intervention. This should generally not be tried until it is clearly in the service of the client's stated goals.

■ Other types of fence-around interventions can be implemented as awareness of the need arises. For example, if you learn that a spouse-batterer is particularly reactive to discussion of a certain issue, you might meet with the couple and arrange to keep that issue off the table for a while to avoid the high-risk situation. If you learn that an alcoholic's high-risk time is after work, you might arrange with a supportive friend to meet your client after work and go together to the gym (instead of the bar).

Chapter 7

Self-Control Skills

In the treatment of problem behavior clients, Self-Control Skills Training is often provided as a stand-alone intervention. In the Fairy Tale model, Self-Control Skills Training builds on the preceding steps in the treatment, and anticipates those that follow. When Self-Control Skills Training is presented as part of an agreed-upon treatment plan in the service of the client's identified goals, he or she is likely to be invested in trying hard to master and use the skills. And by using contemporary daily-life examples for skills practice, the treatment activity addresses the client's current issues and concerns while also working towards long-term goals.

The session after Avoid High Risk, the therapist will, as per the new routine, refer to the treatment plan and then follow up on the previous session by asking whether the client actually did the identified avoidance behaviors, and if so, how it went. As always, it is important for the therapist to maintain a supportive but neutral attitude. Remember, it is the client's decision and the client's life. For example, suppose the client from the previous chapter's example did not avoid the high risk of being with his drinking friends after school and says, "I kept hanging out with the same kids after school. Those are my friends!" The therapist might comment (without sarcasm) that it is up to the client to choose his or her priorities. The therapist may also try to help the client find a more realistic strategy: "Friends are important. Are there times you can still hang with them that aren't such high-risk times for you?" The therapist must balance being willing to help the client in his or her effort to achieve goals without slipping into the position of judging the client or telling him or her what to do.

Similarly, if the client does report having been successful, the therapist should not get all excited about it. This would also be a judgment. If the therapist gets into the habit of making judgments—even positive ones—then the therapist becomes a judge and the client learns to feel that he or she must behave in certain ways if he or she wants the therapist's approval. Regardless of whether the client manages this by trying to please or oppose the therapist, the outcome is bad. We don't want the client focused on complying or fighting with the therapist; we want the client focused on his or her own sense of initiative and power.

The therapist's stance is to be supportive of the client without becoming overly aligned with a particular behavior. For example, suppose the client managed to follow through and says, "I just went to the park every day after school and played basketball. I have some friends there, too. And that way I wasn't around my friends who were drinking." The therapist can say, "So you did what it took to avoid the high risk. How did that work out for you?" This still gives the client the opportunity to be proud and to notice how easy it was to not drink, having avoided the high-risk situation. The therapist is effectively acknowledging the accomplishment and being supportive but without shifting the focus to the therapist's own reaction or opinion.

Therapists can (and should) care about the client and take pleasure in the client's development and success, but in a way that does not sabotage the treatment. The more the focus remains on the clients, and the more the clients retain ownership of their own initiative, the more they are building themselves up for the next steps. Clients learn to feel confident in themselves and learn that they can make progress toward their goals. This is the motivational interviewing (MI) approach and the personal trainer approach.

From Fence-Around to Personal Training

We don't need the client to have consistently avoided every high-risk situation to move on. Although we may hope for this, we don't expect it. However, it is important for the client's life situation to be as stable and supportive as possible. This does not mean that the client has to be completely safe and to feel totally secure. In the real world, this is impossible, and in the world of some of our clients, significant ongoing challenges may remain. However, some work with fence-around interventions can help the client to at least be, and feel, safe and secure enough to take the next step in treatment.

If the client continues to face such pressing issues that he or she is highly preoccupied and cannot focus on anything else, then you stay in fence-around. In other words, fence-around takes as long as it takes. This is true for every phase of treatment. The phase of treatment is completed not merely by performing some specified intervention but when the task of that phase is more or less accomplished.

On the other hand, if the client is making some progress in fence-around but not as much as you might wish, don't worry too much. More opportunities will arise over the course of treatment. And self-management issues may not be fully resolved until after the trauma memories have been worked through and the client's psychological makeup has been accordingly transformed. So we don't expect perfection; we just do our best and hope for "good enough for now." In many cases, the single dedicated Fence-Around session, which is focused on avoiding high risk, is sufficient as long as the therapist continues to address other fence-around issues as they arise.

For example, one 17-year-old boy, who had previously been in a gang, reported at one session, "Yesterday I got hit on the head with a rock. I had gone to the store to buy a soda, and when I came out, someone saw me who had a beef with me from before." For this client, even walking outside on the street was dangerous. So he stayed inside a lot and, when he had to go somewhere, made a point of trying to do it safely (e.g., going with others). Despite the danger, this client felt sufficiently stable and secure that he was able to progress in treatment through personal training and then slaying the dragon.

Getting Safer and Stronger

Getting stronger is an ongoing theme in this treatment approach. Getting stronger involves the ability to tolerate upsetting things (i.e., *affect tolerance*) without doing some stupid thing out of desperation. When people can't stand the bad feeling even for a moment, they are likely to do just about anything to avoid it or get rid of it. This leads to pervasive avoidance, impulsive acting out, substance abuse, and other problems. When people are better able to tolerate feeling bad for a little while, they have a better chance of handling the situation the way they would like to.

Also, as noted in Chapter 1, as clients improve their self-control skills their behavior improves, and in turn others may start to treat them better. As the client's world becomes less hostile and more supportive, clients feel more safe and secure. Thus, a side effect of the personal training phase of treatment is that the fence continues to improve.

Success feeds on itself. The more people become able to handle challenges the way they would like to, the stronger they feel and the more their world reinforces them. This paves the way for the next challenge. This is the personal trainer strategy. We give clients progressively greater challenges while also helping them learn to manage each challenge as it comes. Eventually, the client will be ready to slay the dragon.

In the previous chapter, the focus was on achieving some success by avoiding high-risk situations. In this chapter the focus is more directly on the coping behaviors in those high-risk situations that are not avoided. Developing and practicing the coping behaviors not only improves the client's skills but also to some extent mitigates the high-risk situation. This is because when the client is confident of being able to handle a situation effectively, the distressing emotions become less threatening and feel less overwhelming.

Skills Training with Corrective Reinforcement

To help a client change a habitual problem behavior, it's important to understand not only the trauma-related reactivity driving the impulse but also the reinforcement that the client receives following the behavior.

Imagine that your dog has gotten into the garbage and made a mess. Three days later you scold the dog. What does the dog learn from this? First, getting into the garbage is great fun! Second, the dog's owner is mostly okay but every once in a while gets upset out of the blue. Oh well. It'll pass.

People with problem behaviors have this experience over and over again. The relief or gratification is experienced right away, and the negative consequences happen so much later that they don't seem relevant. What happens some other time doesn't matter because it does not feel connected to the problem situation or to the behavior. Learning occurs best when the consequence—whether reinforcement or punishment—is close to the behavior.

The client's problem behavior is being repeated because it works in some way: It provides relief from the intolerable thoughts and feelings. Negative consequences somewhere down the line do not feel very relevant to the client in the moment. To make matters worse, the client often experiences the so-called appropriate behavior as a punishment because the frustration is immediate and the reward is too far in the future to be reinforcing. Thus, the problem behavior is reinforced by the immediate relief it provides, and the appropriate behavior is punished by the lack of relief. The long-term consequences are too distant to be influential.

To help people change their habits, we must find a way to flip the reinforcement schedule. We must find a way to make the problem behavior less appealing, and the wanted behavior more appealing. This can be done by imaginally rehearsing the challenging situations, along with the different behavioral choices, and by pairing these choices with their respective long-term consequences. Our first goal is to "spit in the soup"—to make the problem behavior less appealing because now it is more closely associated with an unwanted consequence. Our second goal is to "sweeten the pot"—to make the desired behavior more appealing because now it is more closely associated with the wanted consequence.

In other words, we want to provide a corrective reinforcement experience. It is essential to have the client experience (in imagination) his or her behavioral choices immediately followed by the related long-term consequences so that the association of choices and consequences can be reinforced. This encourages the client to reject the old behaviors and acquire the new ones.

Personal Training: Where to Start?

For skills training, the therapist and client choose one example of the high-risk situation, one instance of when the problem behavior happened (or could have happened). Then the therapist guides the client to imaginally rehearse first the quick-relief behavior leading to the bad ending and then the effective behavior leading to the good ending. Then the therapist and client choose another similar example (i.e., another high-risk situation), and practice continues with that—and so on.

When it is time to work with your client on self-control skills, how do you decide where to start? As the personal trainer, your strategy will be to start small so that your client has the best chance of being successful. The following guidelines will help you to choose a high-risk situation most likely to work well for this intervention.

Current Is Relevant

You are looking for a good everyday example of when the client did the identified problem behavior or could easily have done it. Actually, you're looking for the high-risk situation that immediately preceded that behavior, but it may be easier for the client to identify the behavior first. The "something bad" from the check-in might provide such an example. Whether the client handled that event well or badly doesn't matter; it can still be a good focus for practice. This helps the client to stay interested because you are focusing on what is going on in the client's life right now.

Stay Small and Recent

Even if you have to look beyond what was reported at check-in, still choose a minor event, preferably from sometime within the last few days. Do not choose a major event, even if it is recent. And do not choose an event from weeks or months ago. That is likely to have more emotion attached, which will make it harder for the client to overcome his or her emotional reaction and handle the situation effectively.

Avoid Family Members

Choose with a preference for events involving peers, teachers, authority figures, or strangers rather than family members or serious romantic partners; the latter are likely to be more emotionally loaded and thus harder to handle effectively.

Avoid Direct Reminders of Trauma

Avoid examples too closely related to the major trauma. Of course, every high-risk situation is by definition related to the trauma (and associated sore spot reaction), but some events are more closely related than others. For example, if rape is on your client's trauma list, a recent event in which a man grabbed her may be too close; it would be better to find an instance in which she was insulted by a peer. Similarly, if a certain family member was significantly involved in a major trauma in the client's past, virtually any recent event involving that family member will be too close.

Choices Have Consequences

Choices have consequences is an imaginal rehearsal intervention used to help the client to get better at handling the high-risk situations the way they would like to. Once the example situation has been identified, the client is asked to imaginally view a "movie" including the following:

1. The high-risk situation—including time, place, and action—the moment just before the behavioral choice is made.
2. The thoughts, feelings, and physical sensations that follow this. These are the signals that a choice is about to be made.
3. The quick-relief or "bad" behavioral choice.
4. The "bad ending" or negative consequence, paired with the words, "It's not worth it."

Then the client is asked to identify a coping strategy that would get him or her to the good ending instead of the bad one: "What could you do in this situation that would take you toward the good ending?" Many people do know what to do here. However, if the client can't come up with a good idea, the therapist can always offer a menu of what other people have done in this situation. Then the client is asked to imaginally view a movie similar to the first one, except that the good behavioral choice is made that leads to the good ending.

Finally, the client is told to start the movie the same way, but the ending will be determined by the behavioral choice: "Good choice goes to the good ending; bad choice goes to the bad ending." This "surprise ending" is repeated until the client chooses the good ending twice in a row. Then that round is done.

Then it is begun anew, with another example of a high-risk situation that could lead to the same problem behavior.

This is a real workhorse of Self-Control Skills Training and can be used with any number of challenging situations. The following tips will help it to go smoothly and work well:

- It is essential to use a specific situation. If the therapist can't visualize it as if seeing it on TV, it's probably not specific enough yet; for example, you need to know who's saying what.
- This intervention is designed to change the client's behavior only. Use this only when the client's own coping behavior is identified as a problem to be improved.
- Before "running the movie," make sure that the statement, "It's not worth it," feels true to the client for the bad ending that's been selected. If not, extend the bad consequences farther into the future until, "It's not worth it," does feel true. For example, the client may not feel bad about losing a privilege following some misbehavior, but he or she may indeed feel bad about where this habit might lead (e.g., to prison).

■ The therapist should present a neutral response to the client's selected outcome. Many people will experiment with the bad choice before ending up with the good one. The therapist shouldn't become excited either way. That way, the client is deciding for himself or herself and not to please the therapist.

■ This is a rather quick intervention with a very concrete focus. This is not the time or place to ask probing questions about feelings or to work for insight into the source of the problems. We already did that in the case formulation. Now we are focusing on practical coping skills. So don't go therapizing; just help your client get the job done.

The following two exercises will help you learn, step by step, how to set up and conduct the Choices Have Consequences intervention. The setup is the more complicated part. Once you become proficient it only takes a few minutes, but getting used to it does take some practice.

Exercise Part 1: Map Out a Problem

Pair up with a colleague (or try this with a friend or client). This is not a role play. You will each be yourselves, and you will each get a turn as therapist and client. You will be using the Map Out a Problem form shown in Figure 7.1. If you are working alone, complete the form for yourself.

If You Are the Therapist

This can be a challenging exercise because it requires skill and practice to get it right. You may have to say more than you see in the script to elicit all the details you need. Also, this exercise will probably be harder than actually doing the intervention with clients—it just tends to happen that way.

On the practice form, the answer to Question 1 goes into Circle 1; the answer to Question 2 goes in Circle 2, and so on. However, don't start writing just because your client starts talking. Often, you'll have to ask some follow-up questions until the client has given you an answer in the proper format for this intervention. Only then do you write it down. Otherwise, your paper will be so cluttered with stuff you can't use that you won't be able to see the part you need.

Here are some tips that will clarify what you're trying to get in each of the circles. Before you decide that you've finished the job, I suggest that you check back here and review these tips again. People often find that they need to do a few more things to make it right, and it's important to get it right. A proper setup leads the imaginal rehearsal intervention to go smoothly and effectively.

■ The high-risk situation is the moment in time just before the decision is made to either do the quick-relief behavior or the behavior that will lead to the good ending. For example, if the problem behavior is yelling at the mother on the telephone, the high-risk situation is the specific thing the mother says (e.g., "You really should have come by last Sunday") just before your client is tempted to yell.

■ If the desired behavior is going outside to take a walk, the high-risk situation is the moment the client would be going outside or might otherwise decide to sit down and read the paper. Get specific here (e.g., "In the kitchen, it's 7 a.m., just finished my cup of coffee and put the empty cup in the sink").

■ The thoughts and feelings and physical sensations are the signals that a choice is about to be made. These will probably be the same as what's on the treatment plan page (with a real client, with whom you've done that), but they might be different, too. The focus here is on the client's subjective experience in the moment. Your goal is to identify the thoughts, feelings, and sensations that push the client toward the quick-relief behavior.

■ The quick-relief behavior is the behavior that your client is tempted to do instead of what the client wishes he or she would do. This should be a specific action in the moment that the choice is made, not the whole series of steps that follow and lead to the bad ending.

■ The effective behavior is the behavior that the client wants to do in that challenging situation to advance toward his or her goals. Again, it's not a whole series of behaviors, just one first thing done in that moment. The quick-relief behavior and the effective behavior should be mutually incompatible choices—the client must do one or the other. For example, do you yell, "Mom, would you please get off my case already?" or do you say, "Mom, I've got to go now. Talk to you soon"? Do you walk out the door to start on your walk, or do you pick up the newspaper? In these examples, one choice goes to the quick-relief circle, and the other choice goes to the effective behavior circle.

■ The negative consequence (i.e., the bad ending of the movie to come) should represent the worst-case scenario, the definitely unwanted extreme. Normally you can just use the bad ending that was already developed in Future Movies. However, sometimes clients prefer to work with shorter-term bad endings that may seem closer and more real to them. This can also work. As with Future Movies, have your client first describe the general situation before you ask the next question in the script, and get a visual image that represents this. If you can't easily visualize it as if you're watching it in a movie, it's probably not specific enough yet. The image should have a time, place, and action.

■ You want to make sure that "It's not worth it" feels true for the client. If that statement does not feel true, then have the client project the problem farther into the future, to a more extreme bad ending. Until "It's not worth it" feels true for the client, the client has no reason to change his or her behavior.

■ The positive consequence (i.e., the good ending of the movie to come) should represent the best-case scenario, the definitely wanted extreme. Again, the good ending from the future movie can be used, unless your client prefers a shorter-term good ending. In that case, have your client first describe the general situation before you ask the next question in the script, and get a visual image that represents this. If you can't easily visualize it as if you're watching it in a movie, it's probably not specific enough yet. You can ask questions such as, "Where are you? What are you doing? What are you wearing? Who else is there?" and "What time is it?" You won't need to ask all questions to all clients; the point is to get an image that's specific, with time, place, and action. Note that, as long as you are confident that the client can clearly visualize it, you don't need the client to tell you every little detail.

■ Do not allow the good ending to merely be that the client is pleased that he or she handled the high-risk situation the right way. Good behavior is not its own reward; it's important to build in a more powerful good ending, a more inspiring princess, so that the corrective reinforcement will occur. Similarly, do not accept a same-day positive consequence as the good ending. The client has probably experienced such consequences numerous times, and it has not been enough to change the behavior. Go for a better good ending, probably farther in the future, for a more inspiring princess.

■ The thoughts and feelings circle is filled in with internal signals, the red flags that a choice is about to be made. Each of the other circles is filled in with a specific image, including time, place, and action. An image is specific when the therapist can easily visualize it as if watching it on TV.

If You Are the Client

Think of a problem that you would like to work on right now. It must be a behavior that is, in theory, within your power to change. Here are some examples (yes, this is a menu!) of behaviors that people often choose to work on for this exercise:

■ Controlling an angry reaction.
■ Being more assertive in a certain type of situation.
■ Getting more exercise.
■ Controlling overeating.
■ Procrastinating less.
■ Getting certain chores done more efficiently.
■ Doing the things that are a higher priority in your life.

Exercise Part 2: Choices Have Consequences

Continue with the same therapist–client groups, using the Map Out a Problem form (Figure 7.1) as the basis for this exercise. Follow the Choices Have Consequences script that follows. Work only with the problem already detailed

Map Out a Problem - For Behaviors to be Improved
© 2005 Ricky Greenwald

1. So are you always doing this, or just in certain situations? Like what's a recent example, the last time that happened? Doesn't have to be anything big. (Or: When's the next time this could happen?)

2. When you're in this situation, what are the thoughts, the words in your head? Your emotional reaction? The signals in your body?

3. If you let this take you over, what do you do next? (This is, or leads to, the problem behavior.)

4. If the problem habit continues, gets even worse, how bad could things get? What picture could represent that? Does "it's not worth it" feel true — to go that way, I mean?

5. So you're (high risk situation) and (thoughts & feelings). What if you got a handle on this, got it under control, what would you be doing instead (of the problem behavior)?

6. So if this effective behavior got to be a habit, what good things would that lead to? What picture could represent that?

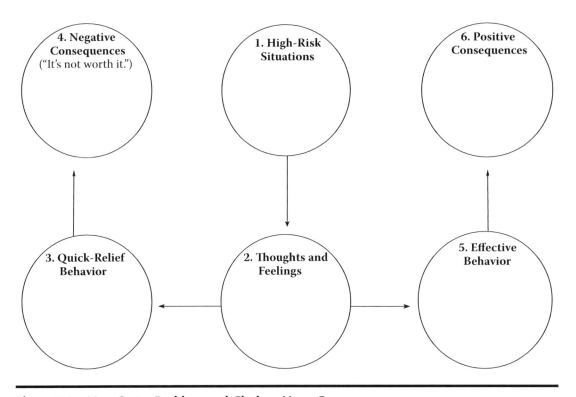

Figure 7.1   Map Out a Problem and Choices Have Consequences

on the map; do not come up with other examples. If you are working by yourself, take yourself through the same script.

Script: Choices Have Consequences

[Work from the map that you just completed.]

I want you to watch this in your mind like it's a movie. Start with [the provocation/situation], then notice [the thoughts and feelings], then [the bad behavior], then the bad ending with, "It's not worth it." (No EM: You can do this with your eyes opened or closed.) Start at the beginning, tell me when it's done. Ready? (EM)

Did you get all the way to the end?

Did you remember to say, "It's not worth it"?

This time the movie starts the same way, with [the situation] and [the thoughts and feelings]. This time, do what it takes to get to the good end. Start at the beginning, tell me when it's done. Ready? (EM)

Did you get all the way to the end?

This time, the movie starts the same way, with [the situation] and [the thoughts and feelings]. This time, I don't know what's going to happen—it depends on you. The rules are bad choice goes to bad ending and "It's not worth it," good choice goes to good ending. Ready? (EM)

Which way did it go?

Did you get all the way to the end?

(If it went to the bad ending: Did you remember to say, "It's not worth it"?)

(Repeat the surprise ending movie routine until positive end is chosen two times in a row)

This time, the movie starts the same way ….

Follow-Up Questions

How did this go for the clients?
What was your experience like?
How did it go for the therapists?

Are you, as the client, now less likely than before to handle this situation the way you want to? No more likely and no less likely? More likely than before?

Discussion

Clients often choose solution behaviors that are not what the therapist might wish. For example, a client may choose a primitive strategy to deal with provocation, such as ignoring it. Or the client may choose an unhealthy strategy such as smoking a cigarette to calm down. As long as the solution behavior can plausibly work to get the client toward his or her goals, the therapist should accept it. Perhaps the client will develop more sophisticated solutions over time (or even within the session, spontaneously) or perhaps not. It's okay.

However, if the client identifies a solution behavior that directly conflicts with going toward the goals, the therapist should challenge this. For example, if the client's proposed solution is to "smoke a joint and calm myself down," the therapist might say, "But didn't you tell me that smoking weed takes you away from your goals?" In such a case, continue to work toward identifying a solution behavior that provides a true (even if minimal) solution.

Sometimes the client chooses the bad way one or more times. This is actually not a problem, so don't worry about it. The client may be struggling with the high-risk situation, and he or she will not prevail every time, at least not at first. On occasion the client may also intentionally choose the bad way, as an experiment or to reinforce the awareness of the bad ending. Indeed, many clients later report that they got themselves to make the good choice in the actual situation by recalling the bad ending and saying, "It's not worth it." As long as the client does not choose the bad way more than twice in a row, it's going well enough. Just hang in there, and the client will eventually choose the good way twice in a row.

Then you're done with that example and can choose another example of the high-risk situation. The preferred strategy is to do Choices Have Consequences with as many examples of one problem as you can fit into the session. Typically you will have time for either two or three full runs of Choices Have Consequences—that is, all the way from the beginning through choosing the good end twice in a row.

Do not have the client address more than one type of high-risk situation in a single session. It is fine to go for different high-risk situations along the same theme, for example, "What else makes you mad?" However, do not go across themes, for example from anger to drug temptation. That's too much to work on at one time and would increase the risk of failure.

Problem-Solving Choices Have Consequences

When Choices Have Consequences goes well, this can lead to unrealistic hopefulness on the part of the clients, which can lead in turn to disappointment and a sense of failure. When Choices Have Consequences does not go well—that is, when the client chooses the bad way more than twice in a row—it is usually because either "It's not worth it" was not true, the example had too heavy an emotional load, or the "effective" behavior was not realistic. These problems and how to resolve them are addressed next.

Unrealistic Expectations

Many people feel encouraged by this exercise and believe that they are now more likely to handle the target situation the way they want to. This may be true, but ask your client,

- How long did it take you to develop the habit you're trying to change now?
- How long do you think it might take to get the new habit?
- What does it take to get a new habit? Practice!

I encourage you to make this point with your clients immediately following Choices Have Consequences. If you do not downplay expectations, there is a risk that clients will expect perfection from themselves and will view anything less as failure. You might prepare your client as follows:

Therapist: It seems like you have this down; you know what to do now in that situation?

Client: Yup, I've got it.

Therapist: So how long did it take you to get that bad habit that you're trying to change now?

Client: I don't know, years I guess.

Therapist: So how long do you think it'll take to change to the new habit you've been practicing?

Client: I don't know.

Therapist: You think it'll happen overnight? Or you think it might take a lot of practice over time?

Client: Practice.

Therapist: I think so too. So don't worry if you're not perfect all of a sudden. But the more you remember to practice this, the sooner you'll get the new habit down.

Following this conversation, it is very hard for the client to fail. If he or she comes back the next week with no progress, the therapist can say that this was expected. Usually at least some progress is noticeable, though. For example, if the problem behavior is still happening sometimes but not as often, the therapist can again say that this was expected and that the progress is encouraging. If, as sometimes happens, the problem behavior has not recurred despite repeated opportunity, the therapist can say, "Well, it wasn't supposed to happen that fast. I'm glad to hear that you did so well this week, but I'm not sure it's a habit yet. If things don't go perfect next week, that just means that it takes a long time to make a new habit." This way the client gets credit for outperforming expectations, and if he or she backslides it's still not a failure—just par for the course. This is the personal trainer strategy: to help the client feel encouraged about making progress one small step at a time.

"It's Not Worth It" Was Not True

When the client chooses the bad way more than twice consecutively, something is going wrong. One possibility is that the bad ending is not sufficiently aversive or unwanted—that "It's not worth it" is not true for the client. If this is the case, then the therapist should guide the client to identify a more aversive ending, typically by extending the problem behavior habit farther into the future.

For example, a 14-year-old boy in residential treatment was working on a recent event in which a peer had said something insulting about his mother and he had physically attacked the peer, leading to being physically restrained and to missing the movie on Saturday night, which everyone else went to. In Choices Have Consequences, he kept choosing the bad way.

Therapist: Why do you keep going the bad way—I thought you didn't want to be stuck there in that room with everyone else out at the movies?

Client: Yeah, well, I want to go to the movie, but it's not that big a deal. A man's gotta be a man. I stood up for myself; I got my pride.

Therapist: But didn't you tell me that you wanted to get out of here and go home?

Client: Yeah—I do.

Therapist: Didn't you tell me that if you keep fighting so much, it'll take longer to graduate and go home?

Client: Yeah. You can't graduate until you're on Level Three [representing a high frequency of appropriate behaviors, with associated privileges] for a month straight.

Therapist: So let's say that every time someone wants some action and decides to say something about your family, you attack him. Your habit continues. How bad could things get?

Client: I could be stuck here a long time.

Therapist: What picture could represent that?

Client: This kid who came in a month after me—it's his graduation party and I'm shaking his hand, wishing him good luck.

Therapist: Does "It's not worth it" feel true with this picture?

Client: Definitely.

If you just use the bad ending from Future Movies, you shouldn't run into this problem. However, sometimes clients prefer shorter-term endings. In that case, do not accept the bad ending that would immediately follow the quick-relief behavior. The client has experienced such consequences numerous times, and that has not been sufficiently aversive to lead to change. Push it farther into the future so the bad ending can be worse and hopefully truly not worth it.

Too Much Emotional Load

If the high-risk situation has too heavy an emotional load, the client may feel so overwhelmed that he or she repeatedly chooses the quick-relief behavior. For example, a 16-year-old incarcerated girl's recent example of a problem behavior was the previous Saturday. She had been on the phone with her mother, for her only allowed phone call for the week, and her mother hung up on her (in anger, before the conversation was really done). Then the girl began throwing objects around and had to be physically restrained. When focusing on this event during Choices Have Consequences, she repeatedly chose the quick-relief behavior.

This case was brought up by a therapist in supervision. A bit of discussion revealed that the client's biggest trauma was abandonment by the mother. If, at first at least, you stay away from events involving family members and if you stay away from events too closely related to the major trauma, you shouldn't run into this problem.

Unrealistic Solution

Sometimes the client will choose the bad way over and over because the so-called effective behavior is unrealistic—something that will not actually work for the client. If you suspect that the client is giving you an unrealistic solution, it's okay to question it on the spot during the setup (in Map Out a Problem; Figure 7.1), perhaps by asking, "Can you do that?" or, "Will that work for you?" If the client confirms that it will work, accept it. If not, help the client find a more plausible strategy.

Sometimes the unrealistic solution slips by, perhaps because it does appear plausible to the therapist. But in Choices Have Consequences, the client goes the bad way over and over. For example, an 18-year-old boy was working on the high-risk situation of being stared at by a peer. The solution behavior was to ignore and walk away. But in Choices Have Consequences, the client chose the bad way again and again.

Therapist: How come you keep going the bad way?
Client: You can't just ignore it when they stare at you. Then you lose respect, and they go after you even more.

Therapist: So what could you do in that situation that might work for you and
    keep you on track toward your goals?
Client: Maybe if I at least say something before I walk away.
Therapist: Like what?
Client: Like, "I'm not going to jail just to put you in the hospital."
Therapist: Could you do that; would that work for you?
Client: I think so.

Once you have identified the problem and have come up with a solution, go
back to Choices Have Consequences and continue to completion.

In subsequent sessions, you can do Choices Have Consequences again, with
the focus on a different theme or type of high-risk situation. For example, the
first Choices Have Consequences session might focus on anger and fighting,
the second on drug temptation, and the third on peer pressure to cut classes.
There is also a wide range of other potentially effective methods of helping
clients to improve their self-control skills. Some of these are discussed in the
next chapter.

Age Variations

With Preteens

No variation; do the session as per the script. However, since you did not do
Future Movies with your client, you will have to come up with good and bad
endings on the spot. Make sure that the endings are meaningful and inspiring to
the client. If one or another ending is not sufficiently inspiring, you can push it
farther into the future to get a magnified outcome; that will hopefully do the trick.

With Adults

No variation; do the session as per the script.

Session 6: Self-Control Skills

Mr. G: Hi. Tell me something good and something bad.
Alex: I made some money.
Mr. G: How much?
Alex: $60. I worked all day Saturday and then a little on Sunday too.
Mr. G: You have any left?
Alex: Yeah, I still have most of it. Feels good to have money in my pocket.
Mr. G: So how did it go, the job?
Alex: It was okay—kind of boring and kind of fun too. Both. My Pops, he's okay.

Mr. G: And something bad?

Alex: I cut my knee; see here (pulls up pant leg)?

Mr. G: Wow—looks like a bad cut. What did you do?

Alex: I was playing basketball on Sunday, two of us went for the ball at the same time.

Mr. G: Did you get it?

Alex: No, didn't even get the ball.

Mr. G: Oh well, at least you were playing. (Pulls out treatment plan). We've been talking about the things you can do to get to your goals. Last week we talked about avoiding high-risk situations. How've you been doing with that?

Alex: Pretty good. I didn't cut through the park; I been going where I'm supposed to go.

Mr. G: How about with the math teacher—have you been talking in his class?

Alex: Not too much. I did ask him a question one time, he was okay about it.

Mr. G: And how about parties? Did you go to any parties?

Alex: No, but there wasn't one, so it's not like I did anything special.

Mr. G: Okay. Let's see what's next: self-control skills. Okay if we talk about self-control skills today?

Alex: I guess so.

Mr. G: You said that anger was the biggest reason that guy would bet against me; let's start with that. When's the last time that someone did something that made you mad?

Alex: Yesterday this kid at school bumped into me.

Mr. G: Then what happened?

Alex: I pushed him back, and he pushed me. Then a teacher came, and we backed off. I don't know what I would have done if the teacher wasn't there. I was mad.

Mr. G: When he bumped you, were you saying to yourself, "I want to hurt him" and the fists, like you told me the other day?

Alex: Yup. Probably would've hurt him, too.

Mr. G: And get yourself in more trouble?

Alex: I know. But I get so mad! And he started it.

Mr. G: I'm not saying you wouldn't have had a right to fight him. But didn't you tell me that fighting takes you away from your goals?

Alex: I know. I'm lucky the teacher came when she did.

Mr. G: Is it okay if we talk about what happened, as an example to practice on?

Alex: I guess so.

Mr. G: Supposing this happens again: Someone bumps you, and you do get mad. What would you like to be able to do, instead of pushing or hitting, to get you toward your goals?

Alex: Just ignore and walk away, I guess. But you can't do that—then they don't respect you and you just get more trouble.

Mr. G: Then what can you think of that might work for you?

Alex: Maybe it's better if I say something first, like, "You're not worth wasting my time on," and then walk away.

Mr. G: Would that work for you?

Alex: Yeah, I done that a couple of times already in the last week or two.

Mr. G: Okay. I'm going to ask you to watch a movie in your mind while you're doing that thing with moving your eyes. The movie starts out, that kid is bumping you. Then the thoughts and feelings. This time, you're going to do your quick-relief behavior: first a push and then hitting. The ending to this movie is that bad ending from the other day; you're behind bars in the orange jumpsuit and the words, "It's not worth it." Start at the beginning, go step by step, and tell me when you're done. Ready? (EM)

Alex: Done.

Mr. G: Did you get all the way to the end?

Alex: Yes.

Mr. G: Did you remember to say, "It's not worth it"?

Alex: Yeah, it's not worth it. I don't want to go that way.

Mr. G: This time, the movie starts out the same way: same bump, same thoughts and feelings. This time you're going to handle it the other way—maybe say something to him and then walk away. The ending to this movie is that good ending from the other day, cutting the ribbon at the grand opening of your second restaurant. Start at the beginning, go step by step, and tell me when you're done. Ready? (EM)

Alex: Done.

Mr. G: Did you get all the way to the end?

Alex: Yes.

Mr. G: This time, the movie starts the same way: same bump, same thoughts and feelings. This time, I don't know what's going to happen. It depends on you. The rules are bad choice goes to the bad ending and "It's not worth it," good choice goes to the good ending. Ready? (EM)

Alex: Done.

Mr. G: Which way did it go?

Alex: The good way.

Mr. G: Did you get all the way to the end?

Alex: Yes.

Mr. G: This time, the movie starts the same way: same bump, same thoughts and feelings. Again, I don't know what's going to happen. It depends on you. The rules are bad choice goes to the bad ending and "It's not worth it," good choice goes to the good ending. Ready? (EM)

Alex: Done.

Mr. G: Which way did it go?

Alex: Bad way.

Mr. G: Did you remember to say, "It's not worth it"?

Alex: No, I forgot that.

Mr. G: That's okay; just pick up where you left off, with that bad ending, and say the words to yourself. (Brief EM until Alex nods.) This time, the movie starts the same way: same bump, same thoughts and feelings. Again, I don't know what's going to happen. Same rules: Bad choice goes to the bad ending and "It's not worth it," good choice goes to the good ending. Ready? (EM)

Alex: Done.

Mr. G: Which way did it go?

Alex: Good way.

Mr. G: You get all the way to the end?

Alex: (Nods)

Mr. G: This time, the movie starts the same way: same bump, same thoughts and feelings. Same rules: Bad choice goes to the bad ending and "It's not worth it," good choice goes to the good ending. Ready? (EM)

Alex: Done.

Mr. G: Which way did it go?

Alex: Good way again.

Mr. G: You make it all the way to the end?

Alex: Yes.

Mr. G: What's another example of a time someone got you mad?

Alex: Well, when I was in lockup, there was this one guy who had a beef with me.

Mr. G: Sorry, I didn't mean from back then. We're looking for more recent things, like since you've been back in the community.

Alex: My math teacher.

Mr. G: What's the last time he did something that made you mad?

Alex: On Monday, the kid next to me asked me a question about the worksheet, and I was trying to explain to him. Then the teacher, he comes up and stands real close to me, leaning over, like, and says, "Mr. _____, if you're not able to do your work now, we can arrange for you to do it after school."

Mr. G: So what did you do?

Alex: I tried to tell him that I was just trying to help someone who asked me a question. So he tells me I'm talking back and sends me to the office.

Mr. G: Then what happened?

Alex: Nothing much. They told me to go back to class and finish my work and to stay out of trouble. They said they didn't want to see me in the office no more.

Mr. G: So they gave you a break, but next time maybe not?

Alex: That's what I'm worried about.

Mr. G: So this math teacher is not so easy to get along with.

Alex: The way he comes up to me like that and be so nasty, it's like he wants me to mess up. He just pushes and pushes. They shouldn't let people like that even be teachers.

Mr. G: You're right. Problem is, there's always someone around like that, making trouble. So do you want to make his day and give him excuses to send you to the office? Maybe even let him win the whole game and get you kicked out of school? Or do you want to make him the loser and keep yourself on track toward your goals?

Alex: Make him the loser. I don't want him to mess me up.

Mr. G: So what would you like to be able to do when he pushes you like that, to stay on track toward your goals?

Alex: Nothing. Just say yes and no, and don't give him any excuses to mess with me.

Mr. G: Okay. We're going to do the movie thing again. Starts out with him standing over you and saying that thing he said. Then your thoughts and feelings. Then this time, do what you might have felt like doing if your anger took over. Then the bad ending with "It's not worth it." Tell me when you're done. Ready? (EM)

Alex: Done.

Mr. G: Did you remember to say, "It's not worth it"?

Alex: Yes.

Mr. G: This time the movie starts the same way, with him standing over you and saying that, same thoughts and feelings. This time, you're going to handle it the better way and then go to the good ending. Ready? (EM)

Alex: Done.

Mr. G: Did it go all the way to the good end?

Alex: Yes.

Mr. G: This time, it starts out the same way: he's doing the same thing, you have the same thoughts and feelings. This time, I don't know what's going to happen. It depends on what you do. Bad choice goes to the bad ending and "It's not worth it," good choice goes to the good ending. Ready? (EM)

Alex: Done. It went the bad way.

Mr. G: Did you remember to say, "It's not worth it"?

Alex: Yes.

Mr. G: This time, it starts out the same way: He's doing the same thing, you have the same thoughts and feelings. Again, bad choice goes to the bad ending and "It's not worth it;" good choice goes to the good ending. Ready? (EM)

Alex: Done. Good way.

Mr. G: Did it go all the way to the end?

Alex: Yes.

Mr. G: This time, it starts out the same way: He's doing the same thing, you have the same thoughts and feelings. Again, bad choice goes to the bad ending and "It's not worth it" good choice goes to the good ending. Ready? (EM)

Alex: Done. Bad way. I really gave him what he deserved!

Mr. G: Did it go all the way to the bad end and "It's not worth it"?

Alex: Yes.

Mr. G: This time, it starts out the same way: He's doing the same thing, you have the same thoughts and feelings. Again, bad choice goes to the bad ending and "It's not worth it;" good choice goes to the good ending. Ready? (EM)

Alex: Done. Good way. All the way to the end.

Mr. G: I guess you know all my questions now! This time, it starts out the same way: He's doing the same thing, you have the same thoughts and feelings. Again, bad choice goes to the bad ending and "It's not worth it," good choice goes to the good ending. Ready? (EM)

Alex: Done. Good way again.

Mr. G: Did it go all the way to the end?

Alex: Yes.

Mr. G: How did it go for you, that practicing?

Alex: I guess it's good; now I'm ready and I know what to do. But it was really boring!

Mr. G: Boring is good. That means you're really getting it. What's your best shot in basketball?

Alex: I can shoot layups, jumpers, fade-aways, anything.

Mr. G: Well, that fade-away, how much did you have to practice before you could do it in a game with someone on you?

Alex: A lot! I used to practice that move for hours.

Mr. G: That's what this is like. You want to practice so much that it's like instinct—so when you're in the situation you have the best chance of doing it under pressure.

Alex: That makes sense.

Mr. G: So how long have you had this habit of reacting in an angry way?

Alex: Long time. Years.

Mr. G: So if all of a sudden you don't have perfect self-control tomorrow, does that mean that you can't ever change? Or does it just mean that it takes time and practice to get a new habit?

Alex: Time and practice.

Mr. G: I think that's how it works. You got some practice here, but now it's up to you to remember to practice in the real situations. You won't get it perfect every time, but the more you remember to practice, the better you'll get.

Alex: That makes sense.

Mr. G: So I hope a lot of people disrespect you this week, so you get a lot of practice.

Alex: Thanks a lot!

Mr. G: That's it for today. Tell me something you liked about the meeting and something you didn't like.

Alex: It was good to practice that stuff. I didn't like that it was so boring.

Mr. G: What's next for you today?

Alex: Homework.

Mr. G: And do you have any plans for the money in your pocket?

Alex: Not really. Probably do something with my cousins on the weekend.

Mr. G: Okay, see you next week.

Alex: See you.

Session 6: Self-Control Skills, Official Notes

Focused today on self-control skills in challenging situations related to anger. Talked about the negative outcome for giving in to impulse vs. the positive outcome for keeping control. Imaginal rehearsal of coping strategies for keeping control in the identified situations.

Session 6: Self-Control Skills, Therapist's Personal Notes

Choices Have Consequences re being bumped by a peer & being disrespected by math teacher.

Session 6: Questions and Answers

Q: What happened to Map Out a Problem? It seems like you sort of did it and sort of skipped it. That's not like what's in the text for this chapter.
A: You're right. I just worked off the treatment plan, which has most of the information on it already. When you're new to this treatment approach, you should probably use the Map Out a Problem form (Figure 7.1). But when you're more used to it, you can go a bit quicker by doing what I did. You're covering all the same ground but just not writing the same things down a second time. On the other hand, some therapists prefer to continue using the map form because it gives the client such a good graphic display of the choices and consequences.

Session 7: More Self-Control Skills

Mr. G: Hi, tell me something good and something bad since last time we met.
Alex: Good, I went to this girl's house on Sunday. Bad, her father don't like me; he don't really want her to mix with me.
Mr. G: Is this the same girl you told me about before—the one from school?
Alex: Yeah. I didn't used to go for just one girl, but maybe this time I will.
Mr. G: You really like her!
Alex: I think so. It's kind of too soon to say. We're not even really going out; at least I'm not sure if we are or not.
Mr. G: What was happening on Sunday?
Alex: It was her little brother's birthday; they had a bunch of people over, she said I could come by.
Mr. G: How come her father doesn't like you?

Alex: He knows I'm in OCFS [the state program that has legal custody of Alex]; he probably thinks I'm gonna do those things I did before.

Mr. G: He's probably not the only one who thinks that about you. I bet a lot of people think you're going to do what you did before.

Alex: That's not right though. People should give you a chance, not just assume you're going to do something bad.

Mr. G: He probably just cares about his daughter.

Alex: I can see that.

Mr. G: But maybe after a while, if he sees that you're doing good, he'll get a different opinion about you.

Alex: I hope so. I'm trying to do good, stay out of trouble.

Mr. G: (pulls out treatment plan) We've been talking about the things you can do to get to your goals. Last week, you were practicing self-control skills for anger. How have you been doing with that?

Alex: Good. I didn't get in no trouble.

Mr. G: What happened—did everyone get nicer?

Alex: No, nothing like that. I just told myself, "It's not worth it" and didn't lose my temper.

Mr. G: How many times did you have a chance to practice?

Alex: That someone got me mad? Um … three times.

Mr. G: And you handled it every time, huh? Well, habits aren't supposed to change that fast, so if you mess up some this coming week, you're still on track.

Alex: I don't want to be messing up.

Mr. G: I can see that. Before, we talked about avoiding high-risk situations. How are you doing with that lately?

Alex: Pretty good. I don't walk through the park; I even skipped a party Saturday night.

Mr. G: How did you get yourself to do that?

Alex: I like this girl, and I been telling her I'm trying to stay away from that stuff. No point lying because she would find out anyway. So I called up my cousins and we got together instead.

Mr. G: How's it going with your math teacher?

Alex: He's still an asshole—oh, scuse me. Anyway I don't let him get to me; I just say yes and no and do my work.

Mr. G: Well, you told me that you cared about your goals. Now you've been proving it.

Alex: Yeah, that's what I been telling my grandparents, but they don't believe me.

Mr. G: I guess it'll take them a little time, too. Like that girl's father.

Alex: I hope so.

Mr. G: Last time we worked on self-control skills for anger. You want to work more on that, or you feel like we did enough already?

Alex: Enough already.

Mr. G: Okay. So is it okay if now we work on self-control skills for another high-risk situation, like when someone passes you a joint?

Alex: But I'm not going to the parties or hanging around with those friends. My cousins, even if they have some, they won't let me smoke. They don't want me locked up again.

Mr. G: And this girl you like, what's her name?

Alex: Alicia.

Mr. G: Does she smoke?

Alex: Not even cigarettes. She's tried it, but that's it.

Mr. G: So the main time would be around your cousins?

Alex: No, I asked them to not even smoke around me. It's not a problem.

Mr. G: So the only high-risk situation left is peers who say "Let's do this," or "Let's do that"?

Alex: Right. That can happen anytime.

Mr. G: When's the last time that someone asked you to do something you're trying not to do?

Alex: Just today at school, I was walking down the hall to class and someone said, "Yo, let's go out and get high," or something like that.

Mr. G: And what did you do?

Alex: I said I can't do that no more; I get drug tested all the time.

Mr. G: So when he said that to you, was it like this (points to Thoughts & Feelings circle) with excitement, "I want to," and "Don't want to say no"?

Alex: Pretty much, yeah.

Mr. G: Okay, so here come the movies. It starts out with the guy saying that to you in the hallway then those thoughts and feelings. In this movie, you're going to let those take you over and do what you feel like doing, Then the bad ending and "It's not worth it." Start at the beginning, go step by step, and tell me when you're done. Ready? (EM)

Alex: My girl said she couldn't see me no more, and I got sent back upstate.

Mr. G: Did you remember to say, "It's not worth it?"

Alex: Yeah.

Mr. G: This time the movie starts the same way: same situation, same thoughts and feelings. This time, do what it takes to get to the good ending. Ready? (EM)

Alex: I just told him, "Thanks but I gotta go to this class," and that was it.

Mr. G: Did you get all the way to the good end?

Alex: Yeah, I was walking Alicia home and telling her how good I'm doing.

Mr. G: This time, the movie starts the same way: same situation, same thoughts and feelings. This time, I don't know what will happen; it depends on what you do. Bad choice goes to bad ending and "It's not worth it," good choice goes to good ending. Ready? (EM)

Alex: Done; good way.

Mr. G: Did you get to the good ending?

Alex: Yes.

Mr. G: This time, the movie starts the same way: same situation, same thoughts and feelings. Again, I don't know what will happen; it depends on what you do. Bad choice goes to bad ending and "It's not worth it," good choice goes to good ending. Ready? (EM)

Alex: Done; good way. Got to the good ending.

Mr. G: What's another time a peer has said, "Let's do something" that would take you away from your goals?

Alex: Someone here—I don't want to say who—he said he had a scheme did I want to do it. He said it would be easy money.

Mr. G: And what did you do?

Alex: I just said no, I'm trying to stay out of trouble.

Mr. G: When he said, "Do you want to do it?" what were you saying to yourself; what were the feelings?

Alex: I was saying no, I want to stay out of trouble.

Mr. G: And was there another part of you saying to go ahead? What was that part saying?

Alex: Sounds good, could do it just once, won't get caught, could use the money.

Mr. G: And what emotion was there?

Alex: Just kind of wanting to.

Mr. G: And signals in your body?

Alex: Nothing.

Mr. G: So this movie starts with him saying, "Do you want to do it?" and then those thoughts and feelings. Then you let them take you over, and you go ahead and do it. Then the bad ending with "It's not worth it." Ready? (EM)

Alex: Done. I went the good way.

Mr. G: Oh, you're ahead of me. Anyway, did you get all the way to the good end?

Alex: Yes.

Mr. G: Okay, but now the bad way, just to check it out, okay?

Alex: Okay.

Mr. G: So the bad way, to the bad end and "It's not worth it," ready? (EM)

Alex: Done.

Mr. G: Did you go all the way to the end?

Alex: Yes, and yes it's not worth it.

Mr. G: Okay. This time the movie starts the same way, same situation, same thoughts and feelings. This time I don't know what's going to happen; it depends on you. Bad choice to bad ending and "It's not worth it," good choice to the good ending. Ready? (EM)

Alex: Done, good way, to the end. I got it already!

Mr. G: Are you telling me it's getting boring?

Alex: It's been boring a long time.

Mr. G: Good, that's what we want. This time the movie starts the same way, same situation, same thoughts and feelings. Again I don't know what's going to happen; it depends on you. Bad choice to bad ending and "It's not worth it," good choice to the good ending. Ready? (EM)

Alex: Done, good way, to the end.

Mr. G: Okay, that's enough for today. Tell me something you liked about the meeting and something you didn't like.

Alex: I don't like all this movie stuff over and over and over.

Mr. G: But you did it.

Alex: And I liked I like that I can prove myself and change people's opinions of me.

Mr. G: What's next for you now?

Alex: I don't know. I got a lot of homework but it's group time; I don't know what they'll make me do.

Mr. G: You got more plans with Alicia?

Alex: Just to see her at school. But I'm going to ask her does she want to go to the movies.

Mr. G: Good luck. See you next week.

Alex: See you.

Session 7: More Self-Control Skills, Official Notes

Followed up on avoiding high risk and self-control in anger-related situations; reports doing well so far. Focused today on self-control skills in challenging situations related to peer pressure. Talked about the negative outcome for giving in to impulse vs. the positive outcome for keeping control. Imaginal rehearsal of coping strategies for keeping control in the identified situations.

Session 7: More Self-Control Skills, Therapist's Personal Notes

- Doing well w/ avoid hi risk and self-control re anger.
- Choices Have Consequences re peer stuff: "Let's do this or that."

Session 7: Questions and Answers

Q: Don't you think you kind of missed the boat by not asking him to work on the high-risk situation of when it's a girl passing him the joint? A few sessions ago he specifically said that when a girl was doing the passing, the temptation was strongest.

A: Yes, you're right. If you read carefully, you'll also see that in a few other places I leave things out that should be there. That's the problem with showing a transcript; you can see that sometimes I forget something or miss something important. Lucky for me he's got some other girl on his mind, but yes, I wish I had done this. The good news is that therapists don't have to be perfect to get the job done. And if something really critical is missed, there's always (or at least, usually) next time.

Chapter 8

More Skills and Strategies

For many clients, the Avoid High Risk session, followed by some sessions of Choices Have Consequences, will be sufficient for effecting substantial improvements in their behaviors and daily functioning. We are not expecting perfection, but we do hope for sufficient improvement, stability, and a sense of success that the client is willing and able to continue moving forward in treatment.

For other clients, additional interventions will also be called for. A large literature exists on how to train clients in self-management skills; the full repertoire is beyond the scope of this book. In this chapter, several interventions are described that are called for with some frequency and that seem to be effective with problem behavior clients.

- *Early Warning System* helps the client become aware of his or her emotional reaction and to have a chance to make a choice before the reaction takes over and it's too late.
- *Tease Proofing* helps the client become more resistant to being affected by provocation and more effective in dealing with it.
- *Sex Talk* helps the client become more likely to protect himself or herself from the risks of pregnancy and sexually transmitted diseases.
- *Job Talk* teaches the client skills to get and keep a job.
- *Money Talk* teaches the client various aspects of money management.

Only one of these interventions, Tease Proofing, is included in the Session Forms section (see Appendix C). The other interventions are not scripted but are described here so that the therapist will be able to adapt them to the client and the situation. In the case example, the Sex Talk and Money Talk are included, but to keep the sessions in order they are not shown following this chapter but later as they appear in the course of the treatment.

The interventions in this chapter are not done routinely with every client. Rather, they are available should the specific need be indicated by a given client's situation. For example, the therapist might initiate the job talk upon hearing that the client is planning to try to get a job. There is also no set order for these interventions, no specific place in treatment that they should go, except for Early Warning System, which if used immediately precedes Choices Have Consequences. Otherwise, these interventions are used when called for.

Depending on your work setting, you may find that additional interventions of this type are frequently called for. Different types of clients have different typical issues and needs. You should not feel limited by what is included in this chapter or in the book as a whole. However, if you are using this treatment approach, you should try to ensure that any additional interventions are consistent with the Fairy Tale model style and approach, with a focus on the client's goals.

With rare exception, these interventions should not be used until after the Treatment Contracting session. Prior to having the treatment contract, clients tend to be less motivated and more prone to perceiving therapist efforts as reflecting the therapist's agenda rather than the clients. Trying to "help" the client too soon—that is, before you have a clear mandate from the client to do so—invites failure with the intervention. This makes your treatment look like those that may have come before: plenty of talk, little benefit. In other words, jump in too soon and you risk losing your chance to really help.

Early Warning System

This intervention is particularly useful for those clients who experience their anger and impulsiveness as coming on so fast and strong that the quick-relief behavior is already completed before the client is fully aware of the situation. Their reaction is experienced as occurring so quickly as to be virtually instantaneous, with no awareness of the various steps leading up to the quick-relief behavior. By the time they realize that they are headed for trouble, they are often past the point of no return. For such clients, Choices Have Consequences may be ineffective on its own because these clients may not be able to think quickly enough to choose the effective behavior, even if they would like to. Therefore, for such clients, Early Warning System is used just prior to (and to prepare for) Choices Have Consequences and in the same session.

Early Warning System helps clients to identify the various steps leading to the explosion so they will be better able to catch themselves earlier in the process when they can more easily choose to go in another direction. This is done by guiding the client to do the following:

■ Recognize the nature of the problem.
■ Identify the internal events that constitute the build-up of the emotional reaction.
■ Identify the order in which those events occur.
■ Practice visualizing those moments in sequence to train the client's awareness.
■ Incorporate this visualized sequence into Choices Have Consequences.

The following example illustrates how this might be accomplished.

Therapist: Did you ever see one of those movies where the bad guy sneaks in the back door at night, climbs up the stairs, and you don't even know he's there until the knife's at your throat?

Client: Yeah.

Therapist: That's what your anger does to you. By the time you know it's there, the knife's already at your throat. It's too late to do anything about it.

Client: I see what you're saying.

Therapist: Did you ever see one of those movies where the people have a guard at the gate, they have the fence around the property, the motion detectors, the video cameras, the dogs—by the time the attacker gets close, they had a chance to get ready. They have an early warning system. That's what you need for your anger so it doesn't get you by the throat. Then you have a chance to be ready and make your own choice about how to protect yourself.

Then the client is asked to focus on a typical problem event, perhaps a recent one, in detail. First the client is asked to describe the situation in terms of the provocation and then his or her internal response. Then the client is asked to examine the internal response in more detail, to discern intervening events that may have been skipped in the first description. The therapist can help by offering a menu of possible responses and by having patience as the client struggles to see this in a new way.

Therapist: So he's talking trash to you and the next thing you know, you punch him out?

Client: That's about it.

Therapist: Now I want you to concentrate on when he's talking trash to you; close your eyes if it helps to concentrate just on that moment. What's going on inside you?

Client: I'm getting heated. No one can talk to me that way.

Therapist: Good. How can you tell you're getting heated? What lets you know?

Client: I just know.

Therapist: Well, what are the signals in your body? Is it hot or cold, is it loose or tense or shaky, is it dry or sweaty?

Client: I get it. Well, I can't see nothin' but the guy, and my whole body tenses up, and my heart's beating fast, and my hands are in fists.

Therapist: Good, that's what we're looking for. And what are you thinking? What are the words in your head?

Client: Kill him.

Therapist: Okay, what happens first? When he's talking trash to you, what's your first sign that something's going wrong?

Client: Well, he's dissing [disrespecting] me I don't like that.

Therapist: Good, so first you notice what he's doing and what you think about it. What happens next?

Client: It just all happens at once.

Therapist: Let's look at it very carefully, like a movie in slow motion. You can close your eyes if that helps you to concentrate. Start with him talking trash, and right away freeze the frame and see what you notice.

This process is continued until both therapist and client are satisfied that a reliable sequence has been identified—for example, (1) provocation; (2) don't like being disrespected; (3) heart races; (4) anger; (5) "kill him"; and (6) hitting. The point here is not to attain insight about the reasons for the client's reactivity but to help the client notice and learn to recognize the details and sequence of his or her own behavioral patterns.

The final step in Early Warning System is to imaginally view a movie in which each step along the escalation is ordered and discrete (with eye movements [EM] if you are trained in Eye Movement Desensitization and Reprocessing [EMDR]). This should be done several times and the client should be questioned after each viewing to ensure that each discrete step was noticed. This should help to slow things down so the client has a better chance to interrupt the process before it's gone too far.

Once the sequence of internal events has been identified and imaginally practiced, it should be incorporated into Choices Have Consequences. This is done by replacing the "thoughts and feelings" step in Choices Have Consequences with the ordered sequence, in the movie script, as follows: "Now I want you to watch a movie in your mind. The movie starts out with [the high-risk situation], then *each piece of your [internal] reaction, one step at a time.* Then you do the [quick-relief behavior] …." This sequence of internal steps is used each time the client is asked to go through the movie.

Tease Proofing

The Tease-Proofing interventions are designed for those who are particularly reactive to provocation by others and for whom this is an identified problem. Sometimes the client is clear that it is a problem: "I hate it when they tease me; I just get so mad, and I lose it and then I'm the one that gets in trouble. I'm sick of it!" When the client is able to clearly identify his or her reactivity as a problem and is motivated to solve it, the therapist can proceed directly to Tease Proofing without further preparation.

However, some clients are conflicted about whether they should be continuing with their reactivity and aggression or are finding some other way to respond to the provocation. They have already identified their reactivity and associated behaviors as a problem, something that takes them toward the unwanted bad ending. On the other hand, some clients perceive the provocations as attacks that legitimately require physical self-defense responses. Other clients may feel that it is proper to stand up for themselves in the face of provocation, regardless of the consequences. Therefore, before addressing the problem of the client's vulnerability to provocation, it is sometimes necessary to help the client to perceive that the reactivity is, indeed, a problem. This can be done with one or both of the following conversations.

Self-Defense

Don't even think about telling your client not to exercise his or her right to self-defense. It would not work, and you would look like a fool. If you have a client who believes that he or she must continue to react to provocation aggressively for self-defense, the best you can do is agree. When you show respect for the client's perceived need for self-protection, the client does not have to argue with you. Then you can try to find some exception, some instance or example of a provocation event that does not require aggression for self-defense. Tease Proofing can be done with this example, and the client will learn the skills.

Later, the client can decide in which situations the skills might apply. It generally turns out that the client will find that relatively few situations actually require aggressive self-defense. It's okay to let the client figure that out over time. To get the Tease Proofing done, all we need is one good example of the provocation to work on. The following conversation can get around the self-defense objection so that the work can be done.

Therapist: Didn't you tell me that fighting can get you arrested again?

Client: Yeah, but you don't know my world. The reason I fight is because if I don't fight, I'm gonna get hurt even worse.

Therapist: So you're talking about self-defense.

Client: That's right.

Therapist: Well, everyone respects self-defense. If you fight for self-defense, and if you can prove that in court, maybe with witnesses or whatever, then they let you off.

Client: If you can prove it. Sometimes they don't believe you.

Therapist: But the point is that you have a right to defend yourself. I'm not here to tell you that you don't.

Client: Thank you.

Therapist: So every single time someone gives you trouble, you have to fight for self-defense? Or are there certain times that someone gives you trouble but you don't really have to fight—that they make you mad but they're not gonna hurt you?

Client: Probably once in a while I wouldn't have to fight.

Therapist: Okay, so we're not gonna talk about the times you have to defend yourself. That's off the table. Let's just talk about those other times—the once in a while— when if you could control yourself better you give yourself a better chance of getting to your goals. Okay?

Client: Okay.

Therapist: When's the last time that something like that happened? That someone provoked you but you didn't really have to fight to protect yourself?

Who's in Charge of You?

Since many who are reactive to provocation feel that they are doing the right thing by standing up for themselves, it can be rather alarming to consider that their reactivity makes them a slave to their enemies. The following cognitive reframe can convert the client in a matter of minutes, from insisting on being reactive to insisting on controlling his or her reaction.

Therapist: So why would that kid say bad things about your mother anyway? Does he even know your mother?

Client: No, he doesn't know my mom. He just has an attitude or something, you know; he wants to get something going, thinks he can push me around.

Therapist: So let's say I'm some kid having a bad day. And let's say that I don't like feeling bad inside me, so I want to get my feelings out on someone else; maybe I'll feel a little better if I can make someone else feel bad. So I want some action; I want to really get someone going. So I walk into the room, and I see you. Are you the kind of guy I can get going?

Client: No, not unless you disrespect my family.

Therapist: So if I want to get you going, all I have to do is say something bad about your mother?

Client: That's right. No one gets away with that.

Therapist: So it's just like pushing a button. I just push the right button and there you go.

Client: I guess you could say that.

Therapist: So you're minding your own business, and anyone having a bad day can make you get all heated and get yourself in trouble?

Client: Well, no one can talk about my mother like that.

Therapist: So that kid who said that stuff yesterday—what's his name?

Client: Claude.

Therapist: Yeah, Claude. I didn't realize you liked Claude so much.

Client: What are you talking about? I hate his guts!

Therapist: Yeah, I didn't realize you liked him so much. Yesterday, you let him decide when you would get angry; you let him decide for you when you would get into trouble.

Client: I don't like him.

Therapist: How come you put him in charge of how you act? You let him run you; all he has to do is press the button and you go off. You must really look up to him.

Client: I told you I don't like him!

Therapist: Yeah, he must be like a father to you. You give him the power, let him be in charge of what you do.

Client: He's not in charge of me; I'm in charge of me.

Therapist: Then who decides how you act? Some jerk having a bad day, or you?

Once the client is no longer conflicted but is willing to work on his or her reactivity to provocation, the Tease Proofing interventions can lead to rapid changes. It would be helpful to review the Session Form for Tease Proofing (Appendix C) before continuing here. These interventions should be done in order, as a package, within a single session.

Play Therapy

This is essentially an imagination version of Play Therapy in which the client can learn to master what was previously overwhelming. The client is instructed to select a typical provocation event, involving (preferably) a peer or authority figure with whom the client tends to be reactive. The client is then introduced to the comic strip (fantasy) context and is instructed to devise a resolution to the problem. Then this sequence is imaginally viewed as a brief movie, including the two frames in the comic strip: the provocation and the resolution. The procedure is repeated, each time with the same initial provocation and a new resolution.

This is a good icebreaker for the other Tease-Proofing techniques, as it can be humorous while increasing confidence in the possibility that such provocation can indeed be mastered. The following are some challenges that may arise in the course of this intervention as well as suggested ways to address these:

- Some clients try to discount this intervention by saying, "This is stupid," because they can't use these strategies in real life. As usual in such circumstances, the therapist will lower the stakes while maintaining an expectation that the client will respond. For example, the therapist can say, "Yeah, we're just fooling around. So what should happen next?"
- Some clients will move too quickly to a prosocial solution. Don't allow that. Play Therapy comes first to help the client feel empowered; if you skip it, you risk having more trouble with the later interventions. But the customer is always right, so find a way to praise before correcting: for example, "You're ahead of me; we were gong to look for good ways of handling this in a few minutes. But for now, we're just fooling around and looking for really funny or bad things that can happen. So what should happen next?"
- Some clients will be uncomfortable with entertaining an aggressive fantasy toward the provoking person in the example situation. This occurs most

often with higher-functioning clients (e.g., your partner for the upcoming practice session) whose provoker is a close friend or family member. You still want to gently encourage the aggressive fantasy endings, but they will probably be much more mild than usual. With a peer antagonist, a ton of bricks might fall on the provoker; with a family member, it is more likely to be a pie in the face.

■ Some therapists will be uncomfortable with encouraging their clients to engage in violent fantasies. Paradoxically, in this treatment context, such fantasies will help the client to feel more empowered and thus less likely to engage in violent behaviors. Remember that this is a variant of Play Therapy, in which the client typically kills the monster over and over. Even play therapists who refuse to provide toy weapons will acknowledge that their clients create weapons out of neutral objects; it's unavoidable. When it comes to symbolism, it is essential to let the clients choose their own so that it will have the most possible meaning and power. Yes, clients often choose violent symbols to help them to feel empowered. This is good therapy. However, if on some rare occasion you should feel concerned that the client will misunderstand the intervention and believe that you are encouraging violent behavior, trust yourself. Then you can say, "You know that we're just fooling around, right? And that I don't want you to really do something like this?"

Walls

This intervention teaches the client to create a boundary between himself or herself and the provoker. As in Play Therapy, the client is instructed to select a typical provocation event, including a peer or authority figure with whom the client tends to be reactive. Generally it works best to use the same provocation situation all the way through Tease Proofing. This time, the therapist teaches the client that the bad feeling is not really the client's, but the provoker's. Then the therapist tells the client to select a barrier to prevent the provoker from having access to the client. The client is then asked to imagine this barrier in detail. Then the client imaginally views a movie in which the provocation is followed by the implementation of this barrier.

This intervention teaches a sophisticated concept, using a concrete metaphor (sometimes literally concrete): that the client does not have to take provocation personally, does not have to take it in or be affected by it. It is the provoker's problem, not the client's.

The primary challenge that may arise with Walls is that the wall doesn't work. That's why the script includes a follow-up question to ask if it worked. If it did not work, the therapist's job is to find out why it did not work and to guide the client to come up with a solution. As always, it is important to resist providing the solution for the client. The client must be allowed to identify his or her own symbol, which will be more meaningful and effective than whatever the therapist might devise, such as in the following example.

Therapist: How did that go?
Client: Not so good this time.
Therapist: Why? What happened?
Client: Well, the brick wall wasn't strong enough; it cracked.
Therapist: What would make it stronger?
Client: Reinforce it with steel.
Therapist: Okay, try that.

However, if the client cannot identify a solution, the therapist can provide a menu of possible solutions, to give the client a nudge (e.g., "Maybe make it thicker, or reinforce it with steel, or add concrete, what do you think would work?"). Once the wall works with the initial provocation situation, it can be tried with another example or two to reinforce the intervention's impact.

Role Model

You may have noticed by now that clients often initially choose rather primitive or unsophisticated ways to cope with their high-risk situations. It is not the therapist's place to criticize the client's possibly effective and self-selected solutions. However, we wouldn't mind if our clients selected more sophisticated and effective strategies! Fortunately, clients are aware of such strategies and are generally able to identify someone who exemplifies the more advanced coping style to which the client may aspire.

In Role Model, the client integrates the exemplar's more adaptive approach to handling provocation. The role model may be a peer, relative, community member, or pop culture figure. The client is asked to describe how the role model would handle this type of situation. The client is first asked to observe an imaginal movie of the role model handling the target situation. Next, the client is asked to "become" the role model and imagine handling the target situation. Finally, the client is asked to try the role model's strategy independently of the role model, again with the movie.

It is important to use the script verbatim when asking the client to select a role model. The question is convoluted. But if you ask a shorter, smoother version of the question, for example, "Who can you think of who can handle this in a good way?" you will not get the answer you want. For example, the client might say, "Hulk Hogan [a famous wrestler]; he'll just pound him into the ground." But if the client emulated this strategy, it would not lead toward the client's goals. For another example, the client might say, "My teacher—she would just send him to the office." But the client does not have the authority to send the provoker to the office. Just use the script, and these problems will not come up very often. Even so, if the client does select an inappropriate role model or coping strategy, the therapist can say, "But that wouldn't help you to get to your goals," and have the client try again.

Exercise: Tease Proofing

Pair up with a colleague (or try this with a friend or client). This is not a role play. You will each be yourselves, and you will each get a turn as therapist and client. You will be using the Tease Proofing script in Appendix C.

If You Are the Therapist

Start by asking the client for a recent (or typical) example of the provocation event. Make sure to get time, place, and action; this often involves a direct quote from the provoker. Then just use the script and follow the suggestions already noted. Use three or four "second frames" for Play Therapy and two examples for Walls. For Role Model, use the first example again (that you used for Play Therapy and that you used first for Walls). Do not engage in extraneous conversation.

If You Are the Client

Be yourself. You will have to identify someone who gets to you or gets on your nerves in some way. Do not look at the script; just respond to the therapist's questions.

Follow-Up Questions

How did this go for the clients? What was your experience like? How did it go for the therapists?

If it seems appropriate and there is time at the end of the session, any of the Tease-Proofing procedures can be extended into a round of Choices Have Consequences. For example, if the client enjoyed turning the provoker into a roach or having the wall go up, that visualization can be invoked in the Choices Have Consequences visualization, perhaps just after the client faces the usual thoughts and feelings. Or if the client came up with a good coping strategy, this can be used as the effective behavior. Building in the good and bad endings with Choices Have Consequences provides further reinforcement for the client's learning.

The entire Tease-Proofing package typically takes about 25 minutes and should always be completed in a single session. Quite frequently, the client will be enthusiastic about learning these powerful new coping skills, and many report immediate and lasting success following the Tease-Proofing session.

Sex Talk

Don't try this too soon; many people have been lectured about safe sex plenty of times already, and you don't want to come off as someone with an agenda to lecture. Hold off until after the treatment plan is done. Then you have the sex talk if or when you become aware that the client may soon be facing an opportunity for unprotected sex. Then this is more likely to be perceived as another way you are trying to help the client to stay on track toward his or her goals.

Condom Access

"Do you have condoms with you? Will you have them with you when you are there (in that situation)? Where do you carry them? Let me see; show me." If the client does not have condoms on hand, either hand him or her some or review the specific procedures needed to get them.

Condom Use

(If yes ...) "Why?" Then give responses that reinforce the client's pride and determination towards the goals, as reflected in the client's behavior. For example: "So you really care about what happens to you, huh?" or "So you've decided that when you're going to be a father/mother, you want to do it right?"

(If no ...) "What would make you not use it?" (Typical answers: "It doesn't feel good" and/or, "Well, when s/he tells me not to, says I don't have to.")

Developing the Self-Talk for Condom Use

"So what if you told him/her that you want to use condoms, what would s/he say?"

"So does that mean that this girl/boy really cares about you, or just wants a good time?"

(If really cares ...) "Does s/he know about how hard you're trying to get to your goals? Does s/he want you to get to your goals?" (If yes, which is usually the case by now ...) "Maybe you could talk about how much you care about the goals, and can s/he support you in doing well by using the condoms even though they don't feel as good?"

(If just wanting a good time ...) "So this is just a feel-good day but s/he doesn't really care about you? Is this the person you want a baby with? Is this the person you want to give up your goals, your good future for?"

"So what could you say in that moment?" (Perhaps something like, "This is how it's gonna be. I'm not going to risk my future for this. Take it or leave it.")

Job Talk

You would do the Job Talk at the moment that the client is ready to look for work. Then this is part of helping the client get toward the stated goals. You might start out with, "What do you already know about applying for a job? I don't want to tell you something you already know." Then the client can tell you what he or she already knows, and you can build on that rather than risk talking down to the client by saying "obvious" things. The purpose of this talk is to give the client information and ideas that will increase his or her chances of obtaining and keeping a job.

What Kind of Job?

Therapist: What kind of job do you want to look for? Some kids just want any old job that pays and that they can fit into their schedule. Others try to look for work that will be more interesting or fun for them, because it's hard enough to show up for a job every day even when you like it; it can be really hard to show up and work when you don't like it. That would be asking for trouble. Some kids try to find work that will give them skills that will help them get to their goals. (Give an example applying to this client, such as, "For example, you said you want to be a mechanic; I wonder if it would be a good idea to get a job in a gas station, and maybe when you have free time you can be helping them fix cars, give yourself a head start" or, "For example, you said you want to be a counselor like me; I wonder if it would be a good idea to get a job taking care of kids in an after-school program to get some experience.")

Note that the therapist's job is not to push kids in a certain direction. It's only to give ideas and help clients become aware of the options and the pros and cons of each option so the client can make an informed choice. Some clients choose to try to find work directly related to their long-term goals, and some choose to get any job. Either is okay; it's the client's choice.

After Putting in an Application

So maybe they have a pile of job applications. How do they decide which ones to call in for an interview? (The ones with experience?) The ones who follow up. Supposing one kid comes back or calls the next day, asks to talk to the manager, and says, "I'm [your name here], I put in a job application the other day. I'm just checking to see if you've scheduled the interviews yet." What's the manager gonna think about that kid? (That he or she really cares, really wants the job.) Matter of fact, I know some bosses that don't call anyone for an interview, unless the person followed up after leaving the job application.

Job Interview

Supposing the boss asks you to come for an interview, to decide whether to hire you or not. What do you wear? (Nice, clean, not-ripped clothes but not too nice. The clothes should be suitable to the type of work, or just one step nicer. Shows that you care.)

What time do you show up? (A few minutes early. That way if something goes wrong, you're still on time, and if nothing goes wrong, you're a little early. What would the boss think about someone who showed up a few minutes early?)

How do you answer the questions? (Straight answers.)

What if s/he asks you if you've been arrested before? (Discussion with client regarding what information the boss is likely to have access to, what the client would like to say, and how it might best be said.)

What questions do *you* ask in a job interview? (This question has never occurred to most teens; they assume that their job is to answer questions, not to ask them.) The thing is, a lot of bosses don't think to tell you—or ask you—some of the important things. What do you want to know about the job? (Job responsibilities/activities, training/supervision for same, work schedule, level of pay, and possibilities for advancement.)

And what do you want the boss to know about you? (Relevant experience/skills, if any. Also: Sure, that you want the job, that you're going to work hard. Let me ask you something else. Suppose the boss has interviewed 10 guys for the job, they all want the job, they're all going to work hard. But one of those guys says, "I want this job because I can learn skills that will help me to get to my goals." Which person is the boss going to hire? Why? Sure, he's going to be saying to himself, "That guy, he's going to be working extra hard because he cares more than the others do." So when you're in the job interview, you want to find something about the job that can help you towards your goals, and find a way to let the boss know about that. Then when it comes time to make a decision, maybe he'll remember what you said, and decide to take a chance on you.

Job Skills

So supposing you get hired, what kinds of things do you do if you want to keep the job, maybe even get promoted, maybe get a good reference for your next job? (Show up early or on time, call ahead if there's an emergency making you late, work hard, don't slack, take initiative.) Note that these activities should not just be therapist orders; rather, the client should be helped to generate these conclusions. For example: "So let's say you're washing dishes and the boss isn't looking your way right now, she's in the other room. What do you do?"

Applying for Jobs

So how do you apply for a job, how do you find jobs to apply for? (Help Wanted ads in the newspaper, seeing the Help Wanted sign on the window, know someone who knows about a job opening.)

If you apply for a job you saw in the paper, how many other people saw that job too? How many other people might be applying for the job? (Maybe 100.) That's a lot of competition, it's pretty tough to get a job when you're only one in a hundred.

If you apply for a job you saw a sign for in the window, how many other people might be applying for that job? (Maybe 10 or 20.) That's better, but it's still a lot of competition. Hard to get that job too.

What if you apply for a job that no one else knows about, how many other people might be applying for that one? (Maybe no one.) Right. So if you really want to have a good chance of getting a job, one trick is to get there before anyone else knows about it. Here's how to do this. Do you have a resume? If you have one, then print up a stack of them. If you don't, that doesn't matter. Is there a printer you can use? What you do is you print up a bunch of papers, maybe print 4 to a page and then cut them up. Put on your name, your phone number, "Wants to work" and then maybe one or two more things, like if you have references, or work experience.

Then you take a stack of these papers and dress nice the way we were talking about, and you start going door to door. You said you wanted to work in [for example] a restaurant, so after school one day you go to all the restaurants around. Even if they're not advertising, even if they don't have a sign up saying they need help. So you go in and what do you say?

Client: I say, "Can I please speak to the manager?"
Therapist: Right. And the manager tells you that they don't need anyone now.
Client: I say, "Can I please fill out an application anyway?"
Therapist: Right. And if the manager says, "We don't have an application"?
Client: I don't know.
Therapist: You hand him one of your pieces of paper. You hold it out until he takes it. Just say, "Well, here's my name and number, maybe if something comes up you can give me a call." And you thank him and go to the next place.

    So here's what happens. Half the time, as soon as you walk out, the manager will take that piece of paper and throw it away. But half the time, he'll stick it on a shelf somewhere and forget about it. So supposing you do this in 20 places one afternoon and another time that week you do it in another 20 places. In the next week or two, what's gonna happen? In one of those places, the dishwasher's going to break his leg, or the cook's helper is going to move to Florida with his girlfriend … Then the boss is going to say, "Damn, I have to hire someone. Put an ad in the paper, answer all those phone calls, schedule interviews, what a pain! Wait a minute! There was this kid in here last week; where did I put that piece of paper?"

What's the boss going to think about someone who came in and gave him that piece of paper when there wasn't even a job opening?

Client: He's going to think: That kid really wants to work!

Therapist: Right. This is a real go-getter, a real hustler. I bet he'll work hard. Maybe I can save all the trouble and just call him up. So this is how you beat the competition: You get there before they do, before there's even a job opening. This is how you give yourself better odds of getting a job. But this strategy isn't for everyone. It takes a lot of work, going from one place to another. And it's easy to get discouraged because when you go to these places, of course they're going to tell you that they don't want you. Some people can't handle being discouraged like that, so this won't work for them. One way to do it is to not be expecting a job that day. If that's your goal, you just get discouraged. But if your goal is to get that piece of paper into 10 people's hands today, then you can accomplish your goal and feel good about it. So I don't know, what do you think about this strategy?

Money Talk

There is no specific moment for this session; however, it's best if you've already completed the Treatment Planning session. You would do the money talk at the moment that the client is wrestling with how to manage, save, spend, and plan around money. Then this is part of helping the client get toward the stated goals.

How to Shop

Let's say you want to buy a TV that's worth $100. Would you rather pay $125, $100, or $75?

Of course you'd rather pay less. Then you have more money for other things.

First, though, let me tell you how to pay more: Get it on credit. Do you know how credit works? They lend you the money, but they charge you plenty for the loan, they call that "interest." The longer you take to pay the loan, the more interest they charge you. So if you buy that TV on a credit card, or on a payment plan from the store, or rent-to-own, how much do you think you've paid by the time it's all paid off? Maybe $125, maybe even $150. Not such a good deal! But sometimes that's worth it to people, to have something right now instead of waiting until they can afford it. The problem is, if that's your strategy, you're always paying so much extra for things, it's hard to save up any money.

So if you only wanted to pay the $100 for the TV, how could you do that? (Just go to the store and buy it.)

Sure. But if you have the cash, why not pay less? How could you do that? (Buy it used; buy it on e-Bay; shop around and buy it on sale.)

It can be helpful to use personal examples, for example if you are wearing some very nice shoes or a nice watch (that anyone would be proud to show) that you got in one of these "bargain" ways.

How Not to Spend

If you don't have a future, it doesn't matter what you do: spend like there's no tomorrow. But you told me you do have a future, and seeing how you've been (going to school, using your self-control skills, etc.) I believe you. To get to your goals, you told me it'll take saving up some money. That doesn't mean you can never spend anything, but if you spend it all, you've got nothing for the future. Do you have any ideas about when you can avoid spending money? Some ideas include self-discipline, walking/biking instead of taking the bus, train or taxi; doing an enjoyable activity that doesn't require cash; giving a smaller gift; etc. Cognitive interventions can also help to make it okay for the client to spend less money. For example:

Therapist: I know you really care about your girlfriend (e.g., mother, grandfather) and want to do something special for her birthday. And she cares about you, too, doesn't she?

Client: Yes, she does; she says she wants to stay together.

Therapist: So is it you she cares for or the gold chain you want to get her?

Client: It's me; she likes the gold chain but it's me she cares for.

Therapist: So do you think she'd want you to blow your savings on a gold chain, if that means you'll have to wait longer to go to college? Or would she rather that you did something else nice for her and started college this coming year?

How to Save

How much are you going to be making in that new job? You told me that you wanted to save up to (buy a car, start your business, go to college, get your own place). What's your idea about how to save up the money?

Do you know how to start a bank account? (You just go there with some money and your ID; they have some forms they'll show you how to fill out. What's the closest bank to where you live? Do you think a savings account would be better for you, or a checking account? Most people like savings accounts better, because they pay a little interest, and because it's not so tempting to write checks and spend the money.)

So when you get your paycheck, if you cash the check and have the money in your pocket, what's going to happen? (Spend it.) What some people do is they set aside a certain amount from every paycheck that goes into the bank. They don't touch it unless there's a real emergency. Then that money builds up, so you can use it for your plans.

If your paycheck is $X, how much do you think would be a good amount to set aside for savings? If the client gives an unrealistically high amount, say, "I don't know, that might be too high. Most people I know, they like to have a little money in their pocket. I'd be worried, if you didn't have any money in your pocket, you might be tempted to go clean the bank out ..." Usually you can help the client to arrive at a reasonable/realistic plan.

Age Variations

With Preteens

Early Warning System and Tease Proofing are the same. You won't have many opportunities for other ones.

With Adults

No variation.

Chapter 9

Reduce Stress

This chapter covers the Reduce Stress session as well as the related sessions that follow, in which the trauma resolution work is done. This chapter does not teach any particular method of trauma resolution, but it does address how to approach and get the client through the trauma resolution phase of treatment within the Fairy Tale model.

Reduce Stress

The Reduce Stress session spans the three major elements of the treatment plan: (1) fence-around; (2) personal training; and (3) slay the dragon. After the usual session-starting routine, the therapist begins by guiding the client to identify (fence-around) strategies to keep bad things from happening—to keep stress from coming along. As in the Avoid High Risk session, a list of time–place–action strategies is made. Then the therapist guides the client to identify (personal training) strategies to catch the stress and cope in a way that reduces the stress and helps the client to regain calm. Another list of strategies is made for the times fence-around was not sufficient and stress came. Finally, the therapist introduces the client to the upcoming (slay the dragon) trauma resolution work and hopefully gets the client to agree to give it a try.

It would be helpful to review the Reduce Stress Session Form (Appendix C) before continuing here.

Everyday Things

The first two parts of the session are straightforward and tend to go both smoothly and quickly. As always, if the client doesn't know what to say, the therapist guides the client with further questions and perhaps menus until the client makes his or her own choices. In general, one or two strategies is too few for a single list; four to six strategies is preferable. The first list should feature behaviors the client can realistically do either on a daily basis or with some frequency. The second list should feature behaviors the client can realistically do either every time he or she is stressed or at least some of the time. We don't expect the client to do all of these behaviors at every opportunity; rather, we are making a list so that the client is aware of his or her choices.

If the client identifies a potential strategy that is not wonderful but is technically acceptable, the therapist should accept it and put it on the list. If the client identifies a strategy that is problematic, the therapist can challenge this by saying, "But didn't you tell me that doing that would take you away from your goals?" Then it is clear that the problem is not that the therapist doesn't like it but that it will interfere with the client's own mission.

The Sore Spot

The most challenging part of the session, and indeed of the whole treatment approach, is getting the client to become willing to face the trauma memories. Even with clients who have made good progress to this point, it can be challenging to get them to be willing to face their trauma memories. Avoidance exists for a reason!

Many clients will reason that they are doing pretty well now without going back to the trauma memories and that it's best to leave well enough alone. Those clients who have made modest but not particularly impressive improvement are also likely to be reluctant to face the trauma memories. Most people do not understand the extent to which healing from trauma and loss is possible, so it can be difficult for them to understand why you would want to put them through pain when they are doing so well. At this point they often feel that they have been as successful as they are likely to be and that treatment should be finished.

Earlier in the development of this treatment approach, we used to lose a much higher percentage of clients at this point—clients who believed that their treatment had been successful and that they were done. We also previously used to lose more clients by going too fast. That happened at various points but most typically when trauma resolution was started. The client would start working on a trauma memory, decide that it was too difficult, and change his or her mind. In such situations, the therapist rarely gets a second chance.

Over the years, to increase client retention and success the following elements of treatment have been added:

■ Completing the Circles and Arrows Case Formulation and Treatment Planning session: Now the case formulation is explained in a graphic format that helps the client to understand how the trauma is related to the presenting problem. Now the client has an explicit treatment plan, including slay the dragon.
■ Using the Treatment Plan form in every subsequent session, which keeps the client focused on making progress on the treatment plan: This also provides

a regular reminder of the role of the trauma memories in the client's problem, even while the focus in a given session may be elsewhere.

■ Predicting the temptation to quit (for those in charge of client's attendance, including in some cases the client himself or herself): This prepares them for the therapist's suggestion, often at this point in treatment, that treatment should be continued through trauma resolution.

■ Implementing the Avoid High Risk session: This builds in some early success and momentum before attempting more challenging types of coping skills.

■ Doing the Reduce Stress session with a trauma resolution sales pitch: The Reduce Stress session adds one more layer of effective, low-challenge coping skills, which help clients to feel successful and in control. This session also provides a transition to slay the dragon and helps to prepare clients for it with a persuasive rationale.

■ Using a personal trainer strategy for selection of trauma resolution memories: This approach to selecting the order of trauma memories to be addressed helps clients to build on their success and reduces the frequency of clients feeling overwhelmed and quitting.

Introducing Slay the Dragon

Many trauma resolution methods stipulate a set way of introducing the method to the client. This typically includes some reminder of the rationale as well as some explanation of what to expect while working on the trauma memory. To the extent that this book's script does not cover the necessary ground, you should still do what your trauma resolution method calls for. However, you should do this script first, and you should do the rest in a way that is consistent with the script's message.

The script provides one example of how to convince the client to go ahead with the next phase of treatment. The script works well with teenaged boys, who tend to appreciate sports. If a sports metaphor is unlikely to work with a particular client, you might want to come up with an alternative metaphor. Even so, your sales pitch should cover the same ground as follows:

■ Highlight the client's success to date.

■ Acknowledge the client's likely and reasonable perception that treatment should be just about finished.

■ Explain what has gone wrong with other, similar clients who terminated treatment at this point. Explain why it went wrong (i.e., because the unresolved trauma's sore spot left the client vulnerable to overwhelming emotional reactions to major stressors).

■ Recommend that the client take care of this vulnerability now, while he or she is strong and doing well, rather than carrying the vulnerability and waiting until a major stressor comes along.

◾ Remind the client that this is your best advice for helping the client, in the long run, to stay on track toward his or her goals.

Once the client is seriously considering this recommendation, the therapist tells the client about the particular method of trauma resolution and explains that it does generally work for other people who are like the client (as per scientific research as well as the therapist's personal experience). To close the deal, the therapist then suggests that the client personally find out if it might work for him or her, by starting with a test run using a minor recent event rather than a major trauma memory from the list. No matter how much sense the therapist has made, many clients remain both nervous and skeptical about the procedure. The prospect of starting with a test run is appealing because it addresses the client's likely final objections: It might be too much, and it might not work for me.

Finally, the therapist reminds the clients of the rules: "What happens if there's something you don't feel like talking about?" The therapist goes on to explain that even though trauma resolution may be planned for the next session the client is not bound to this and can change his or her mind. Personally, I like to tell the clients directly, "Don't go finding some excuse to miss the next session," and say again that they don't have to do this next time and that we have plenty of other things to do. I have found that this reduces my otherwise high no-show rate (even among mandated clients) that would occur when trauma resolution work is anticipated.

In the following session, you'll do the normal session-starting routine. As usual, and especially regarding trauma resolution work, it's important to remind your client about why you are asking him or her to do this activity. Don't think that just because you talked about it last week, the client still knows. People tend to shy away from talking about their trauma memories and can easily forget why it seemed like a good idea when you talked about it before. Clients may feel that bringing up the trauma memory will only make them upset and make things worse for them. Also, clients who are doing better in various ways, often because of your help and guidance, may feel they don't need to talk about the trauma because they're already doing well.

Even if you feel confident you worked all this out last week, remind the client again. You probably don't need to go through the whole sports story all over again, but it may be helpful to refer to it. You'll certainly want to remind the client of the main points that the story is intended to convey.

Target Order

The therapist's suggestion to start small, with a test run, may have already oriented you to one of the primary considerations in selecting an order for targeting trauma memories within the Fairy Tale model. As always, we are the personal trainer, and we do not want to drop that approach just because we are moving to a new phase of treatment. Indeed, because trauma resolution may be the most challenging treatment phase for many clients, it is especially important to keep this strategy foremost. However, other considerations must be made as well, and there is no single correct target order that can be applied across all clients.

Several strategies may be used to decide which trauma memory to address first (assuming, as in most cases, that more than one is listed). Most exposure traditions focus only on the primary identified trauma, that is, the one that apparently precipitated the referral. Another approach, more common with clinicians who use Eye Movement Desensitization and Reprocessing (EMDR), is to go in chronological order, starting with the earliest memory and moving forward. One variant of this approach is to go in chronological order within a certain theme of interest rather than with the entire trauma history. A third strategy, which can also be combined with either of the first two, is to go in order from lower to higher Subjective Units of Distress Scale (SUDS) ratings, that is, from least to most anticipated difficulty. Each strategy has unique benefits and drawbacks.

Go for the "Big One"

This strategy is often used in the exposure tradition. This may be the best choice for clients who were previously high functioning and who had not been exposed to major trauma or loss prior to the primary identified trauma event. One advantage to this strategy is that—if it works—by focusing on only one trauma memory the trauma resolution phase of treatment can be completed relatively quickly. Another advantage to working with the precipitating event memory is that this strategy is relatively easy for clients to understand. If they believe that their problem stems from this event, then it makes sense to them to go after the memory of this event.

However, problems can occur with this approach. For many clients, starting with the big one may prove overwhelming—too much too soon—and backfire by giving the client an upsetting experience that does not lead to feeling better. Also, sometimes when the client starts with a later trauma memory, the trauma resolution work does not go very smoothly because of the influence of untreated earlier memories.

This is a tricky concept but is important to understand. When a client has earlier unprocessed trauma memories, the unprocessed material is kept "behind the wall" and sometimes comes out when triggered by a thematically related stressor. This is the sore spot reaction. When a new trauma event occurs, part of the client's response to the new event will be an overreaction because of the material behind the wall kicking in. The client doesn't know that he or she is overreacting; the client's subjective experience is that the current event warrants this reaction. Later, it works the same way. When we ask for the SUDS rating on that trauma event, some of the reported distress will really be from the sore spot reaction from earlier memories, even though it feels to the client as if it's all related to the identified event.

This is important because when you are trying to help a client process a trauma memory, you want to have a good chance of being successful. When some of the distress attached to the memory is actually from earlier memories that you're not talking about, it's more difficult to get resolution on the memory you are talking about. You can find yourself going through the identified memory over and over, not getting anywhere with it and not knowing why. On the other hand, if the earlier memory is resolved first, the work with the identified memory is likely to go more smoothly (Greenwald, 1999; Greenwald & Schmitt, 2008; Shapiro, 2001).

This was illustrated in the case of Dave, a 34-year-old man who came to treatment complaining of stress on the job for the past 3 years. However, nothing at his work site had changed; everything had been the same for 8 years. It finally came out that his aunt had died 3 years ago. Dave said, "She was like a mother to me, since my own mother died when I was 6." He gave the SUDS rating for the memory of his aunt's death as a 10-plus and the memory of his mother's death as a 4.

Although Dave didn't quite understand why the therapist wanted him to work through the earlier memory (mother's death) first—"that one doesn't bother me"—he agreed to do so on the therapist's suggestion. Working through this memory took three full sessions using EMDR and included considerable intensity of emotion at several points, far more than the initial distress rating of 4. Dave said, "I had no idea that I was still carrying so much pain from that."

Then he faced the more recent memory (aunt's death), which had initially been identified as the primary source of distress. It was still a sad memory, but it took only one session to resolve. There was just not that much left of it once the earlier memory's sore spot reaction had been removed.

Go in Order

This strategy is often used in the EMDR tradition. When more than one significant trauma or loss memory is on the list, often the preferred option is to address each memory in chronological order, starting from age 0 and moving forward. By addressing trauma memories in chronological order, each trauma carries only its own distress burden—no sore spot reaction piled on—and can be more readily resolved. Then when addressing later trauma, the prior traumas have already been resolved so less distress remains.

Go in Order by Theme

This strategy is also often used in the EMDR tradition. This is a symptom-focused approach that, in my opinion, often turns out to be less efficient than hoped for. The technique is to start from either the presenting symptom (e.g., a recent example of having been reactive in a certain situation) or from the major identified trauma and then to have the client "float back" to an earlier memory (as described in Greenwald, 2007). The earlier memory is seen as the "touchstone" (Shapiro, 2001) or source memory—where the sore spot comes from—and is targeted first.

This approach is certainly better in most cases than just going straight for the big one, and it can be a useful strategy in workshop practice sessions, disaster response settings, and other one-shot or short-term therapy opportunities. It can also be cautiously used to address a particularly pressing issue, even if this means going out of the usual target order. It may also be appropriate for otherwise high-functioning, single-trauma clients who are (without the float back) unable to identify any trauma prior to the major identified event. In these situations, going after the source memory can take some of the sting out of the identified memory, which will then be much easier to resolve when the time comes.

On the other hand, the risks entailed in this approach are similar (if less severe) to those entailed in going for the big one. Additional untreated source memories may exist that were not identified in the float back but that contribute to the sore spot underlying the memories targeted for treatment. Then the trauma resolution session is more difficult and more likely to go wrong, either by being too emotionally challenging for the client or by not resolving the memory. Although these challenges can be managed if necessary, it is generally more effective to systematically go in chronological order as described previously.

Personal Trainer Modifications

Finally, with any of these strategies you must also consider whether your client is ready to handle the memory you want to target first. It is often preferable to start with a less distressing trauma memory as a way to help the client become more competent in the method and to gain a track record of success, prior to addressing the more challenging one you might have in mind. For example, what if you want to go in chronological order but the earliest memory on the trauma history list is rated as a 10? Perhaps you'll decide to start with a later memory on the list that has a lower rating to serve as a stepping stone before your client faces the more difficult one. Remember, as the personal trainer you want to give your clients challenges that they can handle. You don't want to offer too great a challenge and invite failure—better to go a step at a time.

Stepping Stone Memories

Targeting memories out of chronological order potentially engenders either of two problems:

1. You risk having a low SUDS memory suddenly become high SUDS as it connects to a more distressing earlier memory (Shapiro, 2001).
2. The low SUDS memory might be very difficult to work through to resolution if much of the unresolved material is actually from an earlier memory that is not being accessed (Greenwald, 2005a).

How do you select a stepping stone memory—a later memory with lower SUDS—that does not incur the problem of being difficult or unresolvable because of the sore spots from earlier memories? The following are the strategies (in order) that tend to work best.

Test Run with Recent Minor Upsetting Memory

For the first (and second) stepping stone, it's often best to start with a recent minor upsetting event, as opposed to a major event from the list. The same principles guiding the selection of a recent example for the Choices Have Consequences exercise (Chapter 7) apply here. You want something recent that would not count as a major trauma and that involves peers, strangers, or authority figures rather than immediate family members. Furthermore, ideally this recent event will not be one event in an ongoing series of similar events with the same person. Selecting a memory with these features gives it the best chance of resolving relatively quickly and easily with the trauma resolution procedure, generally without undue difficulty and without sliding into other more significant prior memories. This gives the client a safe way to try slaying the dragon and begin to develop a good track record of success with it. This track record helps the client to be willing to try slaying the dragon with a more significant memory on the trauma list.

Discrete Major Trauma Memory

When you're ready to tackle the trauma list, if you still need a stepping stone you'll want to identify a discrete memory—that is, a memory that is not thematically related to the other more challenging memories. All losses are thematically related, so if someone has lost many family members, do not attempt to slay the dragon with the memory of a dead pet as a stepping stone. It won't work. Similarly, if a major trauma occurred at the hands of a certain person, anything else that occurred with that person is thematically related. So if your client was severely beaten by a family member, do not attempt to slay the dragon with the memory of a minor discipline incident with that same family member as a stepping stone. It won't work. Likewise, for a teasing, harassment, or bullying memory that was only one of a long series. You get the idea.

Looking for a stepping stone memory does limit your options. Often you'll end up with an auto accident or some other fluke trauma event that is not thematically related to the other events. Even then, of course the helplessness for example in the auto accident will be thematically related to the helplessness from the earlier trauma that you don't want to touch yet. In fact, this is true for any of the stepping stone targets. Even discrete targets are never 100% discrete. However, all we can do is our best. And at least these discrete stepping stone targets have a much better chance of being resolvable and of not sliding into other more challenging memories.

Selecting the order of trauma memories for dragon slaying is guided by clinical judgment and perhaps by the unique features of your preferred trauma resolution method:

- Go for the big one and the hope of quick relief?
- Try a float back and work on a focused theme?
- Use a systematic approach and go chronologically?
- Start small and build up, slower but safer?

Fortunately, order selection is not a single make-or-break decision. The therapist is constantly presenting just-manageable challenges to the client and supporting the client's capacity to manage them. If the challenge is handled well, the therapist can introduce greater challenges; conversely, if the challenge proves too difficult, the therapist can help the client to contain the memory, relax, and back off. Then the therapist will know to go more slowly for a while so the client can build up skills and strength, be successful, and get back on a track of making progress.

This phase of treatment is continued ideally until all trauma memories on the list have been resolved. If you don't have the opportunity to get through the whole list, hopefully you will at least get though the most significant events. But it's better to get through everything because then the sore spot is smaller and the client has a better chance of getting to his or her goals.

Age Variations

With Preteens

The personal trainer target order for preteens can include an additional step. After trying a recent minor upsetting event and before choosing a stepping stone memory from the list, you might work on a current bad dream, if such a target is available and if you are using EMDR. Kids find bad dreams distressing and are glad to get rid of them. In the following session, do not ask if any bad dreams occurred; ask if *that* bad dream came back (then you'll get an answer indicating success). If it did come back, it will be a "resolution dream" and not the same as when it was distressing.

Another option with preteens is to use incentives to encourage them to get through the trauma resolution work. You will still use the same care in selecting the order of memories to target. But the use of incentives, whether provided in session or via the family, can be helpful if the client is otherwise refusing to do this work. Of course you would not want to use such large incentives that the effect would be coercive. Fortunately, small or modest incentives are often sufficient to tip the balance toward willingness.

With Adults

No variation.

Session 8: Reduce Stress Plus Sex Talk

Mr. G: Hi, tell me something good and something bad.

Alex: Good, Alicia said she'll go out with me; also I got an 85 on my math test.

Mr. G: She said she'll go out with you like to a movie or like be your girlfriend?

Alex: Be my girl; we're going out now.

Mr. G: Cool! And did you also go with her to the movies? You told me you were going to ask her.

Alex: Yeah, we went.

Mr. G: She doesn't mind that you're in OCFS [the state program that has legal custody of Alex]?

Alex: She don't like it, but she likes me. She says as long as I stay out of trouble she'll stick with me.

Mr. G: Sounds like she might really care for you.

Alex: I think, maybe.

Mr. G: And what's with this math test?

Alex: Oh yeah. It wasn't so hard; I studied.

Mr. G: I bet your teacher doesn't even know what to do with you.

Alex: That's his problem.

Mr. G: What about something bad?

Alex: She says I can't go over [to her apartment] when her father is home. He don't like me, so she didn't tell him we're going out. I'm going over tonight because he's not there.

Mr. G: Tonight like all night?

Alex: Nah, just until maybe 9 at night, so I can be gone before he gets home.

Mr. G: Will anyone else be there?

Alex: No, because she doesn't want them to know.

Mr. G: I'm not saying you're going to have sex tonight, but just in case, do you have condoms?

Alex: You're not gonna give me that AIDS thing, are you? I had to take all those health classes upstate; I heard all about it.

Mr. G: Good. So do you have condoms?

Alex: Yeah.

Mr. G: Where?

Alex: In my jacket pocket.

Mr. G: Let me see. (Alex pulls two condoms from one of his pockets.) Good. Will you have that jacket with you tonight?

Alex: Yes.

Mr. G: Good. In this kind of situation, would you usually use a condom?

Alex: That depends.

Mr. G: On what?

Alex: Well, I haven't been with a girl for a long time. But before, if the girl said, "We don't need it," I'm, like, "Good." It don't feel so nice when it's wrapped up.

Mr. G: And now that you've been to all those health classes and now that you have goals you're working toward?

Alex: Should prob'ly wrap it. Anyway, I don't want to get no girl pregnant.

Mr. G: You know how that goes. Then you've gotta work at just anything for money to support the baby. But you told me you wanted to start your own restaurant, right?

Alex: Yeah.

Mr. G: Well, that takes a lot of up-front money. A single guy who's working, he can save money. But a guy with a baby? Not so easy.

Alex: I know; I said I would use it.

Mr. G: So what if you told Alicia that you want to use a condom, what would she say?

Alex: Alicia, she prob'ly say the same thing.

Mr. G: Sounds like she has her own goals?

Alex: Yeah, she wants to go to college and everything.

Mr. G: Well, just imagine that you said you want to use a condom and she said, "It's okay, you don't have to do that with me." What could you tell her then?

Alex: I could say, like, "I really care about you and everything, but I don't want nothing bad to happen like you getting pregnant or nothing."

Mr. G: That sounds like a good start. And could you explain why you don't want her to get pregnant?

Alex: Yeah, because she wants to go to college, and I want to start a restaurant, you can't do all that with a baby.

Mr. G: So you could tell her about how you don't want to risk getting pregnant cause it would mess up your goals?

Alex: Yeah.

Mr. G: And maybe if she cares about you, she'll do this to help you get to your goals?

Alex: Yeah.

Mr. G: And if she still said, "It's okay, we don't need to use that," would that mean that she cared about you and what's important to you or doesn't really care, just wants a good time?

Alex: If she said that, I guess she don't care.

Mr: G: So would you want to have a baby with someone who doesn't even care about you? Risk your whole future for a few feel-good minutes with someone like that?

Alex: No. But she won't say that; I think she does care about me.

Mr. G: I hope you're right. Anyway, it sounds like you're ready for whatever she might say.

Alex: I don't think it's gonna go that way anyway. She's not so fast like some of the girls I was with before.

Mr. G: Well, if this is someone you care about, maybe you don't have to be in a hurry anyway.

Alex: No, I'm trying to go slow with her, not mess things up.

Mr. G: That sounds like a good idea. (Pulls out treatment plan) Last week we talked about self-control skills. How have you been doing with that?

Alex: Good, I been doing good.

Mr. G: So is it okay if we talk about reducing stress? That's what's next.

Alex: Okay.

Mr. G: This has some different parts to it. The first part is to make a list of things you can do every day to keep yourself on a good track so the stress doesn't pile up. What kinds of things can you think of, or do you already do?

Alex: I don't know; I guess just do what I have to do—stay away from trouble.

Mr. G: That's part of it. Let me give you some examples of things other kids have told me, see if that gives you any more ideas. Some kids say they have to get enough sleep so they feel good and don't get tired and irritated. Some kids say they like to listen to music every day or get some exercise to stay feeling good.

Alex: I don't really need so much sleep. I can be up half the night and I'm still fine the next day.

Mr. G: Okay, so what kind of things work best to keep you on a good track?

Alex: I like to listen to my music; that's good, keeps me chillin.

Mr. G: Okay, listen to music, what else?

Alex: Get my homework out of the way so I don't have to worry about it.

Mr. G: Okay, what else?

Alex: I like a nice breakfast. Some people they just have a cup of coffee, but me, I like a big breakfast.

Mr. G: What do you have?

Alex: Beans, rice, eggs, a real breakfast.

Mr. G: Okay, what else?

Alex: I like to play hoop, but that's not every day; I have to come here most days.

Mr. G: That's okay; it doesn't have to be every single day to be a good strategy for you. What's good about playing hoop?

Alex: Get my energy out, get my anger out.

Mr. G: Okay. What else?

Alex: Be with my girl.

Mr. G: Like at school?

Alex: School, wherever, yeah.

Mr. G: Okay. Anything else?

Alex: Can't think of anything.

Mr. G: That's a pretty good list; looks like you've got a lot of ways to keep yourself on a good track. The next part of reducing stress is to catch yourself when you notice that the stress is building up and do something to bring it down again. What kinds of things work for you to get yourself to feel good again when you are already stressed?

Alex: I don't know, just get my mind off it, think about something else.

Mr. G: How do you do that?

Alex: Maybe listen to music, or play a video game, or just talk to someone about something else.

Mr. G: Okay, what else might work for you to help bring the stress down?

Alex: Talk to someone, get it off my chest.

Mr. G: Like talk to who?

Alex: My grandmother.

Mr. G: Okay, what else might work?

Alex: Can't really think of anything else.

Mr. G: Some kids tell me that exercise helps. Would that work for you?

Alex: Yeah, if I can play hoop, I'm good.

Mr. G: So if you notice that you're stressed, you have a few good strategies to bring it back down.

Alex: Yeah.

Mr. G: These strategies, these are things you already do or things that maybe you'll try to do more?

Alex: I already do them, but maybe I'll try to do them more.

Mr. G: It's been good to hear how well you've been doing, how well things have been going for you. A lot of the things you said you would do to get to your goals, you've been doing it; you're on track.

Supposing you're on a basketball team, you're one of the key players, you're halfway through the season, and your team is winning every game, and not just by a little. Then your coach says, "I want you to start coming to practice an hour early, do more workouts." Why would he say that?

Alex: I don't know. Doesn't make sense.

Mr. G: I think your coach wants to go all the way. Who are you going to be playing in the playoffs?

Alex: Oh—the teams from the other leagues, they been winning their games too; some of those teams will be pretty good.

Mr. G: So are you going to tell your coach, "No, I don't need to do that. If we start losing games in the playoffs, then I'll practice more?"

Alex: No way; I want to go all the way too. I'm gonna do what the coach says.

Mr. G: Years ago, when I was working with someone like you, he's doing what he has to do, avoiding high risks, controlling his anger, doing well in school. I'd shake his hand and say "Good work. Have a good life." But then, 2 months later or a year later he'd be back.

Here's what happened. The every day challenges, he had gotten pretty good at handling those and staying on track. But sooner or later, something bigger came along. Maybe he cared about a girl and then she cheated on him, maybe someone in his family died—you know how things happen.

Alex: Things do happen. If it's not one thing, it's something else.

Mr. G: Remember when we talked about that sore spot from the past experiences and how it makes reactions extra strong? So if something happens that makes you this mad (hands about 2 inches apart) and it hits a sore spot, how mad do you get?

Alex: Maybe like this (holds hands about a foot apart).

Mr. G: Right, a lot more. So with the everyday stresses, he could handle it, even with that sore spot reaction. But when something really big came along, maybe this bad (holds hands about a foot apart), with that sore spot there, it was like this (holds hands about 3 feet apart). That was too much stress, and he got off his track, went back to his old ways.

So this is like your situation right now. You're doing pretty well with the challenges that are coming your way. You're going strong, you're winning your games. So now, while you're strong, this is a good time for you to do the extra training so that when the big challenges come your way, you'll be strong enough for those, too. That make sense?

Alex: Yeah, it makes sense.

Mr. G: So my suggestion for this part of reducing stress, we would go after some of those memories on that list of worst things, one memory at a time. There's a special way of talking about it—you know how I have you move your eyes sometimes?

Alex: Yeah, that's corny.

Mr. G: You would be moving your eyes like that while you think about the worst part of the bad memory. Every once in a while, we stop and I would ask you what you noticed. And you would tell me maybe that the picture is getting stronger, or weaker, or the same, or that you're getting more mad, or sad, or relaxed, or that you just thought of something else. I never know what you're going to say next; we just kind of trust your brain to know what the next step is. It's kind of like your brain is chewing it up, bite by bite, and digesting it and putting it into the past. Most kids tell me they don't like doing this because it hurts their feelings to think about that stuff. But they also tell me that afterward, the memory feels more like old news, doesn't really hurt as much. And they also say they don't get so mad anymore. What do you think about that?

Alex: I don't know if I really want to talk about that stuff. I don't think it'll help. I mean, no offense or nothing, it's probably good for other people. I just don't think it'll work for me.

Mr. G: It does work for most people. I've probably done it myself with more than 200 kids. It doesn't work once in a while, like if someone changes his mind and decides to stop before it's done. But for most of the kids, if they hang in there, they come out better on the other side.

Alex: Like I said, I believe you and everything; I just don't know if it'll work for me.

Mr. G: I don't know either. I think it will, but I can't promise 100% guarantee. So my suggestion would be to do a kind of a test run on some little thing—nothing big from the list but just some little thing that happened. Then you can see how it goes for you and then you can decide whether to try it on the serious stuff.

Alex: That sounds okay.

Mr. G: So next time we meet, maybe we do a test run and you see what you think. And if we get to something you don't feel like talking about, you know what happens, right?

Alex: I know; we don't talk about it.

Mr. G: Right. So tell me something you liked about this meeting and something you didn't like.

Alex: I like that you see how good I'm doing. Not everyone sees that, like Ms. Burns—she says, "Why wasn't you here at 3:30 instead of 3:45?" even though I got here as fast as I could from school. I don't run the trains; sometimes they fast sometimes they slow. Some people always looking for what you do wrong.

Mr. G: And what you didn't like?

Alex: The AIDS lecture; I heard that enough already. But you did give me some good ideas about how to say things.

Mr. G: I think you figured it out for yourself pretty much. What's next for you now?

Alex: Ms. Burns asked me to help her clean out the supply closet. I bet she gives me some extra snack, too. She did that once before when I helped with something.

Mr. G: Good luck. See you next week.

Alex: See you.

Session 8: Reduce Stress Plus Sex Talk, Official Notes

■ Today talked about safe sex.

■ Mainly focused on reducing stress by doing everyday things to feel good (and to keep things from going bad or becoming stressful) and doing things, when already stressed, to calm down. Reviewed strategies for each of these, including some he is already doing as well as suggestions for other methods.

■ Introduced the idea of trying trauma resolution work to bring down the sore spot stress from old upsetting memories.

Session 8: Reduce Stress Plus Sex Talk, Therapist's Personal Notes

- Sex talk.
- Reduce stress.

Everyday Things

To Keep Feeling Good

- Do what I have to do.
- Listen to music.
- Get homework done.
- Eat a good breakfast.
- Be with a girl.

To Bring the Stress Down

- Get my mind off it—play music, play video games, talk about something else.
- Talk to my grandmother.
- Play hoop.

Intro to EMDR; plan to start with test run next time (?).

Session 9: Trauma Resolution

Mr. G: Hi, tell me something good and something bad.

Alex: Something good, things are going good with Alicia. Something bad, my math teacher got in my face again today. Also my Pops wants me to work more hours, but I gotta be sitting around here all the time.

Mr. G: Hmm. How have you been doing in school?

Alex: Good, I go every day, I didn't skip a class, I bring in my homework, I'm passing all my classes.

Mr. G: And your program here?

Alex: Good. They complain I'm late sometimes from school, but it's not my fault. I do everything I'm supposed to do, I participate in the groups, I talk to you, and my urine has been clean every time since that first time.

Mr. G: When does your Pops want you to work?

Alex: He says I can work there as soon as I get home from school for maybe 2 hours every day. They close at 6 [p.m.].

Mr. G: Why don't you talk to Ms. Burns and see if she'll let you go, at least some of the days?

Alex: I don't know if she'll listen to me. Would you talk to her?

Mr. G: I can if you want, but I think it works better if you do. If you're man enough to work, you ought to be man enough to stand up for yourself and ask for your chance.

Alex: Yeah, I guess.

Mr. G: But you can tell her to talk to me if you want. Here's what I would tell her: That you're working hard with me, I think you're really trying to do good, and that I think having more chance to work would be good for you. I would also tell her that she shouldn't just let you go; she should have some way of making sure you still get your homework done. Because it wouldn't make sense to work a little and then have school get all messed up. So what do you think of what I would say to her?

Alex: Sounds good; maybe she listen to you.

Mr. G: So if she asks you, what's your plan to make sure you get your homework done?

Alex: I get most of it done in study hall [during school] anyway.

Mr. G: And the rest?

Alex: Maybe make a deal with my Pops that I can't start work until the homework is done?

Mr. G: I think Ms. Burns would think that was a good plan. So you gonna talk to her?

Alex: Yeah, I will, when we're done here.

Mr. G: And what's up with Alicia?

Alex: Yeah, it's going good. She's not like other girls. I can talk to her like to a friend.

Mr. G: That's something.

Alex: I think she's the one for me.

Mr. G: Now I'm going to try to ask a rude question in a polite way. If you needed to use the condom, did you?

Alex: You mean did we have sex? I didn't go that night anyway; her father was going to be home early. But I told her about my plans. She told me hers too. We're kind of making plans together.

Mr. G: Wow. It sounds like it's going really well. Any progress with her father?

Alex: Well, he knows we're going out, because we talk on the phone every night. She says he isn't happy about it, but he doesn't say too much. She told him I'm doing better, staying out of trouble.

Mr. G: Well, I hope it keeps going well. Is there anything coming up that you're worried about or looking forward to?

Alex: The quarter [school term] is over next week, so we have all our finals coming up.

Mr. G: How's that going to be for you?

Alex: I'm not sure. I think I'll do okay, but I don't know. I never had to study so much before; I'm not really used to it.

Mr. G: Well, if Ms. Burns gives you trouble about wanting to work more days instead of coming here, maybe she'll listen more if she sees some good grades after next week.

Alex: Yeah, maybe. I think I'll do okay.

Mr. G: (pulls out treatment plan) Let's see, we've been talking about the things you can do to get to your goals, last time we talked about reducing stress. How've you been doing with that?

Alex: Good, I guess. Everything's going good for me now.

Mr. G: And when your math teacher got in your face, how did you handle it?

Alex: I didn't let him mess me up.

Mr. G: What did you do?

Alex: I didn't say nothing; I just waited for him to be done, and then he left me alone again.

Mr. G: So you handled it pretty well.

Alex: I told you, I'm doing good.

Mr. G: So if you remember that now, when he was in your face today, how bad is the feeling right now, on 0 to 10?

Alex: 5. It still pisses me off. He's supposed to be there to help kids, not to mess with them.

Mr. G: And next summer when you remember that, how bad will it be on 0 to 10?

Alex: In the summer? A 1—if I even remember.

Mr. G: So it makes you mad now but it's not really serious, like the memories on that worst things list?

Alex: Right. It's not really serious.

Mr. G: Last week we were talking about how you could bring your stress down from those old memories so you would be stronger for your goals.

Alex: Huh?

Mr. G: Remember I told you about a special way of talking about those bad memories from your list?

Alex: Oh yeah, right.

Mr. G: But we decided to start with a small memory for a test run, to see how it goes for you. How about we use what happened today with the math teacher for the test run?

Alex: I don't think that's a good idea. I'm good now; talking about that will just make me heated again.

Mr. G: It might at first. But if you hang in there a little while, usually it gets better after that.

Alex: I don't know. I get heated up, maybe I go do something stupid, mess things up for myself. I think it's better to leave it alone.

Mr. G: I see what you're saying, and maybe usually you'd be right. But this special way of talking about it is different. Let me ask you a question. I've given you other suggestions before, things that you've tried out. How have those things gone for you?

Alex: Pretty good, really.

Mr. G: I think this one'll go good, too. But just in case, let's make an agreement. If you feel like you're heated up, then you don't leave this room until you feel okay again, until you feel calm. Because I don't want you to leave here heated, either. Okay?

Alex: Okay, I guess I'll give it a try, see how it goes.

Mr. G: Okay. First I want you to practice how to take a break, though, in case you need a break. How does a cop stop traffic with his hand?

Alex: (puts hand up facing forward)

Mr. G: Right. So I'm going to move my hand back and forth, and you make me stop like that with your hand.

(Mr. G moves hand back and forth, Alex puts his hand up, Mr. G stops.)

Mr. G: Good. Let's try it again.

(Mr. G moves hand back and forth, Alex puts his hand up, Mr. G stops.)

Mr. G: Okay. So if you just want to take a break, you know what to do. Now I want you to concentrate on the worst moment from what happened today; you got the picture?

Alex: Yeah. He's right in my face.

Mr. G: What thought goes with that picture? What are you saying to yourself?

Alex: I can't do anything; he's the teacher.

Mr. G: Would it be something like, "I'm helpless" or "I'm powerless"?

Alex: Yeah.

Mr. G: Which one is the best? Which fits the most?

Alex: I'm powerless.

Mr. G: Next time you remember this, what would you rather be saying to yourself?

Alex: He's an asshole.

Mr. G: And what would you like to believe about yourself?

Alex: I can do whatever it takes to get to my goals.

Mr. G: When you concentrate on the picture of what happened and say that to yourself, how true does it feel on a scale of 1 to 7, where 1 is false and 7 is true?

Alex: Like a 4.

Mr. G: And when you concentrate on the picture and "I'm powerless," what emotion comes up?

Alex: Mad.

Mr. G: Where do you feel it?

Alex: All over.

Mr. G: And how bad is it now from 0 to 10?

Alex: 6.

Mr. G: I'm going to ask you to concentrate on the memory while I move my hand and you move your eyes. After a little while, we'll stop and talk about it. Sometimes things will change, and sometimes they won't. There are no "supposed to's." Just let whatever happens happen, and we will talk about it. Just tell me what comes up, even if it doesn't seem important. You remember the stop signal, right?

Alex: Yeah.

Mr. G: Okay. So get back the picture, what you're saying to yourself, where you feel it. Ready? (EM) Now take a deep breath. Okay. So what came up? What did you notice?

Alex: It makes me mad.

Mr. G: Concentrate on that now. (EM) What came up this time?

Alex: More mad. I don't think this is working.

Mr. G: Actually, it's going well. I told you that sometimes you feel worse for a little while. You're doing good. So get that back, got it? (EM) What came up this time?

Alex: A little more relaxed now.

Mr. G: Go with that. (EM) What came up?

Alex: A teacher shouldn't act like that. The man has a problem.

Mr. G: Go with that. (EM) What came up?

Alex: He shouldn't go taking out his problems on the kids. He supposed to be helping us.

Mr. G: Go with that. (EM) What came up?

Alex: I bet he got problems at home, too. Act like that, won't nobody like him.

Mr. G: Go with that. (EM) What came up?

Alex: I just feel sorry for him.

Mr. G: Go with that. (EM) What came up?

Alex: Still, he shouldn't be acting like that; he should be doing his job.

Mr. G: Go with that. (EM) What came up?

Alex: I'm doing my job. I'm not the one with the problem.

Mr. G: Go with that. (EM) What came up?

Alex: I'm getting a B+ in his class. What he on my case for?

Mr. G: Go with that. (EM) What came up?

Alex: I ain't gonna let him mess me up. I can do what I have to do.

Mr. G: Go with that. (EM) What came up?

Alex: I'm gonna move on, graduate high school, have my restaurant, my girl, and he's still gonna be his sorry self, stuck right there in his math class.

Mr. G: Go with that. (EM) What came up?

Alex: Nothing.

Mr. G: So if you go back to the incident you started with, what do you get now?

Alex: Nothing.

Mr. G: I mean like what's the picture, what are you saying to yourself, what's the emotion?

Alex: I can do what I have to do. I'm just glad I'm me and not him.

Mr. G: And where are you now on 0 to 10?

Alex: 0. This is cool!

Mr. G: So concentrate on the incident, ready? (EM) What came up?

Alex: Nothing.

Mr. G: Is it a little better now, a little worse, or about the same as a minute ago?

Alex: A little better.

Mr. G: Concentrate on it again. (EM) A little better, a little worse, the same?

Alex: The same this time.

Mr. G: Concentrate on it again. (EM) Better, worse, the same?

Alex: The same.

Mr. G: Do you remember what you wanted to be saying to yourself, "I can do whatever it takes to do to get to my goals"—is that still what you want to say? Or is there something better?

Alex: I can do what I have to do.

Mr. G: So concentrate on the incident and say those words out loud.

Alex: I can do what I have to do.

Mr. G: How true does that feel now, from 1 false to 7 true?

Alex: 7.

Mr. G: Concentrate on the incident and say those words to yourself. (EM) What came up?

Alex: That's it. I can do what I have to do.

Mr. G: Does it feel more true this time, less true, or the same?

Alex: The same.

Mr. G: Concentrate again on the incident and the words. (EM) More true, less true, the same?

Alex: The same.

Mr. G: Now I want you to concentrate on the incident, the words "I can do what I have to do," and check all through your body, for any discomfort or tension.

Alex: I don't feel anything.

Mr. G: Well, you did it! That was your test run. How did it go for you?

Alex: That was cool! I thought talking about it would just make me more mad. Now it's like it's just gone. I mean I can still remember it, but it doesn't matter.

Mr. G: That's what I was trying to tell you. But it's better that you found out for yourself. So you think you might try that with some of those memories on your list? Try to bring the stress down?

Alex: Yeah, I think it's good. I'll do it.

Mr. G: Okay, we can plan to do one of the memories on the list next time. But remember, if you don't feel like doing it next time, we don't do it. Or even if we start and you change your mind, then we stop. So you better show up even if you don't feel like doing this—we'll just do something else, no big deal.

Alex: I have to come anyway.

Mr. G: I know. I just don't want any excuses.

Alex: No problem.

Mr. G: So tell me something you liked from today's meeting and something you didn't like.

Alex: I liked we made the memory go away. I didn't like the thing with moving my eyes.

Mr. G: What's next for you?

Alex: I'm gonna try to talk with Ms. Burns about my job, if she's not busy with something.

Mr. G: Good luck with that. And you can tell her to ask me if she wants to.

Alex: Thanks.

Mr. G: See you.

Alex: See you.

Session 9: Trauma Resolution, Official Notes

Did a test run of EMDR today, focusing on a recent minor upsetting event. This went well and he reported feeling better about what happened—that it doesn't bother him anymore.

Session 9: Trauma Resolution, Therapist's Personal Notes

- Things going good with Alicia—plans together.
- Wants to work weekday afternoons—still get homework done? Permission to work instead of coming to program? I said need plan for homework—he said get it done before work every day.
- Finals next week.
- EMDR with recent small t [minor upsetting event, not a "big t" major trauma]—teacher in face.
- SUDS started at 6 and ended at 0; went well.
- Next time ask about work deal, finals.
- Memory from list—uncle? Jumped?

Session 9: Questions and Answers

Q: What was that thing you were doing, teaching him to stop by putting his hand up? Why not just use the same old thing where he says he doesn't want to talk about it?

A: That's a technique that's specific to EMDR to help the client feel in control. For questions specifically pertaining to EMDR techniques, I will refer you to other sources (e.g., Greenwald, 1999, 2007) for the details. EMDR happens to be the "sword" used in this case, and I wanted you to see the entire transcript, so there it is. However, the focus of this book is not on a particular method of slaying the dragon but on trauma resolution issues (in this stage) more generally.

Session 10: More Trauma Resolution

Mr. G: Hi, tell me something good and something bad.

Alex: Good, Ms. Burns is gonna let me work for my Pops if I pass all my classes.

Mr. G: Good for you! How many days?

Alex: I'll still have to come here one day a week, to talk to Ms. Burns and to talk to you and to get tested. But the other days I can work.

Mr. G: When do you get your grades?

Alex: I think next Monday.

Mr. G: You pretty sure you'll be passing everything?

Alex: Yeah, pretty sure. The finals are kind of hard, but I think I passed everything so far.

Mr. G: Did you talk with her about making sure to get your homework done before you started your job each day?

Alex: Yeah, I told her that first; I think she liked that. She didn't give me no trouble about it; I was surprised. Just said okay.

Mr. G: Looks like you're getting some respect for how you've been doing. So you'll be pretty busy and making a little more money. What are you going to do with it?

Alex: I gotta get some clothes, some new sneakers. Also I'm gonna take Alicia out Friday night.

Mr. G: Where to?

Alex: To the movies.

Mr. G: What are you gonna see?

Alex: I don't know. We'll decide when we get there.

Mr. G: And tell me something bad.

Alex: All those tests at school.

Mr. G: Is there anything coming up that you're either worried about or looking forward to?

Alex: Friday night. Also I got one more test to go.

Mr. G: Last time you were here, we talked about the time that teacher got in your face. Since we talked about it, did you think about it?

Alex: I forgot about it.

Mr. G: And if you make yourself remember it now, just for a second, how bad is the feeling now from 0 to 10?

Alex: Still a 0.

Mr. G: So how is it in math class now?

Alex: It's okay. I just say to myself, "You do what you gotta do; I'll do what I gotta do." I don't let him mess me up.

Mr. G: So you think talking about it last week helped?

Alex: I think so. Now I just feel sorry for him; he doesn't really get to me no more.

Mr. G: We've been talking about things you can do to get stronger toward your goals. You've been doing a lot; last week we did that test run on talking about the bad memories. Is it okay now to talk about one from the list?

Alex: Which one?

Mr. G: I was thinking of starting with the first one that you said was really bad: when your uncle died.

Alex: Um … Yeah, okay.

Mr. G: You remember the stop signal?

Alex: Yeah.

Mr. G: Good. Now I want to ask you a question. I understand that this really happened, but just for a minute imagine that the whole thing was a bad dream and you had to be back in that dream for a little while. What would you need so that you would be okay?

Alex: My grandmother.

Mr. G: So picture your grandmother, what she says or does, what it feels like to be with her. You have the picture in your mind?

Alex: (nods)

Mr. G: Concentrate on that. (EM) How did that go?

Alex: Good. She's just holding me, telling me everything's gonna be okay.

Mr. G: Concentrate on it again. (EM) Okay. The thing is, when this happened, you were just a little kid, you were stuck in the situation. But now it's over, so all that's left is what's in your brain. So now your brain is in charge, okay? We're going to trust your brain to know just what to do, to digest this memory bite by bite. If your brain wants to bring in your grandmother, fine; if not, fine.

Alex: I never thought of it like that—that it's just in my brain. That's weird.

Mr. G: Now, from when your uncle died, what picture represents the worst moment, the worst part?

Alex: At the funeral, everybody crying.

Mr. G: What negative belief about yourself goes with that picture?

Alex: Huh?

Mr. G: When you see this picture, is there anything you're saying bad about yourself?

Alex: I don't know, not really.

Mr. G: Like maybe, "I'm helpless" or "I'm not important" or "It was my fault" or "I'm all alone" or something like that?

Alex: I'm not important, I'm nobody. It's like I'm invisible, like I'm not even there.

Mr. G: And next time you remember this, what would you like to be able to believe about yourself?

Alex: They do care for me—they was just having a bad time.

Mr. G: So maybe something like, "I am important" or "I deserve to be cared for"?

Alex: Yeah.

Mr. G: What fits the best?

Alex: I am important.

Mr. G: When you see the picture and say the words, "I am important," how true does that feel from 1 false to 7 true?

Alex: Like a 2 or 3.

Mr. G: When you see the picture and say the words, "I'm not important," what emotion comes up?

Alex: Sad, mad.

Mr. G: Where do you feel it in your body?

Alex: In my face.

Mr. G: How bad is it now on 0 to 10?

Alex: It's a 9.

Mr. G: Okay, ready? (EM) What came up? What did you notice?

Alex: Just everyone crying. Now it's a 10.

Mr. G: Go with that. (EM) What came up?

Alex: Same thing.

Mr. G: Go with that. (EM) What came up?

Alex: Same thing. Still a 10. This isn't going so good.

Mr. G: It can be hard, but you're doing well. Can you hang in there a little more?

Alex: Yeah, I guess so.

Mr. G: Okay, get it back, ready? (EM) What came up?

Alex: Same thing. This isn't working.

Mr. G: Would this be a good time to bring in your grandmother?

Alex: Yeah, I think so.

Mr. G: So picture your grandmother there with you. (EM) What came up?

Alex: She told me everything's gonna be okay.

Mr. G: Go with that. (EM) What came up?

Alex: It's gonna be okay.

Mr. G: Go with that. (EM) What came up?

Alex: I just remembered playing with my cousins after the funeral. We were running around and laughing and some people were giving us dirty looks and telling us to stop it, but one of my other uncles he said it was okay, he made them leave us alone, let us play. We were just little kids; we didn't know any better.

Mr. G: Go with that. (EM) What came up?

Alex: Nothing.

Mr. G: Go back to the incident you started with. What do you get now?

Alex: It's the same, but it's only like a 4 now.

Mr. G: Concentrate on that. (EM) What came up?

Alex: More sad now.

Mr. G: Go with that. (EM) What came up?

Alex: Sad.

Mr. G: Go with that. (EM) What came up?

Alex: Nothing.

Mr. G: Get back the incident you started with. What do you get now?

Alex: I can still see it, but it's not so strong now.

Mr. G: What are you saying to yourself now?

Alex: Nothing.

Mr. G: What emotion comes up?

Alex: No emotion.

Mr. G: Where are you now on 0 to 10?

Alex: About a 2.

Mr. G: Where do you feel that?

Alex: Here (touches throat).

Mr. G: Concentrate on that. (EM) What came up?

Alex: It just wasn't right that they didn't take better care of us kids. I mean, I know they were upset and everything, but still, we were just little kids; we didn't understand nothing.

Mr. G: Go with that. (EM) What came up?

Alex: I guess they did the best they could do. It's okay.

Mr. G: Go with that. (EM) What came up?

Alex: Nothing.

Mr. G: Get back the incident you started with. What do you get now?

Alex: Nothing; it's done.

Mr. G: What are you saying to yourself now?

Alex: Nothing. It's okay now.

Mr. G: What emotion comes up?

Alex: None.

Mr. G: Where are you now on 0 to 10?

Alex: 0.

Mr. G: Okay, concentrate on it again. (EM) What came up?

Alex: Nothing.

Mr. G: Is it a little better this time, a little worse, about the same?

Alex: The same.

Mr. G: Is "I'm important" still the right thing to say, or is something else better?

Alex: It's okay now.

Mr. G: Get back the incident you started with, and say the words "It's okay now."

Alex: It's okay now.

Mr. G: How true does that feel, from 1 false to 7 true?

Alex: 7, all the way.

Mr. G: Concentrate on the incident and on those words. (EM) What came up?

Alex: It's okay.

Mr. G: Does that feel more true this time, less true, about the same?

Alex: The same.

Mr. G: Concentrate on it again, the incident and the words. (EM) More true, less true, the same?

Alex: The same.

Mr. G: Now I want you to concentrate on the incident, the words "It's okay now," and check all through your body for any discomfort or tension.

Alex: I don't feel anything.

Mr. G: Congratulations. You just made it through one of the big memories on your list. How did that go for you?

Alex: It didn't start out too good, but after a while it went okay. It's weird though.

Mr. G: Do you think it'll stay a 0, or do you think the bad feeling will come back?

Alex: I think it'll stay 0. I'm done with it.

Mr. G: I guess we'll see. Listen, your brain just did kind of a big thing, going through that memory. So I want you to know that sometimes the next few days can be a little different. You might notice that you think about it more than usual or that you react more strongly than usual even to other things that aren't related. Or that you're not getting as mad when something happens. There's no right or wrong. Anyway, if you notice something like that, don't worry—you're not going crazy or anything. It's just your brain working things out. Next time you come, I'll ask you what you noticed, and we'll go from there. Okay?

Alex: Okay.

Mr. G: So tell me something you liked about this meeting and something you didn't like.

Alex: I liked getting rid of that memory. Didn't like moving my eyes.

Mr. G: What's next for you now?

Alex: They're letting me study instead of going to group. My last final is tomorrow.

Mr. G: Good luck.

Alex: Thanks.

Session 10: More Trauma Resolution, Official Notes

EMDR with an early trauma memory. Continued until no further memory-related distress was reported.

Session 10: More Trauma Resolution, Therapist's Personal Notes

- Permission for working all days but one if passes grades. Finds out Monday?
- EMDR with memory of uncle's death. SUDS 8 to 9 to 0; went well, completed.
- Next: Ask about grades, SUDS on that memory. Next memory: first parent problem?

Session 10: Questions and Answers

Q: He was really willing to go ahead with that trauma work? It's hard to believe, a kid like that.

A: Yes. The hardest sell was the first time, the test run. Now that he knows it works, he's more willing. The other hardest time will be next time, for the heaviest memory on the list. Not every kid is so willing, but quite a few are.

Q: Can you explain that question you asked where the memory was supposed to be like a bad dream?

A: Another EMDR-related technique, used to help clients to access the psychological resources they need to be able to face the memory (see Greenwald, 1999, 2007).

Q: Can you comment on how you used the grandmother later in the session?

A: Okay. It was set up with the dream question, which I routinely do with clients on the way into a trauma memory. Sometimes the setup is the last we deal with that resource, because the session goes smoothly (in part, in my opinion, because we did the resource work up-front). But in a case like this, when the session got rough it came in handy to have the grandmother all ready to come in and save the day.

He was stuck at a SUDS of 10 and no apparent progress following several tries. I don't mind if clients get upset as long as they're moving. But if they're in pain and they're stuck, there's a high risk of premature termination of the trauma resolution work. I think he was close to the quitting point. So I chose to be more active in connecting him with a resource that had a good chance of helping him to tolerate the memory. It seemed to work (as it usually does, by the way; that's why I use it) and he was able to move on.

Q: You did trauma work on the day before a final. Was there any concern that this might affect him the next day?

A: It was a bit of a gamble. Here were my thoughts:

1. The death of the uncle was safer than a parent-related memory might have been.
2. I intended to hang in there until he got all the way to 0, which I thought he would do before too long.
3. He'd been doing tests all week, and somehow it didn't seem like that big of a deal.
4. With problem behavior clients, there's always so much risk that something big will go wrong (and maybe I never see the client again, because he's dead or incarcerated) that I felt that postponing the trauma work would also be a risk. I decided it was better to go ahead and get through this part of the treatment as quickly as possible.

Despite all these nice justifications, I did break a good rule: that you don't do the first major trauma resolution session prior to an important life event that requires full capacity for performance. I had reasons, and it worked out, but I wouldn't recommend routinely taking that kind of risk in treatment.

Session 11: More Trauma Resolution

Mr. G: Hi, tell me something good and something bad.

Alex: Good, I got my grades; check it out (shows printout of grades).

Mr. G: Not bad. You didn't tell me you were going to get any A's.

Alex: I could'a got more, but I didn't start back in school until almost 2 weeks after the quarter already started.

Mr. G: Does this mean you get to work in the afternoons instead of coming here?

Alex: Yeah. I still come one day a week.

Mr. G: Well, you earned your chance. Are you a good worker at that store, or is your Pops just being nice?

Alex: I work hard! He says I get twice as much done as the other kid he has there. That's why he wants me to work more hours; he knows I work hard.

Mr. G: So he's taking care of you and you're taking care of him, too.

Alex: You could say that.

Mr. G: That's a good way for things to be. And something bad?

Alex: Nothing bad happened this week. Things are going good.

Mr. G: I bet you can find something, even if it's little.

Alex: Okay, my Pops is telling me, "Don't talk so much on the phone."

Mr. G: Are you on the phone a lot?

Alex: Maybe an hour or two every night. Alicia's parents don't let her go out on school nights, so we have to talk on the phone.

Mr. G: That's a lot of phone time. I can see why he thinks you're hogging it.

Alex: I guess.

Mr. G: We've been talking about the things you can do to get stronger toward your goals. Last time we talked about when your uncle died. This last week, did you think about that more than usual, less than usual, or about the same?

Alex: I thought about it a lot the first night, and then not after that.

Mr. G: And when you did think about it, how was that?

Alex: It was okay, no big deal.

Mr. G: Did you notice anything unusual this week in how you were feeling, or reacting to things, or anything?

Alex: I kinda felt a little lighter for a couple of days, a little happier. I think I got a little less stress now.

Mr. G: What did you notice that makes you say that?

Alex: Some guy in the train bumped into me and I was all ready to be really mad but it was weird—I just wasn't that mad about it.

Mr. G: So what happened?

Alex: Nothing happened; it was like I didn't even care, just kept on walking.

Mr. G: So when you digest those bad memories, it gets easier to go toward your goals?

Alex: I guess so.

Mr. G: You ready to go after another one of the memories today?

Alex: Yeah, let's get rid of another one!

Mr. G: I was thinking of going after a hard one today—the first time something really bad happened between your parents. Would that be okay?

Alex: Um … I don't really want to talk about that.

Mr. G: Would it be okay to do it if you only think it but don't tell me the details you don't want to say?

Alex: Could we do that?

Mr. G: Yeah, it'll work. I'll ask you the questions I need to ask, and each time, you decide what you want to say and what you don't want to say. Okay?

Alex: Okay.

Mr. G: First the dream question. If what happened was a dream and you had to be back in the dream for a little while, what would you need so you would be okay?

Alex: My grandmother.

Mr. G: Okay, so picture your grandmother, what she looks like, what she's saying or doing, how it feels to be with her. (EM) How did that go?

Alex: Good.

Mr. G: So the first time something really bad happened with your parents, you said you were about 9 or 10, I want you to think of the picture that represents the worst part of it. If you don't want to say it out loud, just tell me when you have it.

Alex: I have it.

Mr. G: What negative belief about yourself goes with this picture?

Alex: I'm scared.

Mr. G: When you see this picture, are you saying to yourself something like, "It was my fault" or "I'm helpless" or "I'm powerless" or "I'm not important" or "I'm not safe" or what?

Alex: Yeah, all of those.

Mr. G: Which one do you feel the most right now?

Alex: Helpless.

Mr. G: And next time you remember this, what would you like to be able to believe about yourself?

Alex: I don't know; I was helpless, I was just a kid.

Mr. G: Maybe something like, "It's over" or "It wasn't my fault" or "I'm stronger now" or what?

Alex: It's okay now.

Mr. G: When you see that picture and say the words, "It's okay now," how true does that feel on 1 to 7?

Alex: Maybe a 4, 4 1/2.

Mr. G: When you see that picture and say the words, "I'm helpless," what emotion comes up?

Alex: Scared, mad.

Mr. G: Where do you feel that?

Alex: In my head.

Mr. G: How bad is the feeling now on 0 to 10?

Alex: 10.

Mr. G: Ready? (EM) What came up?

Alex: Um … No comment.

Mr. G: Go with that. (EM) What came up?

Alex: The same.

Mr. G: Go with that. (EM) What came up?

Alex: The same. Still a 10.

Mr. G: Go with that. (EM) What came up?

Alex: My grandmother's here.

Mr. G: Go with that. (EM) What came up?

Alex: She's taking me away until it's over.

Mr. G: Go with that. (EM) What came up?

Alex: She says I can stay with her and Pops.

Mr. G: Go with that. (EM) What came up?

Alex: I did; I did stay with her and Pops.

Mr. G: Go with that. (EM) What came up?

Alex: Nothing.

Mr. G: Nothing like "No comment" or like "Nothing"?

Alex: Nothing.

Mr. G: Okay. Now go back to the incident you started with. What do you get now?

Alex: No comment.

Mr. G: Concentrate on that. (EM) What came up?

Alex: It's about a 6 now.

Mr. G: Go with that. (EM) What came up?

Alex: Keep going.

Mr. G: (EM) What came up?

Alex: Just keep going.

Mr. G: (EM) What came up?

Alex: No comment.

Mr. G: Go with that. (EM) What came up?

Alex: No comment.

Mr. G: Go with that. (EM) What came up?

Alex: No comment.

Mr. G: Go with that. (EM) What came up?

Alex: No comment.

Mr. G: Go with that. (EM) What came up?

Alex: No comment.

Mr. G: Go with that. (EM) What came up?

Alex: It's better now.

Mr. G: Go with that. (EM) What came up?

Alex: It's okay.

Mr. G: Go with that. (EM) What came up?

Alex: It's okay. Same thing.

Mr. G: Go back to the incident you started with. What do you get now?

Alex: It's okay.

Mr. G: What emotion comes up?

Alex: Nothing.

Mr. G: Where are you now on 0 to 10?

Alex: 3.

Mr. G: What makes it a 3?

Alex: No comment.

Mr. G: Concentrate on that. (EM) What came up?

Alex: No comment.

Mr. G: Go with that. (EM) What came up?

Alex: No comment.

Mr. G: Go with that. (EM) What came up?

Alex: No comment.

Mr. G: Go with that. (EM) What came up?

Alex: Nothing. I think it's done.

Mr. G: Okay, so go back to the incident you started with. What do you get now?

Alex: 0.

Mr. G: Okay, concentrate on the picture you have now, what you're saying to yourself, what you're feeling. (EM) What came up?

Alex: Nothing. It's the same.

Mr. G: Is it a little better than last time, a little worse, or about the same?

Alex: A little better.

Mr. G: Concentrate on it again. (EM) Better, worse, the same?

Alex: A little better.

Mr. G: Again. (EM) Better, worse, the same?

Alex: Better.

Mr. G: Again. (EM) Better, worse, the same?

Alex: Better.

Mr. G: Again. (EM)

Alex: Better.

Mr. G: Again. (EM)

Alex: Better.

Mr. G: Again. (EM)

Alex: Better.

Mr. G: Again. (EM)

Alex: The same.

Mr. G: Again. (EM)

Alex: The same.

Mr. G: Do the words, "It's okay now" still feel like the right thing to say, or is something else better?

Alex: Yeah, that's good. It's okay now.

Mr. G: When you see the incident now and say, "It's okay now," how true does that feel on 1 to 7?

Alex: Feels true.

Mr. G: So what number would you give it, from 1 false to 7 true?

Alex: 6.

Mr. G: Okay, concentrate on the incident and the words, "It's okay now." (EM) What came up?

Alex: It's not really okay. My Moms, she still has some problems.

Mr. G: Go with that. (EM) What came up?

Alex: She's in rehab now for drinking; it's her third time there.

Mr. G: Go with that. (EM) What came up?

Alex: She's doing good there though. And at least I'm not stressing her now.

Mr. G: Go with that. (EM) What came up?

Alex: I try to help out my mother, but I'm not in charge of her.

Mr. G: Go with that. (EM) What came up?

Alex: Same thing.

Mr. G: So when you get the incident back and the words "It's okay now," how true does that feel?

Alex: Like a 6 1/2.

Mr. G: Concentrate on the incident and the words. (EM) What came up?

Alex: It's as good as it can be right now.

Mr. G: Go with that. (EM) What came up?

Alex: Same thing. It's as good as it can be.

Mr. G: And how true does, "It's okay now" feel?

Alex: 6 1/2. That's as good as it can be right now. My father is in lockup where he belongs, and my Moms, maybe she'll make it, but I just don't know. So it can't be a 7.

Mr. G: I want you to look at the original incident, say the words, "It's okay now," and look all through your body for any tension or discomfort.

Alex: Nothing.

Mr. G: So you made it through a big one! Like I told you last time, since your brain just did so much moving stuff around, it might keep shifting around for a few days. So if you notice yourself thinking about it or reacting different than you expect—that can happen—it doesn't mean anything bad. Okay?

Alex: Yeah, okay.

Mr. G: So how did it go for you this time?

Alex: Good, it went good. I never really thought I could get rid of that stuff.

Mr. G: Tell me something you liked about the meeting and something you didn't like.

Alex: I didn't like thinking about that stuff, but I liked that I got rid of it.

Mr. G: You told me that you wanted to get stronger toward your goals. You're obviously pretty serious about it to go through all that.

Alex: Yeah, you could say that.

Mr. G: What's next for you today?

Alex: Try to get as much homework done as I can, while I'm stuck hanging around here anyway.

Mr. G: Sounds like a good idea. When do you start working weekdays?

Alex: Tomorrow!

Mr. G: Good for you. Hope it goes well.

Alex: See you.

Mr. G: See you.

Session 11: More Trauma Resolution, Official Notes

EMDR with another early trauma memory. Continued until no further memory-related distress was reported.

Session 11: More Trauma Resolution, Therapist's Personal Notes

- Good grades, gets to work weekdays now, comes here only 1 day/week for treatment and check-in
- EMDR with big memory of parents (violence? Didn't say). SUDS started at 10 and ended at 0. Went well.
- Father in jail (for hurting mother?). Mother in alcohol rehab for third time, maybe doing okay?
- Next time: Ask about work.
- EMDR with next parent memory?

Session 11: Questions and Answers

Q: Why did you go on and on when he was already at 0?

A: In EMDR, you don't stop at 0; you stop at 0 and no change (Greenwald, 2007; Shapiro, 2001). This is one of the elements of the treatment that facilitates the client in getting as far as he or she can get with resolution of the memory.

Q: How do you know what he was doing or what he got done since he wasn't telling you much detail?

A: I am pretty sure he did really get to 0 (and no change) as he claimed. But with any trauma resolution method, it's always important to follow up to see what was really accomplished and what's still left to do.

Session 12: More Trauma Resolution

Mr. G: Hi. Tell me something good and something bad.

Alex: Good, things are going good with Alicia. Bad, my grandmother is sick.

Mr. G: Sick at home or in the hospital?

Alex: At home. I don't think it's serious.

Mr. G: And what's going good with Alicia?

Alex: No one thing; it's just going good.

Mr. G: Anything coming up that you're worried about or looking forward to?

Alex: No.

Mr. G: (pulls out treatment plan) We've been talking about the things you're going to get stronger toward your goals. The last couple of times we talked about some of the big memories from your list. Have you thought much about your uncle this last week?

Alex: I thought a little about him, but nothing bad. Just remembering some of the times we used to have before he passed.

Mr. G: And when you remember now about when he died, how is it on 0 to 10?

Alex: Still a 0. I told you it would stay.

Mr. G: And last time we talked about stuff that happened with your parents. Well, we didn't exactly talk about it, but you thought about it a lot. Have you thought about that stuff since you were here?

Alex: Yeah, I thought about it a lot, and I asked my grandparents about it, too. I found out why my father was locked up for so long.

Mr. G: You mean before he came back to your family or after?

Alex: Both. I never knew it but he was selling a lot of drugs—before and after.

Mr. G: How was it for you to learn that?

Alex: Good I guess. No one told me before; I was too young. Anyway, I never knew him much. He left when I was a baby, and then he was just back for a year or so and then gone again. He tried to act like my father, but to me he was just some guy beatin' on my Moms.

Mr. G: So you learned more about your family. Did you notice anything else this past week that was different than usual?

Alex: I feel lighter, like a load's off. I feel pretty good.

Mr. G: And if you think about it now, the thing you were thinking about last week, where are you now on 0 to 10?

Alex: 0.

Mr. G: Is it okay if we work on the next thing on the list today?

Alex: Yeah, okay.

Mr. G: What about the next thing that happened with your parents?

Alex: Huh?

Mr. G: You told me before that it was more than one time.

Alex: I did all that last week already.

Mr. G: From all the different times?

Alex: Yeah.

Mr. G: Okay, let's check in on those memories now, too. If you concentrate now on the worst time that something happened, where are you now on 0 to 10?

Alex: 0, I told you.

Mr. G: Okay, and if you concentrate on the last time that something happened, where are you now on 0 to 10?

Alex: 0.

Mr. G: I didn't realize you had done so much last week. Well, let's see what's next—being taken away from your mother.

Alex: I told you, I already did that.

Mr. G: Last week, too?

Alex: Yeah. My father messed her up, and she was drinking so much they wouldn't let me stay. So I went to live with my grandparents, and it's good, and I see my Moms when she's not drinking.

Mr. G: And when you remember that now—being taken away from your mother?

Alex: 0. But I do worry about her, how she's doing. I hear she's doing good in rehab; maybe I'll see her on Sunday.

Mr. G: So what about when you were jumped?

Alex: We can do that.

Mr. G: What picture represents the worst part of that memory?

Alex: When my arm broke.

Mr. G: What negative belief about yourself goes with that picture?

Alex: I don't know.

Mr. G: Would it be "I'm helpless" or "I'm not safe" or what?

Alex: Yeah.

Mr. G: What would be the best one?

Alex: Helpless.

Mr. G: Next time you remember this time, what would you rather be believing about yourself?

Alex: It's okay now.

Mr. G: When you look at that picture and say the words, "It's okay now," how true does that feel on 1 to 7?

Alex: 5.

Mr. G: When you look at the picture and say the words, "I'm helpless," what emotion comes up?

Alex: Fear.

Mr. G: Where do you feel it?

Alex: All over.

Mr. G: How bad is it right now on 0 to 10?

Alex: 4.

Mr. G: Concentrate on the picture, what you're saying to yourself, where you feel it. (EM) What came up?

Alex: I'm feeling my bone crack.

Mr. G: Go with that. (EM) What came up?

Alex: Same thing.

Mr. G: Go with that. (EM) What came up?

Alex: Hospital.

Mr. G: Go with that. (EM) What came up?

Alex: Cast.

Mr. G: Go with that. (EM) What came up?

Alex: Cast is off, I'm playing basketball.

Mr. G: Go with that. (EM) What came up?

Alex: It's okay now.

Mr. G: Go with that. (EM) What came up?

Alex: It's okay.

Mr. G: Go back to the incident you started with; what do you get now?

Alex: There's four of them and only one of me.

Mr. G: Go with that. (EM) What came up?

Alex: I don't have a chance.

Mr. G: Go with that. (EM) What came up?

Alex: I get some good pops in, though!

Mr. G: Go with that. (EM) What came up?

Alex: I did pretty good for having four guys on me.

Mr. G: Go with that. (EM) What came up?

Alex: I did my best.

Mr. G: Go with that. (EM) What came up?

Alex: It's over.

Mr. G: Go with that. (EM) What came up?

Alex: It's over; it's okay now.

Mr. G: Go with that. (EM) What came up?

Alex: Same thing.

Mr. G: Go back to the incident you started with. What do you get now?

Alex: I can still feel the bone cracking.

Mr. G: Go with that. (EM) What came up?

Alex: Same thing.

Mr. G: Go with that. (EM) What came up?

Alex: It's kind of fading.

Mr. G: Go with that. (EM) What came up?

Alex: Fading more.

Mr. G: Go with that. (EM) What came up?

Alex: It's almost gone; I can barely see it.

Mr. G: Go with that. (EM) What came up?

Alex: It's all faded away.

Mr. G: Go with that. (EM) What came up?

Alex: It's gone, all faded away.

Mr. G: Get back the incident you started with; what do you get now?

Alex: Nothing.

Mr. G: What are you saying to yourself now?

Alex: It's over; I'm okay.

Mr. G: What emotion do you get now?

Alex: Nothing.

Mr. G: Where are you now on 0 to 10?

Alex: 0.

Mr. G: Concentrate on the picture, what you're saying to yourself, what you're feeling. (EM) What did you get?

Alex: Nothing.

Mr. G: Is it a little better this time, a little worse, about the same?

Alex: The same.

Mr. G: Concentrate on it again. (EM) Better, worse, the same?

Alex: The same.

Mr. G: Do you still want to say, "It's okay now," or are there better words now?

Alex: I'm okay now.

Mr. G: When you look at the incident you started with and say the words, "I'm okay now," how true does that feel on 1 to 7?

Alex: 7.

Mr. G: Concentrate on the incident and the words. (EM) What came up?

Alex: Nothing.

Mr. G: Does "I'm okay now" feel more true, less true, the same?

Alex: The same.

Mr. G: Concentrate again on the incident and the words. (EM) More true, less true, the same?

Alex: The same.

Mr. G: Now concentrate on the incident and the words, and check all through your body for any stress or discomfort. Anything?

Alex: No.

Mr. G: Wow, that one went pretty fast. You want to try one more?

Alex: Okay, I guess so.

Mr. G: Next would be the first time you got high.

Alex: It's a 0.

Mr. G: Oh—on the list it's a 5.

Alex: It don't bother me no more.

Mr. G: Well, make yourself concentrate on it for a moment—is it still a 0?

Alex: Yes.

Mr. G: Okay, how about getting locked up then?

Alex: Okay.

Mr. G: What picture represents the worst part, the worst moment?

Alex: Being taken away from the court in shackles.

Mr. G: What negative belief about yourself goes with that?

Alex: Helpless.

Mr. G: Next time you remember this, what would you rather believe about yourself?

Alex: I can do what I gotta do.

Mr. G: When you see the picture and say the words, "I can do what I gotta do," how true does that feel on 1 to 7?

Alex: 6.

Mr. G: When you see the picture and say the words, "I'm helpless," what emotion comes up?

Alex: Sad, mad.

Mr. G: Where do you feel it?

Alex: In my heart.

Mr. G: How bad is it now on 0 to 10?

Alex: 3.

Mr. G: Concentrate on it now. (EM) What came up?

Alex: Same thing.

Mr. G: Go with that. (EM) What came up?

Alex: Same thing, but not as strong.

Mr. G: Go with that. (EM) What came up?

Alex: I guess I got through it.

Mr. G: Go with that. (EM) What came up?

Alex: I'm doing good now; I don't really have to worry about getting locked up no more.

Mr. G: Go with that. (EM) What came up?

Alex: I was just thinking about my grandmother.

Mr. G: Go with that. (EM) What came up?

Alex: When we're done I'm going to call and see how she's doing.

Mr. G: You're not afraid of waking her up?

Alex: Oh yeah, maybe I won't call.

Mr. G: Go back now to the incident you started with. What do you get now?

Alex: I can still see it but it's like a long time ago; it doesn't matter now.

Mr. G: What emotion comes up now?

Alex: Just like a 1.

Mr. G: Where do you feel that?

Alex: In my heart.

Mr. G: (EM) What came up?

Alex: It's going away, fading more.

Mr. G: Go with that. (EM) What came up?

Alex: It's just something that happened. It doesn't matter no more.

Mr. G: Go with that. (EM) What came up?

Alex: Same thing.

Mr. G: Go with that. (EM) What came up?

Alex: Same thing.

Mr. G: Go back to the incident you started with. What do you get now?

Alex: Nothing. It's done.

Mr. G: Where are you on 0 to 10?

Alex: 0.

Mr. G: Notice the picture, what you're saying to yourself, what you feel, where you feel it. (EM) What came up?

Alex: Nothing.

Mr. G: Was it a little better this time, a little worse, about the same?

Alex: A little better.

Mr. G: Concentrate on it again. (EM) Better, worse, the same?

Alex: A little better.

Mr. G: Concentrate on it again. (EM) Better, worse, the same?

Alex: About the same this time.

Mr. G: Again. (EM) Better, worse, the same?

Alex: The same.

Mr. G: Is "I can do what I gotta do" still the right thing to say with this memory, or is there something better to say now?

Alex: It's still good.

Mr. G: Get the incident back and say those words to yourself. How true does it feel now on 1 to 7?

Alex: True; 7.

Mr. G: Concentrate on the incident, the words. (EM) What came up?

Alex: It's true; I'm doing it.

Mr. G: Go with that. (EM) What came up?

Alex: Same thing.

Mr. G: Feel more true this time, less true, or about the same?

Alex: A little more.

Mr. G: Again, the incident, the words. (EM) More true, less true, the same?

Alex: The same.

Mr. G: Again. (EM) More true, less true, the same?

Alex: The same.

Mr. G: Now concentrate on the incident and the words, and look all through your body for any tension or stress. Find anything?

Alex: No.

Mr. G: It looks like we got all the way through your list of worst things. Wow!

Alex: I'm glad to be done with that. To tell you the truth, I didn't believe you when you said it was going to work for me. I'm glad I gave it a try.

Mr. G: I'm glad, too. You did a lot of good work.

Alex: You should do this with other kids, too. It does make the anger smaller.

Mr. G: I do it with pretty much whoever decides to go for it. You really care about your goals, so you took the chance and gave it a try.

Alex: But you shouldn't do that eye movement thing; kids will think you're corny.

Mr. G: Yeah, a lot of kids don't like that part. Anyway, you know the routine. My job now is to remind you that your brain just did a lot of work, and you might notice unusual things over the next few days.

Alex: Yeah, I know.

Mr. G: So tell me something you liked about this meeting and something you didn't like.

Alex: I like we got rid of the rest of those memories, didn't like the eye thing.

Mr. G: What's next for you now?

Alex: I'm going to see if Ms. Burns will let me go home early. I'm worried about my grandmother.

Mr. G: Good idea. I hope she gets better soon. See you next week.

Alex: See you.

Session 12: More Trauma Resolution, Official Notes

EMDR with the two remaining trauma memories. Continued (with each in turn) until no further memory-related distress was reported.

Session 12: More Trauma Resolution, Therapist's Personal Notes

- EMDR with rest of memories.
- Parent stuff—all done last week (???).
- First time high—SUDS = 0, no EMDR.
- Jumped, SUDS started at 4 and ended at 0.
- Locked up, SUDS started at 3 and ended at 0.
- Next time: Review and current issues (?).

Session 13: Money Talk

Mr. G: Hi, tell me something good and something bad.

Alex: Something good, it's my grandmother's birthday on Friday. I'm gonna get her something nice. Something bad—there's nothing really bad.

Mr. G: There's always something bad even if it's only little.

Alex: Ms. Burns says I gotta keep on coming here, even though she says I'm doing good. I could be working another day but instead I gotta come here and waste my time. I mean, no offense to you or nothin, I'd just rather be making money than coming here.

Mr. G: I guess she trusts you a lot more, but maybe not all the way yet.

Alex: Yeah, gotta keep on testing me and stuff, I guess. I don't see why they can't do that at school or someplace.

Mr. G: How are you doing in school?

Alex: I'm still doing good. My Pops he checks my homework before I start at his store; he does it every day.

Mr. G: One of those people who care that you were telling me about—one of the reasons I bet on you.

Alex: I guess.

Mr. G: I understand you want to be working more, but you know she's already giving you more leeway than most of the guys who come here, right?

Alex: Yeah, I know.

Mr. G: I want to check on some of the things we've been talking about. When you remember the first time you got high, where are you now on 0 to 10?

Alex: 0.

Mr. G: When you remember the time you got jumped, where are you now on 0 to 10?

Alex: 0.

Mr. G: When you remember the time you got locked up, where are you now on 0 to 10?

Alex: 0.

Mr. G: When you remember when your uncle died, 0 to 10?

Alex: 0.

Mr. G: When the stuff happened with your parents?

Alex: 0.

Mr. G: When you were taken away from your mother?

Alex: 0.

Mr. G: So you think that stuff might really be in the past now?

Alex: It is; I got rid of it.

Mr. G: I forgot to ask: How's your grandmother doing?

Alex: Oh, she's okay. She was only sick a couple of days last week; she's good now.

Mr. G: I'm glad. How old is she gonna be for her birthday?

Alex: I don't even know.

Mr. G: You said you were planning a nice present?

Alex: Yeah, I'm thinking of getting her a parakeet. She used to have one years ago. They're expensive, though; it's like $300.

Mr. G: $300?! You even have that much?

Alex: I will have it by Thursday if Pops pays me then.

Mr. G: Why do you want to get her such an expensive present?

Alex: I just want to do something really special for her.

Mr. G: I guess you really care a lot about her.

Alex: I do.

Mr. G: She must care a lot about you, too.

Alex: She does.

Mr. G: Do you think she'll be more happy that you gave her the parakeet or feel more bad that you used up all your money on her?

Alex: Oh—I don't know. I didn't think about that.

Mr. G: She really cares about you. Does she know about all your plans?

Alex: I told her about it, yeah. She already talked to the guidance counselor for me about getting me into the culinary arts program next year.

Mr. G: If you cared about someone like she cares about you—a young person— and you knew he was trying to save up some money for his big goals, would you want him to spend it all on you?

Alex: I guess not; I would want him to save it for his goals.

Mr. G: Hmm. I wonder if there's some way you can do something really special for her that doesn't cost $300?

Alex: I was also thinking about taking her and my Pops out to dinner. That would be like $25 or $30.

Mr. G: Even that's a lot from a 15-year-old. Do you think she would like that?

Alex: Yeah, they don't go out so much, and there's a little Spanish restaurant she really likes.

Mr. G: That could be a good idea too. I guess you'll figure it out, what you want to do.

Alex: Maybe the dinner is better.

Mr. G: I was wondering how much you know about money. Do you have an idea about how to get enough money to start your restaurant?

Alex: No idea actually.

Mr. G: I think it probably costs about $20,000 to start a small restaurant, if you're willing to buy good used equipment instead of brand new.

Alex: Yeah, I could do that. But $20,000! That's a lot of money!

Mr. G: It is and it isn't. You could probably have most of that within 5 years if you really wanted to.

Alex: How?

Mr. G: Well, not everyone can do it. But if you really care about your goals, I can tell you some ways you could do it.

Alex: Like what?

Mr. G: Okay. Let's say you want to buy a TV that's worth $100. Would you rather pay $125, $100, or $75?

Alex: I'll pay the $75, that's crazy. Everyone would pay $75.

Mr. G: Of course you'd rather pay less. Then you have more money for your goals. But most people pay the higher price. If you want to pay more, I'll tell you how to do it: Get it on credit. Do you know how credit works?

Alex: They lend you money and you pay it on time [in regular installments].

Mr. G: Yeah, they lend you the money, but they charge you plenty for the loan; they call that interest. You know what interest is?

Alex: Not exactly.

Mr. G: It's a percentage they add to what you owe. So if you borrow $100 at 10% interest, that means that if you pay it off in a year, you have to pay back the $100 plus 10%, which is another $10. But a lot of places charge a lot more than 10% for the interest. And the longer you take to pay the loan, the more interest they charge you. So if you buy that TV on a credit card or on a payment plan from the store or rent-to-own, how much do you think you've paid by the time it's all paid off?

Alex: I guess more than $100.

Mr. G: Maybe $125, maybe even $150. Not such a good deal! But sometimes that's worth it to people to have something right now instead of waiting until they can afford it. The problem is, if that's your strategy, you're always paying so much extra for things, it's hard to save up any money.

Alex: I see what you're saying.

Mr. G: So if you always want to be owing money and paying more for things, that's how you do it: You get it on credit. Then all your extra money goes to them instead of to you, and you never save any. So do you want that TV right now, or do you want to wait until you have the money in your hand so you don't have to pay interest?

Alex: Maybe I'll wait.

Mr. G: So if you only wanted to pay the $100 for the TV, how could you do that?

Alex: Go to the store, I guess; just buy it.

Mr. G: Sure. But if you have the cash, why not pay less?

Alex: How could you do that?

Mr. G: That's a good question. How do you get a good deal on something?

Alex: Maybe wait until it goes on sale?

Mr. G: Sure. Or see if one store sells it cheaper than another store. And if you really want to, you can do some other things, too, to get a good deal.

Alex: Like what?

Mr. G: Well, you can buy one used if you want. I don't like that because maybe it's no good anymore, so I think that's maybe not good, unless you know the person and you know it's good. But you can also go to the store and see if they're selling one of the TVs at a lower price—maybe it was the display model or maybe someone returned it and it's really still like new.

Alex: That would be okay; it's still pretty much new, right?

Mr. G: Yeah. Or if you get really serious about finding a good deal, you can even go on e-Bay, at least for some things. Like these shoes here: They're $100 shoes, I got em brand new on e-Bay for $30.

Alex: Really?

Mr. G: Yeah. Sometimes if you take a little trouble to shop around, you can do pretty good. And that means I still have the shoes I want and an extra $70 in my pocket.

Alex: I never tried e-Bay before, but some of that stuff, I could do it.

Mr. G: Not everyone has to be the best shopper. The most important thing is to only spend money you have instead of buying on credit. But shopping around can save more, too.

Alex: Okay, that's a good idea.

Mr. G: Another way to save up some money is to really decide when you want to spend it instead of just spending without thinking first. I'm not saying you should never spend money, but you should decide which times it's really worth it to you and which times it's not.

Alex: Like what do you mean?

Mr. G: Like sometimes there are big things like a parakeet for your grandmother, and she would maybe even be happier with a small present—because she cares about you too. I bet the same thing will come up with Alicia: Do you blow all your money on her, or do you spend enough to have a good time but save some too?

Alex: Yeah, I see what you're saying. She would be cool with that.

Mr. G: Then there are little things. Like some people with good jobs want to spend $10 on a taxi each way when the $2 subway ride is just as fast. Or they have lunch at the deli for $8 every day when they could have the same thing for $3 if they brought it from home. You put those together, you take the subway every day, and bring your own lunch every day, you just saved more than $100 that week. You know how much that adds up to in a year?

Alex: How much?

Mr. G: Figure it out. Let's say 50 weeks in the year instead of 52; 50 weeks times $100 a week is what?

Alex: $5,000? That can't be right!?

Mr. G: $5,000. And you'd never even notice how much you were blowing, it's only a little at a time. So I'm not saying to give up every little thing. If you like your night at the movies, or your ice cream cone, or your cigarettes, or whatever, go for it. Gotta enjoy life too. But people who want to save up money, they think about those little things and ask themself, "Does this really matter to me? Or is this a way I can save some money?" And the money piles up.

Alex: I'm trying to quit smoking anyway.

Mr. G: Yeah? I'm glad to hear that.

Alex: But I never really thought about that stuff.

Mr. G: A lot of people don't. But if you want to get to your goals, you might as well use the tricks that work. So how much are you making now in a week?

Alex: Like $125, after all the taxes and stuff are taken out.

Mr. G: Well, if you want to be saving for your restaurant, what's your idea about how to save up the money?

Alex: I was thinking of asking my Pops to hold it for me so I don't get tempted to spend it all.

Mr. G: You know how I was telling you about interest before?

Alex: Yeah.

Mr. G: Why not get interest to work for you?

Alex: How do you do that?

Mr. G: When you save up enough money in the bank, they start paying you interest just to let them use it while you're saving it there. Do you know how to get a bank account?

Alex: No, not really.

Mr. G: It's pretty easy, actually. You just go there with some money and your ID; they have some forms they'll show you how to fill out. What's the closest bank to where you live?

Alex: There's one across the street from the store my Pops runs. That's the bank the store uses; I been cashing my checks there.

Mr. G: So when you get your paycheck, if you cash the check and have the money in your pocket what's going to happen?

Alex: Spend it sooner or later.

Mr. G: What some people do is they set aside a certain amount from every paycheck that goes into the bank. They don't touch it unless there's a real emergency. Then that money builds up so you can use it for your plans. If your paycheck is $125, how much do you think would be a good amount to set aside for savings?

Alex: Maybe like $100.

Mr. G: I don't know—most people I know, they like to have a little money in their pocket. I'd be worried if you didn't have any money in your pocket you might be tempted to go clean the bank out.

Alex: I can see that.

Mr. G: How about if you take a minute and figure out what you really need money for in the week: how much it costs for what you need, also for the special things like if you want to do something nice for your grandmother's birthday or take your girl out to the movies or something. How much would you want to be able to spend in a week?

Alex: Maybe $40 but some weeks a little more.

Mr. G: So what if you put $75 in the bank every week and had $50 in your pocket; would that be enough in your pocket?

Alex: Yeah.

Mr. G: And if there's a little extra one week, you save it for something special another time.

Alex: I could do that.

Mr. G: So if you're saving $75 a week, how much does that add up to in a year?

Alex: I don't know.

Mr. G: I don't know either. Okay, if $100 was $5,000 in a year, this is three quarters of that, so that's $3,750. That's not bad!

Alex: And in the summer I'll be working more hours.

Mr. G: Oh yeah. So you could sock away $5,000 by one year from now!

Alex: Wow.

Mr. G: When you put your money into a savings account, they don't give you much interest, just like 1% or something. But when you start piling money up, they have something else that gives higher interest, called a certificate of deposit. Have you ever heard of that?

Alex: No.

Mr. G: Well, they have a deal that if you put in so much and promise to keep it there for so long, they give you more interest. So let's say that half a year from now, you take your $2,500 and agree to keep it in a certificate for a year at 4% interest; how much do you get at the end of the year?

Alex: I'm not sure.

Mr. G: Another hundred bucks—just for having your money sitting there waiting for you. It's like getting another week's pay for free.

Alex: Cool.

Mr. G: And then the extra $100 starts earning interest, too. So you see how, if someone was determined, they could save enough to start a restaurant in a few years?

Alex: Yeah. I didn't know it added up so much like that.

Mr. G: That's it for today. Tell me something you liked about the meeting and something you didn't like.

Alex: I liked the ways to save up money; now I see how I can do it. I didn't like, I don't know, nothing really.

Mr. G: See if you can find something.

Alex: Um, no, I can't think of anything.

Mr. G: Okay. What's next for you now?

Alex: Just hang around until they tell me, "You can go now."

Mr. G: Okay, see you next week. Hope you have a good time with your grandmother's birthday.

Alex: Thanks, see you.

Session 13: Money Talk, Official Notes

Reported no further distress regarding trauma memories; doing well in general. Today talked about money management skills and ways to save money in support of future goals.

Session 13: Money Talk, Therapist's Personal Notes

- Doing well. Money talk.
- Next: Ask what he did for grandmother's birthday and if he started a bank account.

Session 13: Questions and Answers

Q: You let him get away with not saying anything bad about the session?

A: In early sessions I push harder until I get something. Then I'm making a point and teaching the client that it's okay (and good) to say negative things if they're true and constructive. By this late in the game, he's got the point and he's comfortable to say what he wants to. So I tried a little, and he just didn't have anything to say. So I let it go.

Chapter 10

Trauma Resolution

Choosing a Sword

When it's time to slay the dragon, which sword should be used? Quite a bit of controlled research has been conducted on the various methods of helping clients to work their trauma memories through to resolution. The clear result is that not all methods are equal. Some tend to be slow and haphazard, whereas others work relatively quickly and thoroughly. The big dividing line is between the traditional talk therapy methods and the structured, focused trauma resolution methods such as prolonged exposure, stress inoculation training, cognitive processing therapy, and eye movement desensitization and reprocessing (EMDR). The structured, focused treatments win hands down (Foa, Keene, & Friedman, 2000). They are faster—often by months or even years—and more effective.

Facing the trauma memory is especially difficult for those with a low tolerance for distressing affect, which is virtually a defining feature of problem behavior clients. Such clients may refuse to try trauma resolution work, or they may try but then quit long before completion. Therefore, acceptability to clients is a primary concern with this population. What makes a given treatment acceptable to a client with low affect tolerance? Primarily how bad it feels and how long it has to feel bad for.

The leading trauma treatments have key elements in common, including client preparation, some variant of persistent exposure (facing the memory), and some way of helping the client to tolerate the exposure rather than becoming overwhelmed. However, the methods also have differences that can variably impact the client's willingness to try the treatment and the client's ability to tolerate it. Selection of a trauma resolution method should be based on evidence of effectiveness, efficiency, and acceptability to clients. The following selective review focuses on how some of the leading trauma treatments address these issues.

Prolonged exposure (PE; Foa & Rothbaum, 1997) is a well-established method that involves having the client tell the trauma story in detail over and over again. Although PE is effective, it can be a grueling ordeal for clients over multiple sessions, and the narrow selection criteria for clients indicate a recognition that many clients cannot tolerate it. Most versions of PE involve homework as well, for example, listening each day to a tape recording of the story told in the exposure session. Although homework may improve outcomes, many problem behavior clients would be unlikely to comply.

One exposure variant, cognitive processing therapy (CPT; Resick, 1993), entails having the client write down the story of the trauma memory rather than telling it out loud. The writing may provide some psychological distance, which would support the client's ability to tolerate the procedure. Several sessions in this treatment focus on cognitive work in addition to the focus on the trauma memory. Although CPT has mostly been used with adult female rape victims, it has also been successful with one group of incarcerated teens with posttraumatic stress disorder (PTSD; Ahrens & Rexford, 2002). CPT requires multiple sessions per trauma memory, plus homework.

Trauma-focused cognitive-behavioral therapy (TF-CBT; Cohen, Mannarino, & Deblinger, 2006), an exposure variant designed for children, breaks down the memory into manageable doses by having the client create a book in which each page represents a significant moment in the story of the memory. The client works on only one page at a time. Children can tolerate this, and it works well. Although TF-CBT has developed a strong research base and is being widely promoted, the treatment requires multiple sessions for each trauma memory.

Traumatic incident reduction (TIR; Gerbode, 1985) provides psychological distance by having the client imaginally view the sequence of events in the trauma memory as if watching it in a movie. Further research is needed before TIR can be considered a first-line treatment; it was included in this review because there is some research support for it (Brisbey, 2005; Descilo, Greenwald, Schmitt, & McSweeney, 2009; Valentine, 2005) and because of the potential value of the method's features for problem behavior clients in that it appears to be well tolerated and to lead to resolution of a memory typically within one to three sessions.

Eye movement desensitization and reprocessing (Greenwald, 2007; Shapiro, 2001) does not require disclosure of details and controls the dose of exposure by using only brief bursts of exposure and by having the client focus on only one portion or aspect of the memory at a time. The intensity of exposure is further controlled by having the client focus simultaneously on the memory and on the therapist's moving fingers; this dual focus may protect against affective overload. EMDR has been shown to be efficient and effective with adults (American Psychological Association, 2004) as well as with children and adolescents (Greenwald, 2006a), typically resolving a trauma memory in one to three sessions. Such efficiency also contributes to ease of tolerance in that the ordeal is over that much sooner. This set of features would arguably make EMDR the trauma resolution treatment of choice, especially for problem behavior clients and others with special difficulty tolerating trauma treatment. Unfortunately, EMDR requires extensive training—the standard training takes 7 1/2 days (EMDR International Association, 2007), with follow-up supervision recommended—and is hard for therapists to learn to do well (Greenwald, 2006b). Although EMDR has been used with this book's treatment approach, it is not taught here because it cannot be taught adequately in just one or two chapters.

The counting method (CM; Ochberg, 1996) is a recently developed trauma treatment that requires the client to imaginally watch a movie of the trauma memory while the therapist counts out loud from 1 to 100. Afterward, the client tells the therapist the details of what was in the movie. The imaginal exposure part of CM enjoys many of the advantages of the other leading methods. It offers the psychological distance of the movie (as in TIR), the ability to do the work without disclosing details (as in TIR and EMDR), and the dual focus' protection against overload (as in EMDR; with CM this is done by listening to the therapist's counting during the exposure). Telling the client that the exposure will stop at "100" also controls the dose (as in TF-CBT and EMDR) while helping clients to tolerate it because they know it will be over soon.

The numerous apparent advantages of the imaginal exposure portion of CM are of particular relevance for those with problem behaviors as well as others with low affect tolerance (e.g., children, adolescents, and those with a history of repeated traumatization). However, these advantages may not persist, in that for the bulk of the CM session, the client is required to discuss the trauma memory in detail with the therapist.

CM achieved equivalent outcomes to PE and EMDR with adult women in a randomized controlled study. However, CM and EMDR took about the same number of sessions, whereas PE took about 50% more treatment time (Johnson & Lubin, 2006). Why should this variant of exposure be so efficient?

> Two additional components of the method are used to intensify the imaginal exposure. First, the event is recalled with eyes closed and without speaking, thus reducing the interpersonal demands during imaginal exposure. This feature is included because clients may be distracted from the memory while speaking to another person and monitoring their reactions. Second, by not requiring the client to translate an embodied and visual experience into words, the exposure to the original sensory experience can be maximized. (Johnson, Lubin, & Ochberg, 2007, p. 3)

Furthermore, the imaginal exposure may allow the client to get right to the important moments without being slowed down by talking or writing as in some other exposure variants.

Progressive counting (PC; Greenwald, 2008c) introduces several modifications to CM that are designed to enhance treatment acceptance, tolerance, and efficiency. Promising outcomes have been reported in case studies of PC with adults

(Greenwald, 2008b; Greenwald, Schmitt, & Borton, 2009), children (Greenwald, 2008a), and even groups (Greenwald, Schmitt, & Borton, 2009); controlled research is in progress. PC is taught here because although it is still under development, it is based on treatments that have been proven effective and (other than perhaps EMDR) is the most appealing of the structured, focused trauma resolution treatments in terms of what it has to offer for problem behavior clients.

Progressive Counting: What's Different?

The standard CM involves three steps (Johnson et al., 2007):

1. Client preparation, including presenting the rationale and identifying the memory to work on.
2. Exposure, in which the client imaginally views the movie of the event while the therapist counts aloud to 100.
3. Review, in which the client describes in detail the memory as viewed during the exposure, and then reports on the exposure experience.

One cycle through these steps takes a full session; in subsequent sessions on the same memory, the preparation would be more a matter of reorienting. The modifications in PC include the following.

A Really Over Ending

In the original CM, the client is instructed to identify the beginning moment in the movie as being just before the trauma event started and the ending moment as being just after the event was over, specifically avoiding extending the story days into the future (Johnson et al., 2007). In PC, the therapist actively guides the client in identifying an ending that represents a point of more complete relief (as in Greenwald, 2005a). For example, in CM a client who was injured in a car accident might identify the end of the event as being told by the emergency room doctor that he or she will suffer no permanent damage. In PC, the client is guided to identify an ending perhaps days, weeks, or months later, at some moment exemplifying that he or she has already healed and regained functioning. This way the movie continues until the trauma is really over and not merely past the worst part. This helps the client to connect the trauma event with the point of greatest relief and also ensures that all distressing aspects of the memory are dealt with.

Minimal Review

In the original CM, following the imaginal exposure the client is instructed to describe the memory sequentially in detail, as it was viewed during the imaginal portion of the exposure, and then to describe the exposure experience (Johnson et al., 2007). This recounting of memory details is essentially another—much longer—round of exposure, although with more therapist interaction. However, the long review phase does not include the tolerance-enhancing advantages of the imaginal portion (e.g., privacy regarding details, psychological distance of the movie, controlled dose of the fixed end point, and dual focus of exposure during therapist counting).

Arguably, CM and PE are for the most part similar. The preparation phase is roughly the same for each method, entailing identifying the memory to be worked on and explaining the rationale. The review procedure in CM is rather similar to the exposure portion of PE; in each method, the client is telling a detailed story of the event. The main difference appears to be the 100 seconds during which, in CM, the client imaginally views the movie while the therapist counts aloud. In the comparison study (Johnson & Lubin, 2006), that 100 seconds of the session was apparently enough to get the job done with CM in two thirds of the time that PE took.

In PC, the client is asked only to briefly comment on the exposure experience. The client may still choose to describe memory details but is not required to do so. This leaves much more time for imaginal exposure plus counting, which is the unique element of CM that makes it so well tolerated and perhaps also so efficient.

Progressively Greater Exposure

In the original CM, the duration of the imaginal exposure is fixed at 100 seconds, one count per second (Johnson et al., 2007). In PC, the count starts at 10, with 10 more added at each round, so that the next round of exposure goes to a count of 20, the next round to 30, and so on, to the maximum of count of 100 (with children younger than 9 or 10, the count increases by only 5 each time). This is to further control the dose and to allow for progressively greater exposure as the client makes progress on mastering the memory. The therapist does have some flexibility based on clinical judgment—for example, the therapist might decide to repeat an exposure of the same duration before progressing to a longer one. Furthermore, as the client gets closer to complete resolution, the duration of exposure is progressively shortened as there is less and less work to do.

Repeated Exposures Within a Single Session

In the original CM, the procedure is done only once per session and is repeated for up to several sessions to resolve a given memory (Johnson et al., 2007). In PC, the review portion is much quicker and the initial exposures are much shorter, allowing more time for repeated imaginal exposures within a single session. This increases the likelihood that the memory will be more fully resolved within the initial exposure session, reducing the risk of postsession distress and problems. Postsession distress and problems are of special concern with problem behavior clients and others with low affect tolerance and can disrupt the client's willingness to continue with the trauma treatment. Quicker resolution also makes for better use of resources while reducing client suffering more quickly.

SUDS to Zero

In the original CM, the procedure is repeated until Subjective Units of Disturbance Scale (SUDS; Wolpe, 1958, as modified in Shapiro, 2001) is 2 or lower, as is standard within the exposure tradition (Johnson et al., 2007). In PC, the procedure is continued until SUDS is 0 and no further change, as is standard within the EMDR tradition (Shapiro, 2001). This increases the likelihood that all trauma-memory-related issues have been resolved, which further reduces the risk of postsession distress or problems.

There is another reason for persisting until 0 and no change. The original CM was designed for a single-incident trauma, not for a cluster of similar memories such as repeated instances of abuse or for addressing the client's entire trauma history (Johnson et al., 2007). When treating PTSD related to a discrete event, getting to a SUDS of 2 may be sufficient for symptom relief. However, if PC proves to be as advantageous as hoped, ideally it will not be limited to use with single-incident trauma. To treat clusters of related trauma events, it is important to fully resolve the (chronologically) first such memory before going after the next one to be treated (only selected memories in the cluster require treatment; see Shapiro, 2001). Also, treating chronologically earlier memories to full resolution appears to take the edge off of later trauma memories (Greenwald & Schmitt, 2008). Thus, a SUDS of 0 is essential, at least until subsequent research indicates otherwise.

Containment Procedure for Closure

In the original CM, no special procedure is specified to assist the client in containing the remaining distress following an exposure session (Johnson et al., 2007), although presumably the client is debriefed and any pressing concerns are addressed. In PC, for any exposure session in which remaining SUDS is greater than 0, the client is guided to visualize putting the memory away in a container (as in Greenwald, 2005a). This is to reverse the in-session activation of the memory and to help the client to regain composure, reducing the risk of postsession distress and problems.

Start Small and Build Up

In the original CM, the most distressing trauma memory is likely to be the target of the treatment (Johnson et al., 2007), as is common in the exposure tradition. In PC, this strategy may also be used in the case of a single-trauma client who is otherwise high-functioning and enjoys strong psychological resources and social support. Otherwise, a nuanced strategy may be used to (1) start small to give the client a success experience with the method, building competence and confidence, and (2) clear up chronologically earlier memories so that when the later memories are faced, the associated distress has been reduced. This strategy, described in detail in the previous chapter, involves first (in some cases) having the client work through a recent upsetting event as a "test run," then (in some cases) one of the less significant trauma memories, and then going in chronological order from the earliest memory on. Although this strategy may sound like a lot of extra trouble, in practice, and when called for, it seems to make the trauma resolution work go relatively smoothly and quickly.

Client Preparation

Progressive counting requires the same level of client preparation that is appropriate to any trauma resolution method. Adequate client preparation may take minutes or months, depending on the situation. The point is to ensure that each task has been accomplished, whether in treatment or elsewhere, so the client has the best chance of success with subsequent steps. For example:

- If the client has not endorsed treatment-related goals, he or she will be unlikely to work hard in treatment.
- If the client does not understand how the trauma history is related to the presenting problem, he or she is unlikely to be willing to do trauma resolution work.
- If the client does not have sufficient affect tolerance, he or she is unlikely to last long enough in the trauma resolution session to achieve resolution.

Rationale

The goal for the imaginal exposure portion of the treatment—during the progressive counting—is for the client to gradually but thoroughly resolve the memory, whether that occurs through emotional processing, desensitization, distancing, or some other (or multiple) mechanisms. Since as yet we don't know which mechanisms are most important or which type of instruction might yield the best outcome, we offer a rationale that encompasses all the major possibilities. This approach helps the client to make sense of the procedure and may also orient the client to possibly effective ways to utilize the experience.

The rationale for why to address the trauma in the first place should have been taken care of earlier in the course of treatment. The rationale for the PC procedure is presented as follows:

You'll be watching this memory like a movie in your mind. It might hurt your feelings for a little while, but you'll be digesting it and making it part of the past so it doesn't have to hurt so much afterward. Going over it and over it, the emotions can get weaker. And looking at it from where you are today can give you some distance so you're not stuck in the experience anymore.

Target Setup

Once you have determined which memory to work on, preparing the memory for PC entails identifying the beginning and the ending so the client will know where the movie starts and stops. Getting the beginning is usually easy; getting the ending can be trickier.

Identify the Beginning

The beginning of the movie should be just before the trauma event started. The therapist asks, "What would the beginning be, before the bad part started?" and the client responds. If the response indicates that the trauma event is already in play, the therapist says, "The beginning of the movie should start before that," and should continue prompting the client until a suitable beginning is identified. If the client does not remember what may have been happening before (as is sometimes the case with early childhood memories), the therapist encourages the client to make his or her best guess as to what the beginning might have been. It is important that the movie starts prior to the trauma event to ensure that the entire trauma event is addressed.

Get to the Good Ending

One thing that's critical to success in this method is to make sure that the client's movie goes all the way to a good ending (Greenwald, 2005a). Even if there is no ending that is really happy, it's essential to find an ending point in which at least the bad part is really over.

One of our goals with trauma resolution is for the client to be able to say, "That was bad, but at least it's over now, and things are okay." Really understanding—on a gut level—that the bad part is over is one of the things that allows people to let it go and move on. One of the reasons that traumatized people stay stuck is that some part of them doesn't really get that the bad part is over now. The memory isn't organized into a story; it's still in fragments. And the fragments that include the worst parts of the memory don't know that it's over now.

So when we are preparing someone to face the memory, we have to make sure that the story goes all the way to a good end—to when the bad part is really over. This can be tricky; it can be hard to find a good end to many stories.

For our purposes, a "good ending" doesn't necessarily mean that what happened was good or even that the ending was good. The goal is to get the client past the distressing fragments of the memory to a felt sense that it's really over. Here are some examples of good endings to bad memories that the therapist helped the client to identify.

- A 61-year-old man became physically disabled from his identified trauma event 6 years before, in an accident at his workplace. Now he is unemployed, less financially well off, and in chronic pain. The good ending was when he came home from the hospital and had dinner with his wife at the kitchen table.

- A 25-year-old woman had been teased mercilessly by her peers throughout high school. Although only two teasing-related memories were on her trauma history list, smaller but similar events were a daily occurrence for some years. So at the end of the event in her memory, she also knew that she faced the same kind of thing the next day. The therapist asked her, "Do you get teased now?" Fortunately, she no longer got teased but got along well with her peers. The ending to her teasing memory story was in the present: The last event in this memory was seeing herself having lunch with her colleagues at work, the day before this therapy session.

- A 10-year-old boy's older brother's fiancée had died 2 years ago in a car accident. The boy missed her then and now; she had been like part of the family, and they had been close. The good ending was seeing himself return to school and playing a game at recess, a week after the funeral.

- A 40-year-old woman had been injured at age 7 in a fall out of a friend's apartment window. She had broken bones and many cuts and had to return to the hospital for treatment on multiple occasions over several months. The story of the trauma memory included those hospital visits. The good end was saying goodbye to the last doctor and then seeing herself playing jump rope with her friends.

- A 5-year-old boy was severely beaten on several occasions by his grandmother when he stayed with her for the summer. He still has to see her at family events, but his parents have told him that grandmother is not allowed to babysit him anymore. The good ending was when his parents told him that and then seeing himself safe with them at their home.

- A 12-year-old girl had been near a building that got bombed. Although her daily life routine is unremarkable, she lives in an area where bombs or other attacks could happen again. Her good ending was that no one she cared about had gotten hurt in the bombing; she visualized eating dinner with her family members all present that evening.

These examples illustrate several possible strategies for identifying the good ending. Ideally, the good ending can represent a true resolution of the event. Sometimes this resolution can be found soon after the event, and sometimes it has to be found much later. Unfortunately, some events do not have true resolutions—for example, when there is lasting damage (e.g., the loss of a family member, a permanent physical injury, or an ongoing related symptom such as anxiety) or when the event seems especially likely to recur (e.g., in an area regularly targeted by criminals or terrorists). In such instances, the best we can do for a good ending is identify a time when the bad event and its aftermath was as finished as possible and things were as much back to normal as possible.

It's important that the good ending be represented in an image of an actual event—an actual moment in time—when a particular thing happened. Many people will describe a status as their good ending; then it's up to the therapist to help the client convert the status into an image that represents that. For example, if the client describes her good ending as, "I wasn't afraid to ride on the bus anymore," then the therapist might ask, "What picture represents that for you? What do you remember doing that let you know that you weren't afraid anymore?" For another example, if the client describes his good ending as, "I didn't feel bad; I wasn't worried about it anymore," the therapist might ask, "So when you didn't feel bad and weren't worried about it anymore, what were you doing?" The point is, this is a story, a movie. In a story, things happen. So for the good ending, it has to be an actual thing that happens—an event at some moment in time. If the client cannot visualize the good ending as clearly as if seeing it on TV, it's not specific enough yet.

Avoid the Middle

We are just getting ready for the exposure here, not getting into it. Do your best to avoid client disclosure of details of the memory until the next step. You don't have to rudely interrupt, but neither do you have to sit there with silence and big eyes while the client goes on and on. That's another kind of exposure, not PC. Normally the client doesn't say too much because you are asking specific questions (for the beginning and end) and the client will respond accordingly. If the client strays, jump in at your first opportunity, get what you need for the setup, and move on.

Imaginal Exposure

The therapist guides the client to imaginally view progressively longer (and later, progressively shorter) runs of the movie of the memory. The following script provides the basic routine for guiding the client through the imaginal exposure portion of PC.

Therapist: I'm going to ask you to watch this in your mind like it's a movie, while I count from 1 to 10 out loud. You can do this with your eyes opened or closed. When I say 1, start at the beginning of the movie, and when I say 10 you should just be finishing up. Make sure you get to that ending, even if you are not there when the count is over. It's very important to get to the end every time. Ready?

Client: (nods yes)

Therapist: Be at the beginning. 1, 2, 3, 4, 5, 6, 7, 8, 9, 10. Now be at the end. Take a deep breath. Let it go. How did that go?

Client: (any comment is okay)

Therapist: And how bad was the worst moment [during the movie], on the 0–10 scale?

Client: (gives a number)

Therapist: Okay. This time I will count to 20. When I say 1, start at the beginning; when I say 20, be at the end. Ready? Be at the beginning. 1, 2, 3 ….

Ending the Set

Make sure that the client gets to the "good end" every time. This is what connects the trauma memory to ultimate relief, and it also helps the client to tolerate the exposure. Since clients are not always so good at pacing, the script includes, "Now be at the end," which can later be shortened to "Be at the end." It's also nice to encourage the client to take a deep breath, to feel the "letting go" of the memory. Many clients report that they appreciate this step.

How Much to Press for Disclosures

The therapist neither pushes nor discourages client comments or disclosures. "How did that go?" is invitation for those clients who may wish to tell details, without pushing those clients who do not. This is an important balance, because on the one hand, some clients may feel the need to tell the therapist details, and this may be an important element of the healing process. On the other hand, some clients may be more comfortable with privacy. Furthermore, if the imaginal exposure is the most efficient component of PC, we should not clutter it up (and slow it down) with talk unless the client indicates a need for the talk. And talking is not necessarily required for the relationship to have a positive effect; even clients who disclosed little detail along the way have reported that the presence of the therapist was important.

The Counting

The therapist makes an effort to speak one count per second, in a steady, soothing monotone with no rhythmic or tonal variation. The movie duration—the counting set—starts with a quickie and gradually progresses so that the client can master a bit at a time rather than facing too much all at once. At the beginning the client is generally in such a hurry to get through on time that the main task is to lay out the events in order. As the sets lengthen, there is more room for recalling details, processing emotion, gaining insights, and so forth. Eventually, when most of the work is already done, the sets get progressively shorter. The guiding principles here are to (1) not push the client too hard too fast; (2) as the client becomes ready, lengthen the movie so more work can get done; and (3) use shorter sets again when only smaller bits of work remain to be done. The progression proceeds according to the following guidelines:

- Start with a count of 10; add 10 each time.
- Continue adding 10s, up to 100 or until the SUDS (of the worst moment of the prior set) is 2 or lower.
- If the set is up to 100 and the SUDS is still higher than 2, continue with sets of 100.
- When the SUDS drops to 2, this is an indication that the client does not need such long sets. Then you can start going down by 10 each time in subsequent sets, as long as you don't go below "double" the most recent SUDS. That is, if the SUDS is 2, don't go less than a count of 40; for a SUDS of 1, no less than a count of 20; and SUDS of 0, no less than a count of 10. For example, let's say you have been adding 10 each time and just did a set of 40, and the client reports having had a SUDS of 2 during that set. You may not go down yet, because 2 is not less than half of the 40. But you can't add, because the SUDS is not over 2. So you do another set of 40. If the next time the SUDS is 1 or 0, climb down by 10 for the next set. On the other hand, if the SUDS is 3 (or higher), add 10 for the next set.
- Even when you are at a set of 10 and a SUDS of 0, continue with further sets until there is no further change. The client reporting new insights, thoughts, emotions, or physical sensations is evidence of change. In lieu of client report, ask, "Was it a little easier (to watch) this time, a little harder, or about the same (compared with the time before)?" As long as it continues to get easier from one time to the next, the client is still making progress and should not be stopped.

It is important to use these guidelines strictly, for long enough to learn how the session should go, before attempting to vary it. After doing PC with a number of clients (perhaps 5 or 10), you will get a feel for what is needed. Then you will still usually follow these guidelines, but with some flexibility.

Closure in an Incomplete Session

The basic rule about working with a trauma memory is that if you take it out, you should put it away (Greenwald, 2007). This "putting away" should be done whenever you've been working with a memory that isn't completely processed; that is, remaining SUDS is greater than 0. After helping the client imaginally put the memory away, you may use another calming intervention such as deep breathing, the safe place visualization, or any of your usual closure activities.

Container

The Container intervention can be used to help calm the client down and regain composure. There is a specific time to use a container: after you've been talking about a possibly upsetting memory. The goal is to help the client feel that the memory is put away again. In the following script, this is a conversation. You have to wait for answers to your questions before you go on to the next one. You don't want to give your client too many ideas; it's better if he or she comes up with his or her own imagery. The questions are designed to help him or her to make it specific enough that it works.

What kind of container can you think of that could hold this memory until you need to get to it again?

What would it be made of? How big would it be? How would you close it (keep it secure)? Where would you keep it?

What I want you to do is imagine packing this memory away in (the container). When it's all put away, let me know.

How did that go? Does it feel all put away or not really?

Problem Solving the Container

Once in a while, the container doesn't really work. You will know this because when you ask, "Does it feel all put away or not really?" your client will say, "No," or, "Not really." Then you have to help your client to improve the container so it will work. Start by asking questions, for example, "What kept it from being all put away?" Then your client will probably tell you that the container was too small, too weak, or not adequately secured. Then you can ask for solutions, for example, "What would it take to make the container work better?" Once the client has improved the container to solve the problem, you try the visualization again.

It is important for the client to be the one to select the symbols and imagery. The therapist's job is to guide the client but not to choose the solution. When the client chooses, the symbolism is likely to have more meaning and impact. Here are some examples of how the problem-solving conversation might go.

Therapist: Is it all put away, or not really?
Client: Not really.
Therapist: Why not? What happened?
Client: It was kind of leaking out the cracks.
Therapist: What could you do with the container to keep that from happening?
Client: I guess wrap it up with plastic.

Therapist. Okay, try it that way. Tell me when it's all put away. Ready?

Therapist: Is it all put away, or not really?

Client: Not really.

Therapist: Why not? What happened?

Client: It didn't all fit in.

Therapist: What would the container need so it could all fit in?

Client: Need to be bigger.

Therapist: Oh? How big?

Exercise: Try PC With a Stepping-Stone Memory

Work with a colleague. When you have finished, change roles and do it again. This cannot be done solo; you need someone else to do the counting and guide the session.

If You Are the Client

- This is not a role play; be yourself. It is up to you to choose an event you are willing to work on right now.
- Please choose a stepping-stone memory so that you can have a similar first experience with PC to what your client might have. This memory should not be part of a cluster; for example, if you have had multiple losses, do not choose a recent loss. It's also generally best to avoid a memory that involved someone in your family doing something to you. A SUDS of 3 to 6 is ideal, but a little higher or lower is okay (don't choose a 10 for this one).

If You Are the Therapist

- Use the following script; note that the "What's the memory?" question is only for this exercise (with real clients, you select the memory). Try to get the setup done efficiently, avoiding conversation. Only use the backup questions if you are not satisfied with the client's first answer; if the client's answer does the job, move on.
- Continue to a SUDS of 0 and no change. If you are unable to get to 0 for any reason, end with the Container (also included in the script).

Exercise Script

What's the memory? (Phrase, not story)

(Did anything like this ever happen before? If so, either pick the earliest example, or find another memory that's not part of the cluster.)

What's the beginning of the movie, before anything bad happened?

(Was that really before it started?)

What's the ending of the movie, when the bad part was over?

(When was it really over?)

(And when would you say it was really over?)

(What picture/event would represent that?)

Progressive Counting

I'm going to ask you to watch this in your mind like it's a movie, while I count from 1 to 10 out loud. You can do this with your eyes opened or closed. When I say 1, start at the beginning of the movie, and when I say 10 you should just be finishing up. Even if you weren't at the end, it's important to get to the end when the counting is done.

Ready? Be at the beginning. 1, 2, 3, 4, 5, 6, 7, 8, 9, 10. Now be at the ending. Take a deep breath. Let it go. How did that go?

And how bad was the worst moment, on the 0–10 scale?

Okay. This time I will count to 20. When I say 1 ….

(When the SUDS was already 0 in the prior movie, then instead of asking, "How bad was the worst moment?" ask:) Was it a little better (this time), a little worse, or about the same?

Container

What kind of container can you think of that could hold this memory until you need to get to it again?

What would it be made of? How big would it be? How would you close it (keep it secure)? Where would you keep it?

What I want you to do is imagine packing this memory away in (the container). When it's all put away, let me know.

How did that go? Does it feel all put away or not really?

(What kept it from working?)

(How would the container need to be different to solve the problem?)

Exercise Follow-Up Questions

If You Were the Client

How did this go for you? What stood out? Did the SUDS during the procedure go higher than you had expected?

If You Were the Therapist

How did this go for you?

Problem Solving

What If the Client Says, "There Is No Good Ending"?

That probably means that you weren't using the script. The "good end" or "happy end" is a concept for therapists, but not what we say to clients—unless the ending really was good. However, many memories (e.g., personal losses as well as trauma memories for which ongoing symptoms remain) do not have a good end. So use the script, which does not imply this, and find the best ending you can to give the client the sense of relief that the bad part is over.

What If the Client Says, "I Went to a Different Ending This Time"?

Then ask what the new good ending was. If you're satisfied that it still does the job, allow it. If the client stopped too soon in the story and the benefit of the really over ending was not achieved, push for a later ending. Most often, the client in this situation has already spontaneously chosen a later good ending that is more effective.

What If the Client Talks a Lot in Between Every Set, Telling You All the Details?

The first time or two, let it go. If it continues, ask, "Are you telling me this because you think you're supposed to or because it feels very important to you to say it out loud to me?"

- If the client really needs to tell the details and be heard or witnessed by the therapist, then allow it; this may be an important part of the healing process.
- If, on the other hand, the client is talking so much just to be a "good client," then you can retrain the client, perhaps as follows: "In some other therapy approaches, talking can be important. With this method, though, it's better not to tell me the details unless there's something you really want me to know."

What If the Client Keeps Reporting the Same SUDS Level Over and Over?

If the client reports the same SUDS level for three sets in a row, then you want to figure out if the processing is stuck or still moving. If the client is still making progress, then you're fine to keep going; if the client is really stuck, then you'll want to shake things up somehow.

If the reported SUDS is the same number three times in a row, then ask, "Is that the same worst moment as it was the time before?" If the answer is no, then although the SUDS level is the same, the client is working on different aspects, so it's going fine. If the answer is yes, ask, "Do you feel like you're making progress, or does it feel stuck?" If the client says that he or she feels that progress is being made, then it's also okay to keep going.

If the client appears to be stuck, then ask, "What keeps it from being a 0?" or "What is the worst part of it now?" or "What makes it stuck?" The client's answer will guide you in selecting your strategy to solve the problem.

- Sometimes a cognitive intervention is helpful. For example, if the client is stuck on irrational self-blame, you might ask questions that will help the client to more appropriately assign blame—for example, "So who was the child in this situation? And who was the adult? And are children usually in charge, or adults?"
- Sometimes a problematic belief is not the issue; rather, the emotion is just too much for the client, in which case additional psychological resources may be helpful. If the client appears to be unable to master the distressing emotion, you might ask the client, "Who would you like to be watching this movie with you?" Once the client responds, suggest, "Why don't you imagine, next time, that (this person) is watching the movie with you."

There is plenty of room for creativity here; these are just examples. However, in general it is more effective to guide the client to come up with his or her own solution rather than simply telling the client what to do or think. Once the client has come up with a useful response, then you can try another movie set and will hopefully get some movement.

What If the Client Is Down to a 1 and It Just Won't Go Any Lower?

First of all, you should try the strategies just described, and usually that will work. However, sometimes it doesn't. For example, regarding the death of a family member, the client may say, "It will just always be a little sad." If the best you can get is a 1, that's the best you can get. But please don't take this to mean that it's okay to just accept the client's rationalization for why he or she can't heal any further. Try all the tricks first before you decide to let it go.

What If You Just Finished a Very Long Set and the Client Reports a Very Low SUDS (2 or Lower)—Do You Still Have to Count Down by Only 10 at a Time?

That depends. If the client got the low SUDS by changing the memory in some way—for example, by including a "helper" who was not actually there, or by acting in some effective way that did not actually occur—then you should just go down by 10 as per the standard protocol. On the other hand, if the SUDS is low without having, in the prior set, distorted the memory in some way, then yes, it's okay to jump down by more than 10. Use the following formula:

- If the SUDS was 2, you can jump down to a set of 50.
- If the SUDS was 1, you can jump down to a set of 40.
- If the SUDS was 0, you can jump down to a set of 30.

What If You Are Running out of Time and the Client Is Still at a High SUDS?

Do a short final set (to a count of 20), and then do the Container. Then do whatever else it takes to help the client regain composure before leaving.

What If You Are Doing the First (Earliest) Memory of a Cluster (of Similar Events) – How Do You Get a "Really Over" Ending If It's Just Going to Happen Again?

In this case, you'll want to have two endings. Guide the client to identify an ending soon after that first event, and then to jump from that soon-after ending to the ultimate ending, without anything else in between. This will help the client to focus on resolving the first memory before facing the rest of them.

What If the Client Is Feeling Better but (Perhaps Because) the Memory Has Been Altered?

If the memory is altered merely by the introduction of additional information or understanding, that's fine. However, if the memory is altered by (for example) including a person who wasn't there, or changing what actually happened to having it happen in a nicer way, that's acceptable as a stage but not as an end point. In that case, once you feel that the client has extracted the benefit from the "wishful" version (which can take several sets), it's important to encourage the client to leave the wishful version aside. For example, the therapist might say, "This time, if you're able, see if you can do it without your father there" (if the father had been added as a helper but was not actually present).

After Exposure

Once the PC portion of your session is over, you can talk over the session a bit. Do not talk memory details—you already put it away; don't take it out again. You might say something like, "You just did a piece of work here; how do you feel?" This gives the client a chance to comment on the experience and the therapist to answer any questions and to point out that the client has made a real effort and perhaps made another step toward his or her goals.

What to Expect Afterward

The therapist should also prepare the client for possible aftereffects of having done trauma work. This is part of the trauma-informed treatment approach of making sure that clients know what to expect and preparing them to cope effectively with what may come. The therapist might say something like this:

> Sometimes when you've done a lot of digesting, moving things around in your brain, things can keep on moving even after you leave here. Some people find that they think about the memory more than usual, or less than usual; that some other memory comes up; that they feel emotionally raw, or exhausted, or better than usual. There's no right or wrong; I just want you to know that things might still be moving. So if you find yourself reacting to something in a way you don't expect, you don't have to worry that something's wrong with you. It's probably just the stuff you were doing here working its way through your system.

If this is the client's first PC session on a major trauma memory, it can also be helpful to provide some extra reassurance and encouragement to contact the therapist if concerned. This is because clients occasionally have had very strong postsession reactions and, despite having already established a good alliance with the therapist, felt isolated and overwhelmed. The therapist might continue from the previous statement as follows:

> However, if you do get worried about how you're doing, I expect to hear from you. I know that you usually don't call, but you just took a

big step and my part in that is to be more than normally available in case you do get concerned.

It is much better to encourage the client to make contact then to have to respond, in the following session, to a client who (however irrationally) says, "I was crying all week long. Why didn't you call me?"

Just as we provide full information prior to initiating PC, it is important to provide information regarding all possibilities postsession. We do not want to surprise our clients. This does not mean that we expect the highly challenging postsession reactions to occur. Because so much of the memory gets resolved within the session, you may be risking fewer "side effects" than with a less efficient trauma resolution method. Also, because you are using the personal trainer strategy of taking your client one small step at a time through the treatment challenges, your client is unlikely to take too big a step and become overwhelmed. Even so, because anything can happen—and occasionally does—we are obliged to prepare our clients accordingly.

Following Up

When a client has done PC, these are the kinds of questions we ask early in the following meeting, typically right after the standard check-in. There are no right or wrong answers, but we do need to know what's going on:

- Have you thought about it (the memory we worked on) more than usual, less than usual, about the same?
- When did you think about it, how was that?
- Have you noticed yourself reacting more strongly than usual to something or less strongly than usual?
- Any dreams?
- Feeling any worse than usual in some way, or better than usual, or different?
- If you make yourself think about the memory again for a second right now, where are you now on 0 to 10?

Learning From the Client's Responses

These questions give you the opportunity to identify possible additional issues to be dealt with. For example, if the client reports recalling a significant trauma memory that was not already on your list, you can add it to the list and take it into account in your target order strategy. The questions also allow you to determine the extent to which the previously targeted memory may be resolved.

An Unresolved Memory

Sometimes a memory that you thought was already completely resolved turns out not to be. So there's more to do. When you go back to PC, you must do the entire routine from a set of 10 on, even if you believe that there is not much work left to do on the memory. Going through the standard protocol gives you the best chance of being thorough and effective. However, you don't need to set up the target all over again; you can use the same beginning and ending for the movie that were used in the prior session.

A Resolved Memory

Sometimes a memory that was left incomplete in the previous session is now resolved! In that case, perhaps the client continued working postsession, whether in dreams, thoughts, or even intentional activities related to the memory. In that case, move on.

No Remaining Reactivity to Trauma-Related Triggers

If the client reports no longer being reactive to a trauma-related trigger, do not be impressed. This does not mean that the trauma resolution portion of treatment is done, nor does it even mean that the symptom is gone. Often following a successful PC session there is a quick flush of apparent cure, but it may not persist. If other trauma memories remain untreated, sooner or later the flush of cure fades and the sore-spot effect may return. So don't let the client's apparent progress throw you off. Stick to your plan and continue with trauma resolution accordingly.

 If, on the other hand, the client reports no longer being reactive following completion of all the planned trauma resolution, this is probably real. Then you can move on.

Remaining Reactivity to Trauma-Related Triggers

If the client reports continuing reactivity to trauma-related triggers or even increased reactivity, do not be discouraged. Increased reactivity is not unusual following even a successful or complete PC session, perhaps because so much emotion has been activated. And we are not expecting symptom resolution following resolution of a single memory if more memories remain untreated or if the related real-life issues have not been addressed. Just stick to your plan, and continue with trauma resolution accordingly.

 The present version of PC is based on available data and experience and may be modified as further data and experience dictate. The following questions (and perhaps others) will be addressed in future research:

- Is it really better to start with the chronologically earlier memories and work your way forward? Or can you just go for the "big one" and consistently get away with it?
- Do client instructions (in the "rationale") matter? Specifically, is it helpful to orient the client to the possible benefit of emotional processing, desensitization, or distancing? Or does it work just as well to instruct the client in the procedure without orienting to possible mechanisms of effect?
- Do you have to go all the way to SUDS of 0 and no change? Or can you end at 1 or 2 and have reasonable confidence that the job was still done adequately?
- Do you have to progressively count back down? Or can you just keep going up each time until the client's SUDS is 0 (or whatever the appropriate ending point turns out to be)?

Age Variations

For Preteens

The system is pretty much the same for children, with a couple of adjustments. First of all, you'll want to use a shorter and less sophisticated rationale the younger your clients are. The goal is to provide a rationale that is meaningful at your client's intellectual and developmental level.

The other adjustment is with the counting system. Younger children tend to have faster brains and lower affect tolerance, so the sets should be downsized accordingly. As a general guideline, halve everything for children younger than 9 or so. Start with a set of 5 and add 5 more each time. For example, "double" a SUDS of 2 is not 40 for a child; it's 20.

The younger your clients are—or more traumatized or with lower affect tolerance for any other reason—you'll want to be that much more cautious in your target selection strategy. It's really worthwhile to start out with smaller earlier memories if you can find them. This gives the client practice and success with the procedure and probably takes some of the edge off the later, more challenging trauma memories.

For Adults

No variation.

Chapter 11

Anticipate Future Challenges

What Next?

When the trauma resolution phase is complete, what comes next? Now is the time to help the client consolidate gains. In general, the strategy is to address, in this order:

1. Remaining trauma-related triggers.
2. Other aspects of daily functioning.
3. Anticipating and preparing for future challenges.

Remaining Trauma-Related Triggers

After trauma resolution has been completed, some of the easiest remaining problems to take care of are those that are trauma related. Often these problems or symptoms will melt away, but sometimes they have taken on a life of their own. These autonomous self-perpetuating symptoms are reminiscent of Ivan Pavlov's dog, which persisted in salivating at the sound of the bell even when food was not present. Some of the "swords"—the trauma resolution methods—may work well when applied to trauma-related triggers. These symptoms also tend to be responsive to cognitive and behavioral interventions, because the driving force underlying the symptoms is no longer present. Incentives can also be helpful in certain situations.

Other Aspects of Daily Functioning

What happens after the dragon is slain? In the fairy tale, there is a celebration, and of course the guy gets to marry the princess. What does this look like in treatment? The essence of this phase of treatment is to help the client to get daily functioning as good as it can be.

After trauma resolution, and once the trauma-related triggers are eliminated, the therapist should take a good look at the client's overall situation. This is the time to take a step back and review the entire course of treatment for anything that can be taken further to help the client get on an even better track toward his or her goals. Check for case management and safety issues, skills and habits, and family dynamics. For anything that still needs work, this is the time to do it. At this point, the intervention strategy should be appropriate to the problem; it's not a trauma issue anymore. Fortunately, at this point, non-trauma-related intervention strategies have an excellent chance of working since the trauma-related sore spot is no longer in the way.

Do not be afraid to revisit issues that were frustrating or only afforded limited progress earlier in treatment. Once the trauma is cleared up, the client is likely to be much more willing to address those issues as well as being more capable of doing so successfully. You may find yourself back in discussions regarding the client's choice of romantic partners or other issues related to avoiding high-risk situations. You may find yourself practicing assertiveness training with your client or practicing Choices Have Consequences with some challenge that previously seemed like too much to tackle. You may also work with the client to take constructive steps toward health, educational, or career goals that previously seemed to be out of reach.

Anticipating and Preparing for Future Challenges

Once the dragon is slain and the knight has married the princess, well, that's nice, but we're not done yet. What can we do to keep more dragons from coming along? And if one should come, what can we do to be ready for it so we can try to keep it from getting in? And if it does get in and do damage, what can we do to be ready to recover quickly?

Now that we've worked out the problems that were bothering the client in the moment, it's time to focus on the future. The client worked so hard with you because he or she has goals. The client's goals do not stop when he or she is doing well this week. The client's goals go into the future. So treatment does not stop until we have done our best to help clients to anticipate and prepare for future challenges. This gives them the best chance of staying on track toward their goals.

Relapse Prevention

Relapse prevention refers to a range of interventions designed to keep a potentially vulnerable person on track despite the challenges and adversities that may arise (Marlatt & Gordon, 1985). It can help to prevent recurrence of an unwanted event and to prepare coping strategies for a stressful situation, and, if and when the bad thing happens anyway, relapse prevention and harm reduction strategies can minimize damage and speed recovery. In trauma-informed treatment, the goals are as follows:

1. To prevent recurrence of trauma.
2. To prepare coping strategies for anticipated challenges.

3. In the event of a new trauma, to develop response behaviors including rapid recognition of the traumatization along with symptom management and help seeking.

The same types of goals can also be applied to problem behaviors and other symptoms. For example, for a client who has overcome a drinking problem, the corresponding goals might be as follows:

1. To avoid high-risk situations regarding temptations to drink.
2. To prepare coping strategies for anticipated challenging situations.
3. In the event of a relapse, to develop response behaviors including rapid recognition of the relapse, along with behavior management and help seeking.

Some of the same concepts and methods that have been used throughout the treatment can be used again, this time focusing on the future.

The approach to relapse prevention is very similar to the approach to self-management skills training that was used earlier in the treatment. In fact, the Choices Have Consequences intervention can be used here as well but now the focus can be on significant anticipated challenges instead of the everyday ones. The strategies in relapse prevention (Marlatt & Gordon, 1985) are as follows:

- To emphasize the client's goals, strengths, and positive intent. Blaming the client only knocks him or her down and makes the client weaker and less capable of handling challenges.
- To externalize the problem. If the problem is personality or temperament, the client is stuck with who he or she is and thus is powerless to cope. If the problem is situational, the client can do something to avoid or manage situations.
- To identify future high risks and strategies to avoid these.
- To identify specific signals as cues to specific actions.
- To identify the signals as early in the risky situation as possible so that the client gets better at managing the situation before it goes too far.
- To label failures as "expected" and not as signifying total failure. If one slip means total failure, the client is more likely to give up. If a slip is expected, the client can still feel that he or she is on track and can maintain his or her efforts.

You can utilize all available resources to help the client implement his or her coping strategies. For example:

- Pair behaviors with their consequences. Involve others in enforcing the consequences.

- Involve family members and others in the planning and implementation of coping strategies.
- Rehearse and practice the coping strategies.

It can be very tempting to end treatment when the client seems to be "all better now"—when the therapist, the client, and interested others are feeling satisfied and successful. There is good reason for this feeling: Everyone did their job; the client is feeling better and acting better; nothing's wrong now. So why not quit? Because if you don't prepare for the future, you could be in for some nasty surprises.

What Can You Do to Keep Bad Things From Happening?

The client as well as family members should be involved in making plans for avoiding potential future high-risk situations. This will probably involve continuing to use the fence-around practices (i.e., staying safe, avoiding high risks) that were hopefully initiated much earlier in the treatment. The latter part of the treatment is also an opportune time for the therapist to prepare the client (and perhaps family members) for upcoming challenges—and related safety concerns—that can reasonably be anticipated.

Coping Skills in Challenging Situations

Of course, it is impossible to prevent every potentially risky situation, so it's also important to prepare the client for challenges that are likely to be faced. Choices Have Consequences is an excellent choice here, focused on the anticipated future challenging situation.

Harm Reduction

What if something bad does happen in the future? What can you do to keep yourself on track? Another part of relapse prevention is called harm reduction. The focus of harm reduction is to help your client anticipate and identify signals that the bad thing has happened, that things are going wrong for him or her, and to catch himself or herself.

Harm reduction can be taught in about the same way as other relapse prevention strategies. It's just that the focus is on a different point in the anticipated challenging situation. The goal here is to anticipate and identify signals that something has gone wrong so that it can be addressed before more damage is done.

As with the other self-management training interventions, it's always important to transform concepts into concrete behaviors and events. Then the chance is better that the client will recognize the problem situation, catch himself or herself, and do something about it. This chance is further improved when the distress signals, the behavioral choices, and the associated outcomes are practiced in imagination using Choices Have Consequences.

Ending Treatment When Trauma Resolution Has Not Been Completed

Relapse prevention and harm reduction strategies should be used at the end of every treatment, regardless of how much has been accomplished already. Treatment may end for a variety of reasons—perhaps because the client is moving or because the insurance policy will not pay for more sessions and the client cannot afford to pay out of pocket. Sometimes treatment ends because the client absolutely refuses to engage in trauma resolution activities, despite the therapist's best efforts—so nothing is left to work on. No matter why treatment is ending, the therapist should prepare the client as well as possible for the challenges to come.

Julio was a 17-year-old boy who came to the United States as a refugee from the Guatemalan civil war at age 11. He had average to high-average intelligence and an accent so good that he sounded native to the United States. He was in treatment while in a 3-month program for first-time offenders at a residential facility operated by the juvenile corrections system in his state. Within the facility, Julio's behavior was excellent. He did well in school, got along with others, did not lose his temper, and did not break rules. The concern was very specific: When he was released, would he go back to stealing cars?

Julio was cooperative in therapy, in part because he was so interested in figuring out what he could do to make sure that he was never incarcerated again. He was able to identify long-term goals that he cared about and was willing to work for. He declined to identify the events on his trauma history list, but, considering where he had come from, it is likely that his trauma history included witnessing of assault, torture, and murder as well as the loss of significant family members. However, as noted in Chapter 3, the specific details are not absolutely necessary to provide a trauma-informed case formulation. The real treatment impasse arose a little later, when the personal training phase of treatment was over and the therapist suggested that it was time to start slaying the dragons.

Julio: No, I don't need to talk about all that stuff [the trauma].
Therapist: What do you mean? You told me about the goals you have for yourself, things you really care about. I thought that you would want to give yourself the best chance of getting there.
Julio: I do care; I'm going to make sure I get there. But now that you explained to me about the traumas behind the wall and the sore spots, I know what to do.
Therapist: What?
Julio: I'll just make the wall stronger so those things don't mess me up anymore.
Therapist: How will you do that?
Julio: I know how.
Therapist: So it sounds like you really don't want to talk about the bad things that happened. You really want to kind of keep them behind the wall and keep them from bothering you.
Julio: That's right.

Therapist: And you also really want to get to your goals, to live the kind of life you were telling me about.

Julio: That's right.

Therapist: And you're feeling pretty confident that you can do both: make the wall stronger, keep those memories out of the way, and get to your goals.

Julio: Yup.

Therapist: Well, my job is to make suggestions, and your job is to make decisions. It's your life. So I'm going to explain a little more about my suggestion, and then it's up to you to make your decision. I've seen other guys try your strategy, and sometimes it works. The problem is, sometimes it only works for a while. Then some new stress comes along and adds to the pile-up. Then even the stronger wall just isn't enough, and the trauma messes them up again, and they end up doing things that get them in trouble all over again. I'd hate for that to happen to you. That's why I'm suggesting that you do the work now, to take care of the trauma memories so they can't hurt you anymore.

Julio: I get what you're saying, but I'm going to do it my way.

Therapist: Okay. I hope that sooner or later you do take care of that stuff behind the wall; when you do it, I think you'll be glad you did. But no one can tell you when it's your time. It could be next year or 20 years from now. You'll have to decide that for yourself.

Julio: Maybe never.

Therapist: Maybe never. Now you're making a decision that I'm kind of worried about. I'm afraid that your way, things might go bad. But I hope you prove me wrong. Supposing that it turns out you're right—say, 1 year from now, what will you be doing? What will be happening in your life?

Julio: I'll be going to work every day, keeping out of trouble. I'll go straight home after work, not hanging out with those guys I used to hang with. I'll be going to that college a couple of nights a week to get my electrician training. I can walk by nice cars without needing to drive them away.

Therapist: In other words, you'll be doing the things you said you would be doing to get toward your goals.

Julio: Yup.

Therapist: And I hope it doesn't happen this way, but what if it turns out that I was right to be worried? What if your wall isn't strong enough and you're getting off track? What would be going on a year from today?

Julio: I'd be stealing cars again, being late for work sometimes, skipping the night classes sometimes. My girlfriend would be on my case all the time.

Therapist: When your girlfriend is on your case, what are you saying to yourself?

Julio: Some things I don't want to say out loud. Also I just want to get out of her way so she doesn't bug me so much.

Therapist: And if you noticed these things happening, what could you do to get yourself on track again?

Julio: Talk to a counselor. Do what you said.

Therapist: How do you find a counselor?

Julio: I know a clinic near where I live. I hear they're okay there.

Therapist: I'm going to ask you to practice this now so that if you're ever in the situation, you'll have some practice in catching yourself before it goes too far. I'll ask you to watch a movie in your mind. In the first part of the movie, you're stealing cars, being late for work, cutting class. Then your girlfriend is on your case. You're saying those things to yourself and trying to get out of her way. This goes to that bad ending we were talking about before, where you're behind bars for a longer time and saying to yourself, "It's not worth it." Start at the beginning and tell me when you're done. Ready?

This therapist used Choices Have Consequences to help Julio practice how to catch himself and get himself to a counselor if he finds that he is going the wrong way. Another therapist might have kept Julio in treatment for longer and tried to work on building affect tolerance to the point where Julio might have been more willing to consider trying the trauma resolution work. That might have been a better strategy. Also, unfortunately, we can't be sure that the counselor whom Julio might find a year from now will know how to help him with trauma resolution. The point of this example was not to second-guess the therapist but to show how a therapist might help a client to prepare for future challenges even when treatment was not completed according to the therapist's agenda.

In many ways, this final part of treatment replicates what was done earlier, but this time with a focus on the future rather than the present. The earlier focus was on avoiding high-risk situations this week; now the focus is on avoiding high-risk situations farther in the future. The earlier focus was on staying on track today; now we are focusing on staying on track tomorrow, next month, and next year. The earlier focus was on managing everyday problem situations in a way that led to a good ending; now the focus is on anticipating more significant and challenging problem situations in the future and managing those.

Ending Treatment

When is it finally time to end treatment? It may be so if the following occur:

- Presenting problems are resolved.
- The client reports little or no distress when recalling the trauma memories.
- The client reports little or no difficulty in managing trauma-related triggers.
- The client's social network (especially family) has made a positive adjustment to the client's improved functioning.
- The client is oriented toward a positive future and is behaving in ways that will make such a future likely to occur.
- The client can anticipate future challenges and stressors and is prepared to avoid or respond to these effectively.

Age Variations

With Preteens

Parents may be relatively more involved with both the present-focused and future-focused treatment activities. However, the tasks in treatment are the same.

With Adults

No variation.

Session 14: Review and Anticipating Future Challenges

Mr. G: Hi, tell me something good and something bad.

Alex: Good, I'm going to start my bank account tomorrow. Bad, I gotta keep coming here. I tried to ask Ms. Burns if I could go to work every day, but she just said, "We'll see." Like what's to see?

Mr. G: You mean she didn't just say no?

Alex: It was sort of no and sort of maybe in a while.

Mr. G: So not right now, but maybe in not too long if you keep doing good?

Alex: Something like that.

Mr. G: So why tomorrow for the bank?

Alex: I asked my Pops to go with me, and he said he can do it tomorrow.

Mr. G: How much money are you going to bring to start it off?

Alex: $250.

Mr. G: That's a good start. The trick is to never touch what you put in until it's time for the restaurant. Otherwise, you know how it goes—there's always one excuse and then another.

Alex: I know, you told me that. I'm keeping $50 in my pocket so I don't get tempted about the bank money.

Mr. G: So what else is going on?

Alex: Nothing really. Just doing what I gotta do.

Mr. G: School still going okay?

Alex: Yup.

Mr. G: Things with Alicia?

Alex: Good. I told her about saving money. She already has her own account with more than $2,000 in it; she's been saving since she was 10 for college.

Mr. G: I guess someone taught her some of that stuff already. Is your Pops still on your case about using the phone too much?

Alex: Yeah, he made a rule that I have to stop after an hour.

Mr. G: At least you get an hour, but I bet you want more. How is Alicia's father now? He still doesn't like you or what?

Alex: No, he's okay. He just didn't want me to mess with her, you know?

Mr. G: Fathers can be like that.

Alex: He's okay with me now, pretty much. He lets her go with me places or whatever.

Mr. G: That's good. What's up with your mother? Have you seen her lately or heard how she's doing?

Alex: Yeah, she came by the other night. She said she was proud of me.

Mr. G: How's she doing?

Alex: She's still living in the rehab place, but she started a part-time job too. She said she's getting ready to get her own place in another few weeks.

Mr. G: She won't live with you guys?

Alex: No, the program she's in, they help her get her own apartment.

Mr. G: And where will you go?

Alex: I'll stay with my grandparents. My Moms wants me with her, but she says not yet, and Ms. Burns says I have to stay with my grandparents anyway. It's all good. She seems pretty good; I think she'll make it this time.

Mr. G: What kind of work is she doing?

Alex: Nurse—that's what she used to do before.

Mr. G: Nurse, that's a good job!

Alex: Yeah, well she's smart.

Mr. G: I hope she makes it this time.

Alex: Me too. Anyway she don't have to worry about my father, because he's locked up. And she don't have to worry about me, because I'm doing good. So there's less stress on her now.

Mr. G: You know, I'm wondering if this might be our last meeting. You've pretty much done all your work with me, you did every step that I had suggested. So maybe you graduate today; what do you think about that?

Alex: That would be cool. I mean, don't take no offense, but if I don't have to talk with you no more, that's one less reason for Ms. Burns to make me keep coming.

Mr. G: Yeah, that's part of what I was thinking, too. If you do keep coming, I hope you'll come by my office and say hi even if you don't have to stay and talk for so long like now.

Alex: Yeah, I will.

Mr. G: So I can't promise without checking with Ms. Burns, but maybe this will be our last meeting. I'll tell her I think you might be done, and she'll decide.

Alex: Okay.

Mr. G: So now I want to check back on some of the things we've been talking about. A while ago we were talking about avoiding high-risk situations like certain kind of parties or being with your friends from before or doing things to get your math teacher mad or walking through that park after school. On 0 to 10, if 10 is perfect and 0 is not at all, this past week how have you been doing with avoiding high risk?

Alex: Perfect, 10. I don't do any of that stuff. No, 9—I did talk in math class a time or two. But that teacher don't bother me anymore anyway.

Mr. G: Okay, and how about self-control skills, for anger and not smoking weed and not giving in to peers when they say, "Let's do this or that" on a scale of 0 to 10 this past week?

Alex: 10. No one really got me mad. I mean, people still do stupid things, but it don't bother me so much; it's no big deal.

Mr. G: And we also talked about the things you could do to keep your stress down, like get your homework done, eat a good breakfast. 0 to 10?

Alex: I do that stuff, too.

Mr. G: Okay. Here's that list of worst memories. Look through the list and see if any of these still bothers you.

Alex: I told you already, they're gone.

Mr. G: Well, a while ago you told me that you really cared about your goals. Now you've gone ahead and done the work, done all these things to make yourself even stronger. So if I ask you now on 0 to 10 what's my chance of winning my bet, what would you say are my chances?

Alex: That I'll make it to my goals?

Mr. G: Yeah.

Alex: 10.

Mr. G: There's no such thing as a 10; that would be a sure thing.

Alex: Okay then, a 9.

Mr. G: I can see why you say that. You're really on track. Is it okay if we talk for a little while about challenges that might come up in the future? So you can be ready and have a better chance of staying on track?

Alex: Yeah, okay.

Mr. G: So what are the bigger challenges coming up that we can think of?

Alex: I don't know, like what do you mean?

Mr. G: Well, when will you be done with OCFS [the state program that has legal custody of Alex]?

Alex: In about 9 months.

Mr. G: A lot of kids I know, as soon as they're not getting tested anymore they go for their chance to get high.

Alex: Yeah, I'll prob'ly do that, too.

Mr. G: So are you the kind of guy who can just have one chocolate chip cookie? Or if you start with one, do you have the whole box?

Alex: I don't know which way I am.

Mr. G: I've seen some guys, they can go get high once or twice, then they forget about it and do their lives. Other guys they do it "just once" and then "just once" and then "just once," and the next thing you know they emptied their bank account, they messed with other girls and they lost the one they cared about, they threw everything away inside a week or two. Then they get so much stress they start doing stupid things and next thing you know, they're locked up all over again. Boom. I've seen it happen plenty of times like that.

Alex: I'm not gonna do all that. No way.

Mr. G: Me, I keep the cookies out of the house.

Alex: Huh?

Mr. G: The chocolate chip cookies. If I have cookies in the house, most days I don't eat them. Sometimes, I just eat one or two. But sooner or later,

I start with one, and boom—the next thing I know, the whole box is empty. So me, I don't have them in the house. What's your strategy once you're not getting tested anymore?

Alex: I'll prob'ly just stay away from it.

Mr. G: Matter of fact, I don't have a TV either.

Alex: For real?

Mr. G: Yup. I can't handle it. Days go by and I'm fine, and then the next thing you know, it's 6 in the morning and I've been watching college basketball all night long.

Alex: I've done that! Maybe not until 6 in the morning though. But for real, you don't have a TV?

Mr. G: Yeah, I just had to decide: Do I want cookies and TV, or do I want to keep my life on track? I chose to go for my goals.

Alex: I can see that. I still can't believe you don't got no TV though.

Mr. G: So when your cousins say, "Hey, let's celebrate you being done with OCFS," and they hand you a blunt, then what do you do?

Alex: Wow, I don't know.

Mr. G: Well, what do you feel like doing?

Alex: Feel like celebrating, having some.

Mr. G: And if you let that take you over?

Alex: I smoke.

Mr. G: And if that becomes a habit again, what kind of negative consequences does it lead to?

Alex: If I do it a lot? Lose my girlfriend, spend my money, do bad in school.

Mr. G: So it all goes, huh, everything you worked for?

Alex: Yeah.

Mr. G: So maybe it even goes all the way to that bad ending we were talking about before?

Alex: Yeah, maybe.

Mr. G: So what would you like to be able to do when your cousins say that to you?

Alex: I do want to celebrate. But maybe some other way.

Mr. G: Like what?

Alex: Go to the beach or to a Knicks [basketball] game or something.

Mr. G: And that keeps you on track to your goals?

Alex: Yeah.

Mr. G: Okay. I'm going to ask you to watch a movie in your mind.

Alex: Another one of those movies?

Mr. G: You remember these, huh?

Alex: Yeah.

Mr. G: The movie starts out, you're with your cousins planning how to celebrate for next week when you're done with OCFS, and one of them says the plan is a party and get you really high now that you're not being tested anymore. Then the thoughts and feelings: Would be fun, just once won't hurt, don't want to say no to my cousins, all that stuff. Then you say okay, and then the bad ending and the words, "It's not worth it." Start at the beginning, go step by step, and tell me when you're done. Ready? [EM]

Alex: Done.

Mr. G: Did you get all the way to the end?

Alex: Yes.

Mr. G: Did you remember to say, "It's not worth it"?

Alex: Yes.

Mr. G: This time the movie starts the same way. Your cousins suggest the plan, you have the same thoughts and feelings. This time you suggest a different plan, and it goes to the good ending. Ready? (EM)

Alex: Done.

Mr. G: Did it get all the way to the end?

Alex: Yeah.

Mr. G: This time the movie starts the same way, your cousins say "Let's do this" and you have the same thoughts and feelings. This time I don't know what's going to happen; it depends on what you do. Rules are: bad choice goes to bad ending and "It's not worth it," good choice goes to good ending. Ready? (EM)

Alex: Done.

Mr. G: Which way did it go?

Alex: Good way. I just told my cousins ahead of time I don't want to go near that stuff anymore, and they were cool with it.

Mr. G: Did it go all the way to the end?

Alex: Yeah.

Mr. G: You had a good strategy to keep the problem from even happening. But just in case you forget to tell them that, this time the movie starts the same way, your cousins say "Let's do this" and you have the same thoughts and feelings. Again I don't know what's going to happen; it depends on what you do. Again, bad choice goes to bad ending and "It's not worth it," good choice goes to good ending. Ready? (EM)

Alex: Done, good way.

Mr. G: Get all the way to the ending?

Alex: Yeah.

Mr. G: What about when your brother Julio comes back; when will that be?

Alex: Not for almost 2 years.

Mr. G: Will he want to do some of that old stuff with you?

Alex: Nah, I already been talking with him about that. He's happy for me, and he wants me to help him do good, too, when he gets out.

Mr. G: So that won't be such a high risk for you?

Alex: No, I don't think so.

Mr. G: Okay. And what if, some day in a year or two, something really bad happens, like someone in your family dies or something, and you have a lot of extra stress.

Alex: I don't really want to think about that.

Mr. G: I don't blame you. We don't have to say this person or that person, but you know how life is: Sooner or later there's something sad happens.

Alex: Yeah, I know; sooner or later it's always something.

Mr. G: So even then, I think there's a good chance you'll be able to keep yourself on track. But is it okay to talk about it for a few minutes just to help you get ready for the worst?

Alex: I guess so.

Mr. G: So suppose that the stress is so much that you go back to your old ways. What kinds of things would you be doing?

Alex: Lose my temper a lot, I guess, yell and stuff. And prob'ly be getting high a lot more. And maybe cutting classes or being late for my job or whatever.

Mr. G: And if you're making excuses for yourself for all that stuff, what might you be saying to yourself?

Alex: I don't know, maybe like, "He deserved it", whoever I was mad at or, "Just this once, no big deal" for the other stuff.

Mr. G: And if you let that take you over, you just keep on doing it?

Alex: I guess.

Mr. G: What if you noticed yourself doing that stuff and making those excuses, what could you do to get yourself back on track toward your goals?

Alex: Maybe talk to my grandmother or start going to church again or go back to a counselor and get myself together.

Mr. G: I'm going to ask you to do one last round of movies for me. This movie starts with you doing all those things again and then making the excuses to yourself. The first time, you're going to listen to those excuses and keep on doing the same stuff—all the way to that bad ending and "It's not worth it." Ready? (EM)

Alex: Done.

Mr. G: Get all the way to the end?

Alex: Yes.

Mr. G: Did you say, "It's not worth it"?

Alex: Yes.

Mr. G: This time the movie starts the same way: You're doing that stuff, making the excuses. This time, you catch yourself and do whatever it takes to get yourself back on track. The last part of this movie is the good ending. Ready? (EM)

Alex: Done. I talked to my grandmother and got a counselor and got back on track.

Mr. G: Did you get all the way to the good end?

Alex: Yes.

Mr. G: This time the movie starts the same way: You're doing that stuff, and making the excuses. This time I don't know what's going to happen; it depends on what you do. Rules are bad choice goes to bad ending and "It's not worth it," good choice to good ending. Ready? (EM)

Alex: Done.

Mr. G: Which way did it go?

Alex: Good way.

Mr. G: Make it all the way to the end?

Alex: Yes.

Mr. G: This time the movie starts the same way: You're doing that stuff, and making the excuses. Again, I don't know what's going to happen; it depends on what you do. Remember, bad choice goes to bad ending and "It's not worth it," good choice goes to good ending. Ready? (EM)

Alex: Done.

Mr. G: Which way did it go?

Alex: Good way again. Got all the way to the end.

Mr. G: Okay. Now we're not quite done, but I'm going to ask my ending questions a little before the end today. Tell me something you liked about this meeting and something you didn't like.

Alex: I liked seeing how much I've done, that I said I was going to do. I didn't like how long it was; it was too much talking.

Mr. G: Yeah, it was kind of long today. Now I want to learn from our whole time together so I can do a better job with someone else in case I ever meet someone else who reminds me of you. What should I make sure to do with him, and what should I make sure to not do with him?

Alex: The best thing was that time talking about my goals and how I could get there. And also getting rid of the bad memories, that was good, helped me to get rid of my anger. You shouldn't do that stuff with moving the eyes; kids will think you're weird.

Mr. G: Thanks for the advice. So just in case this is our last meeting, I want to shake your hand and say, "Good work, and have a good life."

(Mr. G and Alex shake hands.)

Alex: And thank you for all the ways you helped me: You listened to me and you gave me good advice; you're a good counselor, and I hope you help a lot of other kids.

Mr. G: Thank you. And even though we're saying goodbye now, if you're here, you better come by and tell me how you're doing, okay?

Alex: Okay.

Mr. G: See you.

Alex: See you.

Session 14: Review and Anticipating Future Challenges, Official Notes

Possible final session? Reported doing well in every way. Focused today on anticipating possible future challenges. Talked about ways of preventing certain problems from arising. Also talked about if things did go wrong in the future, how to recognize the signals of things going downhill and how to catch himself to get himself back on track.

Session 14: Review and Anticipating Future Challenges, Therapist's Personal Notes

- Doing well. Opening bank account tomorrow.
- Relapse prevention and harm reduction. Goodbye?

Session 14: Questions and Answers

Q: So what happened with this kid anyway?

A: I don't really know. I saw him around for a few months when he came to check in at the program, and he seemed to be doing pretty well. But there was no long-term follow-up.

Chapter 12

Challenging Cases

The focus in this chapter is to increase your facility with using the framework of the Fairy Tale model, both to problem solve challenging cases and to "retrofit" your existing cases so that you can start using this treatment approach with current clients and not just with new ones. The system of analyzing cases presented in this chapter can also be used as a method for providing supervision or consultation. Your supervisees or consultees do not need to be familiar with the contents of this book to benefit from your input as per this framework.

Early in the book, the fairy tale was presented, with elements of the fairy tale then related to corresponding steps in a comprehensive trauma-informed treatment approach. Since then, you've been learning how to do various interventions, to take your clients through the steps in the treatment approach. Now that you've been through each of the steps, it's time to pull it all together again to work with the model as a whole.

Here is a retelling of the fairy tale. Please don't skip this even though you remember it from before. People consistently report that they were grateful to get the story the second time. Read it carefully. As you read it this time, notice what's the same as before and what's different or new.

The Fairy Tale Revisited

Once upon a time …

There was a small kingdom, about the size of a small town. Things were pretty regular there: People did their jobs, kids went to school, some people went to church or temple or mosque and some didn't. Sometimes people would get together to share food, play games, play music, talk. Most people got along, but not everyone. And that's the way things were.

Until one day …

The dragon came. One day the dragon ate a cow right out of a farmer's pasture. Another day the dragon ate a dog right out of someone's front yard. The parents told their kids that they weren't allowed to go outside anymore. But they found out that kids aren't very good at not going outside. So the parents stayed home to guard their kids, to keep them safe from the dragon. And even people who didn't have kids were staying inside; they were nervous about the dragon, too.

Things really slowed down in this kingdom. When people did get together, here's what they talked about: "Why does our kingdom have a dragon, anyway? The other kingdoms don't have one." They didn't know, and they wanted to know. So they started coming up with ideas. This group of people blamed that group of people, and that group of people blamed some others—pretty soon, everyone was blaming someone, and they were all mad at each other.

It didn't take long until this kingdom got a bad reputation. People from the other kingdoms didn't know about the dragon, but they sure knew what was going on. They would say, "The people in that kingdom don't go to work, the kids don't go to school, nobody gets along, they're all mad at each other—they're messed up."

And that's the way things are.

Until one day …

A knight in shining armor came along. Well, he wasn't really a knight, and he didn't have any armor. He was just some guy who happened to be passing through. But the people in the kingdom saw something in him. "You!" they said. "You can slay the dragon; you're just the one to do it!" The guy said, "No, sorry, I'm not a dragon slayer; you have the wrong guy. I've been walking a long way, and I'm looking for this girl I'm in love with. But I don't know where she lives." He pulled a picture out and showed it around. "Have you seen her?" The people said "Yes, she's our princess; she lives here. And what a coincidence: She really wants to get married—to whoever slays the dragon!" When the guy heard this, he said, "Well, in that case, I'm your man. Take me to your dragon!"

So they took him to the dark place where the dragon was sleeping. The guy saw the dragon and said, "Whoa, this is a bad idea! I can't handle this dragon— no way! It's huge, it looks really strong, it's covered with scales, it breathes fire. Let's just forget the whole thing!"

The people said, "No, you can do it; we know you can! Look, you can work out, do exercises, build yourself up. We'll help—we'll get you a personal trainer. And remember the princess!" The guy said, "Oh yeah, the princess!" He was in love with this princess and really wanted to marry her. "Okay, I don't know about this personal trainer stuff, but I'll give it a try and see how it goes."

So they gave him a personal trainer and took him to the schoolyard to start on his exercises. But he couldn't stay focused! Every time he got started on some exercise, he would suddenly stop and look all around—he was afraid the dragon would get him while he was out there, exposed. So he wasn't making any progress. This was clearly not working.

So they took him to a clearing at the edge of the forest where there were high trees on one side. Then they worked to build a high fence around the rest of the clearing. Everybody pitched in, cutting lumber, putting it up, securing it, cooking for the workers. Even the little kids helped: They brought water to people, carried messages, did whatever they could. And it wasn't long until they had a high fence around the rest of the clearing. Then the guy could concentrate on his exercises.

Then he really got to work. He did push-ups and sit-ups, lifted weights, ran laps, did all kinds of exercises. Every day the trainer added a pound or two to the various weights. Every day the guy became a little stronger, a little faster, a little more agile. After a while, he started looking pretty good. When they thought he was almost ready, they had a couple of athletic teenagers dress up like dragons to give him some practice. He didn't use the sword—just a stick—but he got to practice his dragon-fighting moves.

Finally, the day came: He was ready. He faced the dragon, fought it, and slew it.

He did marry the princess. But things didn't just go back to exactly the same way that the kingdom used to be.

For one thing, they now had a hero in their midst. People from the other kingdoms were saying, "That kingdom has a dragon slayer; I wish we had one." And everyone in the kingdom felt proud and walked a little taller; they knew they'd all helped out and been a part of it.

But they were still asking each other, "Why did our kingdom have a dragon anyway? I wonder if we'll get another one?" And they didn't know. And they wanted to know. So they hired a consultant.

The consultant looked everywhere and interviewed everyone, and she finally called a meeting to tell them her findings. "You have two problems here. First of all, you throw all your garbage in the dump; it's this huge pile of garbage that stinks for miles around. That smell attracts dragons." So they decided that everyone would put their garbage in a compost pile in their own yard. Then there would be no big smell to attract dragons, plus compost is good for the gardens anyway.

The consultant also told them, "Here's your other problem. On the edge of the kingdom where the farms are, there are all these low fields—it's flat, flat, flat for miles! Dragons are lazy, and this place is just too easy for a dragon to cruise right in." So they decided to plant clusters of apple trees here and there in the fields. It wouldn't be impossible for a dragon to come, but with all the barricades it wouldn't be as easy as before.

Then they had a lot of apples. So every year at harvest time, they had a big Apple Festival, and people would come from all the kingdoms for miles around. There were all kinds of contests for the tastiest apples, the biggest apples, the best apple pies, and plenty of food, games, music—everything a festival should have.

The highlight of the festival came on Saturday night; it was the event everyone would go to: the dragon-slaying contest. Of course, they didn't have a real dragon, so whoever had won the year before got to play the dragon. All year long, young people from all the kingdoms were practicing, training, hoping that they'd be the one to win the big contest at the next year's festival. Not only was this great fun, but if another dragon ever did show up, they would also be ready!

Then, they did live happily ever after—more or less.

The end.

So what did you notice in the fairy tale this time that was different from the first time?

Give yourself credit for that. The story is exactly the same as before. What's different is you. You know more now, so you are able to notice more elements of the story. You are able to see how these relate to the trauma-informed treatment approach.

Applying the Model

For much of this book, you have been working with one step at a time. The new task for this chapter is to work with the model as a whole.

You probably figured out some time ago that this treatment approach is not just for clients with problem behaviors or just for clients with presenting problems clearly related to trauma. Most therapists who learn and practice this system end up saying, "This is just good therapy. I've been using this with all my clients." They recognize that trauma contributes at least something to virtually every client's problem. They recognize that nearly any symptom can be viewed as a "problem behavior" (even internalizing symptoms) and then can be addressed with this approach. They are still doing many of the things they used to do, with clients, families, and any others involved, but now they are doing it in a way and in an order that takes trauma into account.

Even so, any theory or model has an area of "best fit" and other areas in which the fit may not be so good. One of the goals of this chapter is to help you to test the Fairy Tale model with your own challenging cases to see if, and how well, it might fit your cases and provide you with useful guidance.

Another goal of this chapter is to give you more practice in using the model and internalizing it. When you learn a new way of thinking about how to do your work, at first your focus is on what's new. In the long run, though, you don't want to be focused on the Fairy Tale model; you want to be focused on your clients. So it's important to practice the model until you get used to it. Eventually, instead of focusing on the Fairy Tale model you'll be focusing with it—it'll become your perspective, the way you see a case. This takes practice.

When you are working with the Fairy Tale model, of course it's great if you've started your case that way and have done all the steps in order. But you may have many ongoing cases that you've started some other way or have picked up from someone else. You may also have cases that you are trying to do according to the Fairy Tale model, but they are especially confusing or challenging in some way. And even within the Fairy Tale model, clients may not sit still for us to go along according to our own agenda. Sometimes events happen in their lives that throw off the course of treatment, and when we next see them they're not in the same place we left them.

Because we can't force clients to be where we think they should be, the best we can do is figure out where they actually are. When you know where the client is in the treatment model, you will have a much better idea of what's needed and what you should be doing.

Exercise: Apply the Model

For each of the following cases, speculate about where the client is—that is, which phase of trauma-informed treatment. Or perhaps you will notice and note which essential step has been skipped or done only incompletely. Then make a suggestion as to what the therapist might do to help the client progress. You might wish to refer to the Trauma-Informed Treatment: Tasks and Interventions worksheet (Figure 12.1) later in this chapter for ideas. Remember that until the tasks of one phase have been completed, the client is unlikely to be successful in a later phase of treatment. Also, sometimes a client may leap forward or backslide for one reason or another. Although a single "right answer" rarely exists in this field, some suggested responses are included following the cases. You will probably get more out of this exercise if you formulate your own answers first before looking ahead to the suggested responses.

Case 1

A 17-year-old boy with a history of conduct problems is in treatment as required by the alternatives-to-incarceration program to which he has been adjudicated. He has been cooperative in the first several sessions and appears to be sincerely invested in achieving positive long-term goals. But when the therapist offers him the treatment plan, he rejects it, saying, "I don't need to do that stuff; I don't need counseling." The therapist reminds him of his goals, and the boy says, "Yeah, but I'm going to do all that; I don't have any problems."

What is the phase of treatment (or what's missing)? Based on that, what should the therapist do?

Case 2

A 39-year-old man is in court-mandated treatment for road rage. The first two sessions were focused on rapport building and seemed to go well. In the third session, the therapist is trying to teach the client some self-control skills, but he is barely cooperative and will only participate half-heartedly, and then for only a few minutes at a time. The therapist complains to the man, "This is supposed to be for you. Why does it feel like I care about it more than you do?"

What is the phase of treatment (or what's missing)? Based on that, what should the therapist do?

Case 3

A 26-year-old woman is in an alternative-to-incarceration "halfway house" treatment for substance abuse, prostitution, and child neglect. She shows up punctually for every session (it has been 2 months of weekly meetings) and is clearly engaged in working with you. But every time you meet, she mainly wants to talk about the ongoing interpersonal conflicts she is having with the facility's authority figures and with other residents.

What is the phase of treatment (or what's missing)? Based on that, what should the therapist do?

Case 4

An 11-year-old girl is far along in treatment. She has had two trauma resolution sessions and has done well in each. When she comes for the next session, although she does not report anything special in the check-in at the beginning of the session, she seems angry and abrupt. When the therapist reminds her of how well she has been doing in treatment and suggests picking up where they left off, the girl refuses. The therapist reminds her of her goals and how this work is helping her to achieve them. The girl responds, "I don't want to do it; I just don't care about that anymore."

What is the phase of treatment (or what's missing)? Based on that, what should the therapist do?

Case 5

A 28-year-old man is in court-mandated treatment for domestic violence. He clearly understands that if he hurts his wife again, he will be prosecuted and probably incarcerated. Even so, he continues to minimize the seriousness of his violent past actions and to blame his wife for his behaviors because she did things to make him angry. It's the fourth therapy session, and he still seems to refuse to take responsibility for his actions.

What is the phase of treatment (or what's missing)? Based on that, what should the therapist do?

Case 6

A distraught grandmother calls the clinic to arrange treatment for her 13-year-old grandson, for whom she is the sole custodial parent. She lives alone with her grandson. She complains that the boy has been refusing to go to school for almost a month. The grandmother explains that she is unable to force the boy to go because she is neither healthy nor strong and, in fact, had a heart attack a few weeks ago.

What is the phase of treatment (or what's missing)? Based on that, what should the therapist do?

Case 7

A 17-year-old girl is brought to the in-school therapist because when she took off her sweatshirt earlier in the day, a peer noticed fresh cut marks on the girl's arm and reported it to a counselor. By now the school principal has notified the parents, and the therapist is expected to do whatever is necessary to make sure that the girl is safe and taken care of.

What is the phase of treatment (or what's missing)? Based on that, what should the therapist do?

Case 8

A 17-year-old girl has not been attending school for most of the past several months and is likely to fail her entire junior year of school, which only has 2 1/2 months left. She is finally referred for treatment. In the intake session, the therapist learns of the extended school absence, determines that this is an emergency because of the serious consequences that may ensue, and calls a meeting with the client, parents, and school. At that meeting they agree on a plan, with special accommodations, to help the client to attend school with a reasonable chance of being successful there. The client goes to school for 1 day and then stops again.

What is the phase of treatment (or what's missing)? Based on that, what should the therapist do?

Case 9

A 14-year-old girl has been doing well in treatment and in the previous session worked her most significant trauma through to resolution. That trauma was also the first one, chronologically, on her list, which includes four other traumas rated at a Subjective Units of Distress Scale (SUDS) of 8 or higher. In the next session, the girl reports that the treated memory doesn't bother her anymore. The therapist suggests proceeding with the next trauma on the list, but the girl says that that memory doesn't bother her anymore either—that it's a 0. The therapist checks to make sure that she's really concentrating on it (some kids claim 0 when they really mean that they are making sure not to think about it), and the girl still reports no distress. They go through the same routine with all the other untreated trauma memories on the list, with the same results.

What is the phase of treatment (or what's missing)? Based on that, what should the therapist do?

Apply the Model Exercise: Suggested Answers

Case 1

Phase of Treatment

One small but important thing seems to be missing here. The boy does not seem to perceive that there are any challenges or obstacles between him and his goals. If the boy believes that he is on track to his goals and nothing is in his way, why would he need the therapist?

Intervention

The therapist should find ways of highlighting potential obstacles. Two ways of doing this are described in this book. First is the Future Movies session (see Chapter 4) in which strengths and obstacles are listed, in conjunction with the gambling metaphor and the question, "Why would that other person bet that you're not going to make it?" Later is the Treatment Contract (Chapter 5) session's Problem Behavior Cycle, which has the advantages of being visual and of incorporating the trauma history as the source of the vulnerability. Once there is agreement about possible obstacles, the client is more likely to decide that it's worth working with the therapist and to become more capable of mastering the challenges he faces.

Case 2

Phase of Treatment

In the Fairy Tale model, they are still in the first phase of treatment. The therapist is wishing that the client was ready for personal training, but the foundation is not there. Whenever the therapist is trying harder than the client and wants it more than the client does, it is probable that the princess hasn't been identified. Right now, probably the client's only goals are to get through the required sessions as uneventfully as possible. This is not adequate. If he doesn't have treatment-related goals—some personally meaningful reason to work with the therapist—not much will happen in treatment.

Intervention

If the beginning of the evaluation has already been completed, then the therapist can work with the client on identifying what he would like to improve in his life and making a treatment contract to include treatment activities that will help the man achieve his goals. However, in this case it appears that the therapist has not been following the model at all. If other essential aspects have also been skipped, it's best to start from scratch and do it right; otherwise, problems will continually arise.

Case 3

Phase of Treatment

With the limited information provided, all we know for sure is that if she does have a treatment plan, it's not being followed. Without having and working a plan, it's all too easy for treatment to become "supportive" rather than goal oriented.

Intervention

Do whatever steps it takes to develop a treatment contract. Then if she still doesn't stick to it, interrupt her at some point and remind her of the agreement you made together to pursue a series of steps to help her get stronger toward her goals. This can reorient her to the type of treatment you are trying to do, and together you can work out a way to stick to the plan.

Case 4

Phase of Treatment

The girl is clearly not in the trauma resolution phase today. Since it appears from the case that the case formulation, motivational component, and treatment contracting were done already, the issue probably lies elsewhere. She says she doesn't care about something that the therapist knows she does care about, so something else is going on. Chances are that something has happened to make the girl feel unsafe or insecure in some way and that the phase of treatment would be fence-around. However, it is also possible that the next trauma to be faced is much more upsetting than the ones she has already worked through. It is also possible that the therapist has offended or hurt the client somehow.

Intervention

The first strategy is for the therapist to find out what's on the girl's mind. The second step is to help her address it somehow.

The Story

In this case, it turned out that the girl's mother had gotten upset with her for a minor offense a couple of days prior to the session and threatened to send her into foster care if she misbehaved again. In other words, there was a fresh hole in the fence. The therapist was able to talk with the mother, and the mother agreed to explain to her daughter that she had said that in a moment of anger but did not mean it. Once the fence around the girl had been repaired and she felt secure again, in the following session, she was able to continue with the trauma resolution work.

Case 5

Phase of Treatment

The problem here is that the therapist wants the client to see it the therapist's way. That approach doesn't work. Treatment should be all about what the client wants, not what the therapist wants. Where's the princess?

Intervention

The therapist should be guiding the client to focus on the princess: to identify his own personal goals and how these might be achieved. Then they can discuss what strengths and resources the client can bring to bear on achieving the goals and what obstacles may exist. This provides the basis for client motivation and action.

Case 6

Phase of Treatment

This was a bit of a trick question. In this case, we're in a preevaluation phase, because something urgent must be taken care of before evaluation is even appropriate. If we do an evaluation now, all we will learn is that the boy is afraid to leave his medically fragile grandmother home alone. The principle is "safety first," and urgent safety and survival needs come before anything else.

Intervention

Safety first: In this case, the therapist advised the grandmother to make practical arrangements to ensure that someone would either be with her during the day or checking in frequently to ensure that she was safe and not in need of urgent medical care. Once this was taken care of, the boy readily returned to school.

The top priority is always to take care of pressing safety concerns. This is also a common issue in critical incident and disaster response. Naive mental health professionals may ask people how they are feeling or if they want to talk about it when what's really needed is something more practical. When people are in crisis they need to know what's going on, where their loved ones are, what they will eat, where they will sleep, how they will get home. Safety and survival come first. Often the best "mental health" intervention is giving someone a blanket, a sandwich, or crucial information.

Case 7

Phase of Treatment

In this type of situation, most therapists are trained to conduct a safety assessment for risk of suicide. This might include questions about suicidal ideas, intent, plan, and means to achieve it. If this was your response, don't feel too badly—you're not the only one. But I would argue that these are overly intrusive questions coming from a stranger. And bullets are not whizzing by. The knife is not in her hand right now. Yes, we are concerned, but this concern allows us to take all the time we need to do the job right. I would say that because this is the first meeting, we are at the beginning of the evaluation phase. So she has a presenting problem; everyone has one. This particular presenting problem does have sufficient urgency to require that much of the evaluation is done in the first meeting.

Intervention

This should include introduction to treatment, rules, favorite color, and so on. Make sure you do get to safety contracting before saying good-bye!

The Story

In this particular case, the therapist spent 2 hours with the girl, and they got all the way through the initial interview, family, developmental, medical, school, trauma/loss, and best things history. By this time, the girl felt so comfortable with the therapist that she was glad to explain about the problem with her boyfriend over the weekend and how it made her so upset that she cut her arm. When she contracted for safety, the therapist trusted her because they had a relationship; the girl was not just making a frivolous promise to get some strange adult off her back. The girl did keep her promises and also continued with treatment to a good conclusion.

Case 8

Phase of Treatment

The evaluation has not been completed: There is no princess, no case formulation, no treatment contract. The new therapist decided that the client's long-standing problem behavior suddenly constituted an emergency and jumped the gun with a premature intervention. However, there was no emergency. There was no pressing safety concern, and the consequences of the client's problem behavior, while potentially serious, did not constitute an emergency for the client. Yes, the adults were upset, and the therapist joined with the adults in imposing their concerns on the client in the futile hope that this time, for no special reason, the client would come around.

Intervention

The therapist should have stayed with going in order. Instead, the therapist jumped ahead to attempting to get the client to change behaviors. This was doomed to failure, and all the therapist accomplished was establishment of a poor track record for treatment—not a great start. At this point, the best the therapist can do is apologize and start from scratch.

Case 9

Phase of Treatment

Yes, this does happen sometimes, and it's real. It appears that the trauma resolution phase is complete before the therapist expected it to be.

So how can this be? What happened?

There are three main possibilities, and they are not mutually exclusive. First of all, the high SUDS ratings for the later traumas on the list could have been mainly "me too" reactions: overreactions that had more to do with the earlier memory than with the identified later event. When the earlier event was digested and no longer a source of distress, the discrete reactions of the later events (the reaction not related to the sore spot) just didn't amount to much and weren't significant on their own.

Also, it's possible that when the client works through one trauma memory the new lessons and healing somehow generalize to other trauma memories as well. You can't count on this to happen, but sometimes you find that it did. Even when this does occur, you often still have to treat the other trauma memories, but maybe it'll go easier because of the work that's been done on the first one.

Finally, the client's life situation may have changed in a way that makes the later trauma memory less relevant. For example, a 13-year-old boy's falling out the previous year with his former best friend was rated with a SUDS of 8. He worked through several significant earlier traumas, and by the time he got around to being ready to work on that memory, it was only a 2. The therapist told him that it had been an 8 before and asked why it was so much lower. The boy said, "Well, he wasn't ever really that good a friend anyway; we just kind of did stuff together. And I have some really good friends now, so I don't care about that anymore."

Intervention

It looks like it's time to move on to the posttrauma-resolution reassessment to see what symptoms and problems have disappeared on their own and what might need to be actively addressed. However, if I'm the therapist for this girl, I'll probably keep on checking on the SUDS levels for those untreated trauma memories, at least for a couple more weeks, just to be sure.

The Importance of Using the Fairy Tale Model

Hopefully what you are getting from these examples is the idea that clients will show us where they are by what they say and what they do. They are not always where we think they are or where we wish they would be. But at least they give us clues that we can track down to learn what's going on, and from there we can use the model to figure out what needs to be done. Sometimes a pressing concern or change in life situation causes progress or a setback. Sometimes the therapist has skipped one or more steps and ends up paying for this later when the client is unable or unwilling to do what the therapist wants.

I have been providing supervision and consultation to therapists for many years, and I've learned that certain therapy impasses occur with some frequency. One of the reasons I write books and teach workshops is that I got tired of trying to teach the whole system again and again to therapists within the 1-hour conversations we were having. Here are some of the more typical problems that therapists report, along with my Fairy Tale model response:

Therapist: So that's what's going on. I'm just not sure what to do, where to go from here.
Consultant: What's the case formulation? What's the treatment plan?

Therapist: I'm trying to get him to work with me, but it feels like I'm pulling teeth. It seems like I'm working harder than he is.
Consultant: What are his goals that he believes treatment will help him to achieve?

Therapist: This feels like a good case for [EMDR, Prolonged Exposure], but I don't know if she's ready yet.
Consultant: Do you have a trauma/loss history? Have you done skill building to develop coping skills and affect management? Have you tried the trauma resolution method with a recent minor event? What about starting with an earlier (or a lower SUDS) trauma from the list?

Therapist: I just don't see how I'm going to get anywhere with this kid, the way the home environment is.
Consultant: You're probably right. So the first thing to do is work with the parents to make things more predictable and supportive at home.

In these cases and many others, because therapists skipped steps, they got in trouble or got lost. You can't make a treatment plan without a case formulation. You can't get the client to work on the treatment plan unless the client has personal goals that he or she believes the treatment is supporting. You can't expect a client to focus on goal-oriented treatment activities while he or she is feeling threatened or unsafe in daily life. You can't do trauma resolution unless the client is safe enough and strong enough to handle it.

The Fairy Tale model is a comprehensive system; it covers the bases. When you do the steps in order and you don't skip any, the client tends to be ready and able to do the next one. Of course, some clients can go through the steps faster than others. And because life happens, clients don't always stay in order. Still, proceeding in order and doing all the steps gives you a good chance of getting the job done. When the situation isn't what you thought it was, you can use the model to figure it out and get your bearings.

The Trauma-Informed Treatment: Tasks and Interventions worksheet (Figure 12.1) offers a summary of the Fairy Tale model and the corresponding component in the trauma-informed treatment approach, including goals, tasks, and possible interventions for each phase of treatment. Note that the listed interventions are only suggestions. Other interventions may also be used to accomplish the tasks of the respective phase of treatment. If you do something that works—something that can help the client to accomplish the task—go for it.

Exercise: Case Consultation Using the Fairy Tale Model

This exercise works well either in a small group, pairs, or individually. If you are with a group, have one person present the case, and then the group members can serve as consultants. If you are working with a group, make sure to also do it again on your own, with a different client from the one you may have presented to the group. When you are working on your own, simply do both parts (i.e., presenter and consultant) yourself.

If You Are the One Presenting a Case

- Think of a challenging case, something current and on your active caseload, that's on your mind for whatever reason. It doesn't have to be either a "trauma" case or a "problem behavior" case.
- Do your best to follow the structure without straying or adding extra information.
- Start by taking about 1 minute total to summarize the most essential details of the case: client gender, age, school/work status, living situation, presenting problem, and number of sessions so far. Do not take extra time. You may feel frustrated that you have not conveyed all the important information. For the purpose of this exercise, less is more. Then the focus will be on what you are trying to learn. (If you are working on your own, skip this step; you don't need to introduce yourself to your own case.)

■ Your consultants will ask you questions. Do your best to answer, as you are together figuring out which treatment tasks are already completed, which tasks may have been skipped or only partially completed, and what you might be able to do to improve the status of the case.

If You Are the Consultant

You will be working with the Trauma-Informed Treatment: Tasks and Interventions form (Figure 12.1) and reviewing the course of treatment (for the presented case) step by step. It is essential in this exercise that you proceed in order and restrain yourself from jumping in with questions or suggestions that are out of order. One goal of this exercise is to test the model on this case. If you stick to the Fairy Tale model, can you provide a good consultation? Will you be able to effectively focus on what's most important? Will all of your questions be asked? Will all of your suggestions for interventions have a place in the model?

Another goal of the exercise is to practice using the model in a systematic way that will help you integrate it into your way of thinking about your work. If you just jump in with questions and suggestions as you think of them, you are not doing anything you don't already know how to do, so it's less likely for learning to happen. By going in order, you are, in fact, using the model. It takes discipline to wait for the right moment for your questions and suggestions. It can be helpful to make a note when you think of something so that you have it for the right moment.

Do not take more than 1 minute at any given line or treatment task. This limit may not afford adequate time to thresh out the details of a complex intervention; that's okay. The primary goal of this exercise is not to help the presenter; it is to help you to further integrate the model. If you spend too much time on one spot, you risk getting lost in the trees and not having a clear view of the forest. For now, discipline yourself and keep to the limit, so you can get the learning experience that will help you to grasp the model as a whole. In time, when you have integrated the model, of course there will be occasions in your supervision when you will spend much more time in one spot.

Have the Trauma-Informed Treatment: Tasks and Interventions form (Figure 12.1) in front of you. Go step by step through each line of this form. At each step, your underlying question is, "Has this task in treatment been completed? Or is there some way to take it even further?" Based on what you may already know, you may do the following:

■ Acknowledge that this task has already been completed.
■ Ask the therapist for additional information to determine the extent to which the task may have been completed.
■ Ask the therapist what else can be done to complete any task that still needs work.
■ Offer specific suggestions for interventions that might help to complete the task.

Trauma-Informed Treatment - Sequence of Interventions
© Ricky Greenwald, 2005

<u>Fairy Tale Model</u>

Evaluation   <u>Once upon a time...</u>

- Acculturation: purpose of treatment, treatment activities.
- Rules/expectations/agreements.
- Rapport/trust-building.

- Strengths/resources, internal and external.   <u>The knight and the</u>
- History of relationships and functioning....   <u>kingdom</u>

- along with history of problem development.   <u>The dragon</u>
- Trauma/loss history (then deep breathing, then best things).

- Motivational interviewing/goal setting   <u>The princess</u>
  ‣ Long-term goals (for teens/adults especially); shorter-term goals too.
  ‣ Practical steps to get from here to there.
  ‣ What the bad ending would look like.
  ‣ Strengths/resources in support of goals.
  ‣ Obstacles to achieving the good ending.

- Trauma-informed case formulation and psycho-education.

Remember: Case Formulation + Princess = Treatment Contract

- Trauma-relevant treatment contracting: <u>The plan</u>
  ‣ Fence around, personal training, and slay the dragon; (in other words...)
  ‣ Enhance safety and security, avoid high risk/trigger situations, stabilize, self-management skills, trauma resolution.

Safety, stabilization   <u>Fence Around</u>

- Case management re safe housing, reliable medical care, appropriate educational placement, etc.
- Parent training for increased household routine, consistent/supportive discipline, etc.
- Avoiding/preventing dangerous situations.
- Controlling/limiting bullying and other abuse.
- Avoiding "high risk" situations including trigger/sore-spot situations when possible.

Figure 12.1   Trauma-Informed Treatment

Skill-building, strength-building <u>Personal Training</u>

- Safe Place, deep breathing, etc. for self-soothing/calming.
- Self-management training for anxiety.
- In-vivo exposure to overcome fears.
- Choices Have Consequences (set this up with Map Out A Problem) for control of behaviors.
- Incentive system for habit improvement.

Trauma resolution <u>Slay the dragon</u>

- Introduce Exposure (or EMDR, CPT, or other trauma resolution activity).
- Decide the order for targeting memories (start small!).
- Break down the memory (if you need to, as a step).
- Do the exposure (or other method)

End of session:
- Container with any incompletely processed memory.
- Debrief, calming activities, assist in regaining composure.

Next session:
- Continue with same memory
- or if it's done, go to the next one; or if all done, move on.

Consolidation of gains <u>Marry the princess :^)</u>

- Revisit case management and self-management practices/interventions now that the sore spot is smaller. Get daily functioning as good as it can be.

Relapse prevention and harm reduction

- Revisit case management and self-management practices/interventions, now focused on anticipated future challenges. In particular:
  ▸ Avoid/prevent high risk situations.   <u>Compost</u>
  ▸ Prepare to cope with challenging situations that arise.   <u>Plant Apple Trees</u>
  ▸ If things should go badly, recognize the signs and catch it before it gets too bad.   <u>Dragon-Slayers In Training</u>

Figure 12.1 (continued)

Continue through the form, line by line, until you have gone a step or two ahead of what the therapist has done so far in treatment.

The activity in this exercise is to identify the elements of the treatment that have been completed as well as those elements that have been skipped or perhaps incompletely done and to generate ideas to address any gaps. The focus is not on content but on process. For example, when you ask about the trauma history, you are not asking for details about the client's trauma history; you are asking whether the therapist has learned all that he or she needs to know about the trauma history. And if not, what else might the therapist do to more fully complete this treatment task?

Discussion

Presenter, how did this go for you? Did you feel respected and supported? Did this consultation have any impact on your understanding of the case? Did you find that you had already been doing many things well? Did this consultation give you any ideas for what else to do? Did the Fairy Tale model seem to fit this case?

Consultants, how did this go for you? Did you get a chance to ask all your questions? Did you get a chance to make all your suggestions? Was there a place for them? How does this compare with other ways that you have provided supervision or consultation?

The first time you do this exercise, it should take a total of perhaps 15 minutes per presenter. With more practice, it can go much faster. Going faster has considerable value, because then you are working more with the model as a whole, with less risk of getting lost in the details. When you are doing a speed-practice, try to avoid spending more than about 1 minute at any one point.

Integrating the Model

One good way to work toward integrating the Fairy Tale model as an internalized perspective is to practice this exercise individually for 5 minutes per week. Think of whatever case happens to be on your mind—perhaps one that you feel is not going as you might wish. Go line by line, taking notes on what you would like to do to make the treatment go better (don't worry about full sentences!). Most people report that in about 5 minutes they can develop useful insights and plans that help them to resolve the "stuck" issues in the treatment.

Another good way to integrate the model is to use it as a framework for providing supervision or consultation to others. The exercise that you just completed can be used as the supervision format. It can also be used in group supervision and staff meeting settings.

The more you practice the model, the more you will be aware of where the client is in treatment, what the current task of treatment is, and what interventions might be used to accomplish the tasks. The interventions presented in this book are excellent examples, but you should also incorporate any other interventions that can help to accomplish the tasks.

References

Ahrens, J., & Rexford, L. (2002). Cognitive Processing Therapy for incarcerated adolescents with PTSD. *Journal of Aggression, Maltreatment & Trauma, 6,* 201–216.

American Psychiatric Association. (APA). (1980). *Diagnostic and statistical manual of mental disorders* (3rd ed.). Washington, DC: Author.

American Psychiatric Association (2004). *Practice guideline for the treatment of patients with acute stress disorder and post-traumatic stress disorder.* Arlington, VA: American Psychiatric Association.

Babcock, J. C., Green, C. E., & Robie, C. (2004). Does batterers' treatment work? A meta-analytic review of domestic violence treatment. *Clinical Psychology Review, 23,* 1023–1053.

Bakker, L. W., Hudson, S. M., & Ward, T. (2000). Reducing recidivism in driving while disqualified: A treatment evaluation. *Criminal Justice and Behavior, 27,* 531–560.

Becker, J., & Greenwald, R. (2008). The Family Healing Project: Adapting a trauma-informed treatment to a hard-to-reach population. Manuscript in preparation.

Bloom, S. L. (1997). *Creating sanctuary: Toward the evolution of sane societies.* New York: Routledge.

Brisbey, L. B. (2005). No longer a victim: A treatment outcome study for crime victims with PTSD. In V. Volkman (Ed.), *Traumatic incident reduction: Research and results* (pp. 23-30). Ann Arbor, MI: Loving Healing Press.

Brooks-Gordon, B., Bilby, C., & Wells, H. (2006). A systematic review of psychological interventions for sexual offenders I: Randomised control trials. *Journal of Forensic Psychiatry & Psychology, 17,* 442–466.

Brown, S. H., Gilman, S. G., Fava, N. M., & Smyth, N. J. (2009). *An integrated trauma program as an enhancement in the Thurston County drug court program: A pilot study.* Manuscript in preparation.

Chemtob, C. M., Novaco, R. W., Hamada, R. S., & Gross, D. M. (1997). Cognitive-behavioral treatment for severe anger in posttraumatic stress disorder. *Journal of Consulting and Clinical Psychology, 65,* 184–189.

Chemtob, C. M., Roitblat, H. L., Hamada, R. S., Carlson, J., & Twentyman, C. (1988). A cognitive action theory of posttraumatic stress disorder. *Journal of Anxiety Disorders, 2,* 253–275.

Cohen, J. A., Berliner, L., & March, J. S. (2000). Treatment of children and adolescents. In E. B. Foa, T. M. Keane, & M. J. Friedman (Eds.), *Effective treatments for PTSD: Practice guidelines from the International Society for Traumatic Stress Studies* (pp. 106–138). New York: Guilford.

Cohen, J. A., Mannarino, A. P., & Deblinger, E. (2006). *Treating trauma and traumatic grief in children and adolescents.* New York: Guilford.

Colby, S. M., Monti, P. M., Tevyaw, T. O., Barnett, N. P., Spirito, A., Rohsenow, D. J., et al. (2005). Brief motivational intervention for adolescent smokers in medical settings. *Addictive Behaviors, 30,* 865–874.

Curtis, N. M., Ronan, K. R., & Borduin, C. M. (2004). Multisystemic treatment: A meta-analysis of outcome studies. *Journal of Family Psychology, 18,* 411–419.

Datta, P. C., & Wallace, J. (1996). *Enhancement of victim empathy along with reduction in anxiety and increase of positive cognition of sex offenders after treatment with EMDR.* Paper presented at the annual conference of the EMDR International Association, Denver.

Descilo, T., Greenwald, R., Schmitt, T. A., & McSweeney, L. (2009). *Traumatic Incident Reduction for children: Two open trials with traumatized youth and war refugees.* Manuscript submitted for publication.

Dodge, K. A., & Frame, C. L. (1982). Social cognitive biases and deficits in aggressive boys. *Child Development, 53,* 620–635.

Dodge, K. A., & Somberg, D. R. (1987). Hostile attributional biases among aggressive boys are exacerbated under conditions of threats to the self. *Child Development, 58,* 213–224.

Dowden, C., Antonowicz, D., & Andrews, D. A. (2003). The effectiveness of relapse prevention with offenders: A meta-analysis. *International Journal of Offender Therapy and Comparative Criminology, 47,* 516–528.

EMDR International Association. (2007). *Basic training curriculum.* Accessed August 3, 2007 on Internet: http://emdria.org/associations/5581/files/BT%20Curriculum%20 1-24-07.pdf

Farkas, L., Cyr, M., Lebeau, T., & Lemay, J. (2007). Effectiveness of MASTR/EMDR therapy for traumatized adolescents with conduct problems. Manuscript submitted for publication.

Fletcher, K. E. (1996). Childhood posttraumatic stress disorder. In E. Mash & R. Barkley (Eds.), *Child psychopathology* (pp. 242–276). New York: Guilford.

Foa, E. B., Keane, T. M., & Friedman, M. J. (Eds.) (2000). *Effective treatments for PTSD: Practice guidelines from the International Society for Traumatic Stress Studies* (pp. 106–138). New York: Guilford.

Foa, E. B., & Rothbaum, B. O. (1997). *Treating the trauma of rape.* New York: Guilford.

Foa, E. B., Steketee, G., & Rothbaum, B. (1989). Behavioral/cognitive conceptualizations of post-traumatic stress disorder. *Behavior Therapy, 20,* 155–176.

Ford, J. D. (2002). Traumatic victimization in childhood and persistent problems with oppositional-defiance. *Journal of Aggression, Maltreatment, and Trauma, 6,* 25–58.

Frueh, B. C., Turner, S. M., Beidel, D. C., Mirabella, R. F., & Jones, W. J. (1996). Trauma Management Therapy: A preliminary evaluation of a multicomponent behavioral treatment for chronic combat-related PTSD. *Behavior Research and Therapy, 34,* 533–543.

Garbarino, J. (1999). *Lost boys: Why our sons turn violent and how we can save them.* New York: Free Press.

Gerbode, F. (1985). *Beyond psychology: An introduction to meta-psychology.* Palo Alto, CA: IRM Press.

Giaconia, R. M., Reinherz, H. Z., Silverman, A. B., Pakiz, B., Frost, A. K., & Cohen, E. (1995). Traumas and posttraumatic stress disorder in a community population of older adolescents. *Journal of the American Academy of Child and Adolescent Psychiatry, 34,* 1369–1380.

Girls and Boys Town. (2007) *History.* Retrieved August 8, 2007, from http://www.girlsandboystown.org/aboutus/history/Chapter1.asp

Gowers, S. G., & Smyth, B. (2004). The impact of a motivational assessment interview on initial response to treatment in adolescent anorexia nervosa. *European Eating Disorders Review, 12,* 87–93.

Greenwald, R. (1996, June). *EMDR for adolescents with disruptive behavior disorders.* Workshop presented at the annual meeting of the EMDR International Association, Denver.

Greenwald, R. (1999). *Eye movement desensitization and reprocessing (EMDR) in child and adolescent psychotherapy.* Northvale, NJ: Jason Aronson.

Greenwald, R. (2000). A trauma-focused individual therapy approach for adolescents with conduct disorder. *International Journal of Offender Therapy and Comparative Criminology, 44,* 146–163.

Greenwald, R. (2002a). Motivation-Adaptive Skills-Trauma Resolution (MASTR) therapy for adolescents with conduct problems: An open trial. *Journal of Aggression, Maltreatment, and Trauma, 6,* 237–261.

Greenwald, R. (2002b). The role of trauma in conduct disorder. *Journal of Aggression, Maltreatment, and Trauma, 6,* 5–23.

Greenwald, R. (2002c, June). *Session checklist forms in treatment research: A tool to support supervision and treatment fidelity.* Poster session presented at the annual meeting of the EMDR International Association, San Diego.

Greenwald, R. (Ed.). (2002d). *Trauma and juvenile delinquency: Theory, research and interventions.* Binghamton, NY: Haworth.

Greenwald, R. (2003, Spring). The power of a trauma-informed treatment approach. *Children's Group Therapy Association Newsletter, 24*(1), 1, 8–9.

Greenwald, R. (2005a). *Child trauma handbook: A guide for helping trauma-exposed children and adolescents.* New York: Haworth.

Greenwald, R. (2005b). *MASTR manual, revised.* Greenfield, MA: Child Trauma Institute.

Greenwald, R. (2006a). Eye movement desensitization and reprocessing (EMDR) with traumatized youth. In N. Webb (Ed.), *Working with traumatized youth in child welfare* (pp. 246-264). New York: Guilford.

Greenwald, R. (2006b). The peanut butter and jelly problem: In search of a better EMDR training model. *EMDR Practitioner.* Available Internet: http://www.emdr-practitioner.net.

Greenwald, R. (2007). *EMDR within a phase model of trauma-informed treatment.* New York: Haworth.

Greenwald, R. (2008a). Progressive counting: A new trauma resolution method. *Journal of Child & Adolescent Trauma,* 1, 249-262.

Greenwald, R. (2008b). Progressive counting for trauma resolution: Three case studies. *Traumatology,* 14, 83-92.

Greenwald, R. (2008c). *Progressive Counting: Training manual.* Greenfield, MA: Trauma Institute/Child Trauma Institute.

Greenwald, R., & Baden, K. J. (2007). *A fairy tale.* [Comic book]. Greenfield, MA: Child Trauma Institute.

Greenwald, R., Maguin, E., Smyth, N. J., Greenwald, H., Johnston, K. G., & Weiss, R. L. (2008). Trauma-related insight improves attitudes and behaviors toward challenging clients. *Traumatology, 14*(2), 1–11.

Greenwald, R., Satin, M. S., Azubuike, A. A. A., Borgen, R., & Rubin, A. (2004, November). *Trauma-informed treatment for incarcerated youth: A controlled study.* Poster session presented at the annual meeting of the International Society for Traumatic Stress Studies, New Orleans.

Greenwald, R., & Schmitt, T. A. (2008, September). *Resolving early memories reduces the level of distress associated with later memories.* Poster session presented at the annual meeting of the EMDR International Association, Phoenix.

Greenwald, R., Schmitt, T. A., & Borton, K. (2009). *Progressive Counting: Multi-site group and individual treatment open trials.* Manuscript submitted for publication.

Hamel, J. (2005). *Gender inclusive treatment of intimate partner abuse: A comprehensive approach.* New York: Springer

Henggeler, S. W., Schoenwald, S. K., & Pickrel, S. G. (1995). Multisystemic therapy: Bridging the gap between university- and community-based treatment. *Journal of Consulting and Clinical Psychology, 63,* 709–717.

Herman, J. L. (1992). *Trauma and recovery.* New York: Basic Books.

Hettema, J., Steele, J., & Miller, W. R. (2005). Motivational Interviewing. *Annual Review of Clinical Psychology, 1,* 91–111.

Horvath, A. O., & Greenberg, L. S. (Eds.). (1994). *The working alliance: Theory, research, and practice.* New York: John Wiley & Sons.

International Society for the Study of Dissociation. (2005). Guidelines for treating Dissociative Identity Disorder in adults. *Journal of Trauma & Dissociation, 6,* 69–149.

James, B. (1989). *Treating traumatized children: New insights and creative interventions.* Lexington, MA: Lexington Books.

Johnson, K., Greenwald, R., & Cameron, M. (2002, June). *A single session intervention for violent teens suspended from school.* Poster session presented at the annual meeting of the EMDR International Association, San Diego.

Johnson, D. R., Lubin, H., & Ochberg, F. (2007). *The counting method manual, revised 1/1/07.* Author.

Johnson, D. R., & Lubin, H. (2006). The counting method: Applying the rule of parsimony to the treatment of posttraumatic stress disorder. *Traumatology, 12,* 83-99.

Kazdin, A. E. (1997). Practitioner review: Psychosocial treatments for conduct disorder in children. *Journal of Child Psychology and Psychiatry, 38,* 161–178.

Kazdin, A. E. (2005). *Parent management training: Treatment for oppositional, aggressive, and antisocial behavior in children and adolescents.* New York: Oxford University Press.

Kazdin, A., Mazurick, J. L., & Bass, D. (1993). Risk for attrition in treatment of antisocial children and families. *Journal of Clinical Child Psychology, 22,* 2–16.

Kelly, A. B., & Lapworth, K. (2006). The HYP program: Targeted motivational interviewing for adolescent violations of school tobacco policy. *Preventive Medicine: An International Journal Devoted to Practice and Theory, 43,* 466–471.

Kendall, P. C. (Ed.). (2000). *Child and adolescent psychotherapy: Cognitive-behavioral procedures* (2nd ed.). New York: Guilford.

Kubler-Ross, E. (1969). *On death and dying.* New York: Macmillan.

Lang, P. J. (1977). Imagery in therapy: An information processing analysis of fear. *Behavior Therapy, 8,* 862–886.

Lee, C. W., & Drummond P. D. (2008). Effects of eye movement vs therapist instructions on the process of distressing memories. *Journal of Anxiety Disorders, 22,* 801–808.

Limber, S. P. (2006). The Olweus Bullying Prevention Program: An overview of its implementation and research basis. In S. R. Jimerson & M. Furlong, (Eds.), *Handbook of school violence and school safety: From research to practice* (pp. 293–307). Mahwah, NJ: Lawrence Erlbaum Associates Publishers.

Mallinckrodt, B., & Nelson, M. L. (1991). Counselor training level and the formation of the psychotherapeutic working alliance. *Journal of Counseling Psychology, 38,* 133–138.

Marlatt, G., A., & Donovan, D. M. (Eds.). (2005). *Relapse prevention: Maintenance strategies in the treatment of addictive behaviors* (2nd ed.). New York: Guilford Press.

Marlatt, G. A., & Gordon, J. R. (1985). *Relapse prevention: Strategies in the treatment of addictive behaviors.* New York: Guilford.

McMackin, R. A., Leisen, M. B., Cusack, J. F., LaFratta, J., & Litwin P. (2002). The relationship of trauma exposure to sex offending behavior among male juvenile offenders. *Journal of Child Sexual Abuse, 11,* 25–40.

Messer, S. B., & Wampold, B. E. (2002). Common factors are more potent than specific therapy ingredients. *Clinical Psychology Science and Practice, 6,* 21–25.

Miller, W. R. (2005). Editorial: Motivational interviewing and the incredible shrinking treatment effect. *Addiction, 100,* 421.

Miller, W. R., & Rollnick, S. (2002). *Motivational interviewing: Preparing people for change* (2nd ed.). New York: Guilford.

Miller, W. R., & Sanchez, V. C. (1994). Motivating young adults for treatment and lifestyle change. In G. Howard (Ed.), *Issues in alcohol use and misuse by young adults* (pp. 55–82). Notre Dame, IN: University of Notre Dame.

Mol, S. S. L., Arntz, A., Metsemakers, J. F. M., Dinant, G.-J., Vilters-van Montfort, P. A. P., & Knottnerus, J. A. (2005). Symptoms of post-traumatic stress disorder after non-traumatic events: Evidence from an open population study. *British Journal of Psychiatry, 186,* 494–499.

Morrison, B., & Ahmed, E. (2006). Restorative justice and civil society: Emerging practice, theory, and evidence. *Journal of Social Issues, 62,* 209–215.

Nader, K., Dubrow, N., & Hudnall Stamm, B. (1999). *Honoring differences: cultural issues in the treatment of trauma and loss.* New York: Psychology Press.

Najavits, L. M. (2002). *Seeking safety: A treatment manual for PTSD and substance abuse.* New York: Guilford Press.

Newcorn, J. H., & Strain, J. (1992). Adjustment disorder in children and adolescents. *Journal of the American Academy of Child and Adolescent Psychiatry, 31,* 318–327.

Norcross, J. C. (Ed.). (2002). *Psychotherapy relationships that work: Therapist contributions and responsiveness to patients.* New York: Oxford University Press.

Novaco, R., & Chemtob, C. M. (1998). Anger and trauma: Conceptualization, assessment, and treatment. In V. M. Follette & J. I. Ruzek, & F. R. Abueg (Eds.), *Cognitive-behavioral therapies for trauma* (pp. 162–190). New York: Guilford.

Ochberg, F. (1996). The Counting Method. *Journal of Traumatic Stress, 9,* 887–894.

Olweus, D. (1993). *Bullying at school: What we know and what we can do.* Cambridge, MA: Blackwell.

Ouimette, P., & Brown, P. J. (Eds.). (2003). *Trauma and substance abuse: Causes, consequences, and treatment of comorbid disorders.* Washington, DC: American Psychological Association.

Patterson, G. R., DeBaryshe, B. D., & Ramsey, E. (1989). A developmental perspective on antisocial behavior. *American Psychologist, 44,* 329–335.

Patterson, G. R., & Forgatch, M. S. (1985). Therapist behavior as a determinant for client noncompliance: A paradox for the behavior modifier. *Journal of Consulting and Clinical Psychology, 53,* 846–851.

Polaschek, D. L. L. (2003). Relapse prevention, offense process models, and the treatment of sexual offenders. *Professional Psychology: Research and Practice, 34,* 361–367.

Pynoos, R. S. (1990). Post-traumatic stress disorder in children and adolescents. In B. D. Garfinkel, G. A. Carlson, & E. B. Weller (Eds.), *Psychiatric disorders in children and adolescents* (pp. 48–63). Philadelphia: W. B. Saunders.

Reid, J. B., Patterson, G. R., & Snyder, J. (2002). *Antisocial behavior in children and adolescents: A developmental analysis and model for intervention.* Washington, DC: American Psychological Association.

Resick, P. A., & Schnicke, M. K. (1993). *Cognitive processing therapy for rape victims: A treatment manual.* Newbury Park: Sage Publications.

Ricci, R. J., Clayton, C. A., & Shapiro, F. (2006). Some effects of EMDR on previously abused child molesters: Theoretical reviews and preliminary findings. *Journal of Forensic Psychiatry and Psychology, 17,* 538–562.

Rivard, J. C., Bloom, S. L., McCorkle, D., & Abramovitz, R. (2005). Preliminary results of a study examining the implementation and effects of a trauma recovery framework for youths in residential treatment. *Therapeutic Communities: International Journal for Therapeutic and Supportive Organizations, 26,* 79–92.

Rogers, S., & Silver, S. M. (2003, September). *CBT v. EMDR: A comparison of effect size and treatment time.* Poster presented at the annual meeting of the EMDR International Association, Denver.

Santisteban, D. A., Suarez-Morales, L., Robbins, M. S., & Szapocznik, J. (2006). Brief strategic family therapy: Lessons learned in efficacy research and challenges to blending research and practice. *Family Process, 45,* 259–271.

Saxe, G. N., Ellis, B. H., Fogler, J., Hansen, S., & Sorkin, B. (2005). Comprehensive care for traumatized children. *Psychiatric Annals, 35,* 443–448.

Saxe, G. N., Kaplow, J. B., & Ellis, H. (2006). *Collaborative treatment of traumatized children and teens: The trauma systems therapy approach.* New York: Guilford Press.

Scheck, M. M., Schaeffer, J. A., & Gillette, C. S. (1998). Brief psychological intervention with traumatized young women: The efficacy of eye movement desensitization and reprocessing. *Journal of Traumatic Stress, 11,* 25–44.

Scherrer, J. F., Xian, H., Kapp, J. M. K., Waterman, B., Shah, K. R., Volberg, R., et al. (2007). Association between exposure to childhood and lifetime traumatic events and lifetime pathological gambling in a twin cohort. *Journal of Nervous and Mental Disease, 195,* 72–78.

Seager, J. A., Jellicoe, D., & Dhaliwal, G. K. (2004). Refusers, dropouts, and completers: Measuring sex offender treatment efficacy. *International Journal of Offender Therapy and Comparative Criminology, 48,* 600–612.

Shapiro, F. (2001). *Eye movement desensitization and reprocessing: Basic principles, protocols and procedures* (2nd ed.). New York: Guilford Press.

Shearer, J. (2007). Psychosocial approaches to psychostimulant dependence: A systematic review. *Journal of Substance Abuse Treatment, 32,* 41–52.

Snyder, J., Schrepferman, L., & St. Peter, C. (1997). Origins of antisocial behavior: Negative reinforcement and affect dysregulation of behavior as socialization mechanisms in family interaction. *Behavior Modification, 21,* 187–215.

Soberman, G. B., Greenwald, R., & Rule, D. L. (2002). A controlled study of eye movement desensitization and reprocessing (EMDR) for boys with conduct problems. *Journal of Aggression, Maltreatment, and Trauma, 6,* 217–236.

Solomon, S. D., Gerrity, E. T., & Muff, A. M. (1992). Efficacy of treatments for posttraumatic stress disorder. *Journal of the American Medical Association, 268,* 633–638.

Sommers-Flanagan, J., & Sommers-Flanagan, R. (1995). Psychotherapeutic techniques with treatment-resistant adolescents. *Psychotherapy, 32,* 131–140.

Stein, L. A. R., Colby, S. M., Barnett, N. P., Monti, P. M., Golembeske, C., Lebeau-Craven, R., et al. (2006). Enhancing substance abuse treatment engagement in incarcerated adolescents. *Psychological Services, 3,* 25–34.

Steiner, H., Garcia, I. G., & Matthews, Z. (1997). Posttraumatic stress disorder in incarcerated juvenile delinquents. *Journal of the American Academy of Child and Adolescent Psychiatry, 36,* 357–365.

Steward, S. (1996). Alcohol abuse in individuals exposed to trauma: A critical review. *Psychological Bulletin, 120,* 83–112.

Stewart, K. (1998, July). *Incorporating EMDR in a residential setting for abused adolescent females.* Paper presented at the annual meeting of the EMDR International Association, Baltimore.

Suarez, M., & Mullins, S. (2008). Motivational interviewing and pediatric health behavior interventions. *Journal of Developmental and Behavioral Pediatrics, 29,* 417–428.

Sue, D. W., & Sue, D. (1999). *Counseling the culturally different: Theory and Practice.* (3rd ed.) New York: John Wiley and Sons.

Swenson, C, Henggeler, S. W., Taylor, I. S., & Addison, O. W. (2005). *Multisystemic therapy and neighborhood partnerships.* New York: Guilford Press

Taylor, S. E., Pham, L. B., Rivkin, I. D., & Armor, D. A. (1998). Harnessing the imagination: Mental simulation, self-regulation, and coping. *American Psychologist, 53,* 429–439.

Terr, L. (1991). Childhood traumas: An outline and overview. *American Journal of Psychiatry, 148,* 10–20.

Valentine, P. V. (2005). Brief treatment of trauma-related symptoms in incarcerated females with TIR. In V. Volkman (Ed.), *Traumatic incident reduction: Research and results* (pp. 43–50). Ann Arbor, MI: Loving Healing Press.

Van der Kolk, B. A., Pelcovitz, D., Roth, S., Mandel, F. S., McFarlane, A., & Herman, J. L. (1996). Dissociation, somatization, and affect dysregulation: The complexity of adaptation to trauma. *American Journal of Psychiatry, 153*(Festschrift Supplement), 83–93.

Vrana, S., & Lauterbach, D. (1994). Prevalence of traumatic events and post-traumatic psychological symptoms in a nonclinical sample of college students. *Journal of Traumatic Stress, 7,* 289–302.

Wahler, R. G., & Dumas, J. E. (1986). Maintenance factors in coercive mother–child interactions: The compliance and predictability hypotheses. *Journal of Applied Behavior Analysis, 19,* 13–22.

Ward, T., & Gannon, T. A. (2006). Rehabilitation, etiology, and self-regulation: The comprehensive good lives model of treatment for sexual offenders. *Aggression and Violent Behavior, 11,* 77–94.

Ward, T., & Siegert, R. J. (2002). Toward a comprehensive theory of child sexual abuse: A theory knitting perspective. *Psychology, Crime, and Law, 8,* 319–351.

Weisz, J. R., Walter, B. R., Weiss, B., Fernandez, G. A., & Mikow, V. A. (1990). Arrests among emotionally disturbed violent and assaultive individuals following minimal versus lengthy intervention through North Carolina's Willie M. Program. *Journal of Consulting and Clinical Psychology, 58,* 720–728.

Widom, C. S. (1989). Does violence beget violence? A critical examination of the literature. *Psychological Bulletin, 106,* 3–28.

Wierzbicki, M., & Pekarik, G. (1993). A metaanalysis of psychotherapy dropout. *Professional Psychology: Research and Practice, 24,* 190–195.

Wolpe, J. (1958). *Psychotherapy by reciprocal inhibition.* Stanford, CA: Stanford University Press.

Appendix A

Trauma-Informed Treatment Information and Resources

Things change so fast that I think that the best way to give you good information is to give you access to information as it develops. Here are two good, reliable sites that can help you to find what you need, including up-to-date links to other sites.

Trauma Institute & Child Trauma Institute

As founder and executive director of the Trauma Institute & Child Trauma Institute, I developed and maintain this web site at http://www.trauma.info and http://www.childtrauma.com. It won't overwhelm you with links, but the ones I think are most important are there. The site also features the following:

- Information on training programs related to trauma-informed treatment.
- Information on child/adolescent trauma assessment, including reviews of measures, samples of some instruments, updated data, and abstracts/reprints of published papers.
- A list of publications that can be accessed on site or elsewhere on line.
- Articles for laypeople and other handouts you can use with clients.
- Links to selected sites that offer information related to trauma treatment, motivational interviewing, conduct disorder, domestic violence, and addictions.

Trauma Info Pages

David Baldwin, Ph.D., maintains http://www.trauma-pages.com, which is highly regarded as *the* trauma information site online. This site is comprehensive in providing many types of information about trauma, trauma research, and trauma treatment. Here is a partial list of this site's offerings:

- Information about trauma.
- Trauma articles.
- Trauma resources.
- Disaster handouts and links.
- Trauma links: psychology, research, medical.

Appendix B

The Role of Trauma in Conduct Disorder

Ricky Greenwald

Conduct disorder represents a fairly common pattern of impulsive and antisocial behavior—including, but not limited to, juvenile delinquency—entailing enormous cost to afflicted individuals, their victims, and society (Robins, 1981). We now know a lot about risk factors for the development of conduct disorder, including temperament, gender, low intelligence, attention deficit hyperactivity disorder (ADHD), impulsivity, poor coping skills, social failure, parental psychopathology, inappropriate discipline, affiliation with deviant peers, and socioeconomic disadvantage (see Kazdin, 1995; Moffitt, 1993; Patterson, DeBaryshe, & Ramsey, 1989). We address these factors with a variety of treatment approaches and do help some youth to be successful in socially acceptable ways. Unfortunately, there is as yet no treatment of choice for adolescents with conduct disorder, with even preferred approaches yielding only modest results (Kazdin, 1997b). This may be explained, at least in part, by our failure to address trauma's contribution to conduct disorder.

In this chapter I review child/adolescent trauma prevalence and outcomes, with an emphasis on the conduct disorder population, and then propose a key role for trauma in the development and persistence of conduct disorder. I will discuss current treatment approaches in that light and suggest avenues for further research.

Child and Adolescent Trauma

For present purposes, trauma will be defined as an event in which the child or adolescent experiences intense horror, fear or pain, along with helplessness (Krystal, 1978). Typical examples include auto accident, physical or sexual assault, and witnessing violence. However, there is considerable empirical support for the notion that major loss experiences have a trauma-like impact on children and adolescents (Newcorn & Strain, 1992), except that the hyperarousal response may not be present following a loss (Pynoos, 1990). Therefore, although this discussion will focus strictly on trauma, many of the points probably apply to a wider range of adverse life experiences to which these youth have been exposed.

Prevalence of Trauma Exposure

Some of the data on the prevalence of traumatic events in childhood are indirect and suggestive, yet persuasive and alarming (Finkelhor & Dziuba-Leatherman, 1994; Pynoos, 1990). Recent research has found very high incidence rates for prior experience of at least one Criterion A (major trauma) stressor among young adults—most of which presumably occurred during childhood or adolescence. For example, Riise, Corrigan, Uddo, and Sutker (1994) found an 85% incidence among a military population (only a minority of which were combat related), and Vrana and Lauterbach (1994) found an 84% incidence among college students (for more discussion, see Vrana & Lauterbach, 1994). Trauma during childhood and adolescence is now so common as to be normative (Ford et al., 1996; Greenwald & Rubin, 1999).

Among disadvantaged urban youth, exposure to violence and other potentially traumatic events appears to be a regular occurrence (Campbell & Schwarz, 1996; Jenkins, 1995; Ozer & Weinstein, 1998; Singer, Anglin, Song, & Lunghofer, 1995), a consistent finding despite the underreporting inherent in many study designs (Wolfer, 1997). Many risk factors for conduct disorder also constitute increased risk for trauma: exposure to negligent, coercive, pathological, and/or substance-abusing parents; and exposure to poverty-related violence and crime.

Effects of Trauma

Not all trauma experiences lead to posttraumatic stress reactions (although they may increase future vulnerability), and such reactions, when they do occur, can vary widely in severity and range of symptomatology (Fletcher, 1996; Giaconia et al., 1995). The ability of the individual to recover psychologically from trauma appears to be influenced by numerous factors, including temperament, personality/coping style, severity of exposure, frequency/chronicity of exposure, and posttrauma environmental factors (Fletcher, 1996). Children and adolescents subject to the unfavorable environments that put them at risk for conduct disorder are simultaneously at increased risk for repeated trauma exposure as well as nonsupportive posttrauma environments; thus, they are at increased risk for post-traumatic stress symptoms.

Trauma is experienced as scary, horrible, painful, intolerable. The potentially overwhelming nature of the traumatic experience can lead to a failure to integrate, work through, or "get over" the memory. Then the associated imagery, affect, and cognition may intrude unchecked, outside the control or mediation of the normal, verbally encoded memory storage system (van der Kolk, 1987). Indeed, elements of the traumatic memory are liable to intrude, unless and until the memory has gone through the normal processing system. Thematically related stimuli may trigger the intrusion of trauma-related material, leading to overreactivity in some areas.

Trauma constitutes a violation of the victim's sense of safety and belief in the world as a safe place. This can have the profound effect of reorienting the victim from a complacent to a defensive posture. The posttraumatic "survival mode" orientation can become self-perpetuating through a dynamic of mutually reinforcing symptoms and responses (Chemtob, Roitblat, Hamada, Carlson, & Twentyman, 1988). In a state of heightened alertness and sensitivity to possible danger, minor or even neutral stimuli are misinterpreted as threatening, leading to further arousal and defensive action, such as avoidance, withdrawal, or aggression. This leads in turn to reinforcement of the perception of the world as a dangerous place, preventing recovery from the trauma. In other words, survival mode is perpetuated by the psychological experience of ongoing retraumatization. Classic examples include the combat veteran diving for cover when a balloon pops and the physically abused child who perceives an accidental bump by a passing peer to be an assault. Even the intrusive memory itself can be perceived as threatening. The trauma victim may learn to live in a psychological "war zone" (Garbarino, 1999) and adjusts accordingly, while remaining ever vulnerable to the unprocessed memory elements.

The effects of unintegrated traumatic experiences can thus become permanently established, potentially leading to a variety of posttraumatic symptoms, and forming the basis of many types of psychopathology (e.g., Brom, 1991; Conaway & Hansen, 1989; Famularo, Kinscherff, & Fenton, 1992; Flisher et al., 1997; Green, 1983; Kendall-Tackett, Williams, & Finkelhor, 1993; Terr, 1991; van der Kolk, 1987). The high rate of conduct disorder-related comorbidity noted in the literature (Wierson, Forehand, & Frame, 1992)—mainly affective disorders and substance abuse—may partially reflect trauma effects; at least, one comorbid condition does not cause the other, but both arise from common pathways such as adverse living conditions (Fergusson, Lynskey, & Horwood, 1996), which also engender trauma. Note that trauma may also lead to lasting symptoms in lieu of any formal diagnosis (e.g., Cuffe et al., 1998; Giaconia et al., 1995). This confusing array of responses to traumatization may partially account for the field's general failure to address trauma effects in conduct disorder.

Trauma's Contribution to Conduct Disorder

Although trauma effects can manifest in many ways, when combined with the other risk factors noted above, trauma may be integral to the development and persistence of conduct disorder. Certain key features of the disorder can be explained much more completely by considering the trauma contribution. Trauma can violate basic trust, disrupt attachment, and interfere with empathy (James, 1989), thus reducing inhibitions regarding crimes against others. Trauma can leave the victim in a perpetual state of alert; this sensitivity to threat can lead to a hostile attribution bias, leading in turn to impaired social competence and increased aggressive behaviors (Chemtob et al., 1988; Hartman & Burgess, 1993). Trauma can engender anger and violent acting out (Chemtob, Novaco, Hamada, Gross, & Smith, 1997). Trauma can create intolerable emotion such as intense fear or sadness, sometimes leading in turn to substance abuse (Clark, Lesnick, & Hegedus, 1997; Steward, 1996) and other high-risk activities (Hernandez, Lodico, & DiClemente, 1993). Trauma can diminish the sense of future (Fletcher, 1996; Terr, 1991), fostering an instant gratification orientation and precluding regard for delayed consequences or investment in the long-term. Trauma's unintegrated imagery and intense emotional reactivity can lead to affect dysregulation along with violent and destructive acting out (van der Kolk et al., 1996). Trauma effects can last indefinitely and can become a primary focus around which personality and behavior are organized (Terr, 1991; van der Kolk et al., 1996).

There is a considerable body of literature documenting the relationship between trauma/maltreatment and subsequent aggressive/criminal acting out (see Malinosky-Rummell & Hansen, 1993; Widom, 1989). Prospective studies have identified trauma exposure as a significant risk factor for youth antisocial behavior (Herrenkohl, Egolf, & Herrenkohl, 1997; Luntz & Widom, 1994; Pakiz, Reinherz, & Giaconia, 1997; Rivera & Widom, 1990; Thornberry, 1994). Although not all traumatized youth become antisocial, studies of antisocial youth have found rates of self-reported trauma exposure ranging from 70% to 92% (Dembo, La Voie, Schmeidler, & Washburn, 1987; Lewis, Mallouh, & Webb, 1989; McMackin, Morrissey, Newman, Erwin, & Daley, 1998; Rivera & Widom, 1990; Steiner, Garcia, & Matthews, 1997). The trend of more recent studies reporting higher exposure rates may reflect improved methodology and/or higher rates of exposure for the more recent cohort.

Although much of this research has focused on physical and sexual abuse, exposure to community violence is also a major concern. For example, Wood and colleagues (Wood, Foy, Layne, Pynoos, & James, 2001) reported that 57% of their sample of incarcerated adolescents had witnessed a murder, 17% had witnessed a suicide, and 72% had been shot or shot at.

The effect of trauma exposure is presumably mediated by associated symptoms that may result. Antisocial youth have been found to have high rates of posttraumatic stress disorder (PTSD), ranging from 24% to 65% (Burton, Foy, Bwanausi, Johnson, & Moore, 1994; Cauffman, Feldman, Waterman, & Steiner,

1998; Doyle & Bauer, 1989; McMackin et al., 1998; Steiner et al., 1997; Watson, Kucala, Manifold, Juba, & Vassar, 1988; Wood, Foy, Layne, Pynoos, & James, 2001). Since trauma exposure can lead to a range of problems in addition to PTSD (Giaconia et al., 1995; Kendall-Tackett, Williams, & Finkelhor, 1993), this represents a conservative estimate of trauma-related symptoms and functional impairment in this population. For example, Giaconia and colleagues found that girls in their sample had PTSD 6 times more than boys following trauma exposure; however, boys and girls experienced similar levels of dysfunction following trauma exposure, regardless of diagnostic status.

It is even possible that in some cases conduct disorder is a direct expression of posttraumatic symptomatology. A study of combat veterans found that combat-related trauma predicted both PTSD symptomatology and antisocial behavior, making an additional contribution to the antisocial behavior beyond premorbid predictors (Resnick, Foy, Donahoe, & Miller, 1989). A study comparing adolescents with conduct disorder and PTSD found equally severe behavioral symptoms in both groups (Atlas, DiScipio, Schwartz, & Sessoms, 1991). In another study, adolescents in residential treatment—diagnosis not specified—were indistinguishable from incarcerated adolescents by either psychological symptoms or behaviors (Cohen et al., 1990). However, since there are many possible psychological and behavioral outcomes to trauma (Giaconia et al., 1995; Kendall-Tackett, Williams, & Finkelhor, 1993), it is certain that other factors—such as those noted in the literature—are still very important in determining specific outcomes such as antisocial behavior.

Trauma in Developmental Models of Conduct Disorder

Recognition of trauma's possible role in the development and persistence of conduct disorder does not necessarily entail discarding prior models; rather, those models are enriched. Trauma can help to account for the dynamic underpinnings of the models, why they work. In this light, two prominent models are briefly reviewed below.

The Reinforcement for Coercive Behavior Model

This model of conduct disorder posits that a pattern of ineffectual, combined with intermittently explosive, discipline reinforces noncompliant and coercive rather than prosocial behaviors, because the child's antisocial behaviors lead to positive outcomes such as termination of parental aversive behavior and/or obtaining desired goods or privileges (Patterson, 1986). The child's increasing reliance on noncompliant and coercive behaviors leads to increased parental rejection, peer rejection, school discipline problems, school underachievement, and failure to develop empathy via appropriate family and peer relations. In addition to failing to gain competence in prosocial interpersonal skills, such youth may become socially isolated and depressed. Later exposure to a deviant peer group provides in-group social acceptance along with training and reinforcement from peers for more serious antisocial behaviors (Patterson, DeBaryshe, & Ramsey, 1989).

One plausible role for trauma within this model relates to the affect dysregulation and consequent acting out, which is characteristic of many traumatized individuals (van der Kolk et al., 1996). Some research suggests that affect dysregulation may be as powerful a predictor of antisocial behavior as parental reinforcement for coercive behavior (Snyder, Schrepferman, & St. Peter, 1997). There may be a synergistic effect of mutual reinforcement between these two factors, in that children who are emotionally overreactive are more likely to engage in confrontive, coercive, and noncompliant behaviors (Snyder et al.), leading in turn to more parental reactivity and harshness (Lytton, 1990). This dynamic could also explain the recent finding that trauma exposure was higher among youth with Oppositional Defiant Disorder (a common precursor to conduct disorder) than those with adjustment disorder or ADHD, even after controlling for other risk factors (Ford et al., 1999).

Another plausible role for trauma relates to the question of just what is being reinforced when parents respond inappropriately to children's noncompliant and coercive behaviors. In fact, many of the child's antisocial behaviors lead to apparently negative consequences such as verbal or physical abuse, rejection, or loss of privileges. There is some research to support the notion that, at least on some occasions, what is reinforcing is not that the child gets "what he wants" in some material sense but that by forcing an ostensibly aversive parental response, he has turned a chaotic environment into a predictable one (Wahler & Dumas, 1986). Although a chaotic environment might be uncomfortable for many children, it would be particularly disconcerting for a traumatized child, who may view predictable punishment (or predictable "aversive" attention) as preferable to chaos.

Trauma may also play a central role in the persistence of conduct disorder. Trauma-related hypersensitivity to threat (Chemtob et al., 1988) can lead to misinterpretation of social cues, heightened arousal and anger, and inappropriate aggression in the perceived cause of self-protection. This information processing style is consistent with the "hostile attribution bias" commonly noted among antisocial youth (e.g., Dodge & Frame, 1982), and its use increases as a result of increased feelings of vulnerability or threat (Dodge & Somberg, 1987). This information processing style is self-perpetuating because the perception of threat increases the likelihood of aggression, engendering hostility in others and thus confirming the perception of others as dangerous. Similarly, anger in traumatized youth may serve the function of dampening fear and thus may be self-reinforcing (Novaco, 1976).

Furthermore, trauma-related affect dysregulation may trigger reactivity to a variety of situations and stimuli perceived as thematically related to the trauma. A recent study found that situations triggering trauma-related helplessness, and to a lesser extent fear or horror, accounted for initiating 81% of the "offense cycle" patterns of a sample of adolescent sex offenders, according to therapist ratings

(McMackin, LaFratta, & Litwin, 2000). While the acting-out behavior may provide immediate relief from the trauma-related thoughts and feelings, the consequences of that behavior often serve to confirm the negative lessons initially learned from the trauma, thus reinforcing reactivity and continued susceptibility to reoffending (see Figure B1).

The Cumulative Risk Model

The *cumulative risk* model—more accurately, an atheoretical, piecemeal approach to explanation—posits that the greater the presence of risk factors, the greater the risk that conduct disorder will develop. These factors may have interactive and progressive effects. Trauma may play a role in several of the risk factors that have been identified as contributing to conduct disorder.

For example, various aspects of temperament have been implicated in predisposition to developing conduct disorder (Lytton, 1990; Moffitt & Henry, 1989; Newman & Wallace, 1993); however, what is identified as temperament in the cited studies may already reflect the pervasive effects of early trauma (Perry, Pollard, Blakley, Baker, & Vigilante, 1995). ADHD, widely identified as a risk factor for conduct disorder (Jensen, Martin, & Cantwell, 1997), may sometimes actually represent misdiagnosed PTSD (Cuffe, McCullough, & Pumariega, 1994; Friedman, Harper, Becker, Wilson, & Tinker, 1997).

Learning and academic problems are another widely cited risk factor (Hinshaw, 1997); neuropsychological deficits impeding memory and learning have been linked to child maltreatment (Palmer, Frantz, et al., 1999; Perry et al., 1995). Furthermore, traumatized child, adolescent, and young adult populations do worse than less traumatized controls on a variety of measures of intelligence and academic achievement (Garcia, Lauterbach, Pavlicek, Burns, & Sykes, 1999; Loiselle & Belicki, 1999; Palmer, Brinker, Nicolini, & Farrar, 1999).

The deficits in cognitive processing of interpersonal cues noted in the literature (e.g., Dodge & Frame, 1982; Dodge & Somberg, 1987) may reflect the hostile attribution bias noted among some traumatized individuals who are hypersensitive to indicators of threat (Chemtob et al., 1988; Hartman & Burgess, 1993). Even poor parenting, such as harshness and rejection, can be stimulated by a child's volatility and noncompliance (Lytton, 1990)—again, the child's misbehavior may reflect traumatization (Fletcher, 1996). In sum, the posttraumatic reaction is potentially so pervasive for some individuals that a variety of identified conduct disorder risk factors may be created, mimicked, and/or exacerbated as a result of trauma.

Treatment Issues

Despite the prevalence of trauma history and posttraumatic symptoms among adolescents with conduct disorder, treatment programs tend to address it only in a partial manner. Since trauma effects can be so powerful, this gap in treatment

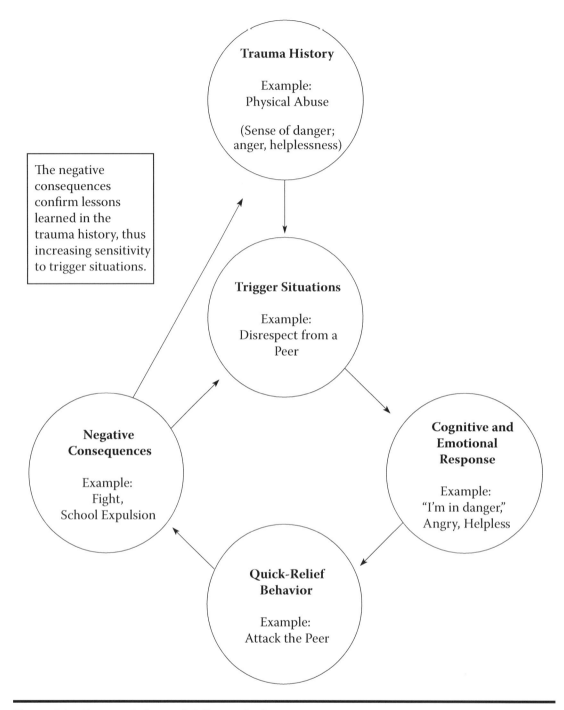

Figure B1   Trauma-Informed Offense Cycle

may leave the youth relatively impervious to the other elements of the treatment program. Until trauma effects are directly targeted and effectively addressed, success rates with this population may remain at the current level.

Trauma treatment involves—to oversimplify—two phases: establishing a sense of safety and then working through the traumatic material (Cohen, Berliner, & March, 2000; James, 1989; Pynoos & Eth, 1986). Safety can be effectively addressed in many ways within a milieu treatment program for adolescents with conduct disorder. A range of physical and behavioral controls helps to maintain a sense of bodily safety. Positive relationships with individual staff members, as well as consistent rules and daily routine, help to foster a sense of emotional safety. In outpatient treatment, parent training contributes to environmental stability, predictability, and supportiveness and indeed has documented effectiveness, particularly with younger children (Kazdin, 1997a). Cognitive-behavioral training also contributes, in that increased self-control allows for increased control over—and predictability of—the environment. For example, in a study of volatile veterans with PTSD, participation in an anger management group led to increased self-control as well as reduction of apparently unrelated trauma symptoms (e.g., intrusive thoughts and images), whereas the routine care for PTSD did neither (Chemtob, Novaco, Hamada, & Gross, 1997). Although cognitive-behavioral interventions do show modest effectiveness with conduct-disordered youth (Kazdin, 1997b), posttraumatic symptomatology has not been tracked in these studies. Consistent with this trauma-informed perspective, Greenwood (1994) observed that the more effective residential programs for juvenile delinquents do feature cognitive-behavioral treatment as well as small, noninstitutional settings in which a relatively secure and supportive environment can be provided.

Unfortunately, current treatment approaches do not address the working through phase very well. In some programs there is at least an attempt to do this, whether individually or in group work, but it's unlikely to be very helpful. (In lieu of directly applicable studies, see discussion of treatment difficulties in Solomon, Gerrity, & Muff, 1992.) First of all, this population is extremely resistant to even engaging in psychotherapy (Kazdin, Mazurick, & Bass, 1993; Sommers-Flanagan & Sommers-Flanagan, 1995). The trauma effects can make them want to avoid close relationships, avoid reminders of the trauma, and avoid even temporary distress for a long-term gain that they don't believe they'll see. Second, even those who are willing to address the trauma in treatment typically make only limited progress toward actual resolution and symptom reduction. Clinical experience indicates that many who attempt to face their traumatic memories only get upset, leading to acting out, negative consequences, and then increased resistance to treatment. The treatment methods used are potentially harmful, generally inadequate, and, at best, inconsistently effective. However, preliminary reports of more successful trauma-focused treatment of conduct disordered youth are beginning to emerge (e.g., Doyle & Bauer, 1989; Greenwald, 2000, 2001; Greenwald, Lundberg, & Smyth, 2001).

Conclusion

Further ascertaining the role of trauma in conduct disorder can be accomplished in several ways. Trauma-related assessment can be included in prospective studies of child/adolescent development. Archival studies and retrospective interviewing can also help to ascertain whether trauma history precedes, or even precipitates, conduct problems. Trauma history and symptoms can also be assessed at intake or at other points when youth with conduct disorder are identified and accessible. In these contexts it will be important to assess not merely for Criterion A events and PTSD but also for the full range of adverse life events and posttraumatic symptomatology, as trauma effects are of clinical and theoretical interest regardless of formal diagnosis.

A fuller elaboration of this traumagenic model of conduct disorder will emerge from studying the interaction between traumatic exposure, posttraumatic symptoms, behavioral contingencies, and other identified contributors to conduct disorder. Since conduct disorder encompasses subtypes (e.g., Christian, Frick, Hill, Tyler, & Frazer, 1997; Moffitt, 1993; Sorensen & Johnson, 1996), these should be considered, as they may prove variably trauma related. Gender is also likely to be a variable of interest, given gender-related differences in behavioral expressions of psychopathology (Zahn-Waxler, 1993), higher rates of PTSD among incarcerated girls compared with incarcerated boys (Cauffman et al., 1998), and somewhat different developmental paths for male versus female juvenile delinquents (Wood, Foy, Gogeun, James, & Pynoos, 2001). Ultimately we should be able to describe the various typical developmental paths that result in conduct disorder and to specify trauma's possible contribution at critical points.

Trauma-focused treatment approaches can also be tested, preferably systematic trauma treatments (e.g., Doyle & Bauer, 1989; Greenwald, 2000, 2001) rather than partial approaches such as psychoeducation or symptom management training. Since conduct disorder seems to be complex and multidetermined, a comprehensive approach including trauma treatment is likely to be more consistently effective than a stand-alone trauma treatment. In treatment outcome studies, both trauma symptoms and conduct disorder symptoms should be tracked to ascertain whether reduction in conduct disorder symptoms is indeed related to the trauma effects.

Existing effective prevention approaches (e.g., Zigler, Taussig, & Black, 1992) can be analyzed for impact on trauma-related issues such as increased environmental stability and reduced risk of trauma exposure, as well as indices of posttraumatic symptomatology. Trauma prevention and treatment components can be added to early intervention/prevention approaches and evaluated for additional yield.

Considering trauma may prove to be key to a more dynamic and comprehensive understanding of conduct disorder, leading to more effective prevention and treatment. Given the ubiquity of trauma in the histories of conduct disordered youth, with potentially profound and lasting effects, trauma may play a central role in the development and persistence of conduct disorder for a large subset—even a majority—of this population. Without negating other important components of prevention and treatment, it may be useful to consider trauma as an organizing principle informing prevention and treatment approaches. Effectively addressing trauma means that other potentially effective interventions may stand a better chance of success.

References

Atlas, J. A., DiScipio, W. J., Schwartz, R., & Sessoms, L. (1991). Symptom correlates among adolescents showing posttraumatic stress disorder versus conduct disorder. *Psychological Reports, 69,* 920–922.

Bowers, L. B. (1990). Traumas precipitating female delinquency: Implications for assessment, practice, and policy. *Child and Adolescent Social Work, 7,* 389–402.

Brom, D. (1991). The prevalence of posttraumatic psychopathology in the general and the clinical population. *Israel Journal of Psychiatry & Related Sciences, 28,* 53–63.

Burton, D., Foy, D., Bwanausi, C., Johnson, J., & Moore, L. (1994). The relationship between traumatic exposure, family dysfunction, and post-traumatic stress symptoms in male juvenile offenders. *Journal of Traumatic Stress, 7,* 83–92.

Campbell, C., & Schwarz, D. (1996). Prevalence and impact of exposure to interpersonal violence among suburban and urban middle school students. *Pediatrics, 98,* 396–402.

Cauffman, E., Feldman, S. S., Waterman, J., & Steiner, H. (1998). Posttraumatic stress disorder among female juvenile offenders. *Journal of the American Academy of Child and Adolescent Psychiatry, 37,* 1209–1216.

Chemtob, C. M., Roitblat, H. L., Hamada, R. S., Carlson, J., & Twentyman, C. (1988). A cognitive action theory of posttraumatic stress disorder. *Journal of Anxiety Disorders, 2,* 253–275.

Chemtob, C. M., Novaco, R. W., Hamada, R. S., & Gross, D. M. (1997). Cognitive-behavioral treatment for severe anger in posttraumatic stress disorder. *Journal of Consulting and Clinical Psychology, 65,* 184–189.

Chemtob, C. M., Novaco, R. W., Hamada, R. S., Gross, D. M., & Smith, G. A. (1997). Anger regulation deficits in combat-related posttraumatic stress disorder. *Journal of Traumatic Stress, 10,* 17–36.

Christian, R. E., Frick, P. J., Hill, N. L., Tyler, L., & Frazer, D. R. (1997). Psychopathy and conduct problems in children: II. Implications for subtyping children with conduct problems. *Journal of the American Academy of Child and Adolescent Psychiatry, 36,* 233–241.

Clark, D. B., Lesnick, L., & Hegedus, A. M. (1997). Traumas and other adverse life events in adolescents with alcohol abuse and dependence. *Journal of the American Academy of Child and Adolescent Psychiatry, 36,* 1744–1751.

Cohen, J. A., Berliner, L., & March, J. S. (2000). Treatment of children and adolescents. In E. B. Foa, T. M. Keane, & M. J. Friedman (Eds.), *Effective treatments for PTSD: Practice guidelines from the International Society for Traumatic Stress Studies* (pp. 106–138). New York: Guilford.

Cohen, R., Parmelee, D. X., Irwin, L., Weisz, J. R., Howard, P., Purcell, P., & Best, A. M. (1990). Characteristics of children and adolescents in a psychiatric hospital and a corrections facility. *Journal of the American Academy of Child and Adolescent Psychiatry, 29,* 909–913.

Conaway, L. P., & Hansen, D. J. (1989). Social behavior of physically abused and neglected children: A critical review. *Clinical Psychology Review, 9,* 627–652.

Cuffe, S. P., Addy, C. L., Garrison, C. Z., Waller, J. L., Jackson, K. L., McKeown, R. E., & Chilappagari, S. (1998). Prevalence of PTSD in a community sample of older adolescents. *Journal of the American Academy of Child and Adolescent Psychiatry, 37,* 147–154.

Cuffe, S. P., McCullough, F. L., & Pumariega, A. J. (1994). Comorbidity of Attention Deficit Hyperactivity Disorder and Post-Traumatic Stress Disorder. *Journal of Child and Family Studies, 3,* 327–336.

Dembo, R., La Voie, L., Schmeidler, J., & Washburn, M. (1987). The nature and correlates of psychological/emotional functioning among a sample of detained youth. *Criminal Justice and Behavior, 14,* 311–334.

Dembo, R., Williams, L., Wothke, W., Schmeidler, J., & Brown, C. H. (1992). The role of family factors, physical abuse, and sexual victimization experiences in high-risk youths' alcohol and other drug use and delinquency: A longitudinal model. *Violence and Victimization, 7,* 245–265.

Dodge, K. A., & Frame, C. L. (1982). Social cognitive biases and deficits in aggressive boys. *Child Development, 53,* 620–635.

Dodge, K. A., & Somberg, D. R. (1987). Hostile attributional biases among aggressive boys are exacerbated under conditions of threats to the self. *Child Development, 58,* 213–224.

Doyle, J. S., & Bauer, S. K. (1989). Post-traumatic stress disorder in children: Its identification and treatment in a residential setting for emotionally disturbed youth. *Journal of Traumatic Stress, 2,* 275–288.

Famularo, R., Kinscherff, R., & Fenton, T. (1992). Psychiatric diagnoses of maltreated children: Preliminary findings. *Journal of the American Academy of Child and Adolescent Psychiatry, 31,* 863–867.

Fergusson, D. M., Lynskey, M. T., & Horwood, J. (1996). Origins of comorbidity between conduct and affective disorders. *Journal of the American Academy of Child and Adolescent Psychiatry, 35,* 451–460.

Finkelhor, D., & Dziuba-Leatherman, J. (1994). Victimization of children. *American Psychologist, 49,* 173–183.

Fletcher, K. E. (1996). Childhood posttraumatic stress disorder. In E. Mash & R. Barkley (Eds.), *Child psychopathology* (pp. 242–276). NY: Guilford.

Flisher, A. J., Kramer, R. A., Hoven, C. W., Greenwald, S., Alegria, M., Bird, H. R., Canino, G., Connell, R., & Moore, R. E. (1997). Psychosocial characteristics of physically abused children and adolescents. *Journal of the American Academy of Child and Adolescent Psychiatry, 36,* 123–131.

Ford, J. D., Racusin, R., Daviss, W. B., Ellis, C., Thomas, J., Rogers, K., Reiser, J., Schiffman, J., & Sengupta, A. (1999). Trauma exposure among children with Attention Deficit Hyperactivity Disorder and Oppositional Defiant Disorder. *Journal of Consulting and Clinical Psychology, 67,* 786-789.

Ford, J. D., Saxe, G., Daviss, W. B., Ellis, C., Rogers, K., Racusin, R., & Thomas, J. (1996, November). *Post-traumatic stress detection and intervention in pediatric healthcare.* Paper presented at the annual meeting of the International Society for Traumatic Stress Studies, San Francisco.

Friedman, M. C., Harper. M. L., Becker, L. A., Wilson, S. A., & Tinker, R. H. (1997, November). *A comparison of Attention Deficit/Hyperactivity Disorder and Posttraumatic Stress Disorder symptomatology in children.* Poster session presented at the annual meeting of the International Society for Traumatic Stress Studies, Montreal.

Garbarino, J. (1999). *Lost boys: Why our sons turn violent and how we can save them.* NY: Free Press.

Garcia, M., Lauterbach, D., Pavlicek, D., Burns, J., & Sykes, M. (1999, November). *Relationship between trauma exposure, PTSD symptoms, and academic performance.* Poster session presented at the annual meeting of the International Society for Traumatic Stress Studies, Miami.

Giaconia, R. M., Reinherz, H. Z., Silverman, A. B., Pakiz, B., Frost, A. K., & Cohen, E. (1995). Traumas and posttraumatic stress disorder in a community population of older adolescents. *Journal of the American Academy of Child and Adolescent Psychiatry, 34,* 1369–1380.

Green, A. H. (1983). Child abuse: Dimension of psychological trauma in abused children. *Journal of the American Academy of Child Psychiatry, 22,* 231–237.

Greenwald, R. (2000). A trauma-focused individual therapy approach for adolescents with conduct disorder. *International Journal of Offender Therapy and Comparative Criminology, 44,* 146–163.

Greenwald, R. (2001). Motivation-Adaptive Skills-Trauma Resolution (MASTR) therapy for adolescents with conduct problems: An open trial. *Journal of Aggression, Maltreatment, and Trauma, 6,* 237–261.

Greenwald, R., Lundberg, D., & Smyth, N. J. (2001). *Trauma treatment for reduction of problem behaviors in an adolescent residential facility.* Manuscript in preparation.

Greenwald, R., & Rubin, A. (1999). Brief assessment of children's post-traumatic symptoms: Development and preliminary validation of parent and child scales. *Research on Social Work Practice, 9,* 61–75.

Greenwood, P. W. (1994). What works with juvenile offenders: A synthesis of the literature and experience. *Federal Probation, 58,* 63–67.

Hartman, C. R., & Burgess, A. W. (1993). Information processing of trauma. *Child Abuse & Neglect, 17,* 47–58.

Hernandez, J. T., Lodico, M., & DiClemente, R. J. (1993). The effects of child abuse and race on risk-taking in male adolescents. *Journal of the National Medical Association, 85,* 593–597.

Herrenkohl, R. C., Egolf, B. P., & Herrenkohl, E. C. (1997). Preschool antecedents of adolescent assaultive behavior: A longitudinal study. *American Journal of Orthopsychiatry, 67,* 422–432.

Hinshaw, S. P. (1997). Externalizing behavior problems and academic underachievement in childhood and adolescence: Causal relationships and underlying mechanisms. *Psychological Bulletin, 111,* 127–155.

James, B. (1989). *Treating traumatized children: New insights and creative interventions.* Lexington, MA: Lexington Books.

Jenkins, E. J. (1995). Violence exposure, psychological distress and risk behaviors in a sample of inner-city youth. In Block, C. R. and Block, R. L. (Eds.), *Trends, risks, and interventions in lethal violence: Proceedings of the third annual spring symposium of the homicide research working group,* Atlanta (pp. 287–297). Washington, DC: U.S. Department of Justice, Office of Justice Programs, National Institute of Justice.

Jensen, P. S., Martin, D., & Cantwell, D. P. (1997). Comorbidity in ADHD: Implications for research, practice, and DSM-V. *Journal of the American Academy of Child and Adolescent Psychiatry, 36,* 1065–1079.

Kazdin, A. (1995). *Conduct disorder in childhood and adolescence* (2nd ed.). Thousand Oaks, CA: Sage.

Kazdin, A. (1997a). Parent management training: Evidence, outcomes, and issues. *Journal of the American Academy of Child and Adolescent Psychiatry, 36,* 1349–1356.

Kazdin, A. (1997b). Practitioner review: Psychosocial treatments for conduct disorder in children. *Journal of Child Psychology and Psychiatry, 38,* 161–178.

Kazdin, A., Mazurick, J. L., & Bass, D. (1993). Risk for attrition in treatment of antisocial children and families. *Journal of Clinical Child Psychology, 22,* 2–16.

Kendall-Tackett, K. A., Williams, L. M., & Finkelhor, D. (1993). Impact of sexual abuse on children: A review and synthesis of recent empirical studies. *Psychological Bulletin, 113,* 164–180.

Krystal, H. (1978). Trauma and affects. *Psychoanalytic Study of the Child, 33,* 81–116.

Lewis, D., Mallouh, C., & Webb, V. (1989). Child abuse, delinquency, and violent criminality. In D. Cicchetti & V. Carlson (Eds.), *Child maltreatment: Theory and research on the causes and consequences of child abuse and neglect* (pp. 707–721). Cambridge: Cambridge University.

Loiselle, L., & Belicki, K. (1999, November). *Trauma/abuse, belief in a just world, and academic failure.* Poster session presented at the annual meeting of the International Society for Traumatic Stress Studies, Miami.

Lytton, H. (1990). Child and parent effects in boys' conduct disorder: A reinterpretation. *Developmental Psychology, 26,* 683–697.

Malinosky-Rummell, R., & Hansen, D. J. (1993). Long-term consequences of childhood physical abuse. *Psychological Bulletin, 114,* 68–79.

McMackin, R. A., LaFratta, J., & Litwin, P. (2000, November). *The relationship of trauma exposure to sex offending behavior among male juvenile offenders.* Poster session presented at the annual meeting of the International Society for Traumatic Stress Studies, San Antonio.

McMackin, R., Morrissey, C., Newman, E., Erwin, B. & Daley, M. (1998). Perpetrator and victim: Understanding and managing the traumatized young offender. *Corrections Management Quarterly,* 2, 36–45.

Moffitt, T. (1993). Adolescence-limited and life-course-persistent antisocial behavior: A developmental taxonomy. *Psychological Review,* 100, 674–701.

Moffitt, T. E., & Henry, B. (1989). Neuropsychological assessment of executive functions in self-reported delinquents. *Development and Psychopathology,* 1, 105–118.

Newcorn, J. H., & Strain, J. (1992). Adjustment disorder in children and adolescents. *Journal of the American Academy of Child and Adolescent Psychiatry,* 31, 318–327.

Newman, J. P., & Wallace, J. F. (1993). Diverse pathways to deficient self-regulation: Implications for disinhibitory psychopathology in children. *Clinical Psychology Review,* 13, 699–720.

Novaco, R. (1976). The functions and regulation of the arousal of anger. *American Journal of Psychiatry, 133,* 1124–1128.

Ozer, E. J., & Weinstein, R. S. (1998, November). *Violence and symptoms in an urban, adolescent sample: A community risk approach.* Paper presented at the annual meeting of the International Society for Traumatic Stress Studies, Washington, DC.

Pakiz, B., Reinherz, H. A., & Giaconia, R. M. (1997). Early risk factors for serious antisocial behavior at age 21: A longitudinal community study. *American Journal of Orthopsychiatry, 67,* 92–101.

Palmer, L., Brinker, C., Nicolini, C., & Farrar, A. (1999, November). *Intellectual and academic functioning in abused versus nonabused children.* Poster session presented at the annual meeting of the International Society for Traumatic Stress Studies, Miami.

Palmer, L., Frantz, C., Armsworth, M., Swank, P., Copley, J., & Bush, G. (1999). Neuropsychological sequelae of chronically psychologically traumatized children: Specific findings in memory and higher cognitive functions. In L. M. Williams & V. L. Banyard (Eds.), *Trauma and memory* (pp. 229–244). Thousand Oaks, CA: Sage.

Paperny, D. M., & Deisher, R. W. (1983). Maltreatment of adolescents: The relationship to a predisposition toward violent behavior and delinquency. *Adolescence, 18,* 499–506.

Patterson, G. R. (1986). Performance models for antisocial boys. *American Psychologist, 41,* 432–444.

Patterson, G. R., DeBaryshe, B. D., & Ramsey, E. (1989). A developmental perspective on antisocial behavior. *American Psychologist, 44,* 329–335.

Perry, B. D., Pollard, R. A., Blakley, T. L., Baker, W. L., & Vigilante, D. (1995). Childhood trauma, the neurobiology of adaptation and use-dependent development of the brain: How states become traits. *Infant Mental Health Journal, 16,* 271–291.

Pynoos, R. S. (1990). Post-traumatic stress disorder in children and adolescents. In B. D. Garfinkel, G. A. Carlson, & E. B. Weller (Eds.), *Psychiatric disorders in children and adolescents* (pp. 48–63). Philadelphia: W. B. Saunders.

Pynoos, R. S., & Eth, S. (1986). Witness to violence: The child interview. *Journal of the American Academy of Child Psychiatry, 25,* 306–319.

Resnick, H. S., Foy, D. W., Donahoe, C. P., & Miller, E. N. (1989). Antisocial behavior and post-traumatic stress disorder in Vietnam veterans. *Journal of Clinical Psychology, 45,* 860–866.

Riise, K. S., Corrigan, S. A., Uddo, M., & Sutker, P. B. (1994, November). *Multiple traumatic experiences: Risk factors for PTSD.* Poster session presented at the annual meeting of the International Society for Traumatic Stress Studies, Chicago.

Rivera, B., & Widom, C. S. (1990). Childhood victimization and violent offending. *Violence and Victims, 5,* 19–35.

Robins, L. N. (1981). Epidemiological approaches to natural history research: Antisocial disorders in children. *Journal of the American Academy of Child Psychiatry, 20,* 566–580.

Singer, M. I., Anglin, T. M., Song, L. Y., Lunghofer, L. (1995). Adolescents' exposure to violence and associated symptoms of psychological trauma. *Journal of the American Medical Association, 273,* 477–482.

Snyder, J., Schrepferman, L., & St. Peter, C. (1997). Origins of antisocial behavior: Negative reinforcement and affect dysregulation of behavior as socialization mechanisms in family interaction. *Behavior Modification, 21,* 187–215.

Solomon, S. D., Gerrity, E. T., & Muff, A. M. (1992). Efficacy of treatments for posttraumatic stress disorder. *Journal of the American Medical Association, 268,* 633–638.

Sommers-Flanagan, J., & Sommers-Flanagan, R. (1995). Psychotherapeutic techniques with treatment-resistant adolescents. *Psychotherapy, 32,* 131–140.

Sorensen, E., & Johnson, E. (1996). Subtypes of incarcerated delinquents constructed via cluster analysis. *Journal of Child Psychology and Psychiatry, 37,* 293–303.

Steiner, H., Garcia, I. G., & Matthews, Z. (1997). Posttraumatic stress disorder in incarcerated juvenile delinquents. *Journal of the American Academy of Child and Adolescent Psychiatry, 36,* 357–365.

Steward, S. (1996). Alcohol abuse in individuals exposed to trauma: A critical review. *Psychological Bulletin, 120,* 83–112.

Terr, L. (1991). Childhood traumas: An outline and overview. *American Journal of Psychiatry, 148,* 10–20.

Thornberry, T. (1994). *Violent families and youth violence.* OJJDP Fact Sheet #21. Washington, DC: Office of Juvenile Justice and Delinquency Prevention.

van der Kolk, B. A. (1987). The psychological consequences of overwhelming life experiences. In B. A. van der Kolk (Ed.), *Psychological trauma* (pp. 1–30). Washington, DC: American Psychiatric Press.

van der Kolk, B. A., Pelcovitz, D., Roth, S., Mandel, F. S., McFarlane, A., & Herman, J. L. (1996). Dissociation, somatization, and affect dysregulation: The complexity of adaptation to trauma. *American Journal of Psychiatry, 153,* Festschrift Supplement, 83–93.

Vrana, S., & Lauterbach, D. (1994) Prevalence of traumatic events and post-traumatic psychological symptoms in a nonclinical sample of college students. *Journal of Traumatic Stress, 7,* 289–302.

Wahler, R. G., & Dumas, J. E. (1986). Maintenance factors in coercive mother-child interactions: The compliance and predictability hypotheses. *Journal of Applied Behavior Analysis, 19,* 13–22.

Watson, C. G., Kucala, T., Manifold, V., Juba, M., & Vassar, D. (1988). The relationship of post-traumatic stress disorder and adolescent illegal activities, drinking, and unemployment. *Journal of Clinical Psychology, 44,* 592–598.

Widom, C. S. (1989). Does violence beget violence? A critical examination of the literature. *Psychological Bulletin, 106,* 3–28.

Wierson, M., Forehand, R. L., & Frame, C. L. (1992). Epidemiology and treatment of mental health problems in juvenile delinquents. *Advances in Behaviour Research and Therapy, 14,* 93–120.

Wolfer, T. A. (1997, November). *"It happens all the time": Overcoming the limits of memory and method in the study of experience with chronic community violence.* Paper presented at the annual meeting of the International Society for Traumatic Stress Studies, Montreal.

Wood, J., James, C. B., & Foy, D. W. (1998, November). *Adolescent witnesses to homicide: An exploration of community violence exposure and PTSD among incarcerated adolescents.* Paper presented at the annual meeting of the International Society for Traumatic Stress Studies, Washington, DC.

Wood, J., Foy, D., Gogeun, C., James, C. B., & Pynoos, R. (2001). Violence exposure and PTSD among delinquent girls. *Journal of Aggression, Maltreatment, and Trauma, 6,* 109–126.

Zahn-Waxler, C. (1993). Warriors and worriers: Gender and psychopathology. *Development and Psychopathology, 5,* 79–89.

Zigler, E., Taussig, C., & Black, K. (1992). Early childhood intervention: A promising preventative for juvenile delinquency. *American Psychologist, 47,* 997–1006.

Appendix C

Session Forms with Scripts and Space for Notes

This appendix includes session forms, with scripts and space for notes, for each of the scripted sessions and interventions. The scripts include occasional backup questions (in parentheses) should follow up be required; if you received a good answer already, do not use the follow-up question. In general, if there is no space, just keep talking; if there is a space, wait for a response.

The scripts do not stand alone; practice should be guided by the considerations addressed in the text, and by your own clinical judgment. These forms can be copied and used to guide treatment, whether to promote treatment adherence in a research protocol (as was done in Farkas, Cyr, Lebeau, & Lemay, 2007; see also Greenwald, 2002c), or simply to help you to remember what to say in your own practice setting.

In a couple of places, portions of the script are designated for either Eye Movement Desensitization and Reprocessing (EMDR) or non-EMDR practitioners. More often, the (EM) indicator to use eye movements is shown for EMDR practitioners. If you are not using EMDR, just ignore the (EMs). The interventions work either way.

It's probably best to start out by writing your notes right into the forms so that you are only dealing with one piece of paper at a time. It's easier to stay on track that way and to still have enough awareness left over to pay attention to your client. When you are more accustomed to the scripts and to the treatment approach, you will probably prefer to write notes on a separate piece of paper, in which case it will look more like the therapist notes in the case example. Ultimately, such notes are easier to work with and refer to over the course of treatment.

Session Forms Included

- Initial Interview
- History
- Motivation
- Treatment Contract
- Avoid High Risk
- Self-Control Skills
- Tease Proofing
- Reduce Stress
- Trauma Resolution (PC)—First session
- Trauma Resolution (PC)—Subsequent sessions

Initial Interview

Client's Name _____ *Date* _____

Introducing Treatment: Acculturation

Hi, I'm _____. Did [your parent/guardian/other] tell you why s/he wanted you to talk with me?

Usually kids come here because someone is worried about them, someone thinks that they could be feeling better, acting better, doing better in some way. My job is to learn a lot about you: what you care about, what you want for yourself, and what might be getting in your way. So I'll be asking you a lot of questions. Then I'll tell you what I think I learned, and you'll tell me if I got it right, or maybe you'll set me straight in some way. Once we agree on what's going on with you, then I'll give you some suggestions, things you can do to get stronger, to have better odds of getting to your goals. Then you'll decide what to do about the suggestions. Okay?

The Rules

Before we get started with the questions, I want to tell you what the rules are for our meetings together. The first rule is about your privacy. Do you know what that rule might be?

That rule is that I don't tell other kids what you say. And I don't tell other grown-ups, either. What you say here is private. But there are exceptions. Do you know what those might be?

One exception is if you give me permission to tell someone about a certain thing. Also, if I'm afraid someone's in danger, the law is that I have to tell. So if you tell me that you have a gun and want to shoot someone, I have to tell the police or someone who can stop you and keep everyone safe. Also if you or some other kid is getting neglected, like they don't get fed meals at home, the law says I have to tell so that they can be taken care of and be safe. So here's a quiz.

What would I do if you told me that you stole a pack of gum from the store but don't tell anyone?

(If "You'd tell," then: Why? ... Is someone in danger? ... Did you give me permission to tell?)

I might tell you that you did something stupid but you're right, I would have to keep your privacy.

[State/explain any additional exceptions to confidentiality, such as parent/guardian access to records, disclosures to third-party payor, records kept for the agency.]

Okay, so that covers the rule about what I can say to other people. The next rule is about what you say. The rule is: You are not allowed to say anything in here—unless you decide you want to. So I'm going to be asking you a lot of questions. What if I ask you something you don't feel like talking about right now? How do you follow this rule? What can you do?

(I don't know if that will work. If you [are quiet; say "I don't know"], then I might get confused and think I didn't ask the question right, and I would ask it again a different way. We need a signal that won't be confusing.)

That would be good. Can I count on you to do that?

Let's try it out. What's 143 times 96?

Good. I'm sorry to take so much time on the rules; I know this is a boring way to meet someone. But I just want to make sure you don't have any surprises.

The Questions

Okay. You remember I said I was going to ask a lot of questions to try to learn a lot about you? You know what to do if there's a question you don't want to answer?

So here come the questions. Ready?

What's your favorite color? (If "No favorite," then, Okay, what are your two or three favorites?)

What's your favorite food?

What's your favorite music?

What's your favorite TV show?

What do you like in school? (Nothing? Not even recess?)

What don't you like in school? (What else?)

Some kids like to keep to themselves, some like to mostly be with one or two good friends, some like to hang with a crowd. Which way are you?

(If "crowd," then) Would you say there are certain kids who are better friends to you? Or everyone the same?

You remember what to do if I ask you something that you don't want to talk about, right?

I'm going to ask you some questions about your friends. Your friends they mostly smoke cigarettes or don't smoke?

Do your friends mostly get high or don't get high?

Your friends mostly drink or don't drink?

Other drugs?

Would you say that your friends do pretty well in school, just get by, or are having trouble?

Do your friends get in trouble with the law or not?

Now some of the same questions about you. You smoke cigarettes or you don't smoke?

You get high or don't get high?

You drink or don't drink?

Other drugs?

What about school? You do pretty well, just get by, or not even?

You get in trouble with the law or not?

What do you like to do with your friends? (Possible follow-up to "hang out": So if I was watching you guys hanging out and having a good time, what would I see you doing?) What else do you do with your friends?

What else do you like to do? (What else?)

What have people told you that you're good at? (What else?)

Here comes a different kind of question. If you could be any animal, who would you be?

What would be good about being a [ ]?

If you could have three wishes, what would they be?

If you could wave a magic wand right now and all your problems would disappear, what would be different tomorrow? (Possible follow-ups: If I'm watching on TV, what would I notice was different? Okay, so _____ would be better. What would be different that would make it better? Would the change be something inside you or outside you?)

Where you live now, who else lives there? (Get a quick genogram including names, ages, what each person does, relationships.)

Standard Ending

Those were the questions I wanted to ask you for today. Because I like to learn, though, I will ask you one more thing before we finish. Can you tell me the thing you liked the most about this meeting we just had and the thing that you didn't like the most?

(If only one answer, ask again for the other, such as, And something you didn't like?)
(If "Nothing good" or "Nothing bad," then, It doesn't have to be anything big.)
(If more help is needed: There must have been one minute that was a little [better/worse] than the others.)

[Talk about what's coming up, etc., to help the client transition from treatment.]

History

Client's Name _____ *Date* _____

Standard Beginning with a Session 2 Introduction

Hi. Because last time was our first meeting, I just want to make sure that you remember the rules, about your privacy and the exceptions and about what to do if there's something you don't want to say.

I like to start with a kind of a check-in, if you could tell me something good that happened since the last time we met and something bad that happened. (If "nothing," then, Doesn't have to be anything big.)

And is there anything coming up in the next week or two that you're either worried about or looking forward to?

I asked you a bunch of questions last time, now I have more.

Developmental/Medical History

I'll start with something you might not even know the answer to. When your mother was pregnant with you, do you know if she might have been smoking cigarettes, drinking, using any drugs?

Were you born early, or late, or on time?

Were you born big, or small, or average size?

Sick or healthy?

Did they tell you what you were like when you were a baby?

When you were maybe a year old, were you the kind of kid who liked to explore and meet people? Or more shy, stay close to Mom?

When you were maybe 2 or 3, old enough to play with other kids, were you like a bully, taking kids' toys? Or did that happen to you? Or was it more like playing fair?

This question is about from being a baby all the way til today. Did you ever get sick or injured to the point that you had to go to the hospital? (If "Yes," then, What happened? How old were you? Any other time? etc.)

Did you ever have to take medicine for more than just a little while? (If "Yes," then, What was it, what was it for? How old were you, how long did you take it for, why did you stop? Any other medicine? etc.)

Did you ever get hit on the head to the point that you were knocked out or got dizzy or headaches? (If "Yes," then, What happened? How old were you? Do you remember having headaches after that or being more tired? Do you remember any other changes, maybe more trouble concentrating, or a shorter temper?)

School/Legal History

When you were in the first grade, do you remember feeling like you were about as smart as other kids, or a little faster, or slower?

What kind of grades were you getting?

Were you getting in more trouble than other kids, less trouble, or about average? (If "More," then, What kind of things?)

Did you have more friends than other kids, less friends, or about average?

So that's how it was in first grade. How long did things stay that way for you in school until something was different? (What grade was that? What was different? What was still the same—did you still get the same grades? etc.)

And how long did things stay that way for you in school until something was different again? (Same follow-up questions as above.)

(If needed) And how long did things stay that way for you in school until something was different again? (Same follow-up questions as above.)

How old were you for the first time you ever did something that, if you were caught, would have gotten you in trouble with the law? (What kind of thing was that? Then how old were you for the next thing? etc.)

Trauma/Loss History

Now I'm going to ask you about something that some kids don't like to talk about. You remember what to do if you don't want to say something?

Good. I won't be asking for the stories today, but I need to make a list of the worst things that ever happened to you. Maybe you already have something in mind, but let me tell you the kinds of things that other kids say, so you know what I'm asking about. Some kids, it would be maybe a car accident, or another kind of accident, or seeing someone else get hurt really bad. Some kids, it's that someone in their family or someone else they care about got really sick or died. Or being taken away from their family. Or if someone hurt you, or made you do sex things, or threatened you, told you they would do something bad. Or seeing parents having really bad arguments or fights. You get the idea—not just a bad day but the kind of thing that could really hit you hard.

So what would be on your list? Okay, how old were you then? What else would be on your list? (Continue until there are no more events to list. For notes, use Worst Things form that follows.)

[If client tries to tell the story of an event: This sounds important. Today we have to get through a lot of stuff. Is it okay if we save talking about this for the right time, when we can do it right?]

[Note: If the client denies *any* trauma/loss, then ask the following questions, to fill out the list:

How old were you for the worst thing that ever happened in school?
How old were you for the worst thing that ever happened with other kids?
How old were you for the worst time you lost someone you cared about?
How old were you for the worst time you ever got punished or disciplined?
How old were you for the worst time you saw parents or other grown-ups arguing or fighting?]

Now I'm going to ask you how bad the feeling is for these, on 0–10, where 10 is the worst feeling in the world and 0 is no bad feeling at all. I'm not asking about how bad it was at the time but, when you make yourself think about it right now, how bad the feeling is right now. So for [the first event listed], how bad is that feeling right now on 0 to 10? (Ask about SUDS—the 0–10 Subjective Units of Distress Scale—for each memory on the list.)

Did anyone ever show you how to do deep breathing, like to relax?

I'm going to ask you to try my way of doing it for a couple of minutes, then you'll tell me whether we should ever do it again or not. You will be taking a very deep, slow breath in, to my count of 3, then hold for 3, then breathe out slowly to a count of 3. Ready? Breathe in 1, 2, 3; hold 1, 2, 3; out slow 1, 2, 3. Again, breathe in 1, 2, 3; hold 1, 2, 3; out slow 1, 2, 3.

This time, when you breathe out look for any bad stuff: tension in your body, upsetting thoughts or pictures. And when you breathe out, imagine the air coming from that place, and the bad stuff going out with the exhale. Ready? Breathe in 1, 2, 3; hold 1, 2, 3; breathe out the bad stuff, 1, 2, 3. Once more, breathe in 1, 2, 3; hold 1, 2, 3; breathe out the bad, 1, 2, 3.

How did that go? Would you say you feel better than before, worse, about the same?

Now I need to make a list about the best things that ever happened to you or times that you felt really good. For some kids it would be a really good birthday or they did something they're proud of or they went someplace special or were having a really good time doing something. What are the best times you can remember? How old were you? What else?

[Then ask for more detail on one or two of the best things.]

Okay, that's it for today. Tell me something you liked about this meeting and something you didn't like.

(If only one answer, ask again for the other, e.g., And something you didn't like?)
(If "Nothing good" or "Nothing bad," then: It doesn't have to be anything big.)
(If more help is needed: There must have been one minute that was a little [better/worse] than the others.)

[Talk about what's coming up, etc., to help the client transition from treatment.]

Worst Things:

Age   Event   SUDS (0-10)

(Breathe)
Best Things:

Age   Event

Motivation

Client's Name _____ *Date* _____

Standard Beginning

Hi, tell me something good that happened since the last time we met and something bad that happened. (Doesn't have to be anything big.)

And is there anything coming up in the next week or two that you're either worried about or looking forward to?

Getting the Good Ending

I've asked about your past and about how things are now. Now I want to know about your future. Since you haven't been there yet I can't ask it the same way, so I'm going to tell a little story, and you'll fill it in for me. Let's say that 10 years from now—how old will you be?

[Fit this story to client's details, but keep it about this vague/general.] So 10 years from now, I stop at the video store on my way home from work and pick up a movie called *The [client's name] Story*. It's about this kid, grows up in a city, starts out pretty good. He has friends, does good in school, his family cares about him …. They have their troubles, too, but it's a good family. But then something bad happens. The kind of thing you wish didn't happen to a kid, but it's a realistic movie. So the stress and anger starts piling up inside. Then more bad things happen, and he gets more angry, more stressed, the bad feelings piling up even more. He gets so stressed he ends up doing some things he doesn't really feel good about, he gets himself into some trouble, it doesn't look too good. By halfway through the movie, he's a teenager, he's locked up, and I'm saying to myself, "I don't even want to watch this movie. I used to work with kids like this. Looks like another good one going down the drain." But I just sit there, and then something good happens. A little thing—nothing stupid like him winning the lottery, it's a realistic movie. Just something he does to make his day go a little better instead of a little worse. And then something else good happens. And then something else. And I don't want to get my hopes up, but little by little, things are starting to go his way. Till finally, by the end of the movie—you know that last picture, when the music's playing and the credits are rolling?—I'm smiling, and saying, "Way to go—you made it!" So tell me: If this was your story and things go the way you wish they would, what would your life be like? (If "I don't know," then: Well, what would it be for this movie?)

(Follow-up questions, as needed) What would you be doing for a living? (What company/business/store/team?)

Where would you be living? In the neighborhood you're in now, or someplace else in the city, or where? Your own house or an apartment? (If "house" then: What color?)

By yourself, with a buddy, with a girlfriend/boyfriend? Maybe married by then?

(If a spouse/romantic partner, then: What's s/he like?)

(If kids, then: How many? Boys or girls? What age?)

Would you have your own car? What kind? What color?

Okay, so if this is your life, what would be in that last picture to let me know how good you're doing? (If needed, guide client to time–place–action good-ending picture.)

And what could you say along the way to encourage yourself toward this goal? Something like, "I can do it," or "I'm gonna make it"?

Okay, now I'm going to ask you to do a concentration exercise. I'll be asking you to concentrate on the picture, the feeling, where you feel it, and what you're saying to yourself.

No EMDR Training

So concentrate on that … take a deep breath …. How did that go?

Try it one more time, concentrate on the picture, the feeling, where you feel it, the words … deep breath …. How did that go?

EMDR Trained: Introducing Eye Movements

At the same time, I'll be moving my hand back and forth, and you will be following with your eyes. Some people tell me this is weird, and I guess they're right, but I think you can handle it. It is a lot to focus on all at once. Ready? [Eye movements (EM).] Were you able to concentrate on everything?

(It can be hard to get used to.) Okay, let's try it again. Ready? (EM) How did it go that time?

[Repeat another time or two until client is able to hold the picture reasonably well.]

Steps Along the Way

The thing is, the movie didn't just jump from the middle to the end; there were all these things that happened along the way to get there. So tell me, if this was your story, what happens in this movie? What would we see you doing tomorrow, next week, next month, next year?

(If needed, ask for specific behaviors that the client would do instead of not doing the bad thing, as well as specific behaviors that would lead to the good outcomes.)

So now I want you to imagine watching the whole movie in your mind—not from the beginning but from today—all the way to that good end you were telling me about. All the things you were saying would happen to get there, step by step. (If no EM: You can do this with your eyes open or closed.) So start from today, tell me when you're done. Ready? (EM)
How did it go? What happened in the movie?

Okay, we're going to do it again, same thing. Ready? (EM). How did it go this time?

Bad Ending Picture

I hope it goes the way you want it to, but just for a minute I want to talk about something else. What if it doesn't go the good way we've been talking about? What if the kid in the movie keeps on doing the same old stuff, things got worse and worse until I'm looking at that last picture 10 years from now I'm sad, I say, "What a waste of a good kid!" What would that picture be? (If needed, guide client to time–place–action bad-ending picture.)

What kind of feeling goes with that picture?

Where do you feel it?

With this picture, **would it feel true to say to yourself, "It's not worth it" to go that way?**

Okay, so just for a few seconds, I want you to concentrate on this bad ending, the bad feeling, where you feel it—the words, "It's not worth it." Got it? (EM) Okay. Did that "It's not worth it" feel more true, less true, about the same?

Okay, let's do this one more time: Concentrate on this bad ending, the bad feeling, where you feel it—"It's not worth it." Got it? (EM) Okay. Is it more true, less true, about the same?

Commitment to Goals

So on 0 to 10, 0 is nothing, 10 is all the way, deep inside how much of you really wants to go for that good ending you were telling me about, or something like that?

Okay, now I know you don't want the bad end, but how much of you, on 0 to 10, still feels like doing the same old thing?

So [most/all] of you really wants to go the good way?

But sometimes that smaller part tries to take over and mess it up for all of you?

Strengths

I'm a gambling [man/woman]. Let's say I put $100 down on the table, says you're going to make it the good way. What makes me think this is a smart bet?

Well, I have some ideas about why this might be a smart bet. See if you think these ideas are right or wrong.

Motivation

Most people I know, if they really care a lot about something, they try harder than for something that doesn't really matter to them. You told me that on 0 to 10 you're a [insert number here], you really want this. So would you say that you're determined, motivated—what's the best word?

Talent

To do what you said, you'd have to [e.g., pass your classes]. Now I know from [some other years that you're smart enough to do well in school if you decide to] (or other evidence of talent needed to achieve steps toward goals). You think that's true?

Also, you're pretty good at [whatever skill is related to the goal], right? So I might bet on you because you have talent.

Support

Would you say that people have a better chance of making it if they're all alone in the world? Or if they have people in their corner that try to help them out sometimes? You have people in your corner, yes?

Persistence

So are you the kind of person who, if something goes wrong, will just give up and throw it all away? Or will you pick yourself up and keep trying?

Good. Because I don't want to bet on a [guy/girl] who lies down and dies every time something goes wrong. Because things do go wrong.

So should we say "Persistence," "Won't quit," "Doesn't give up," "Bounces back"?

Track Record

Now it's one thing for someone to just tell me, "Yes, I want to make it." But you've actually already been doing some of the things we've been talking about that get you toward your goals (give examples). So this makes me think you're serious about it, because you're not just saying it; you're doing it.

So I'm going to write down, "Track record." See, here's the list I made while we were talking. You think these are pretty good reasons to bet on you, or not so good?

Obstacles

Now, you know what's gonna happen as soon as I put that money down. Someone's gonna walk up and say "Sucker! I'll bet you s/he goes the bad way." What makes that guy think he's got some easy money coming?

(If necessary, the therapist can generate a list, including typical things like wanting quick money, temptation [e.g., smoke, drink, easy money, unprotected sex], stress, anger/temper, the don't-care feeling. For example:)

Maybe he'd say, "Sure, he's doing fine now, but pass him a joint and see what he does."

So I'll write down, "drug temptation." Or the guy might say, "Sure, he's doing fine now, but get him mad and he'll do anything, just forget about his goals."

So should I write down "temper" or "anger" or what?

[Continue to a list of the three or four major obstacles. Do not write down "track record" of having done bad, even if the client does mention it.]

So I want to know what my biggest worry is, which of these is the biggest challenge?

[Continue until all obstacles are ranked.] And which one is next?

So it sounds like there are some good reasons to believe that you really could make it on the good track. And also some real challenges, some things that could get in your way.

Today's Odds

So I think I'm going to make my money, but nothing's a sure thing. Now I'm going to ask you to give me the odds, the way you see things right now. On 0 to 10, 10 is a sure thing, 0 is no chance at all, so 0 and 10 are impossible because nothing's ever sure. Today, what do you think my chances are of winning this bet?

And what would it take for you to tell me that it's not a [insert number] anymore, it's a [one higher] now? What would have to happen? (Follow-up questions/reflections as needed)

Okay, that's it for today. Tell me something you liked about this meeting and something you didn't like.

(If only one answer, ask again for the other, e.g., And something you didn't like?)
(If "Nothing good" or "Nothing bad," then: It doesn't have to be anything big.)
(If more help is needed: There must have been one minute that was a little [better/worse) than the others.]

[Talk about what's coming up to help the client transition from treatment.]

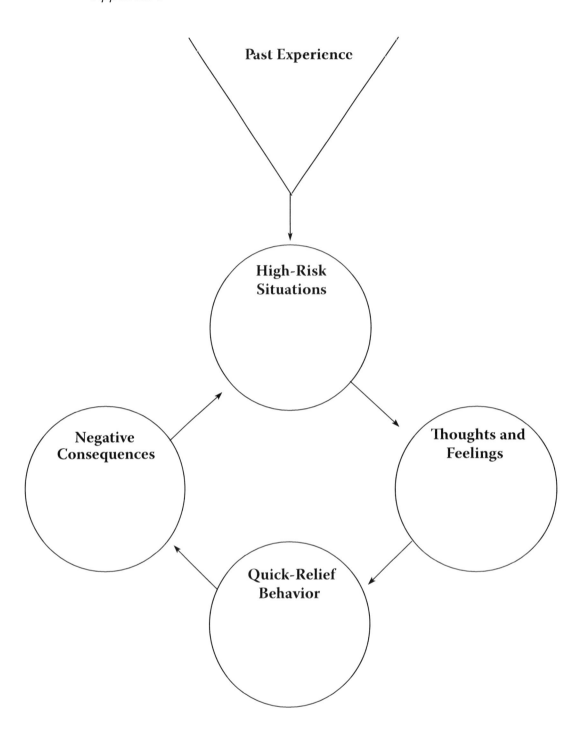

Treatment Contract

Client's Name _____ *Date* _____

Hi, tell me something good that happened since the last time we met and something bad that happened. (Doesn't have to be anything big.)

And is there anything coming up in the next week or two that you're either worried about or looking forward to?

Last time we met, we talked about your goals, the kind of life you want for yourself. We talked about your strengths, things that will help you get what you want —the reasons I'm betting on you—and also about some things that could get in your way if you're not careful—the reasons that other guy was betting against me.
   Have you driven a car before?

Here's a driving question: What do you do if you're driving along and you see a patch of ice on the road ahead?

That's right. Do you know what drivers mean when they talk about "black ice"?

It's from water that melts and then freezes a certain way so you can't see it; you think it's just the road but there's ice on it. What happens if you're driving along and you can't see the ice ahead?

That's right, anything could happen; you could be in big trouble. So I want to talk a little more today about the things that could be getting in your way. The goal is that you can see it clearly and make your own choices; I don't want you to have any black ice. Okay?

You said that the main thing that could get in your way is [your anger, or whatever client's #1 obstacle was from previous session]. So are you [losing your temper] every minute of every day or just at certain times?

Oh, so there are only certain situations that could lead to you losing your temper. I'm going to write these down as your "High-Risk Situations." [Take notes on Treatment Plan form at the end of this form.]

What kinds of things/situations could [make you mad]?

(Or: So when's the last time that one of these things happened?)

So when that happens, what are your thoughts and feelings?

What are you saying to yourself; what are the words in your head?

And what's happening in your body; what are the signals that you're (mad)?

When you're like this, what do you feel like doing?

(Or; If you let this take you over, what do you do next?)
[The client should now state his or her quick-relief behavior. If not, ask further questions to get that answer.]

Okay. But you told me that this kind of thing would get you bad consequences. Like what kind of bad thing might happen to you if you (do that quick-relief behavior)?

[Repeat the above, filling in all four circles for each of the major obstacles that were identified in the previous session.]

So let me ask you another question. These high-risk situations you were telling me about, would you say that you mess up every time someone does one of those things?

Would you say that you have a better chance of controlling yourself when you are feeling good, relaxed? Or when you're already stressed?

So when you get these bad consequences, like [the negative consequences client has named], does that make you more relaxed or more stressed?

So the more you handle these high-risk situations by (doing the quick-relief behaviors), the more you end up getting stressed from the consequences?

Now here's an interesting thing: You know how you told me the things that were your high-risk situations? Other kids, some of them don't mind that stuff, but other things bother them, things that are no big deal to you. I have an idea why these are the high-risk situations for you. Can I tell you?

Okay. To explain this, can I touch your shoulder lightly with this pen?

Okay, pay attention, and tell me how much this hurts, on 0 to 10. [Taps client's shoulder lightly.] How much?

Now I'm going to ask you to imagine something that I would never do and you would never let me do. Imagine that I have a baseball bat and that I swing this bat as hard as I can right to that spot on your shoulder. Not just once, but over and over again for 10 minutes. And then tomorrow, the same thing over and over again—every day like that for 2 weeks. And then you're walking down the hall, and someone bumps you in the shoulder—can I touch you there again?

Okay, now tell me how much this would hurt if someone bumped you like this after that 2 weeks with the baseball bat. [Taps lightly as before.]

How come? I hardly touched you!

Right. The thing is, not all of our sore spots are on the outside. Remember when we made that list of the worst things that ever happened to you, and I asked you on 0 to 10 how much the things still hurt inside? Some of the things on your list had pretty high numbers. I'm wondering if those things make a sore spot inside you, so when something else comes along that maybe feels like that in some way, it hits the sore spot and you react extra strong.

So this thing makes sense to you?

Okay then, we have a pretty good idea of what could get in your way, keep you from getting to your goals. Remember when we first met, I told you I'd ask you a lot of questions, then tell you what I learned, then give you some suggestions?

Well, here come the suggestions. This is my best advice for what you can do to get stronger toward your goals, give yourself better odds. You might be doing some of these things already, and there might be some things you could be doing even better.

First of all, let's say you have a friend, [s/he]'s 21, s/he's an alcoholic but s/he's trying to stay sober. S/he's doing good so far, it's been two months without a drop, but every day's a struggle. S/he needs a job, and s/he says to you, "That bar down the street needs a bartender; think I should try for that?" What will you tell him/her?

Why not?

Good answer. So you already understand the first thing I'm going to suggest for you: Avoid high risk. If you know where the trouble is, sometimes you can just decide to stay away from it. Then it doesn't even have a chance.

So you see your friend a couple of weeks later. S/he tells you, "Thanks for the advice. I got a job at a clothing store; nobody drinks there, I'm doing great. But last Saturday I went to my friend's house for his birthday, I thought it was just going to be a few friends. There were 100 people there! And kegs, bottles, everywhere."

This is a good friend of yours. What do you hope s/he did?

Good idea. Because even when you do everything right, try to stay away from trouble, sometimes trouble finds you.

So you already understand my next suggestion: self-control skills. It's something you're already doing; my suggestion is to get even better at it.

Now you told me that if you're stressed, it's harder to use your self-control skills. So my next suggestion won't be a surprise: reduce stress. Now this one has different parts. One part is to get better doing things every day to keep yourself feeling good so the stress doesn't happen. But no matter how hard you try, sometimes the stress comes, and then the question is do you want to walk around all stressed out? Or catch it and bring it back down?

So there are also things you can do, get better at to bring your stress down.

The other part is to bring stress down from the old stuff—those old memories that make that sore spot inside. Down the road, when I think you're ready, and if you decide you want to, there's a special way of talking about those old memories; it can help to make the sore spot smaller. So something that's a 10 now could end up being a 5 or even a 3. Most kids tell me they don't like that meeting, because they don't like talking about the old memory. But afterward they say things don't make them so [mad] anymore. How does that sound to you?

Well, it works for most people, but I can't promise if it'll work for you or not. Anyway, when the time comes, I'll tell you more about it, and you can make your decision.

And here's my final suggestion: track record of small successes. Let me explain what I mean. Let's say you have someone just like you are today. S/he has his/her goals, but there are things in his/her way, too. So s/he's trying, and s/he's not perfect, but s/he's doing pretty good. Two or three steps forward, one step back. Two or three steps forward, one step back. A month from now, [a typical high-risk situation for the client], and s/he has to decide what to do.

And let's say there's another guy/girl, also starts out like you are today. But every time s/he makes a step forward, s/he slides a step back. One step forward, one step back. S/he's not really getting anywhere. And a month from now, [the same high-risk situation].

Which one of these guys/girls has a better chance of handling this, in a way that will help him/her go toward his/her goals?

Why?
(S/he knows s/he can do it. Also, look how far I've come; why throw it away?)

And what's the other one saying to him/herself?
(Doesn't matter; nothing to lose anyway.)

So when I suggest building this track record of small successes, I'm not just talking about the big things like graduating high school. I'm talking about things like [refer to the client's success in handling a recent high-risk situation]. The more you succeed at doing the things you said you cared about, the more strong you'll feel, the more confident you'll feel, and the harder you'll be willing to work on it.

So what do you think of these suggestions; do they make sense to you?

So is this something you think you might want to work on together when we meet?

Okay. So my suggestion is that when we meet next time, we start at the top. We figure out what you're already doing, and what else you could do if you want to, to get even stronger toward your goals. And in different meetings we kind of work our way down, step by step. And if something comes up that you don't feel like talking about, what happens?

Right. So tell me something you liked about this meeting and something you didn't like.

(If only one answer, ask again for the other, e.g., And something you didn't like?)
(If "Nothing good" or "Nothing bad," then: It doesn't have to be anything big.)
(If more help is needed: There must have been one minute that was a little [better/worse] than the others.)

[Talk about what's coming up to help the client transition from treatment.]

Avoid High Risk

Client's Name _____ ***Date*** _____

Hi, tell me something good that happened since the last time we met and something bad that happened. (Doesn't have to be anything big.)

Is there anything coming up that you're either worried about or looking forward to?

We were talking about the things you wanted to do with your life, the things that could help you get there (the reasons I bet on you) and the things that could get in your way if you're not careful. Last time we met, we talked about a strategy, things you could do to get stronger, give yourself better odds. [Pull out the treatment plan page with circles and arrows.] The first thing on the list is avoid high risk; is it okay if we talk about that today?

Remember, I'm not going to be telling you what you should or shouldn't be doing. My job is to help you see what your choices are so there's no black ice. It will be up to you to decide what to do about it.

Okay, one of the high-risk situations you told me about was [name one of the high-risk situations]. When is that most likely to happen? [It's good to make a list on a separate page so that it can be referred to later.]

If you wanted to avoid that high-risk situation, what could you do?

(If no good answer, offer a "menu" of what other kids have said has worked for them.)

Another high-risk situation you told me about was [name another of the high-risk situations]. When is that most likely to happen?

If you wanted to avoid that high-risk situation, what could you do?

[Continue until all the primary instances of all high-risk situations have been identified along with the associated avoidance strategies for each. Note that both the high-risk situation and the avoidance strategy must be specific, including time, place, and action.]

Then that's it for today; this was a shorter meeting than usual. Tell me something you liked about the meeting and something you didn't like.

(If only one answer, ask again for the other, e.g., And something you didn't like?)
(If "Nothing good" or "Nothing bad," then: It doesn't have to be anything big.)
(If more help is needed: There must have been one minute that was a little [better/ worse) than the others.]

[Talk about what's coming up to help the client transition from treatment.]

High Risk Situation   **Avoidance Strategy**

Self-Control Skills

Client's Name _____ ***Date*** _____

Hi, tell me something good that happened since the last time we met and something bad that happened. (Doesn't have to be anything big.)

And is there anything coming up in the next week or two that you're either worried about or looking forward to?

[Pull out Treatment Plan.] We've been talking about the things you can do to get to your goals. Last week we talked about avoiding high-risk situations. How've you been doing with that?

Okay. Let's see what's next: self-control skills. Okay if we talk about self-control skills today?

You said that [Obstacle #1 from the Treatment Plan] was the biggest reason that guy would bet against me; is it okay to start with that?

[You can either take notes in the respective circles in the following Map Out a Problem form or work off the Treatment Plan page without further writing on that page, in which case your notes would be fewer and elsewhere.]

Choices Have Consequences

I want you to watch this in your mind like it's a movie. Start with [the provocation/situation], then notice [the thoughts and feelings], then [the bad behavior], then the bad ending with, "It's not worth it." (No EM: You can do this with your eyes opened or closed.) Start at the beginning, tell me when it's done. Ready? (EM)

Did you get all the way to the end?

Did you remember to say, "It's not worth it"?

This time the movie starts the same way, with [the situation] and [the thoughts and feelings]. This time, do what it takes to get to the good end. Start at the beginning, tell me when it's done. Ready? (EM)

Did you get all the way to the end?

This time, the movie starts the same way, with [the situation] and [the thoughts and feelings]. This time, I don't know what's going to happen; it depends on you. The rules are: bad choice goes to bad ending and "It's not worth it," good choice goes to good ending. Ready? (EM)

1. So are you always doing this, or just in certain situations? Like what's a recent example, the last time that happened? Doesn't have to be anything big. (Or: When's the next time this could happen?)

2. When you're in this situation, what are the thoughts, the words in your head? Your emotional reaction? The signals in your body?

3. If you let this take you over, what do you do next? (This is, or leads to, the problem behavior.)

4. If the problem habit continues, gets even worse, how bad could things get? What picture could represent that? Does "it's not worth it" feel true — to go that way, I mean?

5. So you're (high risk situation) and (thoughts & feelings). What if you got a handle on this, got it under control, what would you be doing instead (of the problem behavior)?

6. So if this effective behavior got to be a habit, what good things would that lead to? What picture could represent that?

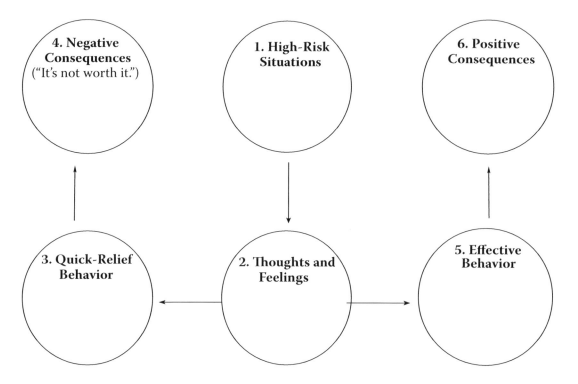

Which way did it go?

Did you get all the way to the end?

(If it went to the bad ending: Did you remember to say, "It's not worth it"?)

[Repeat the surprise ending movie routine until positive end is chosen 2 times in a row.]
    This time, the movie starts the same way ….
[Repeat the entire routine with other examples of the same high-risk situation. Then to end the session …]

So how long have you had this habit you're trying to change?

So if all of a sudden you don't have perfect self-control tomorrow, does that mean that you can't ever change? Or does it just mean that it takes time and practice to get a new habit?

I think that's how it works. You got some practice here, but now it's up to you to remember to practice in the real situations. You won't get it perfect every time, but the more you remember to practice, the better you'll get.

That's it for today. Tell me something you liked about the meeting and something you didn't like.

(If only one answer, ask again for the other, e.g., And something you didn't like?)
(If "Nothing good" or "Nothing bad," then: It doesn't have to be anything big.)
(If more help is needed: There must have been one minute that was a little [better/worse) than the others.]

[Talk about what's coming up to help the client transition from treatment.]

Tease Proofing

Client's Name _____ *Date* _____

Hi, tell me something good that happened since the last time we met and something bad that happened. (Doesn't have to be anything big.)

And is there anything coming up in the next week or two that you're either worried about or looking forward to?

[Pull out Treatment Plan.] We've been talking about the things you can do to get to your goals. Last week we talked about [_____]. How've you been doing with that?

Okay. Let's see what's next: self-control skills. Okay if we talk about self-control skills today?

[Introduce the value of becoming less reactive to peers as per the strategies in the text. Normally you would choose to do this session at a moment when this value is painfully apparent.]

Play Therapy

Imagine that you're an artist for a comic strip. In the first frame, it's going to be that situation [of the provoker calling the name or whatever]. But you're the artist, anything goes, what should happen next?

Okay. So I'm going to ask you to watch this in your mind like you're reading the comic strip. In the first frame, [the provoking situation], and then in the second frame, [the solution]. Ready? (EM)

How did that go?

Well, people liked that comic strip; it sold a lot of copies. So your boss wants you to do another one. It starts the same way, with [the provoking situation]. What's going to happen this time?

Okay, let's try that. Ready? (EM)

How did that go?

[Repeat this procedure 3 or 4 times.]

Walls

Let me ask you something. Do you deserve to be treated like that? Or is it just that [the offender/provoker] has his/her own problems and is trying to take it out on someone else?

So it's really his/her problem? But when it gets through to you, you don't like it?

If you could put up a wall, to keep his/her problems from getting through to you, what would the wall be made of?

Okay. Now you're going to have to put it up pretty fast when the time comes, how will you do that? Press a button, snap your fingers, think it?

Okay, now I'm going to ask you to try this out in your imagination. First s/he's going to [do the provoking thing]. Then you're going to put up the wall, see what happens. Ready? (EM)

How did that go?
(If a problem, ask what happened, and then ask the client how the problem could be resolved. Then try again.)

What else does [that person] do that gets to you?
(Or, Who else pushes your buttons? What does that person do?)

[Then do the wall again with the new situation.]

Role Model

Who can you think of who can handle this kind of thing really well, in a way that, if you did it that way, it would help you to your goal? (Could be someone you know, someone famous, someone in a movie or cartoon …)

And what would [the role model] do in this situation; how would s/he handle it?

I want you to imagine, watch in your mind, [the role model facing the provoking situation] and how s/he handles it. Ready? (EM)

How did that go?

Okay, this time I'm going to ask you to stretch your imagination a bit. Imagine that you are looking at [the role model], you sneak up really close, so close that you can hear him/her breathing. Now imagine stepping into his/her shoes and feel what it feels like to be him/her. Now while you're in there, watch [the role model facing the provoking situation] and how s/he handles it. Ready? (EM)

How did that go?

This time, you're going to be yourself, but handling it the way [the role model] would
Ready? (EM)

How did that go?

That's it for today. Tell me something you liked about the meeting and something you
didn't like.

(If only one answer, ask again for the other, e.g., And something you didn't like?)
(If "Nothing good" or "Nothing bad," then: It doesn't have to be anything big.)
(If more help is needed: There must have been one minute that was a little [better/
worse] than the others.)

[Talk about what's coming up to help the client transition from treatment.]

Reduce Stress

Client's Name _____ ***Date*** _____

Hi, tell me something good that happened since the last time we met and something bad that happened. (Doesn't have to be anything big.)

And is there anything coming up in the next week or two that you're either worried about or looking forward to?

[Pull out Treatment Plan.] We've been talking about the things you can do to get to your goals. Last week we talked about self-control skills again. How've you been doing with that?

Okay. Let's see what's next: reduce stress. Okay if we talk about that today?

This has some different parts to it.

Everyday Things

To Keep Feeling Good

First of all, there are the kinds of things you can do every day to keep yourself feeling good, to keep stress from ever building up. What kinds of things do you do that help you feel good?

[Good to make the list on a separate page so that it can be referred to later.]

Okay, what else?

[Continue until there are about four to six things on the list. If the client has trouble, give a menu.]

To Bring the Stress Down

That's a pretty good list; looks like you've got a lot of ways to keep yourself on a good track. The next part of reducing stress is to catch yourself when you notice that the stress is building up and do something to bring it down again. What kinds of things work for you to get yourself to feel good again when you are already stressed?

Okay, what else?

[Continue until there are about four to six things on the list. If the client has trouble, give a menu.]

So if you notice that you're stressed, you have a few good strategies to bring it back down.

To Make the Sore Spot Smaller

It's been good to hear how well you've been doing, how well things have been going for you. A lot of the things you said you would do to get to your goals, you've been doing it, you're on track.

Suppose you're on a basketball team, you're one of the key players, you're halfway through the season, and your team is winning every game, and not just by a little. Then your coach says, "I want you to start coming to practice an hour early, do more workouts." Why would he say that?

I think your coach wants to go all the way. Who are you going to be playing in the playoffs?

So are you going to tell your coach, "No, I don't need to do that. If we start losing games in the playoffs, then I'll practice more?"

Years ago, when I was working with someone like you, he's doing what he has to do, avoiding high risks, controlling his anger, doing well in school. I'd shake his hand and say "Good work. Have a good life." But then, two months later, or a year later, he'd be back.

Here's what happened. The every day challenges, he had gotten pretty good at handling those and staying on track. But sooner or later, something bigger came along. Maybe he cared about a girl and then she cheated on him, maybe someone in his family died—you know how things happen.

Remember when we talked about that sore spot from the past experiences and how it makes reactions extra strong? So if something happens that makes you this mad (hands about 2 inches apart) and it hits a sore spot, how mad do you get?

Right—a lot more. So with the everyday stresses, he could handle it, even with that sore spot reaction. But when something really big came along, maybe this bad (holds hands about 1 foot apart), with that sore spot there, it was like this (holds hands about 3 feet apart). That was too much stress, and he got off his track, went back to his old ways.

So this is like your situation right now. You're doing pretty well with the challenges that are coming your way. You're going strong, you're winning your games. So now, while you're strong, this is a good time for you to do the extra training so that when the big challenges come your way, you'll be strong enough for those, too. That make sense?

So my suggestion for this part of reducing stress, we would go after some of those memories on that list of worst things, one memory at a time. There's a special way of talking about it. [Introduce your trauma resolution method; briefly explain the procedure.]

Most kids tell me they don't like doing this, because it hurts their feelings to think about that stuff. But they also tell me that afterward the memory feels more like old news, doesn't really hurt as much. And they also say they don't get so mad anymore. What do you think about that?

It does work for most people. I've probably done it myself with more than [insert number] kids. It doesn't work once in a while, like if someone changes his mind and decides to stop before it's done. But for most of the kids, if they hang in there, they come out better on the other side.

I think it will work for you, but I can't promise 100% guarantee. So my suggestion would be to do a kind of a test run on some little thing—nothing big from the list but just some little thing that happened. Then you can see how it goes for you, and then you can decide whether to try it on the serious stuff. Okay?

So next time we meet, maybe we do a test run and you see what you think. And if we get to something you don't feel like talking about, you know what happens, right?

Right. So tell me something you liked about this meeting and something you didn't like.

(If only one answer, ask again for the other, e.g., And something you didn't like?)
(If "Nothing good" or "Nothing bad," then: It doesn't have to be anything big.)
(If more help is needed: There must have been one minute that was a little [better/worse] than the others.)

[Talk about what's coming up to help the client transition from treatment.]

Trauma Resolution (PC)

Client's Name _____ *Date* _____

Standard Beginning, First PC Session

Hi, tell me something good that happened since the last time we met and something bad that happened. (Doesn't have to be anything big.)

And is there anything coming up in the next week or two that you're either worried about or looking forward to?

[Pull out Treatment Plan.] We've been talking about the things you can do to get to your goals. Last week we talked about reducing stress. How've you been doing with that?

Selecting a Test-Run Target

[Select a minor upsetting memory, perhaps the "something bad" if suitable.] You told me about [the recent event/memory], how bad is the feeling now on 0 to 10?

In a month, how bad will it be?

So it bothers you now, but it's not really important?

We were talking about you digesting those old memories that make the sore spot so you don't react so strong to things. I told you there was a special way of talking about the memories that usually helps to digest them. How about trying it out with this one, like a test run? Then you can see how it goes for you.

Rationale

You'll be watching this memory like a movie in your mind. It might hurt your feelings for a little while, but you'll be digesting it and making it part of the past so it doesn't have to hurt so much afterward. Going over it and over it, the emotions can get weaker. And looking at it from where you are today can give you some distance, so you're not stuck in the experience anymore.

Target Setup

What's the beginning of the movie, before anything bad happened?

   [Was that really before it started?]

What's the ending of the movie, when the bad part was over?

>(When was it really over?)
>(And when would you say it was really over?)
>(What picture/event would represent that?)

Progressive Counting

I'm going to ask you to watch this in your mind like it's a movie, while I count from 1 to 10 out loud. You can do this with your eyes opened or closed. When I say "one," start at the beginning of the movie, and when I say "ten" you should just be finishing up. Even if you weren't at the end, it's important to get to the end when the counting is done.

Ready? Be at the beginning. (Count out loud from 1 to 10.) Now be at the end. Take a deep breath. Let it go. How did that go?

And how bad was the worst moment on the 0–10 scale?

Okay. This time I will count to 20. When I say "one …"

Count   **SUDS**   **Any Comments**

(When the SUDS was already 0 in the prior movie, then instead of asking, "How bad was the worst moment?" ask: Was it a little better [this time], a little worse, or about the same?)

Container (If Ending With SUDS > 0)

What kind of container can you think of, that could hold this memory until you need to get to it again?

What would it be made of? How big would it be? How would you close it (keep it secure)? Where would you keep it?

What I want you to do is imagine packing this memory away in (the container). When it's all put away, let me know.

How did that go? Does it feel all put away or not really?

> (What kept it from working?)
> (How would the container need to be different to solve the problem?)

Debriefing

Well, you just did your first session on a bad memory. How did it go for you?

Sometimes when you've done a lot of digesting, moving things around in your brain, things can keep on moving even after you leave here. Some people find that they think about the memory more than usual, or less than usual, that some other memory comes up, that they feel emotionally raw, or exhausted, or better than usual. There's no right or wrong—I just want you to know that things might still be moving. So if you find yourself reacting to something in a way you don't expect, you don't have to worry that something's wrong with you. It's probably just the stuff you were doing here working its way through your system.

However, if you do get worried about how you're doing, I expect to hear from you. I know that you usually don't call, but you just took a big step and my part in that is to be more than normally available in case you do get concerned.

Okay, that's it for today. Tell me something you liked about this meeting and something you didn't like.

(If only one answer, ask again for the other, e.g., And something you didn't like?)
(If "Nothing good" or "Nothing bad," then: It doesn't have to be anything big.)
(If more help is needed: There must have been one minute that was a little [better/ worse] than the others.)

[Talk about what's coming up to help the client transition from treatment.]

Trauma Resolution (PC)

Client's Name _____ ***Date*** _____

Standard Beginning, Subsequent PC Sessions

Hi, tell me something good that happened since the last time we met and something bad that happened. (Doesn't have to be anything big.)

And is there anything coming up in the next week or two that you're either worried about or looking forward to?

[Pull out Treatment Plan.] We've been talking about the things you can do to get to your goals. Last week we talked about [the memory]. Have you thought about it [the memory we worked on] more than usual, less than usual, about the same?

When you did think about it, how was that?

Have you noticed yourself reacting more strongly than usual to something or less strongly than usual?

Any dreams?

Feeling any worse than usual in some way, or better than usual, or different?

If you make yourself think about the memory again for a second right now, where are you now on 0 to 10?

Selecting the Next Target

Is it okay if we work on (the same memory if it needs more work or the next memory according to your strategy) today?

Target Setup

What's the beginning of the movie, before anything bad happened?
    (Was that really before it started?)

What's the ending of the movie, when the bad part was over?
    [When was it really over?]
    [And when would you say it was really over?]
    [What picture/event would represent that?]

Progressive Counting

I'm going to ask you to watch this in your mind like it's a movie, while I count from 1 to 10 out loud. You can do this with your eyes opened or closed. When I say "one," start at the beginning of the movie, and when I say "ten" you should just be finishing up. Even if you weren't at the end, it's important to get to the end when the counting is done.

Ready? Be at the beginning. (Count out loud from 1 to 10.) Now be at the end. Take a deep breath. Let it go. How did that go?

And how bad was the worst moment, on the 0–10 scale?

Okay. This time I will count to 20. When I say "one ..."

Count	SUDS	Any Comments

(When the SUDS was already 0 in the prior movie, then instead of asking, "How bad was the worst moment?" ask: Was it a little better [this time], a little worse, or about the same?)

Container (If Ending With SUDS > 0)

What kind of container can you think of, that could hold this memory until you need to get to it again?

What would it be made of? How big would it be? How would you close it (keep it secure)? Where would you keep it?

What I want you to do is imagine packing this memory away in [the container]. When it's all put away, let me know.

How did that go? Does it feel all put away or not really?

> (What kept it from working?)
> (How would the container need to be different to solve the problem?)

Debriefing

You just did a lot of work. How did it go for you?

Remember, sometimes when you've done a lot of digesting, moving things around in your brain, things can keep on moving even after you leave here. So if you find yourself reacting to something in a way you don't expect, you don't have to worry that something's wrong with you. It's probably just the stuff you were doing here working its way through your system.

Okay, that's it for today. Tell me something you liked about this meeting and something you didn't like.

(If only one answer, ask again for the other, e.g., And something you didn't like?)
(If "Nothing good" or "Nothing bad," then: It doesn't have to be anything big.)
(If more help is needed: There must have been one minute that was a little (better/worse) than the others.)

[Talk about what's coming up to help the client transition from treatment.]

Index